ED

Enjoy the ride

Ed Hill

BUSTED

Library and Archives Canada Cataloguing in Publication

Ed Hill : Busted / Ed Hill.

ISBN 978-1-896238-17-3 (pbk.)

1. Hill Ed, 1948-. 2. Royal Canadian Mounted Police--Biography. 3. Police--British Columbia--Biography. 1. Title. 11. Title: Busted.

HV7911.H45A3 2013   363.2092   C2013-907057-5

Twin Eagles Publishing

Box 2031
Sechelt BC
V0N 3A0

pblakey@telus.net
604 885 7503

twineaglespublishing.com

Dedication

This book is dedicated to the memory of my father and mother, Frank and Mary Hill. Your teachings and example compelled me to write it. Thank you.

It is dedicated, too, to my grandchildren: Keegan, Carter, Mya, Charlotte, Ashton and Mason. It is for you that this book was written. Of course, my daughter and son, Melanie and Bryson and their spouses Brian and Carmen can't be forgotten. It goes without saying that this dedication is for you, too.

And finally, any reader will see that my wife Joy put up with a lot over the years. Most of all, this book is dedicated to you Joy. Thanks for waiting for me. Thanks for the patience, love and understanding.

Thank you

I started writing these stories in 1997. They are all contained in a family collection and now they are presented here in *Busted*. Know that they could not have been presented so well without the patience and dedication of two people. Publisher Paul Blakey helped in the presentation and structure of this book. Neville Judd cut, shaved and shaped my notoriously long story-telling style. He is a skilled editor, to say the least.

This book could not have happened without their creativity, patience and collaboration. I offer Paul and Neville my most sincere appreciation and thanks for all they did to make it happen.

Introduction

As you turn the pages of this book, you are sharing something near and dear to both me and my family. These stories are valuable to all of us, both now and in the future. Some of these stories are being told publicly for the very first time. In some cases I've changed names or locations for reasons that'll become obvious. In other cases real names, dates and places have been used. Those people I've contacted and verified the stories while obtaining permission to use their names. That exercise in itself has been a wonderful way to rekindle old friendships and relationships. One thing I need you to know is that, no matter how strange they may sound, all of these stories are true.

Let me give you some history. First of all, anyone who knows me knows that I'm a storyteller. In fact some would say I'm a bull -shitter. The fact is, I love listening to a good story, and I like telling them.

I probably inherited this trait from my father. He too loved a good yarn and had been known to spin a lot of his own over the years. He was in the Second World War. He never actually saw combat though he was in Britain, Belgium, Holland and Germany, but he had great, funny stories to tell. Some were stories only a son would know and never repeat; others were just great stories of a time gone by. He was a welder by trade after the war, but even in that trade he could find interesting stories to tell. He didn't often relate memories of his youth; in fact I remember very few references to his young days in Guelph, Ontario. My father and I had a very close, fun relationship for the most part. We laughed with, and at, each other until our sides hurt. We both loved scotch and golf and in that we always had something to enjoy together. He was so proud of me when I joined the RCMP in 1968. I never knew when he'd just show up, unannounced, on my doorstep in British Columbia. Of all my siblings, George, Margaret and Madeline, I was the only one who left Ontario for good when I began my career. My father and I had a great friendship. Storytelling and listening to each other's tales was a huge part of that relationship.

Late in 1997 my father was in his last stages of his battle with cancer. I managed to get home to Ontario where he was in hospital in Perth for the last few weeks of his life. He wasn't up much for telling stories at that point; in fact he wasn't able to do much talking at all.

I'd just finished my life altering experience of the VisionQuest Canoe Journey from Hazelton to Victoria with the RCMP. My father had been both interested in and proud of that historic canoe journey of more than 1,600 kilometres. In fact, he and Mom had surprised me by showing up on the beach in Victoria when that journey had ended in August 1997. It was only just over three months ago that we'd enjoyed that time together. Now, he lay dying in his hospital bed in Perth, Ontario.

I'd spend hours with Dad sitting beside his bed and true to our friendship with each other, I'd read my journal of that epic canoe journey to him. He enjoyed the story I'm sure, but a lot of it was read to my Dad as he lay with his eyes closed. For all I know he was sleeping. It was good therapy for him I hope. It was great therapy for me, I know.

My Dad passed away early in November. I'd been able to be with him for his last month or so. I was there for his funeral of course, but then I had to get back to my job as Detachment Commander of Gibsons Detachment.

"So what's all that got to do with this book?" you ask.

As I watched Canada's vast expanse move past below me on my return flight, I found myself in a time of deep reflection and emotion from my window seat of the plane. Losing a father and a close friend has an impact. I was alone on that big jet; well I might as well have been alone. I was acknowledging everything stirring within me. I could identify sorrow, and fond memories. I could feel regrets and laughter. I could recall the good times and the not so good times that any father and son have together. But, there was an emotion I couldn't quite put my finger on and I wrestled with that matter for most of the trip. It was probably somewhere over the Rocky Mountains that it hit me. As I entered this beautiful province that I now consider home, it struck me that within the complex mix of emotions I was feeling at my Dad's passing, one of them was a tinge of anger. Better said, I was mad at my Dad. Why the hell, particularly at a time like this, was I mad at my Dad?

The answer came with only a bit of self-analysis. Mad is the only word I can use, but surely there's a more appropriate one, less harsh or dramatic. I felt that emotion about my Dad because with him died all his stories. Upon reflection, it wasn't his "fault"; rather he was a product of his times. Both he and my mother had always put off or even refused to commit their stories to writing or recording. It was something that just wasn't done, and let's face it, most don't do it even today. The reality was, with my Dad's passing so too did his stories pass. I can remember only a few of his stories, and even those lose their colour and personality in my telling. Through no specific fault of his own, my Dad had left me with only wisps of memory of who he was, what he had experienced and where he had come from. Surely, two generations from now, my Dad will be nothing much more than a name on some genealogical chart. There'll be the odd photograph of him, but his personality, who he really was will have dissipated like some puff of smoke on the breeze.

By the time the plane had landed that bright November day of 1997, I'd made a commitment to myself. In his passing, my Dad had taught me yet one more lesson. I'd be a good student and use that lesson well. I actually remember saying the words out loud.

"I'm not going to do that to my family."

And that was it. The stage was set with those words. For the next year I'd spend huge amounts of time at my computer composing chapter after chapter of my life, from the time I joined the RCMP to the present. Some of the stories were funny and entertaining, others were more dramatic. Some involved my police life and work; some were of personal and family history. Many of the stories were self-deprecating. All were honest and factual to the very best of my abilities.

Christmas 1998, I gave one of the most valuable and powerful gifts I've ever given. Under the tree for both my daughter Melanie and my son Bryson, was a three-ring binder of those stories for each of them. I'd considered having them professionally bound but at the last minute had decided that the three-ring binder was more appropriate for this purpose. In the card attached to this valuable gift I explained that this was a living document. Henceforth, should any of my family want one of my life stories written, all they had to do was ask. Every Christmas morning since 1998 (it's now 2013) there's been a gift under the tree for Melanie and Bryson. It's a gift they've come to expect. Every year there are a number of new stories to add to their books.

And that's how you are the benefactor in reading this book. As you'll see with the pages turning, some of these stories are exciting or take unanticipated twists and turns. Others speak honestly of my alcoholism and how that was managed until I quit drinking forever on October 23, 1984. Some of the stories involve Melanie and Bryson. In short, you are reading but a very few of the family book chapters. Only the family gets to read all of them. Maybe, if you're lucky, they'll publish the rest of the stories after I'm gone.

I suppose I shouldn't go on here without addressing one question that always comes up. It's the proverbial "elephant in the room". As you read these stories, you'll see that I make many references to my alcoholism. The inevitable question is "What happened to make you stop?" The truth is, my family made me stop. Just the thought of what a great family I have and the possibility that I could lose it all with one stupid, alcohol-driven mistake, gave me pause and concern. My personality and the character instilled by my parents allowed me to stop. On the morning of October 23rd, 1984 I woke at 6 a.m. with a severe hangover; the kind of hangover that makes your swimming head feel detached from your churning nauseous body. Lying there with my dizzying world spinning I found myself in a time of self-pity and reflection. Putting all things in the scale, I made an easy decision. All you have to do is read a story like "The Chilliwack Golf Wars" and you'll see but one shining example of some of the things I considered that morning.

So far I'd been lucky. I'd dodged a lot of metaphoric bullets, and some real ones. So too, I was so fortunate to have a great wife in Joy and two wonderful kids. I realized that morning through the fog of yet another all consuming hangover that I was one incident away from tipping those scales. I'd taken this to the very edge.

I rolled over and nudged Joy awake. "I just quit drinking." I said.

"Roll over and go back to sleep," was her response.

Luckily, like my character illustrates in "Taking A Stand," I was willing and able to yet again take a stand. I've not touched a drop of alcohol since that day.

Being an addictive personality though means I'll always have addictions. I suppose mine now is my artwork. I am consumed by that addiction. It's far easier on the head early in the morning and I never have to wake up wondering what happened the night before. Take a look at my website, *www.edhillart.com* and you'll see the fruits of where my addictive personality takes me each day.

For years now, as folks have been entertained by my telling of some of these stories, they've said "Ed, you should write a book!" I'm sick and tired of hearing that, so I hope I've silenced the bunch of you. You've asked for it. Now I've written a book.

I want to add one proviso. You're going to read about accomplishments and mistakes. You're going to read about real human achievements and human frailties, my human frailties. Just know and remember that these were different times in so many ways. Society itself was different then. I was different then. You're welcome to share just a bit of my life and the life of my family in these pages.

I can't close without saying a big thank you to my family for trusting me and supporting me in this process. You'll read about a lot of folks who've had a positive influence in my life. Thanks to all of them too.

A fish story

1959

It seems only fitting that I start my stories with a tale from my childhood. I've loved fishing all my life. This little tale of youthful ingenuity is one I've told often, but that summer morning of 2011 at sunrise, recounting my fishing adventure to a little boy on the shores of Lightning Lake in Manning Park, was something pretty special.

It was August, 2011, and one of the better Manning Park camping trips we'd taken with family and friends. Truth is, every Manning Park visit is good, but this time we'd enjoyed a great stretch of sunny, warm weather. A bear visited our camp at least three times that we knew of, and on the final day, I spotted a wolf. For the entire 10 days, I fly-fished until my fingers were raw from the line.

At Manning, my morning ritual is the same. By 6, I've started a fire in the stove, washed my face and made a coffee. Then, I'll sit by the lake and watch the day come to life as the sun rises over the end of Lone Duck Bay. It is absolutely my favourite place to be in the world every year.

Usually, two quiet coffees are what I'll fit in before the rest of the camp is up. If I do have company at all, it'll be my brother-in-law Wayne, who like me is an early riser. One morning though, things were different.

Just as I was heading down to the lake with my coffee and chair, nine-year-old Eric walked into the cookhouse. The son of a family friend, Eric had wakened early, got up to pee and then decided he'd come and visit with me rather than go back to bed.

I brought an extra chair down to the lake. Together, the two of us welcomed the day as the rising sun warmed us to the core. We talked and listened. Pretty soon the conversation turned to fishing. I'd taken Eric and his Grampa out the day before and we'd let Eric catch a bunch of little trout. He'd brought some home and his family had enjoyed the trout supper he'd proudly provided.

Eric wanted to know the biggest fish I'd ever caught. He wanted to know what kinds of fish I'd caught. He just wanted to hear fishing stories.

I've caught a lot of fish. I've caught a 40-pound salmon, a 75-pound ling cod and numerous other trout and game fish. But the fish I told Eric about that morning was barely more than a foot long. Yet even as I told the story, I could remember the adrenaline rush I'd felt all those years ago.

It had happened to me when I was not much older than Eric. It was the summer of 1959–maybe 1960–in Peterborough, Ontario.

My friend John Coleman and I were fishing fanatics as kids growing up in Peterborough. I lived on Frank Street. He lived up the hill on High Street. We both went to Saint Alphonsus Catholic School and our summers were spent fishing.

Together we'd walk, fishing poles and tackle box in hand, and we'd fish the Otonabee River for miles, walking up and down its shores. We'd fish at the dams on the Trent Canal. We'd fish Little Lake for bass, suckers, sunfish, catfish, pickerel or whatever would bite our hooks.

If we were lucky, we'd get to come home with a fish or two on a string. Probably our favourite fishing though was in the streams around where we lived. We had two streams in particular that we always stalked. The water was clear and clean. When you were thirsty you just dropped down and sucked the cool delight straight from the stream.

We'd often take a backpack with us and at lunchtime we'd build a small fire and cook up a few trout, some frog's legs and fresh watercress from the stream. If I could set back the hands of time for a day, I think I'd return to a day of stream fishing with John Coleman.

The two streams we fished were very different from each other. One was in a forested area about three kilometres from home. The stream meandered through deadfalls and under banks and shelves that hid our prey: Eastern Brook Trout.

Probably the most beautiful of all the trout family, these "Speckled Trout" as they're also known, filled these streams in those days. Eight to ten inches long, they were an absolute thrill to hunt and catch. We'd keep our limit of eight most every day and proudly walk home exhibiting our catch for all to see.

The second stream was a lot closer to home. This stream etched its way through open fields as it left the Kawartha Golf and Country Club. Little did I know at the time that within a few short years my "addiction" would turn to golf at that very club.

The stream ended up going under the highway in a culvert just beside the RCMP detachment where years later I'd begin my career. From there the stream wandered through light brush and into more residential areas.

Generally, we fished just the culvert and across the open fields as far as the golf course. In the dark recesses of the huge culvert you'd usually find the biggest trout. To come home with a 12-incher would be a significant trophy.

I remember it as a hot summer day. John wasn't around to go fishing. I went alone. Rather than do the long walk to the forested creek, I walked to the closer creek up by the RCMP detachment. Geared with my little casting rod that would never be used for casting on these creeks, and my belt bait box, I first fished the culvert.

Sometimes you'd be fooled in the darkness of the culvert. You'd fish the still pools and feel the tug. Setting the hook you'd feel the heavy weight of the giant trout only to find a sucker. Much bigger and heavier, suckers were just coarse fish to be released. They were bait thieves is all, but they had to be endured to get at the trout.

I began making my way up the creek as it snaked its way through the fields of knee-high grass. To the inexperienced eye, you'd never guess that this little creek, no more than six or eight feet wide, would produce Eastern Brook Trout.

I came to a straight stretch of the stream. Upstream was a small riffle of water as it spilled over shallow rocks from the pool above. Below the straight stretch was another shallow collection of small rocks. The clear water in this particular pool was only about two feet deep and the grass and dirt bank above the stream was about a foot high. The water had undercut the banks of the stream such that it provided a cool, shaded area for trout to sit and wait for food to drift downstream.

A rookie wouldn't see the potential, but an aggressive, eager and observant young fisherman knew a fishy area when he saw it.

I stepped quietly to the edge of the pool. Stooped over, so as not to startle a fish with a shadow or silhouette, I dropped my hook into the water at the upstream end of the pool. We'd fish with only about five feet of line extended from the end of the pole and just let it drift, following it quietly by moving the tip of the pole downstream.

As the bait sunk in the water I guided it towards the shadows of the bank below my feet. It was still in the sunlight when out of the dark, black shadows came a huge trout. It was just below my feet. I was looking down as its dark silhouette darted out and I saw a huge mouth open, grab the worm and turn back into the shadows below me.

The tug on the pole was like none I'd felt before. Even as I write this story, my body recalls the shot of adrenaline. The fight lasted perhaps 10 seconds and the fish was gone. I stood on the bank, gasping for air. For the few seconds the fish was on my line, I must have held my breath and forgotten to breathe.

I re-baited my hook with shaking fingers and dropped the offering into the pool again and again. Nothing moved. I knew the fish hadn't gone upstream or down. I'd have seen him splash through the shallows at either end. He was here, right below my feet, but he wasn't going to take any bait I had to offer.

I remember standing and thinking: This is the biggest Speckled Trout I've ever seen but I'm alone. Nobody will believe me, particularly John Coleman. I tried again, this time putting on the biggest, juiciest worm I had in my bait box. Nothing. Not a movement.

I laid my pole down in the grass. On my belly, I edged myself towards the bank. Slowly, I inched forward until I could see into the waters below. The shade of my hat helped. I could look down and under the bank.

There he was, right underneath me. He was the biggest trout I'd ever seen. With his nose facing upstream, he was just sitting quietly in the cool, dark of the undercut.

Quietly I snaked back and away from the bank. I stood and thought. I had a plan.

First, I raced upstream and gathered rocks. Bringing them back to the shallows just above the pool, I built a dam of sorts. My wily trout wouldn't be able to escape upstream. Taking a wide berth into the field, I made my way downstream and did the same thing, building a dam of rocks in the riffles at the bottom of the pool.

Now, no matter what, I had my giant trout cornered.

I didn't even consider trying the bait again. I knew he wouldn't be biting. No, I had another idea. Again, I lay down on my belly and inched toward the bank. Peeking over the edge, I could see my fish was still there, tail languidly swaying against the gentle current.

Holding my breath, I eased my right hand over the bank and down into the water. Slowly, I opened my hand and let it drop over the big trout. Careful not to touch him, my hand was now right over the fish. My thumb was on one side, my four fingers on the other. Gently, I closed my grip. As I touched the fish for the first time, I expected him to shoot away. But he didn't. He just stayed where he was.

I tightened my grip on the fish and actually felt like I could lift him.

I was wrong.

He just gave a powerful thrust of his tail and his slippery skin was gone from my hand. There was no way I could hold against his power and his slick skin. Frustrated, I watched as he quickly darted across the pool.

I could see him there in the shadows of the far bank, nose upstream again, gently pushing against the current. I pulled back from the bank and took a wide run upstream and across the creek. Again I inched toward the bank and again I looked down into the dark water to see the back of my giant trout right below me.

This time I was careful to be extra slow and quiet. My hand slipped silently into the water and slowly closed over the big fish. I closed my grip and again the trout squirted out of my fingers with a powerful thrust. Again he flashed across the pool and I could see him finning gently facing upstream in the shadows of the undercut.

I stood up away from the sight of the creek. My brain was racing, adrenaline coursing, but I forced myself to slow and think. I came up with a new plan and quickly got to work. This time I went downstream to cross the stream. Well out of sight of the pool, I jumped across the water. At a shallow area of the creek I bent down and took a handful of sand from the bottom. With my right hand full of sand, I was again on all fours creeping towards the bank.

On my belly I slithered forward until my eyes could see the fish below me under the bank. He appeared to be a lot calmer than I was, just quietly biding time there in the darkness.

Gently, I lowered my right hand into the water above the fish. This time though my fist was clenched with a handful of sand. As my hand came to within an inch of the trout I released my grip and let the sand fall over the back of the fish. My hand followed at the same speed as the falling sand. Again, the trout let me touch him without flinching. Again, he let my grip tighten. This time though I actually had a grip. As my fingers closed on the trout, I was quick to squeeze.

I could feel his muscular attempt to swim away as he'd done before but this time I had the advantage of a grip that held. The sand had worked.

With one motion, I pulled out and back. The trout came out of the water still in my right hand and as I rolled onto my back I threw him into the field as far as I could. I didn't want him flopping back into the stream. Jumping to my feet I ran to the flailing fish as it glistened wet in the grass.

Quickly, I dispatched the trout and he was mine. I'd done it. I'd caught a beautiful Speckled Trout with my bare hands. God it was big. Later at home I measured it at only 14 inches long, but to me, it was the biggest trout I'd ever seen.

I didn't fish any more that day. I couldn't fish any more that day, I was so excited to show off my prize. Worried that catching a trout with my bare hands might be illegal, I actually took my hook and put a gaping hole in its mouth. There! I'd caught it with a hook! I walked home that day with my prize proudly displayed on the end of a stick.

John Coleman would be impressed, and he'd have to believe. I had the fish to prove it.

Since that day, I've literally caught thousands of fish on all kinds of gear. None of them compare with the adrenaline rush I felt that day as a little boy on the banks of an insignificant stream in Peterborough, Ontario: The day I caught my monster Speckled Trout—with my bare hands!

Taking a stand

1967/68

I've been cursed, or blessed, with a character trait that can be difficult for me, and others. I just can't seem to let things be. If something is right and worth standing up for, I'll stand up without thinking of repercussions. Sometimes it helps me; often it hurts.

In 1967, the year of Canada's 100th birthday, I was in high school. I had started my high school days in St. Peter's High, the catholic high school in Peterborough. Uninspired by French, Latin and my teachers, I failed Grade 9. Mercifully, my Mom and Dad moved from Frank Street to Plati Avenue, which meant a new school. Crestwood Secondary School was where I began to grow up.

The 1960s were an era of free thought, flower children, peace, love and drugs. The in thing was to do your own thing. The education system became a little less restrained too. Crestwood Secondary School meant catching a bus from one side of the city to the other, but it was also a huge lung full of fresh air. Gone were the nuns, priests and staid ways of the Catholic school system. Plus I didn't have to take French and Latin. I could take two art courses and I even took a public speaking course. Subjects like sociology meant that argument and debate were encouraged and I found myself being encouraged to be an individual.

Within a few days of entering the supportive environment of Crestwood Secondary School I began to feel like me. My marks showed that I had value. Leading the way to my personal development was one teacher in particular, Mr. Fenn. George Fenn taught me public speaking and he taught me well; it's a talent that I continue to use, learn and develop to this day. When I argue a point, discuss an issue or take a stand that may be unpopular, I am doing that which I learned from George Fenn. Neither of us has found this way of life easy, but we both feel that it's the only way to face the guy in the mirror.

Doing what's right is far more important than doing what's popular.

I entered the RCMP because of George Fenn. Not because he moved me that way, in fact that was probably the furthest thing from his mind. I got into police work because of the character that George Fenn showed me: His way of committing, of taking a stand, led me to a career in the RCMP.

Not that I was a likely candidate, particularly in the late '60s. I was five-foot eleven and a half inches of skinny determination. I weighed 129 pounds. I could hide behind a signpost. The RCMP hired men only. You couldn't be married when you joined the force. You had to wait two years for permission to marry and even then, the woman you intended to wed had to be approved.

In 1967 though, I had other dreams. I wanted to be a commercial artist. My art teacher, Neil Broadfoot, had been a commercial artist before he taught. He encouraged me and supported me in my dream and I still use a paint box that he gave me in high school. I'm so proud to be a professional artist today and Neil Broadfoot is proud of his former student.

I was president of the student council in 1967, a sign of the personal value I had developed in my short time at the school. My election was due in part to a showdown the year before. The school had fired the vice principal, Don Randal, another great influence on me. Don was not only a vice principal, but he was a personality in the Toronto area. He was a public speaker, a professional artist and eventually ended up being a TV personality for a few years.

When he was fired I went to the principal, Thomas Chilton, and demanded to know why. I was told that it was no business of the kids. It was the first time I had been told that a "kid" had no rights at Crestwood and I wasn't about to accept that. I leaned across the principal's desk and told him that if he didn't communicate with me and the student body then I would take the issue to national television by next Monday morning. With a wave of the back of his hand, Mr. Chilton dismissed me from his office and I was left with my determined words hanging in the air.

The following Monday morning, after a weekend of phoning, planning and meeting, I led the entire student body of 1,400 kids out on strike. We were on the road in front of the school, determined and organized with placards. True to my word, I was interviewed by CBC TV and radio and the story was on national news that evening. Don Randal eventually came and spoke to our group and encouraged us into the gym. There he spoke to the entire student body and encouraged us to return to class. He appreciated our actions and was moved by them. We had made our point and he thanked us. We returned to class and were satisfied, though at the time we had no idea why he had been fired.

Don Randal, our excellent vice-principal, respected by all, was fired for being gay. It was only some time later that we came to know the circumstances. Back then, he would have been fired from the RCMP for the same reason. Society has changed so dramatically.

The strike and my involvement in it led to my election as student council president. I gained yet more personal strength, conviction and determination, and the job taught me much about work and time management. I was learning far more about life, myself and my future, out of the classroom than I was actually in the classroom. Crestwood allowed that to happen.

Several of my student friends were involved in drugs, marijuana, hashish and LSD. I remember them changing. My parents had instilled in me the value of law and order. Drug use was against the law and I couldn't relate to those who blatantly ignored it. Likewise, I couldn't relate to those who sold it. I resented the fear and so-called respect that they garnered.

So in the fall of 1967, I made a decision that would change my life. I decided to take a stand. I decided to do something about the drug traffickers in my school and in my community. I had Dad's car one Saturday afternoon in early September. I drove out to the RCMP detachment and parked in the lot. This wasn't impulse. I'd thought about this for some time. My hair was half way to my shoulders and though 19 at the time, I looked perhaps 15. I opened the door to the detachment, walked in and turned right to the counter. A constable in plain clothes approached and introduced himself as Cst. Jim Simpson.

"What can I help you with?"

After briefly introducing myself, I announced: "I want to help you guys with the drug problem in town!"

Jim's answer was to the point.

"Listen young man, you leave the man's work to us. We'll take care of the drugs, you go back to school!"

The words, I now recognize, were almost identical to those of Thomas Chilton. I was being told that I had no business, no issue, with adult matters. He knew more than I did. I thanked him and turned and left the detachment. Then I sat in Dad's car in the parking lot, thinking and fuming. I drove to a home in the east end of Peterborough. I knew of a guy, perhaps 19 or 20, who was selling dope to the local kids from his parents' home. I drove to the house, parked on the street and went to the door. On talking to the fellow, he obliged and handed me a plastic bag of marijuana. I paid him $15 and drove away. That's how easy it was. It was done. I was now breaking the law.

Less than 30 minutes later I was back at the detachment. Not surprisingly, Cst. Simpson recognized me. From my jeans pocket I took the ounce of marijuana and threw it on the counter in front of him. He looked down at it, then up at me.

"You know that's illegal?" he asked.

"I guess you can either bust me or use me!" I replied, looking him straight in the eye.

"Come on in here," he said as he opened the door to the office.

I followed him to an interview room, taking my first steps to becoming an RCMP informant. That's the word I knew as a kid, "informant, fink, snitch". The reality is, I'd become an "agent" for the next while. For the remainder of 1967 through the spring of 1968 I worked with the local RCMP.

Danny Ashworth was my first bust. Danny was a student selling marijuana to other kids at the school. I was announcing a football game from a high stand. I had ordered marijuana from Danny and he had brought it to the game. Simpson and the plain-clothes members showed up and I gave the signal. They followed as Ashworth and I returned towards the school. Just as we were about to make the deal, the officers arrested both of us. Of course, Danny had the drugs in his possession and I didn't, so I was released and Danny was not. Crestwood now had its first drug bust and no one at the school figured out how it had happened, at least not for another eight months or so.

I spent that fall helping out members of the detachment without my parents even knowing. Dad finally figured something was up and followed me one Friday night. He caught me meeting the detachment members and confronted them. Now Mom and Dad knew and the anxiety began. I kept up the work but it wasn't quite so easy with my parents at home worrying.

In the spring of 1968 the RCMP would drive me to dance pavilions in the Kawartha Lakes area. All of the major lakes had dance pavilions where kids would gather. My job was to go into these pavilions, find the dealers, get a description and report back to the officers hidden up the road. They would then go into the hall, or wait outside and bust the guy. Drug work wasn't nearly as tough as in these modern times.

It was at one such event that my road of life took a more deliberate turn. As we waited down a dark road, watching as cars and trucks filed into the dance pavilion area, Jim Simpson reached into the glove compartment of the unmarked police car and brought out an envelope. He handed it back over the seat to me.

"Why don't you take this home Ed and fill out the papers inside, see what happens."

"What are they?" I asked.

"Application forms for the force," he replied.

I had never thought of it. It just hadn't crossed my mind. Nothing serious about my future had really crossed my mind. But this had a ring to it, a sense of importance. I took the papers and couldn't wait to get a good look at them.

The next morning I devoured the papers. Over the next few weeks I did what I had to do, not only completing the forms, but doing the tests and getting the medicals. I was going to be a Mountie. The idea was exciting and important. I was consumed by the desire to make it. In a matter of months I was accepted. On July 29, 1968, I was sworn into the force in Toronto and within two days I was sitting on the edge of a bed in Regina wondering just how all of this had come about.

That fall, Crestwood Secondary School had its graduation ceremonies. I wasn't there. It was then that Danny Ashworth and the rest of the school figured it out. Their school president had been a narc. That part will never be fun. But then doing what's right is far more important than doing what's popular.

All these years later I wonder how I'd be accepted at a reunion. Maybe someday I'll find out. I do know one thing for sure. There are very few, if any, RCMP members past or present, who willingly broke the law to get into the force. I don't regret my actions over those 18 months. I did it with the conviction learned from some very important people in my life. Sometimes you stand alone simply because you are taking a stand.

Graduation day, January 29, 1969,
Penhold, Alberta

Rat attack

1969/70

This will be your first hint that I had a drinking problem. Better said, I have an alcohol problem. I can say now, I am an alcoholic. I was just enjoying myself. Alcohol played a big role in my life for a time. Luckily, I lived through it. This is but one time when I was lucky.

Gasoline tends to burn fast. I know this because I once blew my eyebrows off. I was 15, working in a restaurant/gas station on the outskirts of Peterborough, Ontario.

One blowing, cold winter day, I'd gone out to burn the garbage at the back of the restaurant. The wind was howling and the 45-gallon drum that held the garbage wouldn't light. The wind would blow the match out before I could get the paper lit.

Like any resourceful 15-year-old, I filled a coke bottle with gasoline from the pump and returned to the drum. I slopped the contents into the drum and threw in a lit match.

Nothing. Again and again, the wind would blow out the match.

What I did next I still can't believe. I unbuttoned my winter parka, spread it open and hunched my chest and face over the drum to break the wind. The match would damned well light this time! With my face buried in the drum and my hands working in the darkness, I fumbled with the book of matches.

I can only remember the WHOMP. I came to, 15 feet away at the rear of the restaurant, sitting with my back against the wall. The drum was burning well. I brushed myself off and got back to work, sure that no one knew of my folly. Sure until people noticed I had no eyebrows and my hair was a curly charcoal mat.

By 1969, as a full-grown adult, I thought I'd learned my lesson. In fact, holding a shovel of burning newspaper at arm's length in the middle of a gasoline soaked backyard in Cloverdale–while drunk–I thought my teenage pyrotechnics had prepared me well.

Perhaps an introduction is in order.

It was the summer of 1969 and I'd been drinking with my buddy Chris. Chris was a bit of a lost soul; 21 years old, living with his parents, Rob and Myrna, in a modest little bungalow. For $50 a month, I rented the basement suite with a fellow cop with whom I had little in common. The RCMP detachment was just a 10-minute walk away and, after my initial training, I had realized my dream of a B.C. posting.

Chris and I bonded over our love of lacrosse and booze. On my weekends off, we'd sit and drink cases of beer and watch sports on TV. By August we'd been enjoying several months of these weekend beer and sports binges. Almost every weekend, we'd spot a rat in the back yard.

Cloverdale is almost at sea level. It's low and wet. Thankfully, my basement suite was dry and warm. Not everyone was so lucky. Basements in Cloverdale were notorious for being damp and impractical. Cloverdale is also notorious for its rats. In the low damp areas, rats live in holes that find their way down to the warm sewer pipes. To some residents, they are simply a common backyard pet.

Chris and I began our first rat hunt with Chris' pellet gun. We sat on the back porch watching, waiting and drinking beer. Our drunken state and wavering aim ensured any rat enjoyed complete safety. But we swore that someday, we'd get the buggers. Weeks later, between bouts of beer and The Wide World of Sports, I spotted a rat flash across the back lawn. The day was clear, hot and sunny. A good day for hunting.

"Chris, those little bastards are out there again. Let's get the sons of bitches!"

The plan was already fermenting nicely in my pickled brain. We'd burn the little bastards out.

"You start finding the holes," I ordered Chris.

While Chris started looking along the fence line, below the shrubs—all the dark places—I raided the garage and found the gas can for Rob's lawnmower.

"Over here!" Chris pointed as I walked from the garage into the bright back yard. Sure enough, there was a hole, a rat hole. I unscrewed the small cap on the red metal gas can and glugged a couple of ounces of gasoline down the hole.

"That'll scorch the little bastards."

"Over here!" Chris pointed again.

Hunting was good. Chris searched and pointed; I poured. He found burrows along the old fence at the back of the property and along the fences bordering both neighbours. He found them under bushes and he even found them right in the middle of the yard. He was a hell of a rat hunter.

I was a good pourer too. After 10 minutes of serious hunting, I think we'd found every one of them. I'd rationed the gasoline such that the last couple of ounces went slopping down the last hole we found. Now all we had to do was light the bastards up.

We retreated to the porch to discuss tactics. A cold beer, freshly cracked, allows for good thinking time, not to mention good percolation time. We decided that one of us would have to pull the trigger on this great rat hunt. We flipped a coin and I won, or lost, depending on your perspective.

Which is how I came to be holding a shovel of burning newspaper at arm's length in the middle of a gasoline soaked backyard in Cloverdale–while drunk.

After my experience in Peterborough, I wasn't going to put my face into a burrow to ignite the gasoline. Taking a crumpled piece of newspaper, I lay it on the shovel. Chris watched from the porch, sipping on a cold beer. I stood by the garage and lit the paper ball.

I started across the grass to the first hole about 25 feet away. I planned to be a good six feet from the hole on ignition. This was a good plan. Thank God I'd learned my lesson as a teenager. Gingerly, I extended my arm as the shovel came to within a foot of the hole in the middle of the lawn.

There was no warning. The whole fucking back yard blew up.

The ground heaved a good two feet. From fence line to fence line the yard wretched with the dull whomp of a gasoline explosion. Chris had found about 15 holes in all and I'd filled each one. From each hole came a geyser of flame 30 feet in the air. Trees and bushes were singed. Wires were scorched and fences were charred.

I can still see the small mushroom clouds that rose from that yard on 57A Avenue that bright, hot summer afternoon. I can still see Chris with eyes saucered in awe. The flames lasted just moments and it took Chris and me only a second to get back into the house. From behind the drapes we could see the neighbours on their back porches. It was the time of the Cold War and those mushroom clouds must have been a wonder to all of them.

To Chris and me it was a source of concern. We didn't talk much as we tried to absorb ourselves in Wide World of Sports. No cops came. No fire department. Why, I don't know to this day. As far as I know, the neighbours never mentioned it to Rob and Myrna, who were away at the time. I don't recall ever seeing a rat in their back yard again, though I purposely never looked too hard.

The next time it rained though, our sins would find us out. That nice dry basement was now filling with water. The explosion had shattered every weeping tile in the back yard. Rob and Myrna had to sell that house because of the leaks, and I lived there for another two years, in a wet basement.

Rob died in 1997 and I was summoned to the funeral. I was glad to be invited but surprised when I was asked to deliver his eulogy. The family wanted me to tell the story of The Great Cloverdale Rat Hunt of '69. I did the story proud and brought a tearful laugh to the family and friends.

I think I know all there is to know about gasoline now. As I write I have a rat living under my deck here on Sargent Road in Gibsons. Perhaps I'll use just a little less gas this time?

Round for the table

1971

Imagine being an alcoholic and getting paid to spend all day in beer parlours. I was working undercover, and a big part of that job was to be in the drinking establishments. The early '70s were a different time. We out here in British Columbia were living in the Wild West. The social mores of the time seem so foreign today. I won't deny my work was fun though. It was!

Let me introduce you to Peanuts.

Peanuts lives in a dingy, hole in the wall room in downtown Victoria. He wakes about 8 and immediately cracks a beer. He watches TV till about 11 and then opens a new syringe. He sticks it in his left arm at the crook of the elbow, gives it two pokes and watches the tracks appear. Next he applies drops to his eyes so they dilate to the size of quarters.

Then Peanuts gets dressed: worn and torn bell bottom jeans held up with a leather belt supporting a leather pouch with some hippy frills on it; confederate boots, a type of square-toed cowboy boot with straps and buckles; a black T-shirt unwashed in six months and reeking of ammonia. All topped off with dark welding glasses and a leather vest with frills.

It's 1971 and Peanuts is ready for work. In case you haven't guessed already, Peanuts is me.

One of the reasons I joined the RCMP was to work undercover. I looked years younger than my actual age. I knew the street and I loved the adrenaline rush of acting and improvising undercover. An undercover police officer is obviously not known by the public, and, probably not even known by police officers in the vicinity. Being undercover is a dangerous and risky business. It's acting but it's not like stage acting. If a stage audience doesn't like your performance they'll boo, hiss and maybe even throw buns at you. Undercover, if the audience doesn't like your performance, they may kill you.

Sometimes I played an asshole. The fact is that assholes don't even like assholes.

My character as an undercover operator embodied filth and slouching laziness. I sat all day in beer parlours, stinking and solitary for the most part. I had developed a character aged 17, a runaway from Ontario with a rich lawyer-father. 'Daddy' still sent bucks the odd time, so I always had cash to supposedly buy drugs.

How did I get the nickname Peanuts?

On my first day of RCMP training, Corporal Johnson had walked down our troop standing to attention in the middle of the gymnasium. He looked me in the eye. I stared back. My 5' 11" frame of 129 pounds stood erect and proud. With my shaved head and hairless face, I probably looked like an escaped high school freshman.

"What's your name?" Johnson yelled into my face.

"Hill, corporal!" I called back in loud, military fashion.

"Where are you from Hill?"

"Peterborough, Ontario, corporal."

"Well, that's where you're going back to Hill. Who the hell let you in my outfit anyways? Look at you. You're too small for this force. You're nothing but a peanut Hill. I'm going to break you Hill. You might as well go back to the dorm and pack up 'cause you're going back to Peterborough. We don't want no peanuts in this force."

Six months later at the passing out ceremony, I asked Corporal Johnson if he remembered that conversation. I was not only graduating but I was second in the troop of 32 guys in physicals.

"Sure I remember that conversation Hill," said Johnson. "It worked didn't it?"

The name Peanuts stuck all through training and into my first few years in Surrey. To this day, if someone says "hi" to Peanuts through someone else, I know they're from those years in the late '60s and early '70s. It was the same nickname that I used when I was undercover and it fit. By the time I was done in Victoria at the end of the summer of '71, I had busted more street level drug traffickers than any other undercover member to that time.

In the fall of 1971 I moved on to Chilliwack, which is where this story really begins. I was part of an experiment at that time. The Force had provided a motorhome for seven of us to work together in—seven undercover members all travelling together in one unit.

One of the problems of undercover work was infiltrating and buying in small, close-knit towns. Small towns seemed almost immune to the efforts of an undercover operation. The theory behind our experiment was that a large group of travelling assholes may have some success. We tried it and it worked.

Together we hit most every settlement from Langley to Hope. We bought dope in every town and busted a lot of dealers simply by driving in and being very loud, visible and crazy. We worked Mission, Abbotsford, Haney, Hope and even Harrison Hot Springs. Not only was it successful, it was fun. It was an all-expenses-paid road party!

We had hit Chilliwack and were staying at a motel in the east of town, near the freeway. From there we'd do daytrips to Agassiz and Mission. It was time to try the local beer parlour, the Empress. We were a varied group of assholes, some with tank tops and tattoos, one with a shoulder-length wig and another billiard-ball bald. We loaded into our motorhome and drove to downtown Chilliwack. Into the beer parlour we trekked as a group and we took over a table in the corner.

Some of us played pool, others just sat and talked. We played a beer parlour game of putting a dime on a napkin that had been stretched like a drum over the mouth of a beer glass. We'd wet the rim of the glass and then pull the paper napkin over it, tearing away the excess. The group would then take turns burning the paper ever so slightly with a lit cigarette. Sometimes the paper would end up holding the dime with hair-thin strips of paper. Whoever burned the paper last, causing the dime to drop, would have to buy a round —with government money of course.

The game not only passed the time, it drew the attention of beer parlour patrons. It was a great way to break the ice, particularly if we could lure some to the locals to join in.

We'd been in the bar no more than 20 minutes when I had to hit the can. No sooner had I begun my business when the door opened and in walked a patron. He used the urinal immediately to my right and I acknowledged his presence with a grunt and a nod. As I finished and turned to walk away, I spoke to him.

"You from here?" I asked as I bent over the sink.

"Yeah," was the short response.

"Do you know where I can get some dope in this town?" I said as I cranked some paper from the dispenser.

"Yeah, sure," came his answer as he zipped up and made for the door. "You're not a narc are you?" he asked.

By now we were both at the door of the washroom. I rolled the paper up in my hands and threw it into the waste basket. I reached and opened the door. He walked out and I walked out behind him.

Pointing to my table of six assholes playing, laughing and just being loud, I asked.

"You see those guys over there?"

"Yeah."

"Well, we're all narcs, every one of us. Now do you want to get me some dope or not?"

I turned and walked to my table, sat down and joined in the fun.

A minute later buddy showed up at the table, asking to sit down. He produced a bag of marijuana and proceeded to expound on the merits of his stuff. With seven RCMP members watching, listening, asking questions and observing, my newest friend in the world proceeded to sell me an ounce of marijuana. Our group sat and enjoyed the beer parlour for perhaps another hour and then we left. It was about three months later that buddy was busted and realized that I'd been telling the truth all along. We were all narcs.

When I attended the court case, almost a year later, my friend pleaded guilty. As the facts of the buy were read into court, he merely sat shaking his head at his own stupidity. Our "experiment" had worked, but I don't know of it ever being repeated. It was expensive and the priority of targeting street level dealers has taken a back seat since then.

Times have changed, but not soon enough for the poor dealer in Chilliwack who sold a round for the table to seven narcs in the

Empress Hotel in the fall of 1971.

A MEMBER OF DRUG SQUAD ON PATROL

Cartoon sketched by Don Ormiston

Bringing Joy into my life

1971

When I met Joy I was smitten immediately. The details of our meeting are truly destiny at work. I tell people to this day, over 40 years later, that I won my wife in a lottery!

Notoriety can be a mixed blessing. In the early '70s, my success as a drug squad member of Surrey Detachment earned me the hatred of anyone involved in the trade. My name had cult value! The Georgia Straight newspaper actually printed a classified ad about me. It stated that if anyone had any information about Surrey's Cst. Ed Hill that could be enacted legally, a legal fund was available to pursue it. To my knowledge, nobody answered the ad; at least I never ended up charged with anything in court.

But with such notoriety also comes respect, meaning informants would generally call me first. I'd already done a year undercover in Victoria. Now I was back in Surrey, living in White Rock with a couple of guys in a basement apartment overlooking the Government wharf and the ocean. We had a pool in the back yard and life was, for the most part, work, golf, drinking and fun. But mostly work.

Working undercover naturally means looking the part. I also specialized in going to jail to elicit information from criminals on the inside. My 'grooming' meant looking like a street person: Grubby T-shirt and jeans, square-toed Confederate leather boots, and a red and white plaid mackinaw coat to hide my snub-nosed .38 gun. To top it off, I often wore a pork-pie golf hat. It became my trademark. Druggies would complain about the cop "with the funny little hat."

Already balding, my thin, greasy hair came down to my shoulders. When my partner, Gary Spence, got married to his first wife Cathy I was best man. Gary's mother actually asked him to have me get my hair cut for the wedding, simply because I looked so awful. Gary explained my job to her, but his mother never really grasped the concept. I showed up for the wedding with my long hair groomed as neatly as I could, but I'm sure in her eyes, I still looked simply awful.

Coming from Peterborough, Ontario, I felt blessed to be transferred to British Columbia. I missed family though and kept in regular contact. At Christmas, I always bought gifts on time and got them home on time. I'd shop at Guildford Mall and go to the gift-wrap department at Woodwards. For two years in a row, the same woman did my wrapping. She was perhaps a couple of years younger than me; slim, with a dark complexion and beautiful, long, cascading black hair. What struck me most was her great and easy smile.

I walked away with my armload of gifts, thinking "Boy I'd love to get close to that lady!" That was it though. I don't recall ever stopping in to connect with her or even just to take another look at the beauty in the Guildford Woodwards' gift wrap department.

Until Christmas 1971.

Sure enough, the girl in the gift-wrap department at Woodwards was still there–in a red dress this year. God she looked good in red. She smiled and did the usual great job. I left again with warm thoughts about this very beautiful lady behind the counter.

About two months later Gary Spence's wife Cathy got a job at Woodwards' gift-wrap and fabric department. I immediately told Gary of the gorgeous lady behind the counter and asked him to investigate. See if there's any possibility of me getting to say hi or not, I asked.

A few days later, Gary told me the bad news. "Her name is Joy O'Bee. She's two years younger, but going out with a guy that she's known since high school."

I set my hopes aside, but told Gary that should an opportunity ever arise, Cathy was to let me know.

A few months later, Gary and I were on patrol. Cathy had come home with news. Apparently Joy had broken up with her boyfriend. She was available to consider going on a date. I immediately asked Gary to contact Cathy. I'd take Joy for coffee at the store, a safe first contact for her. The next day, word came back. Joy would see me for coffee at 10 a.m., Tuesday.

It happened the night before I was due to meet Joy.

I was alone, patrolling Cloverdale and had parked the car for a short walk through the Clover Inn Beer Parlour. Smoke and people filled the place as usual. At the far end of the bar sat a group of guys from a local motorcycle gang–dirty jean jackets, long hair and beards–about 15 of them. For the four years I'd been in the force, I'd known of their activities–drug smuggling, dealing, intimidation and assaults.

I walked the length of the bar and outside into the cool night air. I planned on checking in on the pool hall.

"Hey Hill!" a voice came from behind me.

I stopped and turned around. It was 'Ticker'–real name Howes–one of the gang who'd been in the bar. He was about my size–175 pounds, five-eleven or so. By now he was a foot from me. We were standing in the middle of the main intersection in downtown Cloverdale.

"Are you the asshole that's been busting all the guys around here?" He hit me with his right shoulder into my right shoulder.

"I'm the guy. Why?" I stood my ground, putting my right foot in front of me to protect my groin.

Ticker's shoulder barged into mine again. "Well you better cool it man."

"Cool it or what?" I baited him.

"Or there'll be trouble," he replied, giving me another shoulder.

We were now eye to eye, nose to nose.

"One more of those and you'll be the guy with trouble," I said quietly.

"Trouble from who?" he spit back.

"From me," I barked as my right hand came across his face. It was a glancing blow. He had been ready for what we both knew was coming next.

The talking was over. This guy was being arrested, though I never did get to say the actual words as I recall. We sparred and punched there in the middle of the street for a half a minute or so. We wrestled back towards the corner of the beer parlour. My back was to the pub and my heel hit the curb. I tripped. As I was going down I saw only Ticker's right boot as it smashed into my face.

As I hit the ground I knew he'd done damage. Blood was streaming from my nose and my left eye was already swelling shut as I bounced back up. The stars I saw were only momentary. I bounced to my feet and rushed Ticker, landing a flurry of punches and grappling him to the ground. Only then did I realize that the beer parlour had emptied. This had been a setup. The entire gang was out there and the moment I got the better of Ticker, they started pushing and kicking from behind me.

The policing gods were with me that night. A uniform car was patrolling the area and the cop inside saw the commotion. Still well tangled in my grasp, Ticker was arrested by the two of us and bundled into the police car. (For the record, Ticker was later found guilty of common assault and given a meagre fine. The judge, in his wisdom, ruled that this poor unfortunate man had no way of knowing that I was a police officer, given my appearance.)

The damage was done. My nose was all over my face and my left eye was shut. Together with my long stringy hair and pitiful face, I didn't make a very pretty picture at 10 o'clock the next morning.

Resplendent in my blue jeans, boots, T-shirt and mackinaw coat, I rode the escalator up through the centre of Woodwards and walked to the fabric counter where Joy worked. My hair was combed as neatly as it could be and I took off my dark glasses. With all the confidence I could muster, I spoke.

"Hi Joy, I'm Ed. Got time for coffee?"

Without hesitating, she was away from the counter and we were off. I could feel the eyes of Joy's co-workers. They were all very protective of her. I'd love to have overheard the conversation that day as beauty and the beast walked together down the aisles of Woodwards towards the coffee shop.

Our first encounter was a pleasant one. I explained my appearance and she accepted my story. We used every minute of her available time and we parted company agreeing that we'd get together on Thursday night. I'd explained that I couldn't really relax in Surrey or the Lower Mainland simply because of my job, so it was agreed that I'd pick Joy up from work and head for the border, to the Iron Bull, a club I knew in Bellingham.

I was so excited. Without doubt, she was the most beautiful woman I'd ever dated.

On Thursday, I met Joy. Thank goodness no photos exist of what

I wore that night: a two-piece polyester disco suit. The pants were tight and the vest top was stylish, for the day. The frilly shirt set it all off. Joy of course looked great in a long dress. She'd changed at work to save time and we were off. We talked all the way to Bellingham and already I sensed something special.

I was a very proud guy, bloated face and all, as we walked the block from the car to the Iron Bull. The only thing bugging me was my wallet, bulging in the pocket of my polyester pants. Somehow, it spoiled the look. Joy agreed to put it in her purse.

"Do you have your badge in here?" she asked.

"Sure, open it and you can see it."

She opened it and looked as she walked. Then she put it away in her purse. Inside the club we found a table and Joy opened her purse again. She began looking for something.

"Look at this!" she said, presenting me with her Woodwards employee card.

On the card was her employee number–8853.

By now she had my wallet out and opened again to expose my silver badge and its number–8853.

We danced the night into early morning.

I dropped Joy at her home on 137A St. in Whalley. I walked her to the front step, leaned over and gave her a polite and proper first night kiss on the cheek. We committed to see each other again and she turned and walked in, closing the door.

I turned and walked down the steps and said these words out loud:

"That's the girl I'm going to marry."

August 4, 1972

The Chilliwack Golf War

1975

Read this entire story for the punch line. Of all my stories, this one perhaps best illustrates not only my drinking problem, but also how potentially dangerous it could be.

Some punch lines take longer to deliver than others: 16 years in the case of the Chilliwack Golf War! You could say this story starts in my teenage years when I fell in love with golf. Or it may have begun in the early '70s when S/Sgt. Ray Boisvert and I created the annual RCMP Provincial Golf Tournament.

But let's start in 1975 at the Chilliwack Golf and Country Club, host venue for that year's tournament. Joy and I had been married for a year and we were soon to be transferred to Vernon. This would be my last tournament playing out of Surrey and my intentions of winning were as serious as ever. (That would actually happen three years later at the 108-Mile Ranch golf course—my Masters and US Open all wrapped up in one!)

About 140 of us stayed at a small, two-storey Chilliwack motel, the kind that's shaped in a square U with only a wrought-iron railing obstructing your view of the car park. After the first day's practice round, I'd had my usual pre-tournament night with the guys, followed by the first day of competition. Back then my rule was simple: If, at the end of Day 1, I was within five shots of the lead, I'd go on the wagon for the night. No drinking!

I could hit the ball over 300 yards and scored in the mid to low 70's regularly. In Vernon, I peaked with a three-handicap. I had visions of early retirement and becoming a club professional. But, I had a problem with my game: I drank too much. I simply couldn't go to one of these events without over-indulging. I had a great time, but I was always handicapping myself to the field with a hangover.

So it was in 1975. After Day 1, I was about 10 shots back. It was time to party. After all, if you can't win the tournament, there's always drinking. It was a warm September evening and I was well into my scotch early. I thoroughly enjoyed my scotch, the glow, and the friendship of the guys that I'd see each year at these tournaments. I was wandering the motel, drink in hand, simply looking for familiar faces.

Each room had its door open and inside would be a clutch of guys sitting on beds, bull-shitting away. Card games were in progress. Some would be small games for quarters and dollars. Others would be for hundreds, even thousands of dollars. No matter how drunk I got, I'd never get involved in the big games. I didn't play much poker, but that night I was on a mission. I wanted to play. I guess I was feeling lucky.

It must have been about 10 p.m. as I wandered from room to room looking for a game, but the tables were all full. There was no room for one more, especially one in such a drunken state.

On the second floor balcony, I ran into Cst. Toni Fox with a group of guys. Toni and I had worked general duty in Surrey, and had golfed many a tournament together. Facing me with a drink in one hand, a cigarette in the other, Toni had no intention of playing cards, especially with a drunk like the one standing before him. A stocky, tough hockey player with broad shoulders and a broader chest, Toni is not a man to be trifled with.

"Toni, wanna play some cards?" I slurred.

"Not tonight Eddy!" came the polite brush-off.

"Come on Toni, let's get a game together," I insisted, shouldering my way into the small group.

"No Eddy, not tonight. Go find someone else."

"Come on Toni," I said, reaching up and flicking the cigarette from Toni's mouth.

I woke up some hours later in Ted Thurston's camper. I've known Ted throughout my service. When he found my bloody corpse, he'd merely put me in his camper to sleep it off. I awoke with a hell of a headache, on a blood soaked pillow, and desperately needing another drink.

I got up, found some scotch, and partied on. I was a little more subdued, as I remember it, and I watched the rest of the evening through one eye. All I remembered was Toni's big fist approaching my face. The end result was a split lip, cracked jaw, broken nose, closed eye and a chipped molar.

The next morning, my friend Les Howard came to caddy for me. The expression on Les's face told me how bad I looked. He had hoped to come and caddy for a contender. He ended up caddying for a real winner. At the banquet that night, my prize was a raw steak for my swollen eye. It was actually presented to me at the prize table. I'd certainly made an impression.

Joy's grandfather was visiting when I returned home to Surrey. Joy and I will always remember his fits of laughter as I walked in from a golf tournament looking like I'd just gone 10 rounds with Cassius Clay. Granddad always marvelled at how such a drunk could also be a cop.

That might have been the end of the story, but for a chance conversation some 16 years later. It was in the summer of 1991 and I was fishing on Blane Hagedorn's boat in the Gibsons RCMP fishing derby. In the group was Ted Thurston, who'd taken care of me as my 'cut man' in the one-punch fight I'd had with Toni.

We were sitting at the stern with Blane and the others watching our rods and waiting for no fish to bite. We were reminiscing, laughing and swapping war stories. I took the opportunity to tell the story of the Chilliwack tournament. I hadn't touched booze for seven years by now, so stories of my drinking days seemed all the more unlikely. I'd actually quit drinking on October 23, 1984.

When I finished my story, I noticed Ted wasn't laughing. I can still remember Ted looking at me after 16 long years and saying: "You don't remember that night, do you Ed? Nobody's ever told you, have they?"

It's true, I didn't remember much—just flicking the cigarette from Toni's mouth and then the fist, but that's about it. The next thing I remembered was waking up in a dark place, wondering where I was and what the fuck had hit my head.

Ted looked surprised.

"Ed, everybody there kept this from you because they figured you might sue Toni."

"Sue?" I cried. "Drunks get what they deserve. I got what I deserved that night. Water under the bridge."

I held no grudge.

"Ed, I was in the group with Toni that night," said Ted. "When you flicked that cigarette, Toni took one swing at you. I don't think he even spilled a drop from his glass. He got you flush in the face and you flew backwards right over the railing and down two floors onto the hood of a car.

"If you'd have landed on the ground, you'd be dead.

"We all ran down and checked you out. You were still alive so we put you in my camper."

Ted paused, waiting for my reaction, along with the others on board.

I was shocked. I was also in stitches. I had lived, I was still kicking. I laughed until my sides hurt. I had dodged another bullet and I hadn't even known it. It had taken me 16 years to hear the punch line!

I've seen Toni over the years since. I harbour no hard feelings. In fact, I've never mentioned the incident for fear of stirring up scary memories for him. Ted tells me he was very remorseful and scared to death about what might have happened.

When I look back at the drunken escapades of my life, I realize just how fortunate I was. Perhaps no war story better illustrates that than the tale of The Chilliwack Golf War.

The Mary Milford story

1973

This is the most intriguing story of my undercover days in the RCMP; a tale of murder, chance and coincidence beyond belief. Looking back on the details of these events, I'm still in wonder of how it unfolded. Surely, higher powers were at work.

It was about ten minutes before six when I walked back into the pool hall. As the door swung closed behind me the hair stood up on the back of my neck. I could see Lysche at the table we'd been at earlier in the day. He was playing a rack on his own, waiting for me. Something was different though. There were maybe 20 people in the room. Some played pool. Some merely talked. But something didn't feel right. I noticed furtive glances cast my way. I'd been burned. They were on to me.

*****

Mary Milford was murdered in Stanley Park in 1972. She was strangled, beaten over the head and then buried under brush and left to decompose. Milford's skeletal remains were found in March 1973. Unidentified at the time, she was buried as Jane Doe.

She may have remained Jane Doe but for a remarkable sequence of events set in motion on Wednesday, September 12, 1973. While stranger than fiction, the following is all true.

Vancouver City Police continued to investigate Jane Doe's murder long after she was buried. They got a break when an informant named Andy Lysche told a beat cop that he knew the murderers and was willing to introduce them to an undercover cop. That's where I came in. Detective Ray Peterson called me early that morning and explained what was needed. I was to meet Lysche and the investigating officers at Vancouver City Police offices; go undercover; meet the murderers and solicit a confession.

I'd been working undercover from time to time and in various capacities all over Vancouver Island and throughout the Lower Mainland since 1971. I'd been married to Joy for just over a year. By now she was used to me responding to vague phone calls at all times of day or night. I specialized in going to jail. In total, I've done about a month in jail at various times. A day or two here and there soon adds up. I've been in cells with murderers, rapists, arsonists, bank robbers and extortionists, all with success. I'd portray anything from being a drunk driver to a pervert. I'd live in that confined space with the suspect, gain his confidence and get an admission from him about the crime he'd committed. I even spent Boxing Day in jail once!

Joy was used to me going to jail. I'd dress in my street clothes, knock back a quick belt of scotch, and be gone for a day or two. Such was the life of an undercover RCMP member in those days. Joy was a source of huge support and strength. For the first year and a half of our marriage she slept with a loaded shotgun beside the bed when I was away. We also had Sheena, a trained German Shepherd guard dog. I carried a snub-nose 38 everywhere with me, on duty or off. I had a contract on my head. Few wives would have handled it the way Joy did.

So as the phone rang that morning, Joy thought little of it when I announced I'd be away on a job. I called my office in Cloverdale and advised them where I'd be. At the police station on Main Street I met Ray Peterson and Sam Andrews, a 350-pound hulk of a man –the proverbial legend in his own time. Everyone had heard of him, not only as a crack detective but also because of his size.

Both men outlined the story. After a year of dead ends in the investigation, Sam and Ray had a fink. Andy Lysche was to be my 'buddy' for however long it took to nail our suspects. He was ushered in to meet me.

Andy was perhaps 21 years old, a biker without a bike. He was a street person trying to be someone he'd never be. I couldn't tell if his dark hair was slicked back with grease or dirt. He had small, dark glasses and a clean shaven face. The silver chains and bobbles adorning his black leather jacket jangled and chinked every time he moved. The jacket covered a dark T-shirt and his tight blue jeans showed off his spindly legs. His leather cowboy boots bore yet another chain. He was a cross between an urban cowboy and a '69 Chevy resplendent with all its chrome.

Not that I looked any more appealing. In September 1973, I

was a sight to behold. My greasy shoulder-length hair was long and stringy. I had a scruffy beard and I wore big sunglasses for my sensitive eyes–a holdover from undercover drugs work when I'd put drops in my eyes every day for a freshly glazed look. I'd also poke a clean needle in my arm every day to keep the tracks fresh. (For a more detailed description of how bad I looked and smelled, see 'Round for the table'.)

In short, I looked nothing like a cop, which is exactly the look I wanted. My personality would be that of Ed Mills, a 17-year-old runaway from Peterborough, Ontario. I was an avid pool player and was making money at it. My father had been a lawyer and was still helping me out by sending money now and again. I dressed in a clean T-shirt, blue jeans and congress boots. I looked so young in those days that I could pull the personality off effortlessly.

Immediately Lysche stood, shook my hand and started talking. He had ideas and plans, agendas and initiatives. He was going to get this thing done and I was going to be along for the ride.

Sam beat me to it. He told Lysche to sit down and shut it. Then he laid out the game plan. Lysche and his teenage runaway pool shark buddy would go to Seymour Billiards on Seymour Street. Lysche knew the suspects from that place so naturally that would be where we'd first try to cross paths. We'd play pool until they came in. Lysche would introduce one or both of them to me and I'd be the boss from there on.

The plan was simple and I liked it. One of the most dangerous traps an undercover cop can fall into is to allow others to tell him how to do his job. You must be in character and only you can write the script as it unfolds. The detectives back in the office must trust you. Mistakes can leave you with a face alteration or worse.

It was set then. We'd go to Seymour Billiards and let the play begin.

I drove my own car downtown with Lysche and parked well away from Seymour Street. We walked and talked together and made our way to one of Canada's most famous pool halls of the day. Seymour Billiards was just down the street from another famous institution –The Penthouse.

The Penthouse in those days had its reputation. Right or wrong, the word on the street was that it was well known for its Mafia connections. While The Penthouse survived, Seymour Billiards was torn down in the late '90s. This wasn't a better part of town. Wrong moves here had consequences. Being undercover is like being an actor, but with potentially fatal implications for a poor performance. Andy Lysche and Ed Mills walked in the Seymour entrance of Seymour Billiards and Act One began.

Seymour Billiards was huge, with between 30 and 40 tables. The outside wall featured a large plastic pool cue and coloured balls that were lit from within. The sign itself was a downtown icon. You didn't have to shoot pool to know Seymour Billiards. Unlike the stereotypical pool hall, this one was bright with windows on two sides. The desk was right there beside the front door on the Seymour Street side and we picked up balls for a snooker game making our way to a solitary table at the back. If these guys showed up, I didn't want others listening in.

It felt a bit like a movie as we strode through the hall. Some of the characters wore black pants, patent leather shoes and small shiny vests. Others looked more basic in their muscle shirts designed to show off tattoos and biceps. The smoke hung low in the bright room, tinged blue by the sunlight. The place was half full at 11 in the morning, but by mid-afternoon the place would fill.

We racked the balls and began to play. I had played pool since I was a teenager in Peterborough, and had used my talents as a prop during my undercover work. Until the bad guys showed up I was happy to practice. I cautioned Lysche to let me lead the conversation. His job was to introduce me, and provide chat. My job was to lead the suspects to areas we needed to talk about. He agreed and we played on, waiting for someone to show.

It took just a little less than an hour. I was leaning over a shot and Lysche spoke.

"He's here!"

No matter how long I did this job, I always got a rush at the moment of truth. It's one of the reasons I did the job. I looked up from my shot to the far end of the pool hall and there he was at the front door—my soon to be new friend. He stood perhaps 5' 8" with ratty brown hair framing his young face. Lysche waved the length of the hall and the newest addition to the Seymour Billiards community nodded and walked towards us. I sunk a red ball in the side pocket.

I circled the table while Lysche and our guest talked at the opposite end of the table. Lysche introduced me with "That's Ed!"

I lifted my head from my shooting stance, said "Hi" and stroked the shot. The shot made, I stood and circled again stalking my next red ball. I was on a roll and had little time to talk of less serious things.

"This here is Jean," offered Lysche. I nodded and leaned into my next shot.

Undercover, I never wanted to be the first to talk. I've gone to jail and slept for 24 hours in the cell rather than be the one to initiate conversation. If I can pull that off then the bad guy can always rationalize that I'm not digging. Once the talking starts, I'll do the digging. It was apparent that wasn't going to work here. I didn't know how much time we'd have together, and I could sense right away that Jean was street-wise and wasn't about to invite me out for coffee and donuts any time soon. He was quiet and indifferent. I changed my style and game plan in mid-stream. I began to talk, talk, talk. I told him my life story, the Reader's Digest version, and Lysche and I kept playing pool.

I told him about running away from home. I'd had it with high school and all that shit. My dad was a lawyer, had lots of money, and was glad to see me gone. He'd send money whenever I needed it and I was doing OK. I sure liked the Vancouver scene and I planned on staying for a long while. Who knew, I may even go back to school someday. I used to do pretty well and as long as the old man sent the bucks, why not? I didn't really have any place special to stay yet. Somehow I'd like to get wheels and be able to move around. Maybe I'd even move a bit of weed to make an extra buck or two.

"Green ball in the corner."

For half an hour, I talked and talked. My new friend listened. Lysche played pool and listened. I had to set the scene if my bullshit story was going to work.

"Andy tells me you've got a problem."

I dropped that sentence on the table like spilled coffee.

Now I had his attention. I had touched a nerve and I only hoped that my preamble had sunk in enough to be of value.

"What do you mean?" Jean asked in broken English. Jean was from Montreal and you could cut his accent with the blunt end of a pool cue.

"The problem about the girl in the park," I said.

Jean glanced quickly at Andy. The look said it all. He wasn't pleased. I jumped back in right away.

"Andy told me because he thought I could help," I said.

I explained that I had picked up a lot from the old man over the years and I knew a hell of a lot more about the law than most people on the street. That was one of the reasons the old man kept sending money. I kept telling him that I'd be back to go to Law School and become a lawyer and all that bullshit.

"Hey, if you don't want to talk about it, that's fine with me. If you do, then maybe I can help," I said.

"Want another game?" I asked Lysche and racked the balls.

I felt that Jean was a willing audience. I'd thrown the bait his way and I felt he believed. Sometimes that moment can take days, but I didn't know if I'd have days with Jean. This wasn't just a test of Jean, it was a test of my senses as an undercover operator.

"I don't want to talk about it without my brother," said Jean. It would turn out to be that the two were not actually "brothers", rather that was merely how the two referred to each other as "brothers".

Lysche was surprised, pointing out that Jean had told him that he'd done it with a friend. Jean reiterated that it was in fact his brother that he had done it with.

Either Jean had bought the story and was genuine about wanting to get his brother in on the discussion, or he was merely giving himself an exit, never to be seen again. I sensed though that I had him. Jean asked if we could meet somewhere else to talk and we agreed that we'd all meet at the 616 Club on Pender Street in one hour. Jean would go out and find his brother and bring him to the club where we could talk. With trepidation, I agreed. I really felt that I had this guy and I could have pursued the talk just a bit more. But I didn't want to screw it up, particularly if he was going to bring his brother and implicate him in all of this.

As I stood over Lysche taking a shot I watched as Jean left the pool hall. I was excited, but worried. All I had was a street person named Jean who had admitted in an offhand way that he had a problem with a girl in the park. I didn't know who he was, where he lived, anything at all about him. He was our guy but there he was gone out the door and vaporizing into the streets of downtown Vancouver. I prayed that my story had set the hook deep down his throat, otherwise the memory of him walking out the doors of the pool hall would be all I had to offer the Vancouver City Police.

With an hour to kill, Lysche and I continued to play pool. The 616 Club was just around the corner a block or two away. The hour dragged and my mind wandered. Would these guys show or not?

At ten to two, we left the blue smoke and stale air of the pool hall and turned right on Seymour. We walked to the club—thanks to Lysche—found the non-descript entrance. From bright sunshine we found ourselves in the relative darkness of the 616 Club. Years of walking from bright sun into darkened beer parlours and clubs, on duty of course, had taught me to close my eyes for about two seconds upon entering a room. Those two or three steps between the glare of the sun and the dark of the interior were usually done with my eyes tight shut. That would allow for a quicker adjustment of the eyes when they opened to the darkness. It works—try it sometime. I did the same thing upon entering the 616 club.

Plastic filled the room. Coloured plastic ornaments dimmed the cheap, dull lighting. The chairs looked plastic. The plants were plastic and the canned music sounded plastic. Perhaps 15 people were in the room, which wouldn't have held more than 75. There were high backed booths along two walls, a few tables in the centre of the room, a minute stage, a dance floor and a door that led to a bar/kitchen area.

My eyes adjusted and Lysche was being greeted by someone who obviously knew him. The club owner now welcomed us both and pointed us to the soft leather seats of one of the booths. He was a small man, about 30, neatly groomed with short hair. He wore a long sleeved, pale coloured silk shirt, and a little tight-fitting leather vest. His pants fit tightly from crotch to hem and his little leather shoes came to a point.

Lysche and this little guy kissed—full on the mouth, tongue down the throat, long and wet. I shut my gaping mouth and remembered quickly that this was a play that I was acting in, a play in which the script had just taken a surprising turn. I waved a polite greeting to the owner who had now turned his gaze towards me. I walked towards the booth he had pointed to and slid in with my back firmly against the seat and facing back towards the door. I could see the entire room from my seat. Now I could see everyone. Some sat at tables or in booths. Some were dancing, while others stood and talked. Some kissed, fondled and groped. There were tongues, hands and embraces all around. The slow dancing was merely a vehicle for more elaborate intimate contact. The place had a life of its own, a life that I had only heard about and read about before. I needed a drink.

By now the owner had joined Lysche and me at the table. Lysche sat opposite me, the owner slid in beside Lysche. Scotch was my preference and the owner tootled off across the dance floor to the bar, returning in short order with drinks for us. I paid.

As new patrons entered, they'd spot the owner sitting with us. Most gave a quick wave and went on their way to a table. Some came to the table and said hello with a long wet greeting. My drink never left the front of my face. I perused the play I was in, peeking over the top of a scotch glass. I had to get my eyes back to normal size. I had to get into the play. I had a scene to act in a few minutes. If Jean showed, I had to be comfortable in such a place. I just hoped that nobody wanted to get to know me intimately.

We talked for perhaps 15 minutes before the owner was gone. I'd see him from time to time, flitting around the room, but he never bothered us again. Lysche and I sat talking and I bought a second round.

I saw him walk in as the door opened and the outside light created a natural spotlight. It was Jean. He stopped at the entrance and looked around. I gave a short wave and he immediately walked our way. He sat beside Lysche and asked Jean if his brother had showed up yet. Jean said that he hadn't and I asked if he wanted a drink. He did. I went to the bar and bought him a beer.

Back at the table the three of us talked about the problem in the park. This wasn't a social visit. Jean was fidgety. He wanted to talk, but not yet. He said he'd talk about it only when his brother got there. He'd talked to him and his brother had promised to meet him here. Jean looked around the room and over his shoulder almost every two minutes or so, but no brother. He was concerned that maybe he wouldn't show. I was rooting for his brother to show, too. As much as Jean wanted to talk, I wanted to listen. Where the hell was his brother?

After yet one more furtive glance around the room, Jean quickly got up from his seat and walked to the door. He approached a man about his age, mid to late twenties, standing at the entrance. The two talked for a minute. They talked and looked and pointed. Jean did the pointing, in our direction, then the two walked our way. Jean now sat beside me and his brother sat beside Lysche.

"Hi, I'm Ed," I reached across the table and extended my hand.

With a glance towards Jean first, he turned back to me, extended his hand and gave a weak handshake across the table. His hair was an inch longer than Jean's but the same drab colour of brown. He wore a paper thin white T-shirt and blue jeans.

"What's your name?" I wanted the script to reveal something more than his mere presence.

"Pierre," and he looked back to Jean.

Jean went on to explain that I was the guy he had talked about. I would help them with their problem. I listened as Jean did a feeble job of explaining who I was. It was time for me to jump into the script in a more definitive way. I explained to Pierre my situation. I told him of my lawyer father, the money he kept me in, my experience and learning in law through close association with my father. I spent five minutes setting the stage. I wanted to end this act of the play with all of the players well defined. When we got to Act Two I wanted everyone to know their part and I couldn't wait to hear their lines.

"So what's this problem you guys got?" I asked, sitting back with the cocky confidence of a brash 17-year-old runaway.

Silence. The two looked across the table at each other and neither wanted to say the first word. I waited a few seconds then jumped in again. Someone in this play had forgotten their lines.

"Look, Andy told me something about a girl, over in the park and that you guys know something about it. You were there or something. From what he told me, I think I can help. Fill me in on it and I think you've got nothing to worry about." I waited again.

They shuffled and fidgeted. Their body language told me they were close. Lysche was getting anxious too. He began to try to help by telling the two to tell me what happened. He assured them that I would be able to help.

Seconds passed. Then Pierre spoke.

"It happened last summer ..."

And the story began. As Pierre talked Jean would jump in with details to clarify or add to the tale. In all, their story took no more than five minutes. They handled their part of the script very well.

They had met a girl–they didn't know her name–on Granville Street. They had gone with her to Stanley Park. It wasn't clear how they had gone to the park, walking or in a vehicle. At the park they had gone down to the water and raped her. When it was over, the two young men worried about being identified so they decided to kill her: no witness to the rape, no trouble with the police. While Jean had strangled her with her own belt, Pierre had taken a rock from the beach and crushed her head. Her dead body was then dragged up into the salal brush and undergrowth of the higher ground and buried in a makeshift grave of sand, rocks, sticks and leaves. They left the park and ever since they'd worried about it. That's how Andy knew. They had confided in him.

My heart was racing. I had them. They knew details that only the murderers would know. My job now was to identify these two. Only first names are used on the street for this very reason. It makes identifying bad guys difficult. I determined that they didn't have a vehicle so license plates would be out of the question. They were not offering their place of residence so I had nothing to chase there. I could phone the Vancouver City Police and get Andrews or Peterson on the phone, but who could guarantee that they'd get here before the two left. I'd just have to write another act into the script, that's all there was to it.

"Were you guys drunk when you did this? Drunk or stoned?" I asked.

"We were stoned," offered Pierre.

"And were there any witnesses when you did it?"

"No," said Pierre.

"Have you told anybody else other than Andy or me?"

The two looked at each other and in chorus provided "No."

"Hell, you got nothin' to worry about then. I'll show you," and I leaned over the table and lowered my voice. The brothers leaned in to listen. Andy leaned in too. He had no idea where this script was taking us. So far he'd done a good job as a supporting cast.

I recited what the two had just told me. Each time I'd come to an important part I'd wait for confirmation, or explanation, from the two. They knew the script well and confirmed who did what, adding detail and providing colour commentary. This was really going well. These two were desperate though. They wanted to believe. Their months of torment were driving them over the edge.

I told them that being high on drugs was a defence. I added that maybe she wasn't actually dead when they dragged her into the bush and that somebody else had killed her, particularly if they admitted only to strangling her. Obviously it was somebody else who finished her off. Perhaps she was high herself, which was a huge defence. Lighting too was important. Wasn't it so dark that you really couldn't see a whole lot? I continued with the rationalizations, excuses and defences. Their body language said it all. They were eating the bait in huge chunks. By the time I finished my summary and defence presentation, they were nodding and even smiling. Hell, they hadn't even been there that day. What girl? What murder?

"Look you guys. I'll show you. I'll even be able to build you a better defence," I offered. "I'll rent a car. I got lots of my old man's money. And we'll go over there. You guys show me where it happened, what you did, where you put her and all of that and I'll show you your defence."

Boy had I changed the script for the next act.

That sounded great to Jean and Pierre. I'd rent a car and we'd meet at Seymour Billiards in two hours and drive over to Stanley Park. That would put us in the park in the early evening, at dusk, and we could go about our business in relative privacy, except for the 12 cops I'd have in the bushes videotaping the re-enactment. Except for the cops I'd have monitoring our conversations in the wired car and through the mic that would be on me. Other than that we'd be on our own. The two agreed and in seconds were gone.

After checking to see we weren't being followed, Lysche and I made our way to my car parked blocks away. Our destination of course was right back to Vancouver City Police headquarters. There I told the anxious investigators of what I had so far. They were happier than a bunch of guys getting off shift after 12 hours on duty. Their investigation, time, work and effort were all paying off.

The detectives needed time with me to talk and plan and I had to do my notes so Lysche returned to Seymour Billiards to await my arrival there a few minutes before the appointed meeting time. The detectives frantically prepared for a great closing scene.

It was about ten minutes before six when I walked back into the pool hall. As the door swung closed behind me the hair stood up on the back of my neck. I could see Lysche at the table we'd been at earlier in the day. He was playing a rack on his own, waiting for me. Something was different though. There were maybe 20 people in the room. Some played pool. Some merely talked. But something didn't feel right. I noticed furtive glances cast my way. I'd been burned. They were on to me.

Lysche and I played a very tense game of pool. Instinctively I knew what had happened but I had to play out the scene in case I was wrong. I sank a few shots. In a hushed conversation over the table, Lysche admitted that he had told a friend about our little play. "But everything is cool," he assured me. Everything wasn't cool. Jean and Pierre were nowhere to be seen. They were 30 minutes late. They were gone. I didn't even know who they were. They'd spit the hook, changed the script and run off stage at the best part of the play. Lysche and I left the pool hall with 40 eyes stabbing at my back.

Finks become finks for varied reasons, but the most dangerous finks are the ones who do it for an appreciative audience; to be listened to. That was Andy Lysche. He had left the police station, returned to the pool hall and found friends to visit. He'd shared his adventure with one of them, revealing the fact that I was an undercover cop. Of course he'd sworn his friend to secrecy and of course his friend had immediately told a friend, who told a friend. My cover was blown.

Back at headquarters I told my sad story. Lysche wasn't a popular man. Sam, Ray and I all gave him shit. It wasn't a happy room.

Sam poured me a coffee mug shot of Crown Royal and thrust it in my direction. "You did a good job, Ed. Thank you. Head back to Surrey and we'll work on the rest. Not much more you can do."

I downed my Crown Royal and left. Lysche followed me out the door.

"Are you from Surrey?" he asked. "I know dealers in Surrey. I could help you out there."

"Your kind of help I don't need Andy. Let's call it an experience and we'll see ya later."

He wouldn't take no for an answer. He insisted that he could help. He'd do it better. Just give him a chance.

I stopped and considered.

"Meet me at the Dell Hotel parking lot tomorrow afternoon at four and I'll show you how you can help," I said.

If he didn't show though, all bets were off. I would have bet my next pay cheque he wouldn't show. I had some dealers in the Flamingo Hotel beer parlour that I was working on so if he did show, if he really could help, they'd be my target. I left trying to forget Lysche rather than expecting great things from him.

It was a long drive home. I mused over how I could have done it better. Could I have pressed for last names? Could a cover man have followed them? Chalk it up to life's lessons. The Vancouver cops would work on it, maybe they'd stumble on these guys and maybe someday I'd get to use my notes. The prospects didn't look good though.

It was four o'clock on the day after my Vancouver performance. I drove into the Dell Hotel parking lot and there he was. Leaning against a post, shiny chrome and all, there he was. How he'd got to Surrey I didn't know, and didn't want to know. I stopped the car and he jumped into the passenger seat. It was all business. I was still pissed at this guy. I told him of my problem at the Flamingo and described two heroin dealers who sold their product there. His job was to get close to them, determine if they were carrying dope and where they hid it. I specifically told him not to buy any dope. His job was to collect intelligence and report back to me.

I gave him $50, my home phone number and a verbal kick in the ass as he got out of the car. Any deviation from my instructions and he'd be on his own. As the door closed I put my foot down hard on the gas pedal and sped away. I kissed the $50 goodbye, certain I'd seen the last of Andy Lysche and my money.

At 11:30 that evening I was in the drowsy world between sleep and consciousness when the phone rang.

"Yeah!" I answered on the second ring.

It was a uniform member from the Cloverdale office. He had a story to tell me. Apparently some guy by the name of Lysche had been drinking in the Flamingo. At about 10:30 he'd got up from his table and followed a woman out into the back parking lot. He'd had quite a skin full of booze and was in the throes of forcing her into the bushes when a patrol car drove through the lot.

She'd called for help and the member had responded. Lysche was arrested as a drunk. A few seconds later probably would have resulted in an assault charge or worse. He was now drunk in the cells in Cloverdale, insisting that he was working for Hill. He kept pushing someone to call me and he'd even given them my home number.

I told the member on the phone that Mr. Lysche was not working for me. He was to leave him in the cells and let him sober up. Handle Lysche in whatever way is appropriate, I said. My working relationship with this jerk was over. How could I have let this dork play me, not once but twice?

I went to work the next day with little humour in my heart. Lysche was still in the cells awaiting possible assault charges. They had 24 hours to hold him and they intended to use every minute of it. I found a note on my desk. "Lysche, prisoner in cells–wants to talk to you!" it read. I tossed it into the garbage.

"Hey Ed, how's your fink?" shouted a colleague as I crossed the room for my morning coffee. By now my story was out. Lysche had been stirring up such a fuss that virtually everyone knew about it and I would have to endure the jibes for a day.

By mid-afternoon, in spite of all good intentions, my humour and patience were wearing thin. A uniform member from downstairs poked his head in my office door and said "Ed, that Lysche guy downstairs is really stirring things up to see you: Just thought you'd like to know."

"He'll see me alright." I stood as I spoke and marched downstairs and into the guard room.

"Which cell is Lysche in?" I asked the guard.

"Number 5, third cell on your right, Ed," he said as he handed me the large brass key that opened the main door to the cell block.

This son of a bitch had stung me twice now and he was going to hear about it. I focussed on cell 5 and sure enough, there was Andy Lysche, dressed just the way I had left him yesterday, minus his jacket, boots and belt.

"Listen here, you asshole. The next time I see your face will be too soon. If I ever..."

"Shhhhh!" he interjected, waving both hands. "Shhhh!"

This caught me short. I stopped in mid-sentence. Lysche's hands were still in front of him, palms towards me. With his right hand, he pointed past my left shoulder.

"Look!"

I reluctantly turned and looked over my left shoulder, directly into the cell opposite Lysche, into cell 6.

Sitting on separate bunks were Jean and Pierre.

I still remember my first word.

"Gotcha!"

They sat in submissive positions with heads and eyes downcast, shoulders slumped. I imagine they knew the jig was up when they'd seen Lysche in the cell across from them. After all, they'd got word off the street that he was working with a narc. That's why they hadn't showed up for their appointment.

I left the cell area and immediately returned to my office. I gave specific written and verbal instructions to the jailer directing that the two prisoners in cell 6 were not to be released under any conditions. I started working on the murder investigation again.

Pierre and Jean had fled downtown Vancouver the day before. They'd stolen a car and made for the border. Somewhere in Surrey they'd been in an accident and both had been arrested. Under assumed names they'd appeared in court in Surrey and even as I'd stormed down to see Lysche they were in the process of being released.

Had I not gone down when I did they'd have been gone within the hour. The coincidence of it all amazes me to this day. Had Lysche been in any other cell he wouldn't have seen them and I would likely have never known they were there. In the Lower Mainland, a region of over a million people in those days, what were the odds?

I called Sam at Vancouver City Police and gave him the news. He was in a state of disbelief. I know his was a happy office though. The trial of Jean Francois and Pierre Aubut took place in 1974. Both men were found guilty and sentenced to hang. I believe at least one of them is out on the street again on parole. We now know that they also killed a young boy who apparently witnessed the murder. Like Mary Milford, the boy had been a street kid and to this day his body has not been identified.

It was a high profile trial with famous Vancouver lawyer Harry Rankin defending one of the defendants. The trial also had its own twist. Forensic coroner, Bart Bastien, introduced evidence that the unknown girl murdered by Pierre and Jean was in fact 16-year-old Mary Milford. It was apparently the first time in Canadian justice that a conviction had been handed down when the deceased had been identified by dental records.

I never saw or heard from Andy Lysche again.

Dressed for court, Surrey Drug Squad, 1973

The marijuana detector

1973

A sense of fun is essential to survive almost 35 years in police work. Danger, tedium and endless paperwork are inevitable and part of the job. Whenever the opportunity for fun arose, I seldom passed it up, even at the expense of a marijuana dealer.

Working the Drug Squad in Surrey was the perfect job for me at the time. I was single for most of it, so I could work hard and play hard. Sometimes I'd get an hour during a 20-hour workday, so I always carried my wedge and golf balls. I'd stop at some park and hone my skills with the short game.

The job could be dangerous and it could be tedious. But I loved the work, the life and the energy of it all.

In the summer of 1973, possessing marijuana was still a relatively serious matter. I learned of a small-time drug dealer in Cloverdale, who was selling marijuana out of his apartment. And thanks to an informant, I knew exactly where to find it. My fink told me that the guy hid the drugs in the bag of his vacuum cleaner, just inside the front door of the apartment.

Every cop wants to protect his informant. Sometimes we'd delay busts or design them so the suspect was 'accidentally' collared in a road check. I had an idea how I could keep my fink cool yet search the apartment right now.

Phil Johnson and Mike Maloney were my partners in those days. Phil still had one of the last Writs of Assistance in Canada. That's a blank search warrant allowing an immediate search with grounds: No need to ask a Justice of the Peace or a Judge—just enter and search.

It was a short drive to our man's second-storey apartment. With my long greasy hair and my mackinaw coat, I knocked on the door in full view of the peep hole. I looked like some shitty druggy and I didn't think this guy would recognize me. Sure enough, the door opened and we were in. The three of us spread throughout the apartment and searched high and low; everywhere except just inside the front door of the apartment.

The place was surprisingly neat. He apparently lived alone and though the furnishing wasn't fancy, it was adequate. Confined to the kitchen, Asshole became more cocky with every passing minute.

"I told you guys, I'm not dealing," he repeated. "You got the wrong guy. Search all you want. There's nothin' to find!"

Our futile search continued, but the apartment was as clean as if his mother had just come over and straightened the place out for him. For all I know, she may have. Phil, Mike and I convened back at the front door.

"I told you guys, I'm clean. Why don't you go after the real criminals?" sneered Asshole from the kitchen.

Mike spoke up. "Let's get out of here guys. This place is clean." And we headed for the door.

"Hold it guys," I said. "Wait here, I'll go down and get it. It's worth a try." I quickly ran to my car.

"Where's he going?" Asshole spoke up.

"He's going to get the marijuana detector!" Phil replied.

"The what?" said Asshole.

Phil described our latest contraption that could sniff out even minute amounts of marijuana. By now, I was back at the door with the detector in hand. I don't know which was bigger, Asshole's eyes or his open mouth.

Only this was no marijuana detector. This was a cattle prod.

For any cop hitting a drug house, a cattle prod was useful protection against the guard dogs typically used by dealers. This one looked like a flashlight, at least the part that you held in your hand, and it had an 18-inch shaft. At the end of that shaft was a knob wrapped in bare metal wire and out of that came two metal prongs, like the prongs on a plug. The prongs delivered the shock. They also emit a loud buzz when you press the button.

I was banking on our dealer not knowing what was really in my hand. The look on his face told me all I needed to know. For all he knew, it really was a marijuana detector.

I re-entered the apartment and began a systematic search of the apartment, pointing my ever-silent marijuana detector to all points in the room–under the bed, into the closets, and behind the doors. Asshole followed me; I wanted him to see the entire show. Finally, I searched the kitchen in silence and again, I found nothing. The prod was quiet.

Phil and Mike were waiting by the front door, their lips sore from being bitten so as not to laugh.

"I guess it's clean," I said. "We can go." The two of them turned to walk out the door. I was following.

Buzzzzzz.

"Wait!" I said. Mike and Phil were looking out of the door, trying not to laugh.

I turned and pointed the prod at the closet door. Asshole was silent now.

Buzzzzzz.

"Open that door!" I commanded.

Asshole opened the door.

I pointed the prod up to the shelf. Nothing. I pointed the prod at the coats hanging in the closet. Nothing. I pointed the prod at a pair of shoes on the floor. Nothing.

Then I turned my attention to the vacuum cleaner. I pointed the prod at the vacuum cleaner.

Buzzzzzz.

I couldn't help noticing the beads of sweat on Asshole's face.

I pointed the prod closer now, at the bag on the vacuum cleaner.

Buzzzzzz.

"It's right in there," I cried. "In the bag!"

Mike opened the vacuum bag while I continued to point the Great Marijuana Detector, buzzing all the while. There it was, a nice, neat paper bag around a large plastic bag containing 20 ounces of marijuana. The Great Marijuana Detector had done it–at least that's what Asshole drug dealer thought.

We busted our impressed friend and for a few wonderful weeks, rumours of the narcs' marijuana detector spread. I've always been a practical joker, but this one lives long in the memory. And yes, my informant never got burned. He went on to live a happy life, safe and sound, thanks to the Great Marijuana Detector.

50

Dodging bullets

1975

Canvass most police officers and you'd probably find to your surprise that most have never looked down the wrong end of a gun. Even fewer would have been shot at. Happily, it's just not like the movies. Some police officers though have been shot at, wounded or killed. That's a real part of the job that all of us accept when we join up. When it does happen, it's fast and usually without warning. The lucky ones get to write stories about it.

New Year's Eve 1974 was a cold one in Vernon. Three of us were on duty as the rest of the Detachment enjoyed a function up at the "Hut," an old military barracks kept alive by the RCMP. I'd drawn the short straw this first holiday season in Vernon and I was working the night shift with Doug Greep and Gary Hart.

Our evening had been uneventful and January 1st was an hour old when I made my first mistake of 1975. "God, I wish something would happen, anything just to pass the time," I thought to myself. Almost in conversational response to my words, the radio spoke back.

We had a domestic to attend at Silver Star trailer park on Swan Lake, just on the outskirts of the city. Some guy and his wife were fighting. Only minutes away, we drove through the deep snows of a Vernon winter and into the site, around the circular drive. In our headlights we could see a woman in a housecoat standing knee-deep in the snow.

We stopped and asked what the matter was. It was only then that it became apparent why she was where she was in her nightgown. She was very drunk.

She complained that her husband had slapped her around. She'd had it. She wanted him arrested. She pointed to a singlewide trailer. On the way up the snowy trail, I asked the woman if her husband had any guns in the house. She said he did, but she assured us that he'd never use them.

That's when I made my second mistake of 1975.

In more than 30 years of police work, you'd expect gunplay once or twice. Unlike the movie or television version of police work, it doesn't happen a couple of times every hour. Most police officers will escape being shot at during their career, and even fewer will ever fire their sidearm.

By the time I finished my career, I couldn't say that.

During my undercover career, I pissed off a drug dealer/pimp in Victoria. He didn't like the person I was portraying and he was going to put an end to me. My undercover partners and I ended up in the guy's vehicle. He was taking me out to Goldstream and planned on shooting me with a gun he kept in the consul. My two partners did a lot of fast-talking and saved my life.

A couple of years later I was working drug squad in Surrey when I had my next run-in with a firearm. It was one of my more stupid moves. A call had come over the radio that traffic guys had a car stopped at 176th and Fraser Highway. They were calling for backup to deal with a crazed guy with a shotgun.

When we got there I immediately recognized the suspect. He was Tom Tilson. Tom was a drug addict/heroin dealer middle man. He was a big man, too; well over six feet tall and used to imposing his size on the street. I'd worked with him in my own controversial program. I'd actually taken Tom to Lions Clubs or Rotary meetings as a guest speaker. I wanted these folks to know firsthand about the drug trade in Surrey, and as long as I didn't introduce him by name, Tom would talk about the heroin trade, and answer questions. His presentations were an eye opener and really quite impressive. They were also short-lived. Once my bosses found out what I had been doing, they'd put a stop to it.

When I got out of the car I could see Tom was wielding a sawed off shotgun. He was obviously stoned and making little sense. I simply walked up to Tom, called him by name, and offered to be the guy who took him in.

"It's not loaded, Ed," said Tom, waving the shotgun past my belly.

When we checked the gun after taking it from him, a live shell ejected from the single shot barrel. I was lucky and I was stupid. I knew it immediately and would never make the same mistake again. Firearms surfaced several times while I was stationed in Bella Bella between 1979 and 1981. It was on a weekend when Wolf Presslauer and I received a call of a native man in his early 20s holed up in a house with a .22 rifle. He'd fired off a few shots and was threatening to shoot anyone passing by.

I hunkered down behind an old car abandoned on the front yard dirt, scrub brush and gravel. Wolf snuck around the house to see if the back door was open. It wasn't a great plan, but it was all we had. In Bella Bella, help is 300 miles away.

I started calling the young man's name, while he yelled and ranted at the open front door, rifle still in hand. On the radio, Wolf confirmed that he was up the stairs at the back of the house and through the unlocked back door. I took a calculated risk and stood out from the old car hiding spot. Still waving the gun, he screamed and swore at me. I called into the radio "Now" and continued to talk loudly to the suspect.

Suddenly the gunman was airborne. Wolf had charged half a dozen steps across the hallway and delivered a first-class football tackle. The rifle flew 10 feet in the air and the suspect exploded out of the front door with Wolf and his shoulder buried into his arched back. Wolf stood up immediately and the suspect ended up being checked out at the hospital. No harm done.

It could have been so very different in that snowy Vernon trailer park back in 1975. The second mistake I made that night had been to allow all four of us to approach the trailer in procession. I went first; the drunken, distraught woman was next, followed by Doug and Gary. In our nice neat procession we climbed the steps onto the covered porch of the trailer. We all stopped and listened.

Silence.

I decided to knock to get a sense of what was going on inside.

About the same time that I'd been accepted into the RCMP in 1968, an RCMP member in Newfoundland had been shot through a door and killed.

"Whenever you knock on a door, you stand to the side," my Dad had implored me–proud but worried as he was about my profession. We're taught the same thing in RCMP training, but it was my

Dad's voice that I always heard in that particular situation.

"Everybody stand to the side," I said, and with my left arm, I pushed the woman back against the wall of the trailer. Doug and Gary also backed against the wall.

That was my first good decision of 1975.

I knocked twice.

I don't recall the sound, just the door shattering. Subsequent investigation would show that the shot had been at solar plexus level. Had we all been standing in a neat row in front of the door the rifle bullet would have probably got at least two of us.

There was no need for instructions; we all got the hell off the porch. As Doug bolted to the left of the trailer and Gary behind another trailer to the right, I grabbed the woman's hand and made for a truck and camper right in front of the porch. I heard the trailer door open behind us and the husband yelling and cursing. That's when I heard the next shot. I can still hear the bullet hissing by my right ear. A second later, the woman and I were behind the truck and camper.

Drunk and angry, the woman bolted twice to yell at her husband and twice I had to wrench her back behind cover. Both times I looked up at the husband to see him taking a bead on me with the lever action rifle. Neither time did he fire.

I couldn't risk a third time. I couldn't both contain her and have my sidearm ready. Nor could we flee to safety. I had no choice. I handcuffed the woman to the back of the camper. Now I was committed. Now I couldn't leave this position. The husband wasn't just mad just at us; he wanted to kill his wife too. There was no way to leave her alone. I was stuck with the thin aluminum siding of a camper as cover.

What I didn't know was that the husband not only knew exactly where I was with his wife, he could actually see my feet below the camper's right rear corner. His rifle had a scope on it and from 26 feet away he was taking aim—at my right foot.

The shot shattered the stillness of that cold Vernon night. I jumped. I swear I jumped so high I could see the suspect from over the top of the camper, and I swear I came down sideways. Only when I came down did I realize that the bullet had missed my right foot by a quarter of an inch. The snow had exploded up the inside of my pant leg. I could feel the cold wetness of the melting snow at my knee.

"Son of a bitch! If that had hit me, he'd have fucked up my golf swing forever!" Don't ask why certain thoughts come when they do, but that was my first thought and it made me mad.

Subsequent investigation showed that the bullet had first gone through the fender of the right rear wheel well of the truck. That diversion had been sufficient to make the bullet miss its mark, if only by the smallest measure.

"SOMEBODY SHOOT THAT SON OF A BITCH!" I yelled to my partners. "HE JUST ABOUT GOT ME WITH THAT ONE."

The next sound was another gunshot, but not from a rifle. Gary Hart had been able to get out from behind the trailer and take a shot. The bullet had grazed the corner of a wooden post on the porch, slowing it considerably before merely hitting the suspect's chest and dropping to the floor. Our .38 Smith and Wessons certainly weren't up to the standards of today's sidearms. If they had been, our story would probably have been over then and there.

"You bastards aren't fuckin' around are you!" yelled the suspect, and with that he returned inside the trailer. The lights were all on and he left them on.

We called for additional cover and spent the rest of the night containing the man in his trailer. His drunken wife was spirited away once another RCMP member came. At about 8 a.m., my boss arrived and did what I think was a very stupid thing. Just like some of my stupid mistakes, his turned out OK too.

Wanting to end the situation, he disarmed himself and walked out of cover in front of the trailer and talked the suspect out. It worked and nobody was hurt. It could have turned out very differently.

Inside the trailer we found loaded guns at virtually every window. In one window was a crossbow pulled and ready for action with a bolt in place. We'd dodged a bullet in more ways than one.

Post-traumatic stress syndrome has been the subject of much study over the years. I certainly expected mental repercussions. I even thought about that during the night of containment. In reality, when it was all over, I went home and went to bed.

Over the years, I have had incidents, close calls and files that made an impact. I know I suffer from post-traumatic syndrome from some of them, but this incident somehow fit into my brain the way it should. It was over and done with.

Bottom line—my golf swing didn't change that early morning of January 1st, 1975.

The great B of M caper

1975

I used to share a Force secret with anyone who expected perfection from the RCMP. I'm really not supposed to tell anyone this secret, but if you promise not to tell, I'll let you in on it.

Here it is. From the beginning, the RCMP has been in the unenviable position of only hiring human beings. That's it. That's the secret. We're human and we make mistakes. Here's one of mine.

Their hands caught my eye first; about 25 pairs raised, fully extended in the air, but not moving: 25 people huddled together, facing the vault on the main floor of the Bank of Montreal. On foot and in the middle of Vernon's busiest intersection, I stopped. I crouched, took my portable radio in my left hand and reached for my .38 with my right hand. Inside the bank, nobody moved. Outside, the traffic lights had turned green and a few cars back, horns began honking. But motorists at the front could see a uniformed cop at work; radio to his mouth and gun at his fingertips. Time stood still.

It was midweek, late November, about 4:30 p.m. and getting dark. Shoppers were out and traffic was just picking up. I was walking the beat, one of my favourite duties as a police officer. Foot patrol offers fresh air, exercise, conversation and crime prevention. Everybody wins, except for the criminals. The assholes never know when we're going to show up! I'll bet I've walked more foot patrol miles than almost any modern RCMP member.

I worked in Vernon from 1974 to 1979 and was assigned the duty of Crime Prevention Officer–a new title for the day, but an old, old concept simply being reborn. No matter the weather, I walked a foot patrol in downtown Vernon almost daily. I cherished that time each day and I made friendships that lasted for years.

Highway 97 runs through the middle of Vernon. Downtown, traffic could be busy and impatient, especially during the summer as tourists made their way through the Okanagan. I remember walking the beat one hot summer day when a flatbed truck stopped suddenly for the amber light turning red. It stopped in time but its cargo kept going, dislodging a box and breaking it open in the process.

The box happened to be a beehive and now downtown was swarming with thousands of confused and upset bees. Homeless bees don't possess a sense of humour and several people got stung during a few chaotic minutes. Luckily, a good Okanagan breeze blew that day and within 20 minutes, the swarm had dispersed.

At the same intersection stands the Bank of Montreal. In those days it was a fairly modern building; two glass-fronted storeys cut on an angle to the intersection. You could see directly into the bright bank from all corners. Behind the bank was a small parking lot but in front were the two streets, always busy with pedestrians and traffic.

By 4:30 that November day, the bank was brightly lit, its neon lights in stark contrast to the dusk outside. I was half way across the highway when I noticed people assembled on the ground floor. It was only on reflection that I recalled that upstairs was empty. The bank's vault was situated in the back corner of the main floor and that was where my focus was drawn. There in the corner, in front of the vault, 25 people were huddled together with their hands in the air.

Crouched in the middle of the busy intersection, I could hear more motorists growing steadily more impatient. I didn't transmit on the radio because I knew that if there was a getaway car, they would probably be monitoring. I might only get one transmission and I wanted to make it a good one, conveying as much information as possible. The honking grew louder. Motorists could see the green light. They couldn't see the cop crouched and ready for action.

I looked to the rear of the bank for a suspicious vehicle or someone who might be a part of all of this. Nothing! I scanned past the front of the building again, past the employees with their hands in the air, and onto the main street. Nobody!

The seconds passed. It was time for a transmission. Would that be the ignition point? Would my transmission calling for backup be the catalyst? Where would I find cover? What about the pedestrians outside? What about the people in the bank? So many questions: So many doubts.

The honking intensified and as I looked back into the bank, I could still see hands in the air. I looked for anyone I could describe in my transmission, so I scrutinized the group more closely. That's when I noticed something odd.

They all had one hand in the air, all 25 of them. Now they seemed quite animated. I focused and realized that they all were laughing.

I quickly looked around. Pedestrians had stopped to look at me. Highway 97 now resembled a parking lot. I returned my radio to its belt and released my sweaty grip on my revolver before securing the holster. Hoping that no one had noticed, but feeling like I'd just emerged from a still-life painting, I waved traffic on and walked to the sidewalk.

Back at the office, a phone call to the Bank of Montreal confirmed my suspicions. I had just witnessed the entire staff, finishing work, with one hand in the air, huddled in a corner, voting on where to host their staff Christmas party: Crime prevention at its best.

The only shot fired that day was the bolt of adrenaline coursing through my crouched body at the busiest intersection in Vernon. It's a moment forever forged into my memory, the indelible image of the Great Vernon B of M Caper.

Honkie girl

1979

An RCMP officer can expect transfers during a career. That was true for me and my family. My children, Melanie and Bryson, don't have a home town. They grew up in Armstrong, Bella Bella, Ottawa, Tofino, Gibsons and Hope. That's the reality of being an "RCMP brat". Moving has its positives. I wouldn't have traded those transfers for the world. It can also mean unforeseen twists for family members. Melanie found that out on her first day of school in Bella Bella at the tender age of four.

You never know when life will teach you a lesson. School might be an appropriate venue, but the lesson our daughter Melanie learned on the first day of school in Bella Bella had nothing to do with the curriculum.

It was 1979 and from the day we'd arrived in this remote Indian village, we'd understood what it's like to be different. How could we not? At the time, Bella Bella comprised 1,300 native people and about 40 whites–teachers, doctors and nurses, clergy, cops and their families.

Melanie was four years old. School consisted of four buildings. There was an old elementary school to the north end of the field, beside the hall. (It burned down the day Ottawa denied Bella Bella funding for a new building. The funds were found for a new school soon after the fire!) There was a new high school directly behind the police detachment, which was across the road from the church.

Beside that school was another building which served as an intermediate school and right beside the RCMP detachment was a trailer that served as the pre-school building. Here Melanie would attend her first day of school. We lived facing the water, across the road from the hospital, so our walk to the office and to school was about three minutes.

The big day arrived clear and sunny, and Melanie was primped and proudly dressed by Joy. This was a big day for all of us. Hand in hand, Melanie and I walked up the dirt roads of Bella Bella, her in a dress and me in my uniform. This was long before Melanie and her brother Bryson were embarrassed by Dad in his uniform. When we got to the trailer school, I walked Melanie right up the stairs and into the class. In the classroom, not yet in session, were about 20 kids of the same age, all native, all equally excited. I proudly handed my little girl over to her teacher before walking over to the detachment for work.

Melanie was only attending half days at this pre-school stage, and noon came quickly. She was waiting for me on the school steps and we walked hand in hand down to the house where Joy waited for the news of the first day.

Joy had a great lunch ready and the four of us sat and began to eat. We all talked and asked questions and Melanie was full of her first exciting day. Finally, there was silence. It was then that Melanie, our blonde, blue-eyed little white girl, in her sweetest most innocent little girl voice, spoke.

"Mommy, Daddy, what's a fuckin' Honkie?"

I don't remember our exact response, just the immediate eye contact between Joy and me.

Melanie was the only white kid in the class. The native kids had long heard their parents refer to us white folk as "Honkies." Melanie was a "fuckin' Honkie". Joy and I took the time to explain about being different, about the word "minority" and boy did Melanie understand. She wasn't hurt by the comments–she didn't know how to be–but now she learned.

Being who she is, Melanie easily won over the kids of her class and the other kids that she knew in the village. By the time we left Bella Bella she was singing their songs, and dancing their dances at potlatches. She had learned some of their language and was even given a button blanket and apron by Evelyn Windsor, a village elder. She won the social struggle that can come in such a place and that experience stands her well to this day.

A couple of years later, Melanie drew upon those lessons. Now stationed in Ottawa, Joy and I had the kids going to a Catholic elementary school near our home. We got a call one day from Melanie's teacher, telling us how proud we should be of our little girl.

Melanie's Grade 1 classmate, Carlee, was afflicted by a terrible case of eczema. Her body was a mass of scabs, bloody sores and blotches. Her hair was patchwork interlaced with the redness of the disease. She was different and the class treated her as such. They teased her and taunted her.

Melanie had stood in front of her classmates and told them how she had been different at one time and how she had been treated. She told the class that Carlee was sick, not different, and that they all had to treat her better. Melanie's Bella Bella lesson had been learned well and was now passed on. To this day, Carlee's family keep in touch with us. They remember how a little girl stood up for their very special daughter. They remember and appreciate.

Bella Bella was a special place for all of us: Special for its friendships, its memories, and most of all for its lessons. It will always be a place that I look back to with pride. I am proud of my work there, of how Joy and I worked together there, and how my family adapted. One of my fondest and proudest memories though will always be of the lesson taught and learned on that first day of school. I'll always remember my very special little Honkie girl.

Daddy's little Honkie girl

Gotcha

1980

Over the span of a career, you can expect to work with people that you'll never forget. Lifelong friends are made at work, if you're lucky. That's how it is with Garry Rodgers, one of the good guys I had the great fortune to work with. And how do I show affection for those I like? I get them of course. One rainy day in 1980 I got Garry Rodgers in Bella Bella. See if you can figure out how.

Garry Rodgers had it coming. The day Garry said he'd never be the victim of a practical joke sealed his fate. I hatched my plan. All I needed was a rainy day. Not a long wait in Bella Bella!

Garry was a good worker, a good cop and most of all a good friend in Bella Bella. We shared many a laugh, many, many drinks and our fair share of dangerous work while policing a 10,000-square-mile 'beat'. He had my back and I had his.

You needed good friends and family in Bella Bella, my favourite posting during 34 years in the RCMP. The cultural experience shaped who I am today. I wouldn't be an artist were it not for the First Nations people of Bella Bella. My love of paddling big ocean canoes came from Bella Bella's profound influence. It could be a fisherman's paradise, but it could also be a lonely, isolating place, especially during weeks of rain and winter storms.

Family and friends were vital in diffusing that isolation. So was having fun. Garry got a kick out of my sense of humour, particularly the practical jokes I played on others. One rainy November day in 1980 Garry was to become my next victim.

Garry and I were working: me in my office, performing the mundane duties of an NCO in charge; he working at the equally mundane task of report writing at his desk in the main office. The rain was falling in typical Bella Bella fashion for November: relentless and in sheets. Just walking from the office to the car would leave you drenched, even while wearing rain gear. Perfect!

"Garry, would you mind running over to BC Packers for me," I asked, innocently enough. "Sorry to send you on such a shitty day, but I'm expecting mail and it hasn't come here so my guess is it's over there."

I knew the answer even before he spoke. Garry wasn't one to complain. "Sure Ed. I'll get it."

In those days, Bella Bella, located on Campbell Island, had a post office and on Denny Island–about a mile across the channel–so did BC Packers. Bella Bella's post office is known by the First Nations name of Waglisla. In its final days, the little BC Packers settlement had been an outpost of homes, buildings and docks. Some of our mail would end up at their post office. While I'd check the Waglisla mail daily through the week, perhaps once a week we'd take the police boat over to BC Packers to check for mail there.

Today is was important that Garry make the trip to BC Packers and check the mail. In the pouring rain.

Half an hour later, Garry got up from his paperwork, donned his Force raincoat and RCMP forage cap in preparation for the trip to BC Packers. Taking the boat keys off the hook, he exited the front door. With a fiendish smile, I watched him–shoulders slumped to the rain, head tucked deeply into his raincoat collar–run to the police truck.

The truck drove away and I returned to my mundane work, chuckling out loud. I'd already got Garry and he didn't even know it.

There was no quick way to get from the BC Packers' boat dock, up the ramp and into the ancient building that served as a general store and post office. Quite the opposite. Run on the docks and you risked finding yourself on your butt, or worse still sliding right off the dock and into the salt chuck. No, for Garry this would be a slow, careful walk in the wind-driven November rainstorm.

All part of the plan.

About 45 minutes later, Garry came in the front door of the detachment and did the human version of a dog shaking himself off. Garry's coat dripped a trail across the office floor. Water had collected in his hat, making it droop. He dropped the few bits of mail in the mailbox on the secretary's desk and returned to his paperwork. I looked up from my desk. "Thanks Garry."

The plan had worked so well, I struggled to conceal my satisfaction.

"OK boss," came the reply.

I waited about five minutes, then looked up from my work out through the open door of my office, over to Garry at his desk.

"I gotcha!"

Garry looked up.

"What was that?" asked Garry.

"I gotcha, Garry. I gotcha!"

"What the fuck you talkin' about?"

"I told you I'd get you someday, Garry. I gotcha! You'll see."

I returned to work and Garry did the same, albeit far more distracted now. It was just a matter of time.

It took only a few minutes, but for me it seemed like an hour. I forced myself to keep my head down in my work. Garry got up from his desk and walked to the washroom. I put my pen down, sat back in my chair and waited.

"You son-of-a-bitch!" came the shout from the washroom. I chuckled for the second time that day.

Out came Garry from the washroom with a paper towel crumpled in his hand. His entire face was green—the most beautiful deep emerald green. It streaked down from his brow like so many green fingers gripping his face all the way to his chin where it dripped away unnoticed.

Garry was trying to wipe the dark green stain from his face. He wasn't laughing—yet. He was still trying to figure out what had happened. It didn't take long though; he's no dummy. Cops know about malachite green.

"You got me! You completely got me!" he laughed. It would be a full day before the green completely disappeared from Garry's face.

Malachite green was commonly used in police work to identify people with light fingers in the till. We'd help stores who suspected a thief on staff by simply dusting a large bill with a minute amount of malachite. Eventually the guilty party would help themselves. When they noticed the green stain on their fingers, they'd try to wash it off and it would spread. The wetter it got, the more it spread.

I'd been saving my stash of green crystalline powder for a rainy day. For Garry! I'd lined the brim of Garry's police forage cap. On the way to BC Packers, the powdery concoction had worked its technicolor magic.

Garry recalled the folks over at BC Packers looking at him strangely. The locals on our dock had given him a wide, silent berth as he'd made his way back to the police truck. Being "had" sunk in for Garry. It all made sense. They probably wondered if their local Constable was green with envy or turning into the Incredible Hulk.

I keep waiting for the other shoe to fall, even as I write this in 2013. Garry's not one to forget, nor is he one to let this slide. My day is coming–but when?

Silent flight

1981

Policing in isolated posts can be a mixed blessing. Bella Bella was the highlight posting of my career. Were I given the chance to work my career all over again, Bella Bella would be my first choice. That said, policing in isolation is challenging. It can have its close calls, too. I'm glad Silent Flight is just a good story to tell.

January 1st, 1981, dawned calm and clear in Bella Bella. The evening before had been anything but. We'd spent the night wrestling and arresting drunks. The village was a mess. One of the local bootleggers had brought in a shipment and the community was not a pleasant place to be.

The travelling judge, Cunliff Barnett, came to our community every six weeks or so and on that particular night I certainly felt like he was of little help. He'd allow anyone in Bella Bella to possess a case of whiskey in their house and the bootleggers knew the drill. If they could hide their excess stash they'd be safe from enforcement and seizure. But, they'd always have a ready and "legal" supply on hand in their home. Fighting the bootleggers was a perennial battle, but as long as they plied their trade we were destined to strife, injury and death in the village.

I'd resorted several times to entering bootleggers' homes and finding their booze. With my diamond ring I'd etch my initials in the bottles in front of them. I'd tell them that if I found any of the bottles anywhere in the village, I'd charge them. My bluff had minimal success. Other times I'd get wind of a bootlegger returning from Ocean Falls with a shipment of whiskey. They'd usually go over in a herring skiff and return with as many as a dozen cases of Five Star Rye Whiskey, Bella Bella's drink of choice in those days. Knowing that I'd get little support from the system, I had to find a way to stifle the flow. A few times I managed to do just that.

The return trip from Ocean Falls takes you through a very narrow channel called Gunboat Passage. It looks more like a river than an ocean pass between two islands. After hearing that a bootlegger was making a run to Ocean Falls, I'd take the police boat over to Gunboat Passage. Backing into a small hidden bay, I'd wait. Soon enough the herring skiff would power its way through the channel on its return trip to Bella Bella, its two-man crew eager to cash in. When they were a quarter of a mile away I'd fire up the police boat to full power, put on the siren and charge from my hiding spot.

At full speed I'd make for the offending vessel and you can imagine what they'd do. That's right; they'd throw every case of bootleg whiskey overboard. I'd control the speed of the police boat to ensure that they had time to jettison every last piece of evidence. Then I'd just motor by and wave a friendly hello. At least those shipments didn't make it to Bella Bella. Somewhere in that channel you'll find those abandoned cases of whiskey, well preserved in the chilly inland Pacific waters.

Today we had to get into the bootlegger's house to seize what was left, if for no other reason than to cool the village down in its consumption. Liz Wilson, our Justice of the Peace, was out of town and without a JP's signature, a search warrant was unavailable. I'd have to charter a plane to Port Hardy.

When I was posted to Bella Bella in 1979 I knew a few things for sure. I'd be isolated with my family for two years. I'd get in lots of great fishing and I'd fly a lot in small planes. All proved true. The isolation turned out to be a blessing rather than a curse. To this day I love visiting the other world that is Bella Bella.

The Bella Bella posting covered the communities of Oweekeno, Klemtu, Namu and many, many logging camps. To quickly and effectively patrol and police them, you had to fly. Boats took too long and were vulnerable in bad weather. My men and I flew in Beavers or Cessnas several times a week. Odds were that eventually one of us would experience a close call. That's just a reality when you fly in so many small planes on the west coast of Canada. Every bush pilot has his or her stories.

Normally, we'd rent a smaller, cheaper Cessna. On New Year's Day, 1981, the only plane available for charter was a Beaver floatplane. In full uniform I met the plane at the main dock and climbed in, briefcase in hand. I had the necessary documentation and I'd called ahead for an appointment with the Justice of the Peace in Port Hardy. It would only be a 35-minute flight, but take-off signalled a chance to relax after last night's trouble.

The sun beat through the windshield into my face. There wasn't a cloud to be seen. The air hissed through the cupped window vent, providing fresh oxygen and amplifying the drone of the engine to soothe my brain. We rocked, bounced and rolled gently and within a minute or two I was out for the count.

Had I known what awaited us up there, sleep would not have come so easily.

The truth is, after so many flights, the novelty of flying had worn off long ago. Toby Miller did most of our charter work. A drinker and card player, Toby became a friend as well as a pilot to us. He was a daredevil, too. I've since learned that many of his stunts could have resulted in disaster. Beavers aren't meant to climb vertically until they stall and fall out of the sky while the pilot restarts the engine and powers out of the earthbound spin. We did that anyway, just for the thrill of it. He'd drop full rolls of toilet paper out of the plane window then circle the plane repeatedly, seeing how many times he could cut the unraveled roll as it fluttered towards the ocean. Then he'd have to shake off all the toilet paper from the wings before we landed in civilization again.

I'd been weightless in Toby's plane as he'd taken it up, then over the top and powered back towards the water. Holding a pen in a flat, open palm I could actually see it float in front of my eyes for a few seconds.

I'd flown many times, watching for boats in dense, dark fog. The pilot would watch his wing tip as he flew as close to shore as he dared, simply searching for a reference. Then at the last minute he'd ascend to narrowly avoid the mast of a fishing boat or ferry. I'd been a passenger when the pilot had to put down and taxi the plane for miles in the fog simply because it was safer to be a boat than a plane in such conditions.

January 1st, 1981 was different though.

From my deep, dead sleep, my eyes bolted open so fast, so wide that I almost hurt myself.

Dead silence.

No engine drone, just the whispering hiss of air in the window vent.

I looked wide-eyed at the waking pilot beside me just as his head jerked upright. His eyes were twice as big as mine. The silence had awakened both of us almost simultaneously.

We were gliding, fuel-less in one tank at least.

Frantically, the pilot began flipping switches, turning dials and pumping levers. Switching tanks and priming the engine again takes time. The Pacific Ocean loomed getting closer; the silence grew ever more oppressive.

Neither of us said anything.

And then I heard it; the glorious, stuttering, chugging sound of a Beaver engine reluctantly turning over for its first rotations. Then it caught and we were a powered aircraft again. The drone of an engine never sounded so good. It hypnotized neither of us this time. No, we flew wide-eyed on to Port Hardy and back.

I executed my warrant and did my job. The odds had almost caught up with me and I still feel lucky to have lived to tell about the silent flight.

Old man

1985

When I quit drinking in 1984 it changed my life forever. I replaced one addiction for another. That new addiction was painting. This is the story of the very first painting I ever did under the tutelage of Roy Henry Vickers.

For me, this is where it all began, my art career that is. Being in charge of Tofino RCMP Detachment, I spent a few hours each week walking the beat. My foot patrols took me to all 20 stores in downtown Tofino.

One of those businesses was the Eagle Aerie Art Gallery, the artistic home of Roy Henry Vickers. We quickly became friends and I watched him paint for about a year. I didn't realize at the time that I was learning as I watched. More as a practical joke than anything, I decided to try a painting in the Vickers style. My plan was to finish a painting, hang it on my wall and then watch Roy's reaction, as he found a piece similar to his style. My plan fell apart one day when I'd only half finished the painting. Roy happened to come over to my home for a visit. He knocked and walked in. Catching me in the act, he leaned over my shoulder and took a long studied look. Without warning he reached to the table, picked up the half-finished painting and tore it in two. His words at the time were, "If you're going to copy my style then do it right." He left my home and went to his gallery. He returned in a few minutes with proper brushes, paints and paper and began teaching me. The end result was my first painting in the Vickers style–"Old Man." It was a few months later, when my painting was framed, hung and on my living room wall that the next development took place. Roy and I were sitting in a hot tub one colourful west coast evening and we had a conversation. Roy insisted that prints of my painting would sell in his gallery. I had no money to invest in such a fanciful project so Roy told me how he would tackle the project to prove his point.

Investing his own money, Roy took my painting and had it reproduced in a limited edition of 100 serigraphs and hung them in his gallery. Before the end of that summer all 100 prints were sold and had gone around the world. I was a believer–in myself. Roy Vickers gave me a gift that summer. The gift was a look inside myself. He showed me something of me that I didn't know was there. I continue to paint and print my works to this day. I will be forever grateful to my friend and teacher–Roy Henry Vickers.

Old Man

Jail bird

1986

Melanie wasn't the only kid in the family to learn lessons in her early years. Bryson learned a life lesson at age nine. Some say the teacher was too harsh. Bryson is today a Corporal in the RCMP. I'll let you decide, but in passing judgment, I'd ask that you consider Bryson's comments at the end of this story.

I made countless arrests during my RCMP career but none as tough as the one I made in the little town of Tofino. Tofino was a special place for my family, especially for my son Bryson. Tofino turned out to be his schoolhouse of life.

In Tofino, Bryson was old enough to rise early, don his lifejacket and fish all day down at the docks. With a friend, he'd fish for dock perch or shiners, or just hang out enjoying the sea life at the tideline. Growing up in Peterborough, Ontario, I'd walk four miles to a trout stream and not return till supper time. I could relate to the freedom that Bryson was enjoying.

One memorable afternoon, Bryson called us from Safric's Dock, excited to have caught a 62-pound skate. Together with his friend Sean and some of the locals, he'd pulled the skate in. We ate great fish that night.

If Tofino was a place of fond memories for Bryson, it was also a place of hard-learned lessons. When he got his new bicycle I told him what every dad tells his son: put the bike away when you're not on it. On the very first afternoon of the very first day that Bryson had his new bike, he left it in our driveway, right up by the road.

I drove by in the police car and wasn't surprised by what I saw. I loaded the bike into the trunk and drove it to the detachment. I stored it in the garage and returned to work. About two hours later Bryson called the detachment in tears to tell me his bike was gone. I feigned surprise and had him tell me that he'd left it in the driveway. He was remorseful but the lesson wasn't over yet.

For the next half an hour I drove Bryson around in the police car while he checked the water at the end of each dock–the usual resting places for bikes stolen by local joyriders. The bike wasn't to be found. With that I told him we'd write a police report, so we headed back to the station. At the detachment I sat at the typewriter and began 'filling out a report.' I told the tearful victim to go back to the garage and get me a form off the shelf and off he went down the hallway. It wasn't 30 seconds later when he returned, eyes welled with tears.

"Why'd you do that to me Dad?"

I was about in tears myself as I tried to explain that I hadn't done something to him, but for him. That day of life-school was hard on both of us. Bryson understood and, I believe, he forgave me for the harsh lesson. I know one thing. He never left his bike in the driveway again.

A bigger lesson was yet to come, though.

It was in the fall of 1986. I was called to Wickinninish Elementary School one Monday morning. The principal took me to the back door of the school and showed me that the locking mechanism had been jammed with chewing gum. While the door actually appeared to be closed and locked, it wasn't. The gum prevented it from locking. Nothing else appeared to be amiss so the principal agreed to simply have the door cleaned out and restored to working order.

I thought nothing more of it until Thursday afternoon of that same week. I was walking the beat and had dropped in at the Maquinna Hotel Beer Parlour–a must stop on any foot patrol. Even in the middle of a fall afternoon you never knew who you'd find pissed in there. I walked into the dim light, took my hat off and put it under my arm, and sauntered through the pub. Between the door and the bar sat a local sipping his beer alone. As I walked by and said hi, he mumbled something.

I stopped and turned back to him. I thought I'd heard him mumble something about my kid.

"What was that?" I asked.

"Sure, your kid can get away with breaking into the school, but nobody else's kid can get away with it!" came his more audible and concise response. He had my attention.

"What the hell are you talking about?" I asked as I walked closer, pulled out a chair and sat down.

As he sipped his beer he told me what almost everyone in Tofino knew. Bryson and his friend Steven had jammed the door with gum last Friday afternoon. On Saturday they'd entered the school through the jimmied door and helped themselves to sports equipment. They'd played with it on the field before returning it to the school. Then they decided to look around inside. Among their discoveries was that teachers kept chips in the staff room. So they each helped themselves to a bag and left the school.

Of course, the boys had to tell all of their friends and their friends told anyone they knew, including their parents. Everyone knew!

Now I knew. And I planned on doing something about it. I thanked the guy in the beer parlour and assured him that he would soon hear of the results. As I walked from the dim light of the hotel into the bright daylight outside I knew already exactly how I'd handle this one.

Back at the office I called Steven's dad, one of the few people who didn't know of the incident. He gave his blessing to my scheme. Then I drove to the school, parking directly in front of the main entrance. I walked in and didn't have to wait long to see Bryson, who was between classes. Better yet, he was with Steven.

"Hi Dad," said Bryson, flashing me his great smile.

My face wasn't a friendly one. I reached out with both hands, putting one on Bryson's shoulder and one on Steven's shoulder. There, in front of a corridor full of people, I said:

"You boys are under arrest!"

Bryson's eyes searched mine and his eyes grew as he realized I meant business.

"What's the matter Dad?"

"Don't say anything. You are under arrest for breaking into the school, now come on out and get into the police car."

This wasn't easy, but it had to be done.

In the car Bryson tried to catch my eye.

"What's the matter Dad?"

"I'm not your Dad, Bryson, I'm Corporal Hill and you are under arrest for breaking into the school last weekend. Now shut up and sit quietly. You boys are in a lot of trouble."

They both obeyed in stunned silence. In the rear view mirror I could see them both eyeing each other.

I parked the car at the office and silently marched the two into the building. Once inside I merely pointed to the cells. With my hands gripping their shoulders, I directed them inside, leaving them both sitting on metal bunks to stew in their own cells. I slammed the doors shut. Through the bars I saw Bryson turn and look me in the eye. This was tough business and without doubt the toughest arrest I'd ever made.

I sat at my desk for 10 minutes. I wanted my emotions in control. This was an extreme lesson and I had to do it right. I called Whitey Bernard, then Mayor of Tofino. He'd help with the lesson.

Whitey has his enduring moment of fame as a four-year-old. He's the bleached-blond boy photographed in New Westminster running to hold the hand of his father as he marches with his regiment off to the harbour and World War II. It's a photo immortalized in posters for the war effort and still seen every Remembrance Day.

I explained the problem to Whitey and he immediately agreed to help, arriving in his best suit about 15 minutes later. Whitey took his place in my chair behind the desk and I went back to the cells.

I opened Steven's cell first, told him to come out and stand in the hall and wait. Next it was Bryson's cell. I felt so badly for him just sitting there with his knees up to his chin, his arms wrapped around his legs. He looked up for some reassurance but I gave nothing back.

When the two were in the hallway I finally spoke.

"You're going out to see the Mayor. He's your judge. Now keep your mouths shut and march!"

The two boys followed orders and marched straight to my office.

"Stop there, in front of the desk."

Whitey sat watching the performance. I spoke.

"Your Worship, these two boys broke into the school last weekend, took some sports equipment out to play with it and put it back. Then they went into the staff room and each stole a bag of chips. They're guilty and they're here for sentencing."

We got through the trial part of the process real fast. That's my kind of trial, straight to the sentencing. The boys stood at attention, straight faces staring Whitey right in the eye. They weren't being tough or belligerent; they were being scared little boys.

"Is that what you did?" asked Whitey, and both boys nodded.

Whitey spent a few minutes talking to the boys about the seriousness of their misbehaviour and he went on to explain how, as mayor, he represented the community. It was in that capacity that he was now going to sentence the boys. They listened without a word.

Whitey sentenced the boys to each write a letter of apology to the teaching staff. They would be expected to hand deliver that letter to a staff meeting and to each read their letter to the staff.

At the same time they would pay back the money to the staff for the two bags of chips. That wasn't all though. No, Whitey had a little more for the boys. They were each sentenced to 40 hours of community work around Tofino.

The sentence was stiffer than many judges hand out for armed robbery, but it was appropriate for these two boys learning a life lesson.

And so it was done. Bryson's time in jail–his 'hard time'–was over. Now he had a debt to pay for his crime. For the next three weeks he and Steven spent each evening after school, in the pouring Tofino rains, wheeling hog fuel from a pile in the park to all of the Rhododendron beds around town. In their raincoats they'd work after school for a few hours and their debt eliminated only when every minute of their 40 hours was paid back to the community that they had violated.

Everyone in Tofino knew who was out there paying off their debt to society. There was nothing quiet or anonymous about this punishment. It was very public and to their credit, both boys did their time without complaint.

I've since used this story in public speeches about parenting. Usually a parent tells me that I was perhaps too tough on the boys. To those parents I remind them of what Bryson said in giving me permission to use his story.

"That was one of the best things you ever did for me Dad!"

Bryson, who is now a Corporal in the RCMP himself, often tells the story to parents with their own kid problems. He cherishes his life lesson and the good it did for him. The lesson was tough for both teacher and student. It was born out of love and necessity. But it was done for Bryson. He got it.

Yes, Tofino was a place of life lessons for all of us, but especially for my son, my very special son, Bryson–The Jail Bird.

Bryson and his big skate

Asshole on the loose

1986

I have long been known as a practical joker. It's my kind of humour and within my circle of friends I have a reputation to uphold. Few are the friends who haven't fallen victim to one of my setups. I guess it was only a matter of time before someone got me.

Everyone has a quota of alcohol to drink in their lifetime. I finished my quota earlier than the rest of you; on October 23rd, 1984, to be exact. That's one of my very good memories of the time we spent in Tofino, one of my favourite postings.

It was in Tofino that I met Roy Vickers and discovered my artistic talents. The fishing was good too!

Tofino provided good police work all year round. The Meares Island protest happened during my tenure and the dynamics of handling that situation suited my personality and policing style. The place was well on its way to being a tourist centre in the summers, but in the winters it was quiet, it was ours.

My colleagues made Tofino special, too. One in particular was Randy Koch. Randy and I went through a lot together and would always be there for each other in a crunch. I've kept in touch with Randy over the years, in spite of this story. If I ever picked an all-star RCMP team, Randy would be in it. I just might have benched him that fateful fall day in 1986 though.

My morning routine was under way: 6 a.m., coffee in hand and enjoying the peace of the house and the rainy view of Meares Island. Tofino gets over 12 feet of rain a year and fall, winter and spring is when most of it comes down.

Looking out the front of the house, over the rim of my coffee cup, something caught my attention. The front passenger window of my police car didn't reflect any of the morning light. Lowering my cup, I leaned and peered through the blinds for a closer look.

"Damn it!" I said out loud.

I'd left the front passenger window down overnight. The damned car would be full of water by now. It had rained all night. A second look confirmed my suspicions.

"Damn!"

Wearing only my dressing gown, and with coffee mug in hand, I walked briskly to the front door. I stepped into my rubber boots, opened the door and stormed out into the rain. I walked straight across the front lawn, keeping my head down into the wind and rain. What I saw made my already lousy start of a day even worse.

There on the ground beside the car, was a strewn mess of broken glass. On the seat was a rock the size of a softball and more glass peppered throughout the vehicle.

"Fuck!"

I looked closer, leaning in the window not wanting to touch anything.

"Fuck!" This time I didn't just think the word, I spoke it out loud.

The shotgun was gone from its rack. How anyone had removed it, I didn't know, but it was gone. I even took a second look at the rack to confirm it.

"Fuck!"

I stood back and surveyed the scene, oblivious to the wind and rain. I must have been a sight: The local police chief in his dressing gown and rubber boots. I gulped a mouthful of coffee, my mind working overtime in full police mode.

I hadn't heard a thing. Someone must have heard the damned glass breaking. Maybe Jim McBride next door had heard something. His bedroom, like ours, faced onto the street. I sloshed across the lawn and up Jim's steps. It was about 6:45 a.m., the lights were off, but this was an emergency.

I rang the doorbell and knocked loudly for good measure. It only took a few seconds and Jim was at the door. He looked a bit stunned, possibly from being awakened so abruptly or from the sight of the police chief in his dressing gown and boots, holding a mug of coffee.

Or both.

I explained the situation quickly and asked if he'd heard anything.

80

He hadn't. He closed the door slowly, his eyes peering through the diminishing crack.

I walked back across the lawn to the police vehicle for one more look. Maybe I'd missed something. I leaned in again and surveyed the interior. I'd left my portable radio on the seat the night before so it would be ready for any emergency. I realized it was gone too.

"Fuck!"

Now we not only had some asshole on the loose with a shotgun, he had one of our radios, too. I shuddered in the cold morning rain. Finally, I woke up to the fact that I was outside in a deluge. I turned and rushed back in the front door.

My first phone call was to Randy Koch. Together we'd get to the bottom of this. He was already up when I called and agreed to be right over.

My next call was to Port Alberni. I advised them to guard their radio transmissions because of the missing radio. We had no way of knowing who may be listening. I also asked them to notify my Section NCO in Courtenay as well as the OC. Then I told them to contact Ident, that's the section of the Force that does fingerprint scans at crimes scenes among many other jobs, and have them on their way over here immediately. We had work to do.

By the time those calls had been made I was cold. The rain soaked dressing gown wasn't doing its job of keeping me warm. Joy had heard the commotion and was up by now. She had poured herself a coffee and was looking out the window at the car. She could see Randy approaching the front door. He had driven up while I was on the phone, so she let him in. He entered the kitchen, looking concerned.

"What happened?" he asked. I explained the situation and directed him to immediately canvass the neighbourhood to see if anyone saw or heard anything. I'd have a quick shower to get warmed up; then I'd get into my uniform and find this asshole. I wanted him in jail by evening. The last thing I needed in Tofino was some transient running around with a shotgun and a police radio.

In the shower, my mind raced. Was it someone local? Was it someone from a boat? You never knew who was down there from day to day. It could be someone who'd driven in, too. I was out in a minute and dressing in my uniform. I walked down the hallway, still fastening my gun belt. Entering the kitchen, I was stunned. Randy was still there.

"What the fuck are you still doing here Randy? This is serious shit! We've got to get neighbourhood enquiries done!"

Didn't he understand how serious this was? I'd called him to get his ass out and start neighbourhood enquiries. What the hell was he doing standing here–drinking coffee? This was so unlike Randy, the guy I trusted and depended on.

Randy never took his eyes off of me as he took another sip of coffee. He lowered the coffee and spoke directly to me.

"I got ya!"

The words had no meaning to me.

"I got ya!"

Lights started to come on, not quickly, more like a dimmer switch that slowly turns up the brightness. The light got brighter and Randy spoke again.

"I came over at 4 this morning and rolled the window down on the police car. I took out the shotgun and radio and put them in the trunk. I put the rock on the seat and spread the broken glass around inside and out. I got the glass from Happy Keith's Service Station."

Randy smiled as he lifted the coffee mug for another satisfying sip. His eyes appeared to be laughing as they peered over the rim of the coffee mug. Joy laughed too.

I'm a practical joker and a practical joker must always be alert, to avoid being the victim and to be ready to turn the tables. How was I going to turn this one around?

"That's a good one Randy," I said with what little bravado I could muster. "But we've got a bit of a problem. I've just called the OC, the Section NCO, Ident, Telecoms in Port Alberni and the entire free world. Ident's already on its way over here. You'd better call and cancel them!"

There, I had some measure of control and revenge. It was the best I could do.

Randy listened from behind his coffee cup, all the while his eyes laughing at me over the rim.

"I called them all yesterday, Ed. They all knew this was going to happen. They were all in on it."

He barely removed the coffee mug from his mouth. His smug, smiling eyes told the story.

I had the reputation as a practical joker, but he had me. It was done, and done well. Of all the gags pulled on me over the years, this is without doubt the very best. I tell the story often and enjoy the telling as much as I laughed and enjoyed the real thing.

The day Randy Koch had an asshole on the loose is one of my favourite memories of Tofino. The only thing that I've never yet paid him back for, and I will someday, is that in this case, I was the asshole on the loose.

Enough is enough

1995

It's just one of those stories where the old adage applies: "You had to be there!" It is a true story!

Visible from the eastbound lanes a few minutes' drive west of Hope there's a tree stump. The stump has been there at least 18 years because that's where the bloody man was sitting when I questioned him in 1995.

Every time I pass it on the highway the stump summons memories of this story and I feel compelled to tell whoever's in the car with me. Perhaps I won't have to anymore now I've finally written it down–at 4:30 a.m. on my first coffee of the day. It's probably the shortest story in this book!

I was in charge of Hope Detachment from 1993 to 1997. Located on the one major highway from Vancouver to points east, Hope is a pee break for many who left the big city a couple of hours ago. It was summer and as Staff Sergeant I was at my desk while my officers were out policing a sizable area; from half way to Boston Bar, to the Summit of the Coquihalla Highway and to the top of the Hope-Princeton Highway.

Both highways on either side of the Fraser River were ours to police and the dirt roads heading south were ours all the way to the border.

When the call came in there was no one else available to attend. There had been an 'incident' on the highway about a minute or two out of Hope on the Vancouver side on the eastbound lanes. The report wasn't clear. It didn't look like an accident but cars and people had stopped on the side of the road. An ambulance had been dispatched, too.

I was gladly out of my chair, free of my desk and into my unmarked car heading west out of town.

It didn't take long to reach the scene. Just as the caller had described, half a dozen vehicles had stopped on the side of the road on the eastbound side of the highway. About a dozen people had gathered beside the cars or out on the grass beside the highway. I drove until I was able to make a U-turn across the median. With emergency lights on, I arrived moments later.

Most of the people had collected around a woman standing beside her vehicle at the side of the road. She was obviously distraught but didn't appear to be injured. Over in the grass a couple of men were tending to another man sitting against a tree stump. He was bloodied but conscious and communicating. There was no vehicle damage. What the hell was going on?

"What's happened here?" I asked.

I was introduced to the woman at the centre of the gathering. She had been driving the vehicle parked on the side of the road. She was in her 40s, about five foot four, dressed casually, and was very upset. I pulled her aside. Through her tears she told me that she and her partner, the guy by the stump, had driven from Vancouver. They had been arguing since Vancouver, she said.

"I was driving the speed limit when all of a sudden the door opened up and he fell out," she said.

The woman had pulled over and raced back to her partner. "That's him over there, sitting with his back against the stump," she said.

It's worth considering a few facts at this point. The speed limit is 100 kilometres an hour. The woman appeared in no way intoxicated or on drugs. She simply didn't know what had happened.

While some of the other people present stayed with the woman, I walked through the grass to the man at the stump. The ambulance was on its way and the two Samaritans continued tending to the man's wounds while I asked the questions.

He was in his mid-40s, too, about the same size as me and covered in cuts and abrasions. His clothes were pretty torn up and despite being in obvious pain, he insisted nothing was broken. Like his female companion, he seemed perfectly sober and was remarkably lucid under the circumstances.

"What happened?" I asked him.

He looked me in the eye with a gaze that was both helpless and frustrated.

"I'd had enough," he said. "She'd been driving all the way from

Vancouver and bitching at me the whole way. I couldn't take it anymore. So I jumped."

The ambulance came and took buddy away. I think the woman followed on in the car. The Samaritans dispersed. No crimes had been committed and no cars had been damaged. I often wonder about that couple, who I very much doubt are still a couple today. But most of all I wonder how someone could jump from a moving vehicle travelling at 100 clicks and not hurt themself more seriously.

And on a more selfish note, I'm so glad he wasn't pushed. The paperwork would have been hell.

Remembering Cst. Mike Buday

1995

With age comes perspective on life's pivotal moments. It's those times that shape who we are today. My time spent in the Yukon searching for an image to paint, is one of those moments. My sobriety combined with my "addiction" to painting is one of the most positive changes in my life. The same combination took me to Teslin in an attempt to remember my friend, Cst. Mike Buday.

TIME TRAVELLER

Mike Buday had wanted to join the RCMP since he was four years old. He died in a Mountie uniform on a desolate lake connecting Yukon and B.C. in March 1985. The 27-year-old was fatally wounded in a shootout with Michael Oros, a violent, mentally unstable loner dubbed the Mad Trapper II.

Almost 10 years to the day after Cst. Buday's murder, I awoke in a Whitehorse hotel room. I had come to the Yukon with a group of RCMP members, media representatives and my friend and fellow artist, Roy Henry Vickers.

The tragedy on Teslin Lake 10 years prior had ended with another bullet. My friend, Cst. Garry Rodgers had returned fire on Buday's killer, shooting Oros dead. The purpose of our visit was to find an image to remember a fallen policeman. Vickers and I would paint that image and create a print edition to raise money for a recovery centre on Canada's west coast, an initiative that would be known as VisionQuest.

Little did we know at the time, of the magical experiences awaiting us.

We started early that Friday, March 17th, 1995: Breakfast at 6 followed by an appointment with a native man near Carcross. Insp. John Grant, Cst. Jack LeCerte, Roy Vickers and I were to meet Harold Gattensby at a restaurant on the shores of Naars Lake. We wanted to ask his permission to use his sweat lodge.

At the restaurant we were told he wasn't there and to try his home. So began a step back in time. Dog sled teams were being mustered and harnessed for a trip down Naars Lake, destination–Atlin. It was a clear, minus one day and something about the sights and sounds of all of those dogs yelping at the harness touched a chord with me. Were I ever stationed in the north, I know dogs would have been in my life.

We returned to the car and drove to the head of Naars Lake and found Harold's home, the epitome of a Yukon homestead. A round, self-made two-storey log structure; Harold's home was snuggled in willows and pines with a frozen lake at the front door, stark mountains all around. This felt like a step further back in time. Compared to southern B.C., the mountains here don't impose. They are stately and feel a part of the life in some participatory way. They present possibilities rather than hide them.

A white man on a snowmobile came up the lake. He stopped and asked our business. When he knew we were looking for Harold, he turned and left on the machine to find him and bring him back. Half an hour later, he returned to tell us that we had to go to Harold, not him to us. He would take us. On the back of the snowmobile was a long metal sled, with one-foot-high sides. With space limited in our 'taxi', John stayed behind. Harold's daughter, perhaps 20, stood at the back like a dog musher on her sled.

Under watchful giant peaks we travelled down frozen Naars Lake and passed dog sled teams navigating the centre of the lake. I watched from my comfortable vantage point as this scene from the past played out before my eyes.

We arrived at Harold's camp at the narrows of the lake. Five or six canvas winter-walled tents dotted the landscape among the willows, pine and poplar. Native children played baseball in the snow and women walked the paths, acknowledging us with a glance. Not an indifferent, unfriendly glance, rather one of acceptance. We were part of the moment. We had completed yet another step back in time.

"Welcome!" From behind the meal tent came Harold, a big man with long black hair tied back, in a scene reminiscent of those ancient sepia photographs. He was comfortable in the past or the present. Which were we in?

We exchanged greetings and were promptly invited into the meal tent. Inside was a large wood fired cooking stove with griddle top. A long table with wood chairs along one wall held women, children and infants. Others were preparing breakfasts. We were welcomed only with shy glances and then we were forgotten. We were from another time and life went on in spite of us.

Harold sat and drank coffee with us and talked. He had a strong yet soft voice, but he spoke with authority. We talked no business, rather we avoided that. Finishing his coffee, Harold stood up. "Let's go to my tent and talk," he said.

The three of us followed Harold through the snow paths. I stepped off once and went over my knees in deep snow. We walked to a white canvas walled tent. A stove pipe came out of the wall of the tent and it billowed grey smoke into the clear, cool day. At the stove where sweet grass burned in a pan, Harold washed himself with the smoke–a ritual called smudging. Jack did the same. Roy and I waited, but the invitation never came. We stood in this warm, dry and bright room. The floor was wood on bare ground with a worn all-weather carpet on top. Besides the stove, there was a chair and a small table between two rustic wooden bunk beds. The room slept four. We were completely comfortable.

For a moment we were all silent then Jack, our medicine man, stood up and approached Harold. He extended his arms and offered Harold tobacco in a red pouch, bearing an RCMP crest and pieces of cloth. The cloth was a yard in length for each of the two colours, white and green. White signifies the Creator and green the earth. In a voice barely audible to us, Jack began to speak. He explained that he was offering these gifts in the hopes that we could use Harold's sweat lodge back at Carcross. He explained that our purpose was to bless this trip, to cleanse ourselves and to heal members of our group. He explained that we were in search of an image for Roy and me to paint.

Jack was humble, slow and deliberate, trying to choose just the right words. It was a difficult job and Jack was trying to do it properly. Harold took the gifts without saying anything and placed them on the bunk beside him. Jack turned to me. I was dressed in my

RCMP parka and had my Staff Sergeant hooks visible on the shoulders. It was obvious who I was. I stood and approached Harold and presented him with an art card image of my painting "Old Man." I told him of my job and position in the RCMP. I told him of my connection to Roy and my native name, Klakleeleekla, bestowed by elders during my RCMP posting in Bella Bella.

I told him of our joint venture to remember Mike Buday and of the recovery centre we hoped to build. I thanked him for his time and for receiving us and then sat down. After a silence, Harold began to speak. He thought it significant that the RCMP should be approaching him. His people were having problems with the justice system, the police included. He talked for some time but was honoured to receive our gifts. He granted us permission to use the sweat lodge but asked that no cameras or media be present. We agreed. He also gave Jack a pouch of tobacco and asked that Jack include the well-being of his people in his ceremony. Jack agreed.

Shortly after, the same man who had brought us down the lake earlier that morning entered the tent. Harold introduced him as an Anglican minister. The minister said it was a great privilege for us to gain Harold's trust and respect. He told us of fasts and sweats that Harold had performed to earn his position. He explained how Harold had climbed Naars Mountain to fast. Finally he asked that we respect the sweat lodge and the ground around it. He was silent after that. After a final handshake and verbal agreement, we left the tent and returned to the cool, still air of the camp.

Outside there was excitement as younger natives returned on the snowmobile from a successful fishing trip. They had set a net under the ice and caught three Whitefish, perhaps three pounds each. Harold offered to drive us back to his home so into the sled we loaded and over the snow bank onto the lake we went. As we headed up the lake I could feel our bodies returning to the present. I was reluctant to leave the past behind. The closer we got to our van, the more I felt time speeding up again. We were happy and excited to have our sweat arranged, but I wanted to linger awhile in the past.

Like grudgingly awakening from a particularly comfortable dream, we surrendered to reality. We were returning. We weren't returning empty handed though. We had our sweat arranged but more than that, we had touched a placid and peaceful place.

We drove back to Whitehorse with our news, met the others and then returned to Carcross. Of the nine headed to the sweat lodge, six were to experience it for the first time and what an experience it was to be. If we had travelled hundreds of years back in time already today, our sweat, and all of its ancient rituals, represented thousands of years of tradition and ceremony. The best was yet to come. The heat was yet to come.

THE SWEAT

There's work to do for a 24-rock sweat. Heading back to Carcross, we stopped to cut our own wood, finding poplar dead falls alongside the highway. We waded through thigh-deep snow, cut, dragged it and loaded it into the back of our vehicles.

The sweat lodge at Harold's house was in a stand of small willows, pines and other scrub brush. At first glance, it looked like nothing more than a white walled canvas tent. It was however, sacred native ground. Supported by lodge poles, the tent stood about seven feet tall. Tucked neatly inside was a domed enclosure–a canvas and cloth igloo would be a good way to describe it. It had an arched doorway and inside at its centre was a pit full of football-sized rocks. At the outer edge of the lodge were pine boughs covered with folded blankets.

The sweat lodge closes simply by dropping a canvas and cloth drape over the doorway opening. This leaves the inside pitch black. Long willow sticks were placed in the ground then bent over to meet in an arch where they were tied and secured. Over that was placed black plastic, blankets and canvas. It was a surprisingly sturdy structure and it was created in accordance with spiritual and traditional specifications. For instance, tobacco was placed in each willow pole hole in the ground before the pole entered the hole. Outside, at each corner of the canvas tent, were poles. On each was a coloured cloth embodying spiritual significance.

Jack placed logs on the fire pit about 20 feet from the tent. Just in front of the tent was a small mound of dirt, an altar of sorts created from the rock pit inside the lodge. Having placed a layer of logs on the ground Jack then placed rocks in a specific sequence on those logs. One went to the centre to represent the creator, then four more–one in each direction. Then we helped place all 24 rocks on the pile. Over that we placed all of the wood we had cut. The rocks were completely buried in firewood. We set the whole works on fire with a bull torch and in no time we had a raging blaze. Jack now went to work on the next phase.

While the fire burned, Jack squatted in front of the mound and took several items from a bag. He put a small frying pan on the mound and burned a pile of sage. Jack took a small root from the bag. He broke off small pieces and gave one to each of us to chew. He called it "Rat Root," telling us it was "Indian antibiotics." We were not to swallow the pulp, only swallow the juices from the root. It was the first physically intense moment of the day. There were a lot of screwed up faces and pursed lips. "Strong" would be an understatement to describe the taste. Jack continued to work. He wrapped tobacco–tobacco that each of us had given him when we met him at the plane in Smithers two days earlier. He wrapped it in the corners of the cloth that we had also given him. These were offerings to the Creator and were put inside the lodge once prepared, to remain there for our sweat.

When that was done, Jack removed the frying pan. He had blessed each cloth and all of the tobacco with the smoke of the sage in the pan. Now he placed a buffalo pipe on the mound. We were closing in on our sweat. Throughout, Jack explained the symbolism of the preparations. Now he told us the order in which we would enter the lodge, explaining that we'd circle everything clockwise in recognition of the sun. I was to enter second last. Roy was the "doorman" and last to enter. We all stripped down to our shorts or bathing suits and Jack invited us into the lodge. Roy and I were to serve as "rock men" so we stayed outside for the time being.

With everyone seated on the blankets around the empty rock pit, Jack, to the immediate right of the door as we entered, called out and asked for the rocks. Roy took a four-prong pitch fork and began lifting rocks from the fire pit. He carried them to the lodge and Jack directed where they were to be placed. I brushed the rocks on the fork with a pine bow, cleaning off dust and ash that would otherwise cause smoke in the lodge.

Jack placed the rocks, one in the centre of the pit, representing the Creator; the next four placed appropriately around the centre rock to represent north, south, east and west. Then we brought in the rest of the rocks. It was hot and heavy work so Roy and I took turns. As we brushed the rocks they hissed at the touch of the bow and when we dropped the rocks in the dim light of the lodge they glowed pink. They were extremely hot. All the rocks were placed, at Jack's direction, on specific spots in the pit until finally we had 24 rocks piled in a neat mound.

Now it was time for Roy and me to enter the lodge. I entered first and found my place to the left of the door. Roy sat immediately beside me, next to the door.

Once we were all inside, Jack took control. He spoke in a quiet, fatherly and authoritative voice. We started by passing a pipe filled with tobacco. We were to think of and list our wishes and requests as we smoked the pipe. When the pipe finally returned to Jack, he loaded it full again and lit it. He smoked the entire pipe until it went out. The smoke wafted out the door of the lodge carried by the heat of the waiting rocks. Jack placed the pipe down on the mound immediately outside the front of the lodge and put tobacco on the hot rocks. It burned and smoked immediately. Jack spoke again, encouraging us to allow the spirits within to come out. He asked Roy to close the door, leaving us in complete darkness. The rocks no longer glowed.

Jack spoke softly, preparing us for the unknown to come. There was silence. It was warm but very comfortable.

The sound of the tin cup broke the silence. Tied to the end of a stick, it clattered and rattled into the bucket of water that had been brought into the lodge earlier. There was a hissing of water pouring onto the rocks. It took only a few seconds to experience the result. Steam heat hit back, shoulders, face and then the entire body. Then there was more water, more steam, more water and more steam. In seconds the temperature was hotter than any sauna I have ever experienced. Jack sang. He had given Garry Rodgers and me rattles and we were to rattle them whenever he sang. The heat was so intense that I forgot to rattle. I couldn't take this. A loud voice of panic and shock screamed within me.

"What would happen if I leave?"

"What would the others think?"

"I'm here as one of the artists. I can't leave."

"God, I want to get out of here!"

"Would Jack be offended?"

Jack was singing but I wasn't hearing. Neither Garry nor I were rattling. My thoughts were coming in a blitz of emotion.

"Was everyone else OK?"

"Shit this is HOT!"

"Rattle!"–a word in the song I understood. "Rattle!" Jack said again and I realized he was speaking to us. Garry and I both started a feeble rattle in unison. Jack sang on.

By now I was on my hands and knees. The heat was so intense I dropped to my elbows and put my face to the ground. In the darkness I must have been a sight, like some religious devotee bowing to the east. Jack sang on and more water hissed on the rocks.

"How long is one of these things anyway?" I thought in panic.

"I thought it was supposed to be cooler on the ground."

"I can't take this!"

Jack stopped singing and my feeble rattling stopped. A short silence was followed by words as sweet as any cool water I have ever drunk. "Open the door." It was Jack's voice that had spoken those kind and merciful words. At that, Roy opened the flap and the light poured in. I looked around at the circle of stunned, red, dripping faces. Little was said. More shock than healing was going on here!

Outside we reassured each other that we had all felt the pain and the heat. Thank God I wasn't alone. I rubbed snow on my body and it felt so good. I started to return to room temperature when Jack's voice called from the lodge. "OK, let's go again."

As I crouched and entered for the second round, how was I to know the worst, and the best, was yet to come?

We weren't exactly quick to rush back in but we had cooled down, we could take it. I rationalized that the hot rocks heated the lodge. We had cooled those rocks hadn't we? Jack had thrown a lot of water on them? My red skin was testimony to that fact. The second round would be better, surely not as hot. And even if it was as hot

–I could make it!

As I took my place inside the lodge, I felt the air inside the structure. The lodge had cooled to a very comfortable level again. That first round had been a shock for a rookie like me, I thought. It really wasn't that bad at all, I reassured myself.

My defences were working well.

Jack spoke for a while about our purpose here. He asked for blessings for all of us and in particular he asked that our journey be blessed. He also asked that Roy and I find the image that we sought with the help of the Creator.

Jack asked that we all talk of our wishes openly. He asked that we express our desires and in particular ask for blessings. We did so with a trust and calmness that none of us expected, I'm sure. Most of us were new at this and the open honesty of the moment came as a surprise to us all. We were for the most part a group of strangers. We were there for many reasons. Yet our first round had broken those differences and barriers. It had established a focus within the group. Its physical effects had been dramatic. Its effects on the soul had been subtle. We felt something in common and for 15 minutes we sat peacefully and talked, listened, prayed, relaxed and cooled. The placid, comforting warmth of the lodge embraced all of us. Time slowed and we enjoyed the moment together.

"OK, close the door," Jack said quietly to Roy.

I have never heard such softly spoken words sound so loud. I snapped from the relaxed state that I had let myself slide into. Rationalization took over again. The rocks had to be cooler, I thought.

The lodge was black. Jack led us to the second round. He prayed that we allow ourselves to accept the wisdom and teachings of the Creator. Teachings that present themselves to us each day, if only we will look for them we will see them, he said. He suggested that we forget our bodies amid the rising heat, that we listen to his song, that we chant and pray. He told Garry and me to rattle with his song and to listen to the rhythm of the rattles. In our efforts to rattle and in those sounds within the lodge we would find peace from the pain of the heat. Let our minds take charge and our bodies would be there when we come back, said Jack. There was a warm, still silence. In that silence I could hear everyone listening for what was to come next.

Rattle, rattle–Hissssss.

The blast hit with a slap, first on my back then it hit my entire body. Before that wave disappeared there was more rattling and hissing, more waves hitting hard. The rushes came one after the other. I was back to my position, praying to the east. Then Jack sang.

"He started singing before it got this hot last time, didn't he?"

Reality was already hitting me. This session was even now at the same heat that the last round had ended on.

As Jack sang, I rattled. I had been told to rattle harder and to concentrate on the rattling to help me get through. God I rattled! The singing went on. From my devout position on all fours, my right hand held the rattle close to my right ear. I rattled on with the instrument immediately beside my face. I kissed the ground in search of cool air. The singing continued and more water was splashed on the rocks–the rocks that were supposed to be cooler.

I screamed more thoughts to myself.

"This song is longer than the last one!"

More water, more song.

The heat was now so intense that I was convinced that Jack was doing actual bodily harm to us. My ears were hurting from the heat and from the intense rattling right beside my face.

"To hell with the beat–just rattle."

"God damn it Jack, that's a long song!"

Hissssss.

"NO WAY!"

Another blast.

The moaning from around the lodge told me that I was not alone in my agony. Roy and Jack were the only ones who really seemed to have control, but they were sitting by the door!

Hissssss.

Jack sang on. I inhaled dirt in my desperate attempt to find cool air.

A rush of super-heated air blasted me.

"What the hell was that?"

Moans continued from around the lodge. Jack was fanning us! I had wondered what those eagle wings were for. They had been up in the willow rafters of the lodge when we came in.

I wasn't going to make it. Hell, we were only half way. We're not even half way. We aren't finished round two of a four-round sweat. The moaning and chanting weren't doing the trick for me. No matter how hard I rattled, I couldn't forget the pain.

"Open the door."

As Jack spoke those words I made for the light of the opening flap. I scrambled on weak and unsure hands and knees. The sweat wasn't beading on my body, it was gushing from every searing pore. "Don't stop Roy or I'll climb right over you."

As I stood outside rubbing myself with the cool snow, I knew I'd make it. I said those words out loud with the determination that I know of myself. Once spoken, I am committed. In that emotion, with the speaking of those words, I found strength. I must have looked almost as bad as I felt though, as a few of the group asked if I was OK and was I going to make it. I assured them and myself that I would. I was ready for round three.

"OK" was all Jack needed to say this time. We filed in quicker this time. A lot of my fear was gone. I knew I'd be there at the end of this. Even with my newfound strength however, as soon as the lights were out, I was praying to the east again. I didn't even wait for the foreboding sound of the rattling tin cup. After a few guiding words, Jack began to sing and immediately stoked up the heat. I could feel the heat but I rattled my rattle with purpose this time. I even kept time with the song that Jack sang. When I felt painful blasts of heat, I rattled and listened and the heat was secondary. People had talked of seeing visions and I wanted so much to see one myself. I looked and listened, forever the skeptic. I absorbed the moment. I began to lift my head into the heat. I'd drop it again to refocus, but I'd lift it again just as quickly. Was I the only one becoming more sure of myself?

I was fully up on hands and knees as Jack's song ended. The blast of eagle wing heat hit me. I was expecting it this time and I felt strength from my endurance of it. I saw no visions. I heard no distant voices. I heard only the chants, sighs and moans of friends in the lodge. Where was my vision? Where was the image I had asked for?

"Open the door."

The third round was already over. But wait Jack. I was almost there. I had found strength. I was passed the fear and pain. I'd left it somewhere else.

I stood this time outside the lodge and I appreciated where we were. Clear skies showed beautiful Yukon mountains all around us. The willows and pines told of the slightest breeze. The temperature was just above freezing. What a powerful place, if only for the beauty around us. We were together, strong and with a singular purpose. We were in the perfect place at the perfect time. The snow cooled my skin and I was calm and determined in anticipation of round four.

"Let's begin." Jack's voice no longer conjured fearful anticipation in me. Rather it was strangely welcome. This was special and powerful. I entered the lodge with purpose. I sat upright with legs crossed, head held high. I was soaked with sweat and melted snow. As the lodge flap closed, I waited for that sound in anticipation rather than fear.

Rattle, rattle–Hissssss.

The heat immediately embraced my body. I began to rattle even before Jack sang and I invited the moment to be powerful.

Rattle, rattle–Hissssss.

My head remained high. Wave after wave came and I actually heard Jack's singing. My rattling maintained a rhythm and my body quietly endured. Was everything in rhythm and in time sequence? I looked for my vision. I strained for "the image." I listened for a voice but only the intensity of the moment prevailed. Was I failing? Was I not doing it right?

The song ended and the eagle wing fan went to work. The heat blast was the hottest, most intense moment of the entire ceremony. The heat was incredible yet I only sucked a lung full of air and quietly endured. Fear and panic had left me. As the eagle flew twice around the lodge I knew it was coming to an end. It was hot and I wanted to cool but I didn't want this to end. At Jack's direction, the flap was opened and the light revealed the circle of faces. This time those faces showed confidence, pride and smiles of contentment. They were hot, sweaty, dripping faces. They had been exposed to extremes, but through it all they had endured. We left the lodge for the cool air but without the desperation of before. Once cooled, the group returned to the lodge. Jack didn't have to call us. We came back on our own.

I am told that the lodge represents Mother Earth's womb. I can say that we all felt warm and protected in that place at that time. It felt like home. We lay and sat in peaceful contentment. It was perhaps one of the most peaceful and calm times of my life. We had entered this lodge with fear, nervous anticipation, bravado and ignorance. Now we relaxed in an air of friendship having mutually experienced something that would somehow bond all of us for life.

There was talk of visions. I hadn't seen any. And there was talk of personal triumph over the heat. We could have stayed there for hours but again Jack took control.

"I think we should get out now, time to go."

Like his first words in the lodge some time earlier, Jack's voice stirred a mild resistance in me. All that time ago when he had invited us into the lodge I had felt a resistance. I hadn't wanted to sacrifice the comfortable world outside to endure the pain I knew would be there in the lodge. Now Jack was calling us from the warm embrace of the lodge to the reality of the world outside.

We reluctantly left the lodge, all hoping that someday we would experience this again. I hadn't seen the image I had sought, but I had something in me that wasn't there when we started all of this.

I will never be able to talk of that event, of my first sweat, without becoming emotional. I wish I could have left it all there. I wish I could have done it right the first time, or done it better. I must endure and experience another sweat.

I was not to know then how soon one of my wishes, that of seeing the image, would come to me. It was to come with the power of the heat blast of the eagle's wing. The time, for at least that wish to come true, was close at hand. Teslin Lake was only two days away.

THE IMAGE

On Sunday, March 19th, 1995, we flew in to the western side of Teslin Lake on a plane fitted with skis. Half of the group had gone ahead, enjoying a trip by snowmobile leaving just after six o'clock that morning. We arrived later and unloaded the plane on a snow-packed runway, marked with Jerry cans and snowshoes. Once unburdened, the plane turned to the wind and flew into the blue sky, leaving us alone. A small camp was established close to the dramatic events of 10 years ago. Packed snow sidewalks soon materialized throughout camp and if you stepped off those white walkways, you sank thigh-deep in the snow. Soon the camp was well packed down and snowshoes were no longer necessary. On the lake, snowmobile tracks provided firm roads, which invited exploration. I walked the area, familiarizing myself with the location of the cairn erected to remember the event. I was told the incident had taken place "up there," generally the area of bush hugging the shore beside our camp.

The weather was kind again–perhaps minus 5, and some broken cloud providing depth and perspective to the huge landscape before us. All was still but for the treetops rustling occasionally.

Garry Rodgers tacked a picture of Cst. Mike Buday and his police service dog on a tree behind the cairn. I felt alone, despite all the people present. My job was before me. I had the entire day, but I felt urgency. I looked to the trees where the events had unfolded. No faces appeared; no images became apparent.

I wandered alone for a few minutes, but felt no bristle within me. I walked back to the campfire and sat above it on a snowshoe, on the point of land. Thick ice covered the lake and open water flowed north away from us. In the distance was Big Island, the resting place of a Tlingit Shaman, and there were the Aces–a stand of mountains, four peaks in all, three of which all but matched symmetrically. The locals called them the Aces–four aces standing alone.

The treed distant shore of the lake contrasted with the whites and blues of the proud peaks. I sat looking, but not seeing. I was lost in my search, working too hard. I watched the mountains and lake, but my mind remained in those trees. The policeman in me was reenacting the shootings. The policeman knew the image must be in the bush. As I sat there, oblivious of the activity around me, I took my coat off and relaxed in the warm comfort of the sun. I listened and waited for something, but received nothing. Roy and I had not really talked to this point, only smiled at each other when our eyes met. Our dream of being here, in this place, had come true. Now we were searching. We were both working in our own way.

Now I noticed Roy walking north on the lake. The policeman left me quickly. I stood up and followed. I knew that walk. Many times we'd seen each other on point. Surely it wasn't as simple as the mountain. I surveyed the scene as I walked several metres behind Roy. It was beautiful and powerful but it didn't hit. I saw only Aces standing alone.

Roy had stopped and as I approached, I felt it: The bristle. In front of us, close to our feet, the open water was blue, black and steely cold. The ice that etched its shore showed bright white and crystal blue. Its sharp, icy shards created shadows and shapes.

As I stood beside Roy I looked up and the image was before us: The open water, the mountains and trees and Big Island. All were visible, yet walk 10 feet one way or the other and the scene was lost. We were standing immediately on the spot for which we had been searching some eight years. That was when the dream had begun; when Roy and I had agreed to someday do a painting to honour Cst. Mike Buday. Only this spot showed us the image we had been looking for. We talked. Mostly I talked. Roy tends to reflect quietly at such time. I bubble over verbally, describing every detail of the painting to be. Roy usually smiles at this point. He looks me in the eye and smiles.

"We've got it!" was all he said.

We'd only been on the lake for a few minutes really, but we had it. That spot, that time, that light—it was all in rhythm, like the rattles in the sweat lodge once I had let my mind relax. It was there, so simple, so evident, before us. We enjoyed the bristle and emotion together and then Roy was gone, walking back to camp. I couldn't leave that special spot, not yet. I had something to see, something more to experience.

Standing only in my boots, snow pants and shirt, I was warm from the sun now glowing through the broken clouds. I stepped off the snowmobile track that we had used as a platform and I sunk into the snow. I leaned forward and dropped to my knees. Sitting back on my heels, folding my hands under the bib of my snow pants, I relaxed like I haven't done in years. No sound, no wind, only the image before me. I was part of it. I was completely at peace.

Almost 20 years later, I still call upon the feeling of that moment on the ice. I use it as a touchstone, a remembrance of when everything was right, everything was in rhythm.

I fell asleep in that position. Some might call it a trance, but I fell asleep. I dreamed. I don't remember of what I dreamed but they were happy, peaceful and calm experiences. The Trickster awakened me. The native people call the Raven "the Trickster" and it was his cawing and cackling that brought me back to the real world. I awoke to find my eyes full of tears. I turned and looked through watery eyes over my left shoulder to watch the Raven disappear over the trees, the very trees in which the drama of 10 years ago had played out. I resented that Raven. I had been so relaxed, so peaceful. Now I was back in the real world. I turned back to the mountain. Could I catch the moment again?

What I saw hit me hard. Now I knew why I had waited. Before me was a flock of Trumpeter Swans flying right at me. They were framed by the dark tree line of the distant shore. Had I looked a moment earlier, or a moment later, that image would have been lost to me. The flock flew in unison showing me many and varied formations as if to pose for my artistic purposes. As they dropped to the snow and ice of the lake, their show ended.

I jumped to my feet, eyes welled with the tears of my sleep. Roy had missed it! I turned to look at the camp some 400 metres away. I could see Roy looking my way. I motioned in the direction of the Trumpeters. "Did you see it?" I cried. He acknowledged with an exuberant wave of his arms high over his head. We had seen it together.

An emotional charge suddenly hit me. My breath left my lungs in one powerful blast. My legs weakened and I slumped with my hands to my knees. I stayed in that position for only a few seconds. It wasn't unpleasant; rather it was a comfortable blow. I sucked cool air back into my lungs, stood and turned.

I didn't look back at the mountains. The moment had gone. I walked a peaceful walk back to camp. By the time I got there my tears were mostly dry. I hadn't only seen the image, I had experienced it. It had hit me with the same intensity as the eagle's wing in the sweat lodge. Is that what a vision is?

Roy and I hugged and agreed that that portion of our job was done. The Aces quickly became "Sheep Standing By Himself". That's what the local native people call these mountains in their own language. The rest of the day was spent enjoying the area and listening to stories from Garry of that day 10 years ago.

Sometime later, Roy, Garry and I sat in the exact spot where Mike Buday had died. Garry talked and told us of the spiritual events he had experienced on that day in 1985. We smoked a pipe that Roy prepared and were again at peace in a proper place. As we talked I looked over Roy's shoulder. Through the trees I could see the mountain range of our image. I could see Big Island and the open water. It was then I realized that this had been Mike's final sight of the world. The spot Roy and I had found on the lake earlier that day lined up directly with the spot where Mike had died. The straight line intersected the mountain range known as Sheep Standing By Himself. The line intersected exactly where the Trumpeters had been. It cut through the point of ice we had chosen for our piece. No wonder we weren't allowed to wander a few feet either way on the ice. We had been at the perfect place at the perfect time.

I pointed this out to Roy and he smiled again with that "I told you so!" look he gives me at such times. We smoked on and enjoyed the moment: Three men at peace in a very powerful place. We had found the place, the moment and the emotion. It was the birthplace and time of an image to remember a fallen Mountie. Mike Buday, you will never be forgotten.

Sheep Standing By Himself

The Port Mellon landmine

1991

The Howe Sound Pulp and Paper Mill is a huge operation here on the Sunshine Coast. Other than a strike, what could possibly shut the place down? A phone call from an observant worker made that happen. We even called in the Armed Forces.

Looks can be deceiving. Ask anyone involved with the Port Mellon landmine incident in 1991.

The beginning of the 1990s was a time of transition for Gibsons. Filming of The Beachcombers was winding down, while at Port Mellon, expansion of Howe Sound Pulp and Paper was ramping up. That meant 1,500 men working, some of them living on-site in ATCO trailers or at motels, B&Bs and basement suites in Gibsons. Times were good for everyone but the police.

Our meager detachment had received the paltry upgrade of one member to acknowledge the huge influx of men to our community. Our tired staff was on call for over a year. Overtime eased the pain financially, but the constant bouncing from one file to another took its toll. In 1991, our crime statistics spiked. Everything from sexual assaults to shoplifting jumped. There were fights at the camps on-site, and fights at The Cabaret nightclub and fights at the pubs. There was even a dust-up at a local restaurant between rival trades working at the mill. Car accidents were up, thefts were up–even armed robberies were up!

You never knew what the next phone call would bring.

And so it was, at 8 o'clock one summer morning in 1991 that the phone rang at my home. A worker had been walking the beach on his time off out at the mill. It was low tide and there below the tide-line he'd found a landmine. How did he know it was a landmine? He'd seen landmines while growing up in Czechoslovakia. This was a landmine.

I drove to the mill and met the man who had sighted the mine. Tall, slim and about 60, the man spoke with a heavy accent. After his nightshift, he'd gone for a walk along the beach north of the mill. Spotting what he recognized as a landmine, he'd edged closer and confirmed his suspicion.

As a boy in Czechoslovakia, he'd grown up during World War II. He and his chums would search for ordinance left over from the fighting. They'd collect shell casings from the battlefields near their village. They'd bring home any artifact that they could locate. They'd even find landmines. Some they'd point out to adults, and others, being kids, they'd pick up for their collections. He insisted that he knew landmines. He insisted that Port Mellon had its very own landmine.

The tide was coming in. I encouraged the man to show me and Gord Brittan, who ran the mill camp. I'd only seen landmines in the movies. We drove over Rainy River and around the chip piles, making our way down to the beach just north of the mouth of the river. Getting out of our vehicles, Gord and I walked down to the beach following our witness.

"There it is!" he pointed.

Barnacles, slimy seaweed and sandy debris covered the rocks of the beach. There, perhaps 10 feet from the incoming tide, was a landmine. At least it looked like a landmine to me. Shaped like a flying saucer, about 15 inches across, it had a small button or dome at its peak. Encrusted in barnacles and other sea life and debris, it had all of the appearances of a landmine. It was just like the ones I'd seen in the movies, and that alone dictated that I wasn't going to touch it. Our witness described every nuance of the bomb, confirming in his own mind, and in ours, that this was a landmine. He'd seen lots of them before. It was decision time.

I called my office for backup. I'd remain at the scene until they arrived, serving as security. Within an hour the tide would serve as security. The mine had obviously been there for years and to this point, the ocean had done a good job of security.

With the scene secure, I could now deal with the next phase of my plan. Returning to the office, I called our bomb disposal unit in Vancouver and was referred to the Canadian Forces Ordinance Disposal Unit at CFB Chilliwack. Our bomb, apparently, was military in origin. They didn't laugh when I called them. They asked questions—lots of them. Over the years, they'd recovered enough 'souvenirs' to know that they couldn't dismiss any call.

I'd sketched the mine in my notebook and faxed it to them with estimated dimensions. Within minutes, they called me back to say they'd be on their way tomorrow morning at low tide. Based on the dimensions and sketch, it appeared we had a landmine at Port Mellon.

During the next 24 hours, as the tide line receded, RCMP members or auxiliaries patrolled the site. Nobody was allowed within 100 yards of the bomb. It had obviously been there for years, but I wasn't going to have anyone blowing themselves up on my watch.

The next morning, off the first ferry came two military explosives experts. I led them from the detachment to the mill and was happy to turn a lot of the decisions over to them.

We all watched from afar as the two men approached our bomb. Standing over it, we could see them taking pictures, measuring and writing in their notebooks. They turned with purpose and came back to our small group. Gord and I leaned in with interest as we huddled there on the beach, well back from the bomb.

"From what we see there, you guys got a landmine on the beach," said one of the military men.

They described and named the device, based on its size and description. How it got there was a mystery. There was no telling how volatile the device may be.

Back at the car, the two experts brought out a book and turned to a page showing the picture and description of our bomb. Our experts were convinced that we had a bomb on the beach, even though it was deeply encrusted in sea life. Security would have to be maintained for yet another day while a plan was devised and resources for disposal brought to the site. There'd be more overtime and hours of volunteer work for a few auxiliaries.

We spent hours at the mill offices and in our detachment. Working with mill executives, the bomb experts and Gord Brittan, we devised a plan for tomorrow's low tide. Rather than move the bomb, it would be destroyed.

The next morning, everything was in place. This would involve a lot of people and inconvenience many, many more. There was no way of knowing just how powerful this device may be. The mill would have to shut down and staff would have to leave the area. We couldn't chance anyone getting hurt. Hundreds of people got a paid break that morning. The train had to be moved, too. That's right–the train! Port Mellon has the only train tracks on the Sunshine Coast. Barges bring in rail tanker cars full of chemicals used in the pulp and paper process. Once emptied, they return to the barge, which in turn off-loads a couple more railway tanker cars. The rail cars had to be moved and protected at the far end of the mill.

With everyone at a safe distance and the mill secure, the second phase of the plan moved into action. Blasting equipment was already on-site and being used to accommodate the mill's expansion. They had cranes and blasting blankets–large spreads of old tires lashed together by wire that act as shock absorbers.

The military experts now directed the crane oh so carefully and quietly down the beach, as close to the mine as they dared. With its long reach, the crane lowered a few blasting blankets over the mine. The military men guided them into place, creating a tent of heavy blasting blankets over the bomb. Satisfied with the tent structure, the crane was moved back out of range.

Standing bravely back at the police tape, some hundred yards away, we held our breath as the two explosives experts disappeared into the tent. They were loading a charge right up against the bomb. I was glad to see them emerge slowly and carefully from the cover. Unreeling wire from a large spool, they came to us. They'd blow their charge, destroying the bomb in the process. If it was live, there would be a large explosion. Nobody, including the experts, knew what to expect.

By radio, Gord checked with the mill. Everyone was clear of the north end. The trains were secure at the far end of their track. Police scanned the immediate area. Nobody had breached the secure area. It was safe to blow.

There were loud-hailer warnings, followed by an air horn. It was time.

"Five, four, three, two, one!"

A military thumb threw the military switch.

The explosion was loud, but muffled. The huge blankets heaved in their effort to contain the blast, and smoke belched from within their folds. It was over in a second. Now we'd wait 10 long minutes, just in case of residual danger.

The experts approached the tent, all eyes fixed on them. This wasn't over until they'd again crawled in, right up to the beast, and were able to declare mission accomplished. They disappeared again into the tent. Within a minute, they re-emerged.

This time, they walked more briskly, appearing more relaxed. In their hands they carried the remnants of the bomb.

Except it wasn't a bomb.

It was a hubcap.

All of that time; all of those resources; all of that money - for a hubcap.

The bomb experts had no regrets. The job they do allows for no errors. One mistake and your widow gets a small pension cheque. They again compared the photographs they'd taken of the 'bomb' and compared it to the photographs of the real thing. They were absolutely the same in every way.

Gord Brittan has since passed away, but Bill Hughes, who was president of Howe Sound Pulp and Paper in those days, still laughs about it. Both Bill and I are retired now, but I know we'll never forget when Port Mellon was threatened by a World War II landmine.

As for the military men, they called me a few weeks later to tell me that there are two new photographs on the wall of their office: one is of a real landmine; the other is of a barnacle encrusted hub cap.

Cop in the kitchen

1992

Police work can be dangerous, exciting, tedious and a blur of paperwork. But it can also be fun. I'm sure even the star of this story–a drunk who went to jail–is laughing about it somewhere today.

The annual women's bonspiel in Gibsons could be a rowdy affair. You'd usually hear the commotion from the street. Some years, patrons of the Gibsons Motor Inn next door would come over to complain and the side-doors would have to be closed so they could sleep.

But this is how we pass our long, wet winters on the Sunshine Coast; coming together over curling or some other social activity. Traditionally the men would help in the kitchen for the women's bonspiel and when it came time for the men's event, the women would return the favour. Somehow when let loose the women would always have more fun than the men and make a lot more noise.

It was at one such Saturday evening event that I was happily washing the dishes. The women had enjoyed their meal and were upstairs partying it up. I could hear laughing, yelling and loud music. Half a dozen of us men were now downstairs, elbows deep in dishwater, just in the throes of putting the kitchen back in order. We were telling stories and jokes while collecting dishes, washing, drying and cleaning up. That was when one of the men spotted a young guy staggering in the front door. He didn't belong to the club, and no one recognized him as a friend of anyone upstairs. There might have been 150 women up there, but you get to know who belongs and who doesn't.

This guy was just drunk, heard the noise, and smelled a free drink. I was the lucky one in the dishwater so I didn't see him come in. When someone told me, I immediately left the sink, drying my hands on my apron. It was one of those big, flowery aprons with the bib and all and had obviously been the pride and joy of someone's gramma. It clashed with my blue jeans, runners and plain T-shirt. As soon as I saw the young man at the door I knew I had a problem. A cop knows a drunk from a troublemaker and I figured I had the latter.

He stood at the door, listening and getting his bearings. It was obviously the first time he'd ever been in this building, and indeed in any curling club. He was looking at the glass partition towards the ice. His wavering, staggering gaze then turned up towards the stairs and his liquor radar confirmed the location of the action.

He made the right turn, almost falling in the process, but now he was pointed in the right direction, heading up into the party. Only I was in the way, on the first step looking down, resplendent in my blue jeans and floral apron. His first unsteady step put his face directly in my chest, concealed by all those beautiful flowers. He looked straight ahead at the floral obstruction and then he looked up into my face. The smell of booze confirmed that which didn't need confirmation. He said nothing, perhaps more confused than anything. He was probably wondering where I had materialized from.

"That's a private party happening up there pal!" I said calmly but firmly. "You'd do well to just head on out and go home."

"Fuck off!" he said, stepping towards me.

I backed one step up and he stepped onto the first step. We had begun our little dance.

"Listen, I'm a member of this club and I don't think you should be here. I'm asking you to leave."

"Fuck off!" he replied with a full blast of booze breath right up into my face. He stepped up to the next step and I backed up one more.

Unbeknownst to me, one of the men in the kitchen had called the police. They were patrolling Sunnycrest Mall, only seconds away.

"I am an executive member of this club," I said. "It's a private club and you're not welcome. I'm telling you to leave—now!"

"Fuck off!" came the answer. His breath carried the message directly up my nose.

He took the next step and I retreated yet one more time.

I reached into my jeans, pulled out my black leather wallet, unfolded it and flipped it right into the face of the drunk. A cop with a badge and a flowery apron confronting a drunk–it might have been a scene from a movie. I don't know if a script writer could have dreamed up a more bizarre scene.

"Listen to me. I'm the Chief of Police here in Gibsons and I'm telling you to leave now! Either you turn and leave now or I'll arrest you and you'll spend the night in jail."

I didn't have to wait long for his reaction.

"Fuck off!"

He reached up to push me in the chest.

I leaned forward from my step and put my weight on his. We tumbled backwards down the few stairs right into the front door of the club. I landed on top of him and in his struggle he twisted and turned over onto his belly–right where I wanted him! It must have looked impressive! I reached for his arm and twisted it up behind him. My other hand went for his hair to pull his head back into a submission hold. It only took seconds and then with perfect timing, through the door came the two cops who had been called. They reached down, cuffed the drunk, stood him up and ushered him out the door. He protested all the way and we could hear him yelling as the police car door slammed shut. The car drove away and we resumed our dish washing duties.

It wasn't until the next day before the story fully unfolded. That was when one of the arresting members told me of what had happened back at the office as my drunken friend was being booked in.

It is of course normal procedure to take all possessions from a prisoner. Pens, coins, papers, belts and the like are held for safe keeping and also to ensure that nothing can be used to hurt either the prisoner or the guards and staff working with the prisoner. That was done in the cell block area. My friend was emptying his pockets for the two members. The usual drill includes the members patiently waiting while the drunk staggers and sways his way through the process, all the while protesting or joking with the members. Contrary to popular belief, most drunks are OK once we get them back to the cell area.

My friend began asking why he was going to jail. One of the members responded by saying that he was drunk and that was why he was going to jail for the night. That wasn't enough though. The drunk insisted on knowing why he was going to jail. Finally in exasperation, one of the members responded by saying.

"You were drunk in public. You were told to leave and given a chance to go on your own and you didn't. You've been arrested and are being held for the night until you sober up and that's it. You shouldn't have been up there at the curling club. You were a problem."

Without a moment of hesitation the drunk retorted.

"I'm a problem?" he questioned loudly.

"I'm not your problem! I'll tell you where your problem is. Your problem is up there at that curling rink. There's some asshole in a flowery apron up there who thinks he's the Chief of Police. That's your problem."

The drunk went to jail. I washed my dishes in my beautiful flowered apron and a war story was born.

Transition

2002

The transition from S/Sgt. Hill to "Mr. Hill" would be difficult and I knew it. I loved my job and my career. I was proud of it. As my career came to an end I devised a plan. On April 1st, 2002, I'd say goodbye in style.

When I started police work the cars were black and white. There was no screen separating front and back seat to protect the police officer. The light on the top of a police car was a single dome; a bubble gum machine is how they were best described. There were no computers in the office, let alone in the police cars.

Criminal records and other data were filed and stored by hand, usually by the junior constable. Confidential messages were sent via a noisy telex machine; that's one step up from Morse code if you haven't seen one before. Stolen cars and property were recorded on a blackboard, not in cyberspace.

To check a vehicle and occupants on the road could take up to 15 minutes simply to transmit all necessary information back and forth between your police car, the office and Vancouver. Those record checks were all done manually by checking a filing system in Criminal Index Section Headquarters. Such checks now take seconds, even before the vehicle has stopped sometimes.

On April 1st, 2002, I began my first day since July 29th, 1968, as a member of the public–not a member of the RCMP. Having worked as a police officer for 34 years, in five different decades, I had seen so many changes, so much growth and so much deterioration. Not all changes have been positive.

During my early days in the force, members received absolutely no overtime pay. You worked a shift and you kept working until your work was all done. You were called in on any day to work endless hours of unpaid overtime. Even the most minor investigation was usually typed in triplicate by the investigating constable. And they were typed letter perfect. One mistake would see the Sergeant put a red pen stroke through the report and you'd do it again–on your own unpaid time.

Women were not admitted to the RCMP until 1974. That was when both women and married applicants could be accepted. When I joined the RCMP I had to wait two years before I could apply to get married. Permission was only granted after an investigation had been conducted into Joy's background and character.

In all of those 34 years of police work I had changed in so many ways. During my last posting here in Gibsons I could see that I had changed physically, emotionally and spiritually. Over the years I had been shot at and commended, beat up on the street and looked up to by entire communities. I had been loved and hated because of the uniform I wore. I had been feared and I had been sought out as a comforter, advisor, mentor and leader.

I worked with people who thought I was the very best at what I did, and I had worked with those who thought just the opposite. I had recognized my alcoholism and quit drinking in 1984. Joy, Melanie and Bryson had followed me happily, if not always willingly, to some of the most remote communities in British Columbia. They gave up a home base for the transitional life of a travelling RCMP member.

Indeed, my wife and children and most of my friends had only known Ed Hill the police officer. They had never known "Mr. Hill." I had been adopted by two different native families in my career, so even my name had changed twice. My rank changed over those 34 years, too. By the time I retired I was a Staff Sergeant - Staff Sergeant Hill. That's who I was, day and night. I was the man in charge.

Oh, I had become an artist. I had become involved in community. I had found canoe paddling as an obsession, but always–I was Staff Sergeant Hill. When my eyes opened in the morning I knew who I was. When I looked in the mirror, I looked at Staff Sergeant Hill. I took my job very seriously. It consumed me.

I was told many times by retired members, that I would know when it was time to retire. By 2000, I knew. Stress was taking its toll. Over the last five years, the face in the mirror had aged. Sleep was a fleeting luxury. The changing face of the force and the younger members were becoming something I didn't completely recognize.

Not always did I agree with policies, tactics or work ethics. These were different and difficult times.

Long ago I recognized that everyone carries their own private backpack. It's invisible but it's always there on your back. It's your Stress Pack. In it you load those things that cause stress in your life. It carries the worries of everyday life; a leaking roof, bills to be paid and that nagging pain that the doctor can't quite put his finger on.

Your pack also carries the stress of others. It carries the weight of the argument you had with an employee. It carries the load of seeing a fellow police officer die at the hand of a murderer. Or it carries the weight of someone confiding in you with their problems. When someone comes into the office to share something with you, what they are usually doing is relieving weight from their own Stress Pack at the expense of yours.

Someone once said, "Why is it, whenever someone wants to share something with you, it's never money!" The reality is that, particularly as a police officer, your Stress Pack becomes overloaded. When you weigh yourself on the scales you can actually see that load in real kilograms. Your health suffers because of the weight of the Stress Pack and that's often reflected in excess body weight caused by neglect, lack of time and energy.

It was time for me to consider retiring.

I looked at my pension and realized that I'd never be a millionaire, but I would have enough to live on. I considered what I'd do with all of that spare time. How would I fill my days? I knew that part would be easy. I had always been involved in community. I played sports, participated in organizations and organized events constantly. I looked forward to having the time to do what I loved most.

For many years I'd been a productive artist. My work was selling well, and though I wouldn't want to have to make a living at it, the funds would nicely supplement my pension. I had grandchildren to play with and I had friends to spend more time with. I wouldn't ever have to worry about sitting at home, growing old and wondering what there was to do. There would be no regrets. Hell there wouldn't be time to look back!

No, the toughest part would be the transition. The time I both feared and longed for was the moment when Staff Sergeant Hill became Mr. Hill. How would I handle that? I needed to think that through. I needed a defining moment.

There is an old saying that your level of stress is directly proportional to the number of keys on your key ring. One day in 2002, as I contemplated my transition dilemma, the lights came on. My transition would be a time of lightening the load. My transition from Staff Sergeant to Mr. Hill would be a time of emptying my Stress Pack. I would begin this new phase of my life with a much lighter pack, and I would do it by design. It was then that I planned my last hours as Staff Sergeant Hill. I knew how I'd handle it. I knew how I'd become Mr. Hill.

Friday, March 29th, 2002, would be my last day as Staff Sergeant Hill. I was at my desk, in full uniform, at the usual time–8:30 a.m. Though the routine was somewhat different in many respects on that final day, much of it was the same. Police work still happens even on your last day. There were phone calls and decisions to be made. Final reports were composed and signed and people still had their problems.

I managed to get my desk emptied and the walls cleared by late in the afternoon. I walked downtown for a final foot patrol as Staff Sergeant Hill, saying my goodbyes to several of the merchants and community. A few phone calls were made and received to say goodbye and the time approached. I kept busy all the while knowing the transition was coming.

Throughout my career I always prided myself, particularly during 22 years of being a detachment commander, as being someone who works Friday afternoons right up to the last minute. Many commanders take Friday afternoons off as a matter of course, feeling that it's owed to them somehow. I never fell into that and today, my last day, would be no different. I would work until five, to the minute.

At about four in the afternoon, Cst. Kim Hall received a call of a domestic problem on Franklin Road. Not knowing all of the details, she advised me of her call. Immediately, I told her I'd go with her, if only long enough to determine that all was OK. By the time we finished that file, which turned out to be nothing, it was 6:30 p.m.

It was somehow fitting that my last minutes as a police officer were spent as they had begun–working voluntary overtime.

116

Transition time was at hand. I dropped Cst. Hall back at the office. Turning my unmarked police car back towards the ocean I drove to Gospel Rock, parked the car and walked to the top of the rocky prominence. As I stood proudly in my uniform looking over the ocean and the area that Staff Sergeant Hill was in charge of, my eyes were shaded by the peak of the police hat.

The hat and my dark glasses hid the tears now welling up. The evening was clear and calm and my community looked so beautiful. It was such an honour to serve as the NCO in charge of the RCMP detachment here. With the same thought though, I felt the weight. I could feel my Stress Pack. I reflected on the weights in that pack. Some were mine, but many, too many belonged to others. It was time. There was no turning back.

I held a large ring of keys. I had long been known for my large key ring. Some keys served a purpose; others had served their time but had never been discarded. I knew what each key was for and I knew that they were heavy. Each key represented a brick in my Stress Pack.

One by one, I took the keys from my key ring. The first one was the hardest. I stood with it in my hand for quite some time as I looked at the world before me, and ahead of me, through teary eyes. Then I did it, I threw the key from the top of Gospel Rock into the waiting ocean. As it dropped on its arc to the water below, I yelled "It's over, let it go!"

As the key splashed, I felt my Stress Pack lighten. It felt good. I had come to the threshold and made it over the edge. The next key came off the ring easier, and it flew further. "It's over, let it go!" Time and again the keys flew, the words were spoken out loud, and the load got lighter. Each one felt better than the last. By the time I was done, I had a big key ring with two keys on it; the car key and the office key. Alone on Gospel Rock and feeling like I could float back to the office, I turned and faced Gibsons. I saluted and spoke.

"That's all I've got!"

Back at the office I asked Kim Hall to drive me home. I put the keys on my desk and without looking back I walked out the back door of Gibsons Detachment. I did feel lighter, and I did feel better. This had been a good thing–I think!

On the drive home Kim insisted that I close with appropriate words on the radio. The police car stopped in the driveway and I took the radio in hand. I called up telecoms and, once acknowledged, I spoke my final words as a police officer.

"After 34 years on the job, Staff Sergeant Hill off shift at my res. That's a wrap!"

Staff Sergeant Hill put the radio microphone back in its cradle and he got out of the car. Mr. Hill walked to the door, waved goodbye to Cst. Hall and closed the door on a wonderful career.

The next day, as I enjoyed an extra coffee at home in the morning, I felt so good. None of the anticipated remorse, regret or self-doubt materialized. I felt so energized and so sure. I had done the right thing at exactly the right time. To this day I feel the same way.

Life still has its way of loading the Stress Pack, but it is a whole lot lighter and healthier. Joy and I have too many things to keep us busy. I look back though and realize that transition was important.

I liked that old Staff Sergeant Hill. He brought me to where I am today. But I really like Mr. Hill. I am very comfortable in his presence and I look forward to where the future takes us.

Made in the USA
Charleston, SC
01 December 2013

dom. The footsteps that chased her triggered panic, and an involuntary scream crawled out of her like the evil trying to escape this place—the same evil that was trying to kill her.

Intricate glass carvings of the family's crest lined the windows framed in the large double doors, breaking up the moonlight. Unlike the rest of the windows in the house, those had been meticulously cleaned, and it had been Maggie who'd done it.

Maggie grabbed the polished brass handle, but the door remained locked.

"No." The defeated whisper left Maggie's lips, which were distorted into a frown. "No!" She pounded against the glass and then turned away from the door, searching for another way out.

The house itself was a maze. Maggie had lived here for the past month, and she still hadn't seen all of the rooms. She tried to drown out the heavy footfalls growing louder and closer, thinking of another way out. She gasped and popped her eyes open. *The drawing room*, she remembered. It was in the east wing, and she'd seen that one of the windows had a broken latch.

Just before Maggie reached the drawing room, she glanced down the hall to find the darkened figure of her attacker. Her heart skipped a beat, and she burst into the room. With her eyes already locked on the window to freedom, she tripped over the edge of the rug in the room's center. She caught her balance on the coffee table and wove around the vintage desks and chairs.

Maggie thumped against the glass, fumbling to keep her fingers still beneath the window's sill. She pushed upward, but the window moved only an inch before the worn tracks stopped the motion.

"C'mon!" She pounded the window frame's sides, trying

to loosen the track's hold, then managed to open it halfway, where she was greeted with a blast of frigid night air.

Maggie thrust her head outside, and a pair of hands grabbed at her waist.

"No!" Maggie screamed and latched onto the window's frame, her grip weakening as the attacker pulled. One finger was plucked loose, then another, as her bloodcurdling cries echoed through the night air. "HELP ME!"

The muscles along her arms burned with fatigue as she clung to the last bit of hope that someone would hear her in the town below.

One last forceful tug sucked Maggie back into the room, where she landed hard on the floor, and the window was quickly slammed shut.

Maggie scooted backward along the dusty floor, crying on her retreat.

"I'm sorry. I know I broke the rules. I shouldn't have been snooping around." Her tears mixed with the sweat and dust on her cheeks, offering the illusion that she was crying black tar. "I won't tell anyone what I found. I promise."

The man turned, silhouetted in moonlight, his facial features indistinguishable. He stepped toward her, tracking dirt from his boots, the laces untied and dangling precariously to the sides.

Maggie shuddered when she backed into a chair, and she turned her face away, shutting her eyes as the man neared. The tickle of his hot breath against her neck transformed her skin into gooseflesh. He sniffed and then wrapped his rough, leather-gloved hands around her neck.

"Please," Maggie said, choking as he squeezed.

The pressure eased, but then he quickly lifted Maggie off the floor and slung her over his shoulder.

"NO!" Maggie fought, impotently smacking her fists

against his back, as she was carried swiftly to the fifth floor. "STOP!"

Blood rushed to her head, triggering a dull throb through her skull, her view limited to the floor and lower portions of the walls they passed.

The higher they ascended, the dirtier their surroundings became. Thick layers of dust covered the floors, walls, and furniture. Cobwebs filled the space between the paintings on the wall and the ceiling. Wide cracks separated the floorboards, the blackened empty spaces between them traveling like fault lines.

The attacker opened a door at the end of the fifth-floor hall and heaved Maggie through it. She thumped against the floor, triggering a plume of dust. She coughed and lifted her head in time to watch the door slam shut, followed by the heavy turn of a lock.

Maggie crawled to the door. "No." Still on her knees, she wiggled the knob and then beat her fists against the door. "Let me out!"

But with her pleas ignored, Maggie spun around, sobbing, and pressed her back to the door.

The room was colder than the rest of the house, and Maggie rubbed her arms, her bare palms sliding quickly over the long sleeves of her uniform. She let the tears run their course then regained control of her breathing and pushed herself off the floor. Shivering, she walked to the room's only window and pressed her nose against the dirty glass.

Five stories separated Maggie from freedom, and the ground below was nothing but concrete. She looked to the left and right, hoping to see a ledge that she might be able to climb onto, but found nothing.

Maggie turned away from the window, examining the rest of the room. There was a four-post king-sized bed, neatly made, though the sheets had been permanently greyed with dust and neglect.

Time had frozen the room upon the previous occupant' death, their belongings trapped and forgotten. She was standing in a mausoleum.

Distracted by her own thoughts, she didn't hear the groaning of the closet hinges, and when the doorknob knocked against the adjacent wall, Maggie jumped.

The open door exposed the sleeves of a few ratty jackets near the front, but the back of the closet was concealed in darkness.

Maggie stared into the void, and the hairs on her arms stood up, and little pins pricked the base of her skull, triggering a tingling sensation down her spine. She tried to avert her gaze, but she couldn't.

The darkness in the closet crawled forward, spreading into the room. Maggie retreated, watching it cover the floor, the bed, the dresser, moving closer to her. She shuddered when her back pressed against the window.

Maggie shut her eyes, fists clenched, as a numbing cold soaked through her clothes and into her skin. Her heart rate slowed, and the blood in her veins transformed into a thick slush like the dirty ice found on the side of the road a few days after a snow storm.

It spread to her fingers and toes, her skin turning a light shade of blue as her nails frosted over. It numbed her tongue, silencing her screams of pain as it crept into her brain and shoved her consciousness into the corner of her own mind. She watched helplessly as it took control of her body and turned her to face the window.

Unprovoked, Maggie unlocked the window's latch, pushed it open. She placed her palms against the windowsill and climbed on top of it. She pushed herself up and onto the window's ledge, her toes dangling over the side. She stared into the quiet night of the sky, but never looked down.

Maggie closed her eyes and smiled as a falsetto voice whispered, "You're one step away. One step from the freedom you seek."

"Yes," Maggie whispered to herself. "I want to be free."

The cold that consumed her awoke memories of summers during high school, the wild nights with friends, boys, and the thrill of adventure. The cold connected those thoughts with the idea of falling, and the nostalgia offered the final push over the edge.

Maggie leaned forward, falling slowly at first, still smiling. But past the point of no return, she opened her eyes, the smile gone as the ground rushed at her. She screamed, the bloodcurdling elation of fear reaching a crescendo that ended with the heavy splat of her body against the concrete.

_T_he inside of the semi truck's cab was littered with fast-food wrappers and crushed beer cans. Any time Sarah moved her feet, the trash would shuffle and draw the attention of the truck driver who had picked her up outside of Springfield, Massachusetts. She didn't like his stare. She'd seen it all her life from men like him.

It was the dead gaze of hunger, a longing to satisfy his sexual appetite by way of the cute little blonde. But despite the driver's hungry eyes, he didn't touch her. And for a girl in her position, it was the best that she could have hoped for.

Sarah had dressed for the cold, but her wardrobe was limited. She wore a grey beanie that concealed most of her short blond hair, and a matching colored scarf that swallowed her neck. Jeans, boots, and a thick Carhartt jacket that was two sizes too big rounded out the rest of her attire. She rarely found clothes that fit, her petite frame always swallowed up in even the smallest sizes.

The rest of her belongings were zipped up in her backpack, which she kept on her lap, both arms wrapped around it. When you barely had anything left, you made sure to keep it close.

The cab's windows were dirty and frosted over from the cold, which offered her blue eyes a distorted view of the scenic country roads. Fall was nearly done, and those colorful leaves that so many flocked to watch change in the northern parts of Maine had fallen and turned black along the roadside as the country teetered on the cusp of winter.

However, Sarah hadn't come all this way for the changing seasons. It wasn't a luxury she could afford even if she wanted too. All she wanted was to keep moving, but when the truck started to slow down, she knew that she was running out of space.

The inside of the cab rumbled as the driver pulled off the road, and then the brakes on the eighteen-wheeler squealed all the way to a stop.

"Well, here ya go." The trucker grunted as he shifted the big stick into neutral. His stomach pressed against the steering wheel even when he was leaned all the way back. He gestured to the welcome sign outside of Bell, Maine. Population: one hundred twelve. "This is the last stop before the Canadian border."

Sarah leaned her face closer to the window until she felt the chill coming off the glass. She didn't want to stop here. But with no passport, this was the end of the line.

"Do you have family here? Someone that you can stay with?" The trucker scratched his beard and then pushed his baseball cap higher on his head, exposing his receding hairline. He squinted at Sarah's silence. "Are you in some kind of trouble?"

"Thanks for the ride." Sarah opened the door, slid off the seat, and landed onto the asphalt. She heaved the door closed without a goodbye, slid her arms through the straps of her backpack, and skirted the shoulder of the two-lane road into town.

The semi lingered for a moment, and Sarah was afraid that the trucker might try and follow her, but she exhaled with relief when the big diesel drove off.

It wasn't until the noise of the truck's engine disappeared that she finally turned around, finding the road empty save for the scattered leaves that had been flattened into the asphalt.

Sarah adjusted her pack and then stared at her boots. The leaves beneath her feet were so dead they'd lost their crunch. Winter had already started its purge of life. One of the many reasons she hated the cold.

Sarah wiped her nose, which burned red from the cold and constant run of phlegm. Matching red marks appeared on her cheeks, striking in contrast with her pale skin.

She tugged at her left sleeve and stared down at her hand. The cold, dry air had already caused the flesh over her knuckles to crack, and her left pinky had grown so dry it started to bleed. She tucked her hands back into her pockets and tried to focus on anything but the cold.

Clouds of grey blanketed the sky above, blocking out the sunlight. The road stretched ahead as she tramped several miles, and the sky darkened as the afternoon faded into evening. And just when Sarah was about to turn around, thinking that the town didn't exist, she saw the house on the hill.

She used the term "house" loosely. It was massive, even from a distance, and the treetops ahead blocked most of it from view. Sarah stopped, glaring at the towers on either side of the mansion that thrust upward and the dozens of windows that lined the front of the house on the top floor. If someone in Bell could afford a house like that, then she might be able to find some work.

The road continued its curving path for another mile before Sarah glimpsed the rest of the town, and found it lacking the shock and awe that the mansion provided.

Seven buildings had been erected on the side of the road, three on the left and four on the right. Before and after the main-street buildings were several one-lane paths that stretched off the paved road and disappeared into the woods.

The buildings on the left side consisted of a grocery, hardware store, and a bar. But then as Sarah walked a little farther she saw another structure appear at the end of the buildings, or at least what was left of one.

All that remained of the building was the skeletal structure. Everything had been burned down, the remaining wood scorched and blackened. But even from what was left Sarah could tell that it was a church. She'd been forced to go to enough Sunday services to recognize the high-pitched roof and the charred rubble from the rows of pews.

The four buildings on the right housed several small businesses that ranged from lawyer to doctor, providing the town's residents with their basic needs.

A small diner was the last business in the row of buildings on the right. The scent of food worsened the grumble in her stomach, and Sarah was drawn to it like a bug to a light bulb.

Through the windows that lined the front of the diner, Sarah saw only one patron, an elderly woman who was gingerly bringing a soup spoon to her mouth. She was dolled up like she was heading to the city, wearing a floral dress complete with an extravagant pink hat with a peacock feather sticking straight up out of the back.

A bell chimed at Sarah's entrance, and a blast of warmth loosened the cold's grip on her senses. The scent of bacon and bleach flooded her nose, and the mix of smells caused her stomach to churn.

Old stools with torn red cushion seats lined the bar, and

Sarah sat down, hands folded together, as a man stepped from the back.

Like the trucker who had given her a ride, the man behind the counter was overweight, thickly bearded, and balding on top save for a few greasy black wisps. Brown stains covered his shirt, and his sleeves were rolled up to his elbows. Sweat beaded on his forehead, and he removed a small pad of paper from his apron pocket. Without looking at her, he placed pen to paper. "What do you want?"

The heat from the kitchen warmed Sarah's front, while her backside remained frosted. "Are you hiring?"

The fat waiter placed the paper and pen back in his apron pocket then pressed his hands onto the counter. He gave Sarah the once-over then tilted his head to the side. "No. Now are you going to order something or not?"

Sarah had half a mind to walk out, but the warmth prompted her to stay. "Coffee."

The waiter tapped his finger against the counter. "Can you pay for it?"

"Only if it doesn't taste like piss water."

"I'll be sure to brew a fresh pot." He smirked and then returned to the kitchen.

Sarah planted her elbows on the counter, the rough sleeves of the Carhartt jacket providing a thin layer of cushion, and let her body thaw.

After a while, she started to grow hot, but she resisted the urge to take off her jacket and scarf. She didn't need people asking any questions.

Sarah swiveled on the stool, sneaking a peak at the old woman, who was still working on her soup. She didn't slurp, but Sarah noticed that after every mouthful, she'd dab her face with a new napkin. Every time.

"Dollar fifty." The waiter set the cup down roughly, some of the coffee spilling onto the saucer.

Sarah reached inside her jacket and removed a crumpled wad of cash. She plucked out two wrinkled one-dollar bills and placed both on the counter.

The waiter snatched up both then smoothed out the bills along the side of the register. He tossed two quarters back to her, and Sarah made sure he saw her pocket his tip. He laughed and then shook his head as he pulled the rag from his shoulder and wiped down the counter.

Sarah sipped the coffee sparingly, knowing the moment it was done, the grease ball would either force her to buy something else or kick her out. Neither of which she wanted. Money and warmth were in short supply. And if she couldn't find a job, then her dwindling cash supply would only shrink.

"How long have you been on the road?"

Coffee in hand, Sarah turned to her right, finding the elderly woman finished with her soup, which she had set aside. Her tone sounded friendly, but the old woman wore no smile.

"A few days," Sarah answered then returned to the warmth of her coffee.

"All by yourself?"

"Yup."

The old woman chuckled. "Well, aren't you brave."

Sarah ignored the old woman's remarks.

"Where are you from?" the woman asked.

"Not here."

"Oh, for heaven's sake, will you come over here and just sit down," the old woman said. "We're the only two people here, and Frank isn't much of a conversationalist. I'll even buy you dinner."

Almost on cue, Sarah's stomach rumbled. It'd been more than a day since she'd eaten. Turning down a free meal wasn't just stupid, it was crazy.

Sarah brought her coffee along, and the old woman smiled in triumph from their battle of wills. The old bat could have the victory so long as Sarah could eat.

"Frank! Bring me another butternut squash soup!" The old woman nodded to Sarah. "What do you want?"

She reached for the menu still on the table and immediately spied the meatloaf and mashed potatoes as Frank returned with the woman's second bowl of soup.

"I'll have the number two," Sarah said.

Frank didn't bother jotting the order down, but did make it a point to glare at her before he stepped away.

"Don't mind him," the old woman said. "He's just sore because it was another bad tourist season." She pushed the soup toward Sarah. "Go on. It's quite good. What Frank lacks in customer service he makes up for in product."

Sarah hesitated but then snatched up the spoon and shoveled a mouthful down her gullet. It really was good. She shoveled another dozen spoonfuls down before she stopped herself. If she ate too quickly, she knew she'd toss it right back up.

Sarah plucked a napkin from the dispenser and wiped her mouth then took a closer look at the woman across the table. She wore thick, almost comical layers of makeup. And Sarah noticed the old woman had purposely smeared red lipstick onto the skin around her thin lips to make them look thicker.

"My name is Iris Bell." She lifted a weathered hand, making an effort to keep it above the table.

Sarah regarded the old woman's hand. "Bell. Like the town?"

"Pretty *and* smart," Iris replied. "You're just the whole package."

Iris kept her hand extended, and Sarah eventually accepted the greeting. She barely squeezed the woman's hand, but the bones inside smooshed together like sticks in a bag.

Iris reclaimed her hand and grabbed the wooden sphere at the end of her necklace. The simple piece of jewelry stood out amongst the rest of her gaudy attire. She twirled it in a practiced motion between her fingers as she narrowed her eyes at Sarah. "What are you doing all the way out here?"

"Looking for work," Sarah answered.

Iris laughed. "If you wanted to find work, you wouldn't have come to Bell." The laughter transformed into a cough that started slowly but turned into a crippling hack. Iris released the wooden sphere and grabbed a tissue and covered her mouth, coughing into the cloth.

When Iris peeled the tissue from her lips, she stared at its contents for a moment then folded it and placed it back in her purse. She noticed Sarah's stare. "Age comes for everyone eventually, dear. But I'm sure someone so young doesn't think about that."

Frank returned with a plate stacked with meatloaf, gravy, and mashed potatoes and slid it right under Sarah's nose.

Knife and fork scraped the white porcelain, and Sarah no longer cared about eating too fast or the pain that would follow from so much food. All that mattered was filling the aching pit in her stomach.

Iris was silent while Sarah ate, but the old woman stared at her through the entire meal. Once the meatloaf was gone and only a few lines of gravy were left, Sarah pushed the plate away and leaned back, the vinyl seats groaning as she moved.

"I'm surprised you remembered to breathe while you ate that," Iris said.

Full and warm, Sarah loosened the scarf around her neck. "It's just been a long day, and I had to walk from—"

Iris's gaze had fallen from Sarah's eyes to the bruises on

her throat. Realizing what she'd done, Sarah quickly adjusted the scarf, her cheeks blushing redder than Iris's makeup.

"I suppose those might have something to do with your visit to our little town," Iris said.

Sarah cleared her throat, keeping her face tilted down. She reached for the coffee, drained it quickly, and then slammed the cup back down on the table. "Thanks for the meal, but I need to get going."

"If you're looking for a job I might be able to help with that," Iris said.

Sarah was halfway out of the booth when she stopped. "Doing what?"

"I'm in need of a maid," Iris answered. "I'm not much use for cleaning anything, and the house needs a lot of work, but I can pay you five hundred dollars a week."

Sarah repositioned herself in the booth, straightening up a little. She hoped that she didn't look too eager. With that kind of money coming in every week, she could save up enough to start over somewhere after a few months.

"You live in town?" Sarah asked.

Iris nodded. "I'm sure you saw my place when you came in." She leaned toward the window and then pointed north, extending a bony, frail finger.

Sarah inched her way toward the window, following the indication, and spotted the mansion on the hill. Slowly, Sarah turned around. "*You* live in that house?"

"Me and a few staff," Iris said. "So what do you say?" She grabbed hold of that sphere again, twirling it between her fingers.

Sarah examined the old woman and then looked back up at the mansion on the hill. It had been three weeks since she'd slept on a proper bed, and six days since she'd taken a shower. Not that she was counting.

But what was more, Sarah had reached the end of the

line. The only thing north of Bell was Canada, and Sarah didn't want to risk more legal trouble by sneaking across the border. And with winter a breath away, she knew she couldn't survive the cold without shelter. At the very least, she might be able to lift some jewels or valuables off the old woman.

"Well?" Iris asked, her patience thinning.

Sarah turned back around, looking at the old woman who had offered her the best, and only, lifeline she was apt to receive. "When do I start?"

_T_he closer Sarah moved to the mansion, the larger the structure grew. But what it gained in size, it lost in luster. Distance had hidden much of the mansion's decay, and up close it looked more like an extension of the old woman than the beacon of decadence that had been its original incarnation.

The steps leading up to the front doors were crumbling, some of them completely missing, worn away by time and neglect.

The evening sunlight breaking through the gray skies exposed the dirt and grime that covered the windows. Large cracks ran the length of the building's five stories, and each of the gargoyle statues posted on the roof was missing some type of limb, head, or wing.

But the mansion wasn't completely without awe-inspiring features. Two massive columns ran the height of the house on either side of the doors, each of them engraved with beautiful, intricate designs and elements of the forest, and though they had been weathered by the seasons, time and nature couldn't detract from the craftsmanship.

"Damn steps keep multiplying." Iris stopped at the top of the stairs and leaned up against a statue for support. She was short of breath, and despite the cold, she was sweating. "I just need... a minute."

After a few minutes of rest, Iris straightened herself and smiled. "Age will do a number on you, darling. Don't take that young body of yours for granted." She gestured toward the house. "Now let's go inside before we freeze to death."

The front double doors weren't locked, but they groaned loudly and opened slowly. Iris entered, but Sarah hung back a moment, examining the scrollwork on the wood. It was a carving of the town below.

Sarah saw the road that cut through the middle, the buildings on either side, and on top of the hill was the mansion itself.

"Get in here," Iris snapped. "It's drafty enough in this damn place."

When Sarah finally crossed the threshold, it took her eyes a moment to adjust to the dimness, and Iris closed the doors behind her.

"You'll get used to the darkness," Iris said, scooting past Sarah. "Powering this house costs a fortune, and while the Bell name still carries value in town, I'm afraid the family bank account doesn't share the same clout." She struck a match and lit a candle.

"I hope it has a little something left," Sarah said, staring at the back of the old woman's head, that ridiculous feather sticking out from the top making her look like a weathered bird. "I don't plan on working for free."

Iris turned, the glow from the candle shifting the shadows on her face. "You'll get your payment, dear. Don't worry."

"Good." Unsettled by Iris's glare, Sarah stepped past her, head tilted up, and gazed at the massive crystal chandelier hanging from the ceiling then at the grand staircase that led to the upper floors. Red carpeting draped over the steps, and the stairs' railing was engraved with more scrollwork, though it was too small for Sarah to decipher. The floor of the foyer was marble, though the stone needed a good polish to restore its shine.

Iris moved past Sarah and stopped at the foyer's exit onto the first-floor hallway. "Coming?"

Sarah nodded then followed.

"The job is quite simple. You will work Monday through Friday from eight o'clock in the morning until five o'clock in the afternoon. You will be given one forty-five-minute lunch break and two fifteen-minute breaks to use at your leisure." Iris abruptly stopped in the hallway and spun around. She pointed a long, arthritic finger at Sarah. "But don't you try and take advantage of that and think you can use that time to start late or leave early. Got it?"

Sarah leaned back, her forehead wrinkling as she frowned. "Yeah, I got it."

"Good." Iris spun back around, candlelight illuminating the golden-flecked wallpaper on either side of them, which made it feel as though they were walking down a hallway of stars. "At the beginning of each day, I will assign you a room that needs tending. You will be tasked with cleaning it from top to bottom, including any furniture or belongings that are inside. Should you find anything broken or beyond your capacity to fix, you will notify Dennis."

"Who's Dennis?"

"The groundskeeper."

"How many people do you have working in this place?"

"A few," Iris answered, her tone ending the conversation. "Now, you and Dennis will be part of the day crew, and there is another shift that works at night. You're not to disturb them, and they won't disturb you, understand?"

"What do they do?" Sarah asked, goading the old woman into a flurry.

"Whatever I tell them to," Iris said, again clutching that wooden sphere, and then tapped her arthritic finger against Sarah's shoulder. "Do you have a problem with following directions?"

Sarah walked over to a nearby table and picked up an empty vase, wondering if it was worth anything. "So long as the money comes on Friday I'm all yours, lady."

"Good," Iris said. "I'll show you your room."

A second staircase was revealed at the end of the hallway. It was much more modest than the grand staircase. The space was narrow and cramped, winding tightly, with the steps so small it gave the impression it had been built for children.

Sarah followed Iris onto the third floor, and the pair stopped at the seventh door on the left.

"Here we are." Iris reached into her pocket and removed a silver key. "This is your room."

Inside, light flooded through an open window, exposing a modest room that boasted only a bed, a nightstand, and a vanity. The furniture was from the last century, but the sheets on the bed looked new, and the fresh scent of bleach signaled it had been recently cleaned. A fireplace was on the wall opposite the bed, logs stacked next to it.

"Bath is next to the closet. The shower is small, and it takes a while for the hot water to kick in, but it'll come." Iris set the candle down as Sarah walked to the window. "You'll have your privacy, but keep in mind that I reserve the right to search any part of this house without a warrant." She held up the silver key as a threat. "So mind your sticky fingers."

Dust covered the window, the scent growing stronger the closer Sarah moved to the glass. Her room boasted a view of a garden in the back, which was surprisingly vibrant. Amid the changing leaves and the black and white of the coming winter, there was nothing but green.

"I'll expect you downstairs at the front door, dressed and ready for work tomorrow. Uniforms are in the closet. I'm sure you can find one your size." Iris grabbed the candle, turning to leave, and then stopped before she closed the door behind her. "You have free run of the house, so long as the doors you try aren't locked. But I don't want you snooping around on the fifth floor, understand?"

"Sure," Sarah answered.

"I'm serious, girl," Iris growled, pressing her chin into her neck. "That is one rule that is unforgiveable. I will throw you out without pay if I find you up there."

Sarah finally peeled her gaze away from the window, slung her backpack off, and placed it on the bed. "I got it."

"Good." Iris stepped toward the door, and then stopped herself. "Oh, and no smoking in the house." She wrinkled her nose. "I could smell that disgusting habit on you the moment you walked into the diner."

"Of course, my lady." Sarah gave a deep curtsy, keeping her head down until the door slammed shut, and Iris was gone.

Sarah lifted her head and flipped the bird at the door, lip twisted in a snarl, then flopped down on the bed next to her backpack.

The mattress swallowed her up, and while it was soft, it didn't offer much support. With effort, she finally sat up and opened her pack, dumping its contents over the sheets.

A few shirts, an extra pair of jeans, thick wool socks, another scarf, a sweater, and a few pairs of underwear were her spare clothes. She had one bra but never wore it. The bulky Carhartt jacket took care of concealing her breasts, and she wasn't complaining about not having to wear one.

Aside from the clothes, she had a can of pepper spray, two

packets of beef jerky, a flashlight, a lighter, and her last pack of cigarettes. With money scarce, she had been forced to cut back on the habit, and she had bummed as many smokes on her trek north as she could, which were few and far between since most people had kicked the habit or were too smart to start in the first place.

Staring into the backpack now, anyone would have thought it was empty. But Sarah reached toward the bottom and pulled at a loose corner. The fabric gave way and exposed the tough leather underneath, and she removed a folded photograph.

Holding it, Sarah shivered, then tucked it into her pocket. She stacked a few logs in the fireplace, dumped some lighter fluid over them, then struck a match.

Flames brightened the room, and a quick blast of heat warmed her cheeks. But the initial blaze died down quickly. She added more lighter fluid, and it helped the flame catch permanently.

The room warmed quickly, and Sarah sat down at the vanity, the mirror offering a cloudy and scratched reflection. She unwrapped the scarf and examined the bruises along her neck.

The finger marks didn't look as bad as they had when she'd first hit the road. The worst of the purple and black had faded, leaving only a few lingering marks from the middle and index fingers. But the area was still sensitive to the touch.

Starting to sweat, Sarah removed her jacket, the long-sleeved shirt underneath loose against her body, and then rotated to the left and lifted her shirt to examine her side.

Like the marks on her throat, the bruises on her ribs had started to fade. She dropped the shirt and placed her hand over her side, gingerly leaning back in the chair. She hadn't pissed blood since the fight, and it didn't hurt to breathe anymore, so she was glad to discover her body was healing.

Sarah glanced around the room once more and sighed. Once again, she found herself in a stranger's home where she never wanted to be in the first place.

But it was a dance she was familiar with, and she had started it young, after the death of her parents. For fifteen years, she had ping-ponged around different foster homes, fighting for her life and the right to see tomorrow.

Her childhood had been spent fending off a drunken foster parent who wanted to knock her around, and then as she grew older, protecting herself from the molesters that wanted to take what she wasn't willing to give.

She hoped that she wouldn't run into those types of people here, but if Sarah learned one thing, it was to never trust a book by its cover. And while Iris Bell played the part of cranky old woman well, Sarah bet there were more than a few pages the crow wished she could burn.

Sarah turned to watch the fire and placed her hand over the pocket that held the picture. She liked keeping it close whenever she was in a strange place. It had been that way ever since she was little.

After a few minutes of gazing into the crackling flames, she realized how tired she was. Travel, cold, and her injuries had drained her energy, and she hadn't had a full night's rest since she'd left New York.

With an actual bed to sleep in, Sarah crawled beneath the covers and shut her eyes. Two minutes later, she was sound asleep.

* * *

DESPITE SARAH'S desire for rest, the nightmare returned. It was the same nightmare that she'd experienced every night for the past week. She was running through the streets of New York, cutting down alleys, tossing quick glances over her shoulder at the dark figure in pursuit.

It was night, her path illuminated by yellowed and flickering streetlights. There was no traffic and no one else on the sidewalks, just her and the man with the gun. But no matter how far she ran, or how fast, the man always caught up.

Sarah tripped and skidded to the concrete, tearing the skin from her palms and knees. When she turned to look behind her, the man was silhouetted from a nearby streetlight. He had the gun aimed at her head, his finger on the trigger.

But he never pulled it. He lowered it, a smile stretching over his face that pulsed cold chills through Sarah's body. He'd step closer, until he was practically on top of her, and he'd just stare down at her with those dead, dark eyes and that cold smile.

Sarah trembled, incapable of doing anything but wait for the end. And then, just when she thought he might walk away and let her live, his hand would strike out quick as a snake bite and clamp around her neck.

Sarah sprang awake, gasping for breath as she instinctively reached for the imaginary hand around her neck. She coughed then drew in hyperventilated gasps as she checked the room to ensure she was alone.

"It's not real." Sarah shut her eyes, whispering to herself. "He's not here. It's not real." Slowly, her heart rate calmed, and she collapsed back onto her pillow. She regained control of her breathing and then flung the covers off of her bed, letting the air cool the sweat that had drenched her body.

Sarah rolled her head to the left, checking the old windup clock on the nightstand. It was three o'clock in the morning. She groaned and then rolled the opposite direction, knowing it would be difficult to go back to sleep.

Groggy, Sarah rolled out of bed, still dressed in her jeans and t-shirt, and grabbed the pack of smokes from her pack. Having one usually calmed her down. She walked to the window and tried to open it, but the lock was jammed shut.

"Shit." Sarah turned from the window and then walked over to the dying amber glow of the fireplace. She pressed the end of her cigarette against the hot log, and then puffed the smoke into the chimney. "Sorry, Santa."

After only a few hits, Sarah felt the nicotine calm her down. And while the rest of the room had become drafty again, it was still warm by the dying coals. The combination of the cigarette and the warmth helped rock her back into a sleepy daze, and just when she was about to nod off, a loud bang echoed in the hallway.

Sarah jerked her head toward the door. She frowned, pausing before she took another hit of the cigarette. She waited for the sound to return, but heard nothing. She stood and then flicked the nub of her smoke into the fire.

Sarah made it one step toward the door when the knock returned, this time hitting against her own bedroom door.

Sarah froze, her heart once again beating quickly in her chest. "Hello?"

Another knock.

"Um, just a minute." Sarah was approaching the door when another knock made her jump. "All right!"

The pounding grew quick and violent against the door, and Sarah grabbed the fire poker from the hearth. She raised the piece of iron in her hands and reached for the doorknob, the knocking reaching a crescendo. "I'm trying to sleep, so if you don't knock it off—"

Sarah swung the door open, muscles tensed and poised to swing the rusted iron at whatever was on the other side. But the hallway was empty.

Sarah stepped into the hallway, checking both ends of the

hall, but saw nothing but paintings and wilting flowers in expensive porcelain vases.

With the hallway clear, Sarah lowered the iron. She turned back toward her door and made it one step before—

"Can you see me?"

Sarah spun around, raising the iron with both hands toward the sound of the voice. She traced the voice to a patch of darkness in the hall where the moonlight from the window couldn't reach. She stared harder. "Who's there?"

"You can, can't you?"

Slowly, the darkness took shape, and from it emerged the figure of a woman who kept her back toward Sarah. Long black hair fell down her back, and she wore a dark dress that blended her with the night.

"You have to help us," she said.

A cold sweat broke over Sarah's body, and the hairs on the back of her neck stood up. The whisper tickled her ear as if the person were right beside her.

Sarah kept her distance and the iron raised. "Listen, I'm new around here, so if you need help then you can talk to Mrs. Bell."

The woman remained silent and motionless.

Sarah lowered the iron, no longer having the energy or the patience to deal with the lady. "Listen, I'm going back to bed."

"No Bell." The words were hissed between lips with disdain.

Sarah stopped. "What do you mean, no Bell?"

"No Bell. No Bell. NO BELL!"

More chills pulsed through Sarah, and she lifted the iron again. "You leave now or I'm going to call the cops. I don't care if you work here or not, understand?"

"Please," the woman said, her voice softer. "You must help us."

"Help you do what?" Sarah hissed back angrily, the frustration mixing with her exhaustion.

The question triggered the woman to slowly turn, but she kept her head down. As she spun, the darkness seemed to shift with her, and Sarah retreated, a fierce cold seeping into her bones. It was raw and sickening, and triggered panic through her veins.

A scream that she couldn't control crawled up and out of her throat, and she retreated faster, the woman growing closer and closer, her head down but her arm stretched out to try and grab Sarah.

"NO!" Sarah slammed into something behind her, tripping to the floor and dropping the iron in the fall.

"Hey, are you all right?"

Still on her back, Sarah smacked at the hands grabbing at her shoulders and then snatched the iron as she quickly stood. It was hard to make him out in the darkness, but he was a man. He wore a white T-shirt, flannel pajama pants, and a pair of slippers. She looked him up and down, still gripping the iron with both hands. "Who the hell are you? Are you with her?" But when Sarah turned, she found the woman gone.

"I'm not with anyone." He kept his hands raised in a passive gesture. "My name's Kegan Bell. I'm Iris's grandson."

Sarah regarded the young man. He was tall, with broad shoulders, and handsome.

"I got in late tonight," Kegan said. "I didn't want to wake her, so I thought I'd surprise her in the morning." He offered a hand to shake. "Are you the new help?"

"I'm the new employee."

"Right. Sorry." Kegan smirked, one of those half smiles that were common practice for pretty boys who'd never had trouble getting girls.

Sarah finally lowered the iron and then turned back to

where she'd seen the woman. "You didn't hear anyone?" She faced Kegan again. "Talking to me just now?"

"The only person I heard was you," Kegan answered. "Are you sure you're all right?"

Sarah walked past him. "I'm fine." She returned to her room and shut and then locked the door.

She laid the fire poker back on the hearth before getting back in bed. And the longer she lay there, the more she questioned what she had seen. She lifted her head and looked at the door one more time before flinging the sheets off. She retrieved the fire poker from the hearth, set it next to her bedside, and climbed back under the covers.

4

After the disruption in the night, Sarah struggled to fall back asleep and ended up watching the sun come up. She stayed in bed until about seven thirty and then decided to get ready.

Still groggy, she flung the covers off, shivering as she placed her bare feet on the wood. She furiously rubbed her arms and walked to the closet, remembering that Iris had mentioned wearing a uniform. But when Sarah opened the closet doors, she frowned. "What the hell?"

Several articles of clothing hung from the racks, each varying in size, but all of them in the same style. The uniform was a simple black gown complete with a starched white apron with frilly lace around the edges and a mob cap to wear on her head. If it had been nineteen twenty-six, she'd have fit right in.

Sarah sighed, shutting her eyes. "Five hundred dollars a week." She repeated it like a mantra and then undressed and picked the smallest size she could find. Then she headed downstairs.

"Well, there you are!" Iris said, tapping her foot as Sarah came down the hall. "I was beginning to think you'd run off." The old woman was still immaculately dressed, her make-up layered on thick, and clutched the wooden sphere at the end of her necklace with fingers that were crooked and swollen from arthritis.

"It's seven fifty-five." Sarah fidgeted with the uniform. It was stiff and constricting. "I'm early."

"Well, I've already been up for three hours," Iris snarled and then gave Sarah a once-over. "Probably a bit more modest than what you're used to." She smirked. "Of course, if I still had your figure, I'd flaunt it too." She sighed. "Well, c'mon. We're burning daylight."

Sarah followed Iris to the third floor, where they stopped at a small door, Iris unlocking it with that same silver key.

The room was small but crammed with furniture covered with sheets stained with dust. The curtains were drawn over the windows, extinguishing the morning light and keeping the room in darkness. Two of the walls contained book-shelves that stretched the length of the wall from floor to ceiling, where a smaller version of the foyer chandelier hung, cobwebs strung between the crystals.

"I expect you to be efficient," Iris said, staying in the door-way. "Like I mentioned yesterday, anything beyond repair or a good cleaning just set out in the hallway and Dennis will pick it up in the evening. Cleaning supplies are in the kitchen in the west wing on the first floor. Pick what you want from the fridge during your lunch break, but—Wake up!"

Sarah snapped her head forward, jumping a little as she swayed on her legs.

Iris narrowed her eyes, turning her nose up at Sarah. "Do you think you can handle this, or do I need to end our agreement?"

"No," Sarah said. "I just didn't get much sleep last night. One of the night crew woke me up."

Iris arched her eyebrow, pausing before taking a step back. "Well, be that as it may, I still expect you to perform your duties efficiently. Now, get to work." She quickly clapped her hands together twice and then left.

Sarah waited for Iris to leave before she headed back down to the kitchen, which was massive. After piling what she thought she'd need into a bucket, Sarah lugged the supplies up the stairs and then got to work.

Sarah opened the curtains, letting light spill into the room, and then pulled the covers off the furniture. Dust flew about, swirling and dancing in the rays of sunlight.

Never having done any type of maid work before, Sarah started with the simple things like the windows, then dusting, and dusting some more, and then dusting up the dust that she'd just dusted.

All the while, Sarah examined the room for anything valuable. She checked under cushions and in old clothes pockets for cash, and drawers for jewelry, but found nothing but lint.

Sarah picked at her uniform, which became even more constricting and uncomfortable as time passed. She didn't understand how women could have worn this kind of stuff. Just layer after layer of cloth, corsets squeezing them until they couldn't breathe anymore... she couldn't have imagined living back then.

It had taken her until lunch to rid the room of the thick layer of grime, and that was just on the surfaces of shelves, windows, and furniture. She hadn't even touched the floor.

When lunchtime finally rolled around, Sarah was convinced that she had inhaled more shit from that room than in her seven years smoking cigarettes. Coughing and with her stomach rumbling, Sarah headed toward the kitchen.

Having already seen most of what the kitchen had to offer when she was searching for the cleaning supplies, Sarah grabbed a plate and made herself a turkey sandwich with a side of chips and grabbed a bottled water from the fridge.

With her meal ready, she started to sit down at the table but then caught a glimpse of the weather outside. Remembering the garden she'd seen from her window, she decided to take her lunch out there.

Outside, the late morning was a stark contrast from the day before. Nothing but blue skies and sunshine, though a chill lingered in the air despite the sun. But after working up a sweat in the house, she found the cold refreshing.

A concrete path led her from the side of the house toward the garden in the back, where she was greeted with the bright green of hedges, accented with bursts of color from a variety of flowers.

Plate of food in one hand and her bottle of water in the other, Sarah found a seat on a wooden bench nestled under a lattice that was covered in green ivy.

"Hello."

Sarah jumped, which flung the plate off her lap. Turkey, bread, lettuce, cheese, and tomato splatted against the concrete, and her heel crunched the chips as she stood and spun around.

A tall man in a dirty blue jumpsuit, gloves, and work boots held up his hands in apology. "Sorry." He smiled, exposing crooked and yellowed teeth. "Didn't mean to startle you." His voice was rough like the dark stubble along his cheeks. "I'm Dennis." He removed his glove and extended a big, calloused hand with long fingernails that matched the yellow of his teeth.

Sarah regarded the hand, and Dennis retracted it, looking a little self-conscious over her dismissal.

Dennis dropped his gaze to the spilled food and then frowned. "Oh no, look what I did. Let me run in and fix you something real quick."

"No, it's fine. Really." She bent down and scooped the sandwich up, dusting off the bread

"Are you sure? I promise I can make it just like you want it," Dennis said.

Sarah reassembled the sandwich and took a bite to end his attempts to reconcile. "See? Good as new." She tried to smile through the chomping, but the bite she had taken was too big.

"You must be the new maid." Dennis cleared his throat and then ran his palm over his head, sneaking a quick glance at her figure. He probably didn't think she noticed, but she always did. All women did. "Glad to have some help around here, though my expertise is somewhat limited to the yards."

Sarah finished the bite and then glanced around the garden. "You do all this yourself?"

"Yup." Dennis crossed his arms and then rocked back on his heels. "Mrs. Bell likes to have a place to come outside and rest. It's a challenge keeping everything alive, especially this time of year." He frowned. "Once the first snow hits, it's goodbye clementine."

"Right," Sarah said, still holding her sandwich and still standing. She kept quiet for a while, looking at anything but Dennis's face, hoping the man would get the hint that she wanted to be left alone, but he kept staring at her, flashing those yellow teeth. "Well, I should finish up." She raised the sandwich. "Need to get back to work soon."

"Oh, sorry." Dennis quickly donned his glove. "Well, if you need anything, don't be afraid to reach out. Lovely to meet you, um—"

"Sarah," she said.

Dennis smiled. "Sarah." He lingered a moment longer than necessary then disappeared behind the tall hedges.

Sarah shivered once he was out of sight, but it wasn't from the cold. It was the way that Dennis had said her name. There was a hint of adoration, almost as if he was tasting the words as he spoke.

She ate a few more bites of the sandwich, but she'd lost her appetite. Leaving the crushed chips on the ground, she returned to work.

By the time five o'clock rolled around, Sarah could barely stand up straight. She'd finished the room, or at least she thought she had until Iris walked into the room with a tornado of insults, exposing every dirty nook and cranny she had missed.

"This crown molding needs to be replaced," Iris said, looking down at the floor, then ran her finger over one of the cushions on the seat. "And these need a wash." She flashed the dirty print toward Sarah. "It's filthy!"

Too tired to protest, Sarah kept quiet, focusing her energy on keeping her eyelids open.

"You'll start in this room again tomorrow, and give it a *proper* cleaning." Iris pointed at the windows. "You didn't even reach the top sections of the glass!" Shaking her head in disgust, she stormed out of the room, her grumblings trailing her.

Sarah rubbed her eyes, smudging the dust and grime deeper into her skin, and left the cleaning supplies in the room, since she'd be back in the morning.

She made a pit stop at the kitchen before retiring to her room, making herself a sandwich and snagging two bottles of water. Because she had practically skipped lunch, the sandwich was gone before she returned to her room.

Sarah chugged half the water bottle and then turned on

the shower to let the water start to warm. The pipes groaned, and the showerhead rattled, but the faucet eventually spit water as Sarah disrobed.

She peeled the uniform from her body like a second skin, and as she wiggled out of her clothes, the scars etched along her back were revealed.

The smallest of them was less than an inch and the largest no more than three inches. They crisscrossed along her back from the base of her neck all the way to her waist. She reached for a few at the top of her shoulders, feeling the raised keloids.

They were much older than the bruises she'd received last week, and they'd be around long after the bruises were gone. They were tattoos of pain that she had never requested.

At the time, Sarah was living with the angriest prick the world had ever known, and despite his repeated warnings for her to keep out of his personal food stash, hunger finally drove her to steal.

The bastard had caught Sarah red-handed, shoveling crackers into her mouth to help ease the nagging ache of hunger in the pit of her stomach.

But when he closed his bedroom door, locking the two of them in the room, there was no anger on his face. He simply pointed toward the dresser and told her to open the bottom drawer.

Sarah had received the belt before, so she didn't think anything of it as she trudged over toward dresser, keeping the box of crackers in her hand. She knew the belt would hurt, but the pain was temporary.

She frowned, her mind transporting her back into that dingy, poorly lit bedroom, her feet crunching against the stiff carpet that hadn't been cleaned in decades. She saw the dresser in her mind, the faded oak and the dirty brass handle.

Except this time when she opened the drawer she didn't

find any belts or switches. And it was the first time in her life that she'd experienced real fear. A fear that no seven-year-old should ever feel.

She dropped the box of crackers and then sprinted toward the door, pounding on it and screaming to be let out, but the coward scooped her up and tossed her back onto the bed.

The sheets had wreaked of body odor and stale booze, and the man pinned her down, pointing the knife that had been in the drawer at her face.

"It's time you learn there are consequences for your actions, girl!" He spit the words at her face, and then flipped her to her stomach.

Sarah screamed and cried as he cut open her shirt, but when the tip of the knife dug into her back for the first time the pain was so intense that her voice disappeared. She gasped for breath, spasming on the bed like a fish being descaled.

Her entire body lit up with pain, but after a few the first dozen cuts her entire body went numb.

By the time he finished, her back was slick and covered with blood. She felt nothing as he dragged her from the bed and onto the tile in the hallway.

"Remember this, girl."

And the memory ended with the slam of the bedroom door.

Sarah dropped her hand, shaking the bad memories from her thoughts, and checked the water, which had warmed, and then stepped into the shower.

The room had fogged with steam by the time she finished, and Sarah trailed watery footprints toward the fire-place as she dried off with her towel.

Steam rose from her skin as she stacked fresh logs over the ashes of the previous night's fire. She lit another flame before the warmth from the steam faded and then dropped the towel to the floor on the way to bed, sliding beneath the covers.

The sheets were cool but soft against her bare skin. She ran the bottom of her foot against her leg, feeling the stubble that had grown. She watched the fire as she rubbed her leg, waiting to drift into sleep, and her eyelids fluttered closed.

But like the night before, this one was plagued with restlessness. The scars on her back revived the nightmares of her childhood. She was forced to relive the horrid conditions of her foster homes, and fight the monsters that had been charged with keeping her safe.

* * *

MORNING CAME FASTER than it had the day before. Sarah groggily slid from bed, donning the same uniform from yesterday and headed downstairs to meet with an already irate Mrs. Bell.

"It's ten after," Iris said and then gestured at Sarah's attire. "And you don't even bother making yourself presentable!"

Sarah smoothed her hair under the white cap and examined the dirt on her apron. "I didn't think it mattered since I'm just going to get dirty—"

"Save it," Iris said, her tone snappy and mean. "You're redoing the room from yesterday. When you've finished with it, and I mean really finished, come find me."

Iris stormed off, and Sarah had determined that after only five minutes of consciousness, she'd already reached her daily limit for bullshit.

The cleaning supplies were right where she'd left them upstairs, and with her brain still half asleep she tried to think of where to start. She glanced up at the windows and remembered Iris's comment from yesterday.

Grabbing a rag and glass cleaner, Sarah pushed one of the chairs over to the window. On her tippy toes, she stretched as high as she could reach, barely able to wipe the top corners.

Scrubbing decades' worth of filth off the glass, Sarah reminded herself that she only needed to stay long enough to earn a couple grand, and then she was gone. And as she scrubbed she started to think about where she would go.

California sounded nice. She had a friend in San Diego who told her it was always sunny and seventy-two degrees, no matter the time of year. It was stable, it was safe, and it was warm. But more importantly, it was far away from *him*.

With the top panels of the window clean, Sarah rechecked her work on the other windows from the day before, giving them an additional wipedown to avoid further scolding.

Still on the chair, Sarah dropped the rag and was about to turn away from the window when she saw Dennis emerge from the woods. He walked slowly, dragging a shovel behind him, and he was covered in dirt.

Unsure if she could be seen, Sarah leaned to the side of the window, tucking herself behind the curtain.

Below, Dennis dropped the shovel and then ran his fingers through his hair. He swiped at his eyes as if he'd been crying and paced back and forth very quickly. After a minute, he seemed to calm himself down, and then he headed toward the house.

Sarah emerged from the curtain and then stepped down from the chair, processing what she'd seen. Her imagination ran wild, but she attempted to keep it in check. He was a groundskeeper, so being covered in dirt and dragging around a shovel was hardly anything to trigger accusations. She plunked the sponge into the bucket and returned to work.

Everything was rewashed, and Sarah paid particular

attention to the cushions, which she removed and cycled through with a load of laundry. While they washed, she ticked off a list of items needing repair to hand over to Dennis, and then she took her lunch break.

She entered the kitchen warily, wanting to avoid any run-ins with Dennis, and when she determined that the coast was clear, she made herself a grilled cheese, which she paired with a can of tomato soup.

But with all of the kitchen's modern updates, she still found no microwave. "Of course." She sighed and then turned on the gas burners and found a pot in one of the lower cupboards. She found an old wooden spoon to stir the red sauce in the pot, and she munched on some grapes while the soup heated.

"What's for lunch?"

Startled, Sarah spun around, clutching her chest, finding Kegan smirking. "Is that just how you greet people? Scaring the shit out of them?"

"At least I kept my distance this time." Kegan stood at the kitchen's entrance and eyed the spoon in her hand. "Think you could set that down before you decide to hurt me with it?"

Sarah tossed the spoon back into the pot and then opened cabinets.

"Bowls are at the end," Kegan said, pointing to the last cupboard above the stove, then sat at the table. He smiled, that natural, easygoing charm on display. He reminded Sarah of the football players from her high school. All confidence and no substance. "So how are things working out for you here?"

"Fine." Sarah kept her back to him.

"Good, good." Kegan rubbed his hands together. "Any constructive feedback you'd like to suggest to management to improve your work environment?"

Sarah poured the soup from the pot to her bowl, careful not to spill and burn herself. When she was done, she turned and lifted the pot so Kegan could see. "Get a microwave." She tossed the pot into the sink and then grabbed her grilled cheese.

"Good to know," Kegan said.

Sarah passed Kegan, and was almost free when he called out to her.

"I'm sorry about the other night," Kegan said. "I spoke to the maid who woke you up. It won't happen again."

"How many people work here anyway?" Sarah asked.

"What's going on here?" Iris appeared at the kitchen's entrance, her nose turned up at the sight of her grandson mingling with the help. But the sneer was made impotent by the seven layers of makeup on her face.

"Morning, Grandmother." Kegan spoke sweetly and smiled widely.

Iris grunted and then regarded Sarah and her lunch. "Hurry up and finish that, so you can get back to work. Clock is ticking, my dear."

Sarah repressed the urge to respond and instead decided to take her lunch to her room. But before she made it up the staircase, she heard Iris and Kegan arguing. She stopped, curious to hear what they were saying, and crept back toward the kitchen's entrance.

"What do you think you're doing?" Iris asked, her voice an angry whisper.

"I'm just being friendly, Grandma," Kegan answered. "There's no crime in that."

"I don't want you getting close to her, understand? You've got enough on your plate as it is. The last thing you need is some tramp to slip into your bed."

Kegan laughed. "You're being a little over—"

A harsh slap ended Kegan's reply.

"You have a job to do, and she will only provide a distraction. You hear me?"

At the sound of Iris's shuffling footsteps, Sarah sprinted soundlessly up the carpeted grand staircase before Iris saw her.

5

*T*he end of the day came quickly, and when Iris never showed up to assess Sarah's work, she retired to her room.

Once she was undressed and showered, Sarah caught a look out the window of the dying evening light over the mountains to the west. It was golden and beautiful, and a stark contrast from the old, stuffy house that she had been cooped up inside for the past two days.

She needed a break.

Sarah donned her Carhartt jacket, along with her scarf, before stepping out of her room. The bruises were still visible, and she didn't want to call any more attention to herself.

Outside, the air was crisp, and the temperature plummeted with the sunset, which left streaks of pinks and purples in the sky as the town of Bell transitioned into nightfall.

Sarah flipped up the collar of her jacket, guarding her cheeks from the stiff wind blowing in from the north, reminding her of her disdain for the coming season.

For Sarah, winter had always been associated with death.

It withered everything that was green and turned nature brittle and skittish, weeding out the weak and old, burying them under freezing sheets of snow.

And her parents had died in winter.

But this winter, somewhere out in the growing cold, was a man who wanted her dead. He was as relentless as the Grim Reaper himself, and she'd be looking over her shoulder for the rest of her days.

A few cars were still parked outside the buildings on either side of the street on Bell's main drag. They must have belonged to people just finishing up their workdays.

Sarah veered toward the burned-down church, kicking at an old piece of wood before peering through the windows of the small grocery and hardware store before heading across the road.

The first store on the other side was the diner, followed by an accountant's office, a doctor's office, an antique shop, and finally, an empty building with a "for lease" sign hanging at an uneven tilt from the window.

A bell on a door jingled behind her, and Sarah turned around to find a small man, bundled up in a jacket that looked far too big on him, stepping out of the tax accountant's office.

He kept his back turned toward her as he locked up, and when he turned around and spotted Sarah, he froze.

The man was old, his face shriveled up like a raisin. A pair of thin-framed, round glasses magnified his eyeballs beyond their normal size. He blinked twice and then pocketed his keys.

"Who are you?" His tone held more accusation than curiosity.

"A new neighbor," Sarah answered, throwing the same indignant tone back at him. "Who are you?"

Raisin Face threw his hands in the air, shaking his head as

he walked away. He waddled toward a rusted Cadillac El Dorado and struggled with opening the door. He put one leg inside and then stopped, looking at Sarah through those thick lenses. "I find anything broken tomorrow morning, I'll know who to tell the authorities did it, understand?" He lowered himself into his driver seat and slammed the door shut.

The El Dorado squealed when it started, and its dirty headlights flashed Sarah as the old man backed out of the parking spot and headed toward the highway, giving her a dirty look as he passed.

"Don't mind him."

Sarah jumped, spinning around to find a man standing behind her.

"Old man Dunst doesn't like anything that he can't enter into a spreadsheet." He smiled warmly, hands in the pockets of his jeans as he walked toward her. His hair was grey and peppered with spots of white, which gave the impression of old age, but the face that was underneath was smooth and taut. A few wrinkles appeared at the corners of his mouth and eyes. He was tall with broad shoulders, and he wore a long-sleeved black-and-red flannel shirt that was open and untucked, showing a white T-shirt underneath.

"Good to know," Sarah said, taking a few steps back to keep a comfortable distance between herself and the newcomer as he moved closer.

"Pat." He removed his right hand from his pocket and extended it, but when Sarah didn't take it, he returned it. "I don't have any ID on me, but, uh…" He gestured across the street.

Sarah glanced to the other buildings across the street, finding a larger building with the name "Pat's Tavern" painted above the door in bold white letters.

"Best watering hole in town," Pat said.

"Not much competition," Sarah said.

Pat laughed. "No, there isn't. You the new help up at the Bell house?"

"I wouldn't necessarily call it a house," Sarah answered, glancing past Pat and toward the five-story structure.

"Well, I was just about to head over and open up if you'd like to have a drink. I don't mean to brag, but I happen to be in cahoots with the owner. Could probably get you something on the house." He added an exaggerated wink.

"Are you always this awkward, or is it just when you're meeting new people?"

"Always," Pat answered. "But after a while, people just stop noticing it as much. Like a mole they found on their back three years ago that just keeps growing."

Sarah laughed, relaxing a bit as she lowered her guard. It had been a while since she could afford a drink, and she wasn't about to turn down a free one. She nodded and then followed Pat across the road and into his tavern.

He flicked the lights on, illuminating an open space lined with square tables and chairs, a jukebox at the far end radiating neon yellows, pinks, and blues.

While Sarah examined the décor, Pat rolled up his sleeves and stepped behind the bar. "So, what'll you have?"

"Whiskey," Sarah answered, her eyes locked on the variety of hunting trophies along the wall. Most of them were deer, but Sarah stopped on a massive grizzly bear head.

The bear's mouth was open, the long, yellowed teeth exposed and sharp as daggers. Judging from the head's size, the grizzly must have been huge. The head was half the size of Sarah.

"Stood ten feet tall," Pat said. "The paws on the bear were as wide as my chest." He dropped some ice into a glass and then poured in a generous amount of whiskey. "Took three men to carry it back."

"It was killed in the woods around here?" Sarah asked, turning around.

"Yes, ma'am." Pat placed a square white napkin on the bar as a coaster for the glass. "We tried to get those Guinness World Record folks to come and look at it, but I never got a response. I read somewhere once about a polar bear around the same size, and it was marked as the biggest bear ever recorded." He shook his head. "Shame we couldn't get them to come up here. Might have been able to get some traffic coming into town."

Sarah sat down on the stool closest to the drink. "You guys look like you could have used it."

Pat's face slackened, his expression grave. "Been slow lately."

Sarah took a sip of her drink. The liquor flooded her veins, warming her cheeks and nose, which turned a light shade of red.

"Why not move?" Sarah asked. "Sell the bar?"

Pat smiled, and reached for a dirty glass that he wiped down with a rag. "It didn't always use to be like this here. Once upon a time this town was a beacon for anyone wanting to make a fortune." He gestured to the stuffed bear. "Bell was founded by a trapper over one hundred and fifty years ago. Back then the forests were overflowing with game. Deer, bears, beavers, if it crawled in the forest, we had it. Allister Bell recognized that and bought up every acre of land he could afford, and some he couldn't. And anyone that wanted to hunt, or fish, or live on this land had to pay for it."

"So what happened?" Sarah asked.

"A lot of things," Pat answered. "But the nail in the coffin came a year after he dumped all of his money into the land. That was when the textile mills were born, and practically made the fur trade obsolete. He couldn't afford the payments on the loans he used to buy the land, and those that had settled in the makeshift town were leaving by the dozens every day for work at the textile mills in the city."

That warm sensation spread throughout Sarah's body, and she examined her glass, finding it halfway empty. It had been a while since she'd had a drink, and she set it down, knowing she shouldn't go too hard too fast.

"But," Pat said, raising a finger, "a woman heard of his trouble and came to visit. She was a strange woman, an outcast who had settled the land long before Allister Bell had arrived. The townspeople whispered that she had been in league with the devil."

Sarah snorted, spinning the drink on the napkin, watching the condensation collect on the glass. "She must have pissed off the wrong man to start those rumors."

"At the end of his rope, Allister decided to speak with the woman. She told him that she could make him rich and powerful beyond his wildest imagination. And all it would cost was his soul." Pat finished with the glasses and flung the white rag over his shoulder and leaned closer to Sarah. "He'd never been a religious man, and with his family starving and broke with winter on the way, he had nothing to lose."

A combination of Pat's storytelling and the whiskey pulled her into the tale. "And so the woman just made all of it happen." Sarah snapped her fingers. "Just like that, huh?" She laughed and then took another sip. "Sounds like a hell of a deal. Hey, you wouldn't happen to know if that witch is still around? I could use a get-out-of-jail-free card."

Pat smiled. "Don't mind giving up your soul for it?"

Sarah swirled the ice and the liquor, staring down into her glass. "Not sure I ever had one to begin with." She took another drink, this one lasting a few gulps before setting it down, and Pat's silence brought Sarah's face up from the cubes floating in liquor. "So what happened? Did she come and claim his soul?"

"That's where the waters get a little muddied," Pat answered. "The exact terms of the agreement vary, but there is one consistency to the story, and that was what happened on Allister Bell's deathbed. The woman returned, and while he looked withered and old, the woman hadn't aged a day. I don't know what was said, but after she left, Allister Bell died, and the town started its slow decay into what you see now."

Sarah arched her eyebrows. "An old man dying on his deathbed. There's a shocker." She drained the glass and dropped it down on the table. "And you still didn't answer my question. Why not leave?"

Pat smiled. "Because this is my home. Been here my whole life, and while it may not be much, it's mine." He finished wiping down the glasses and reached for the bottle of whiskey. He freshened Sarah's glass and then leaned onto the bar top. "But what about you, my weary traveler? What brings you to Bell?"

Sarah picked up the whiskey glass and stared at the melting ice cubes floating in the brown liquor. "Nothing good." She took a smaller sip and then set the glass down. She reached for her cigarettes and lit one up.

"Mysterious," Pat said.

Sarah shut her eyes and inhaled. The smoke funneled down her throat and into her lungs. She held her breath for a moment, and then exhaled through her nose, her body thankful for the hit.

"I'm glad it's working," Sarah said.

"And does my mysterious traveler have a name?"

She puffed smoke, Pat's face growing hazy from the cloud. "Sarah."

"You running from trouble, Sarah?" Pat asked, keeping his tone innocent.

Sarah smiled and reached for the whiskey glass. "A girl

never reveals her secrets, Pat." She winked, and Pat laughed.

The door opened behind her, and she watched Pat's reaction brighten in surprise.

"Well, if it isn't the prodigal son returned home."

"Prodigal grandson."

Sarah turned slightly to her right, finding Kegan approaching the bar. She quickly looked away, returning her attention to the whiskey and cigarette. If she hadn't been down to her last pack, she would have snuffed it out and left, but she wasn't about to let some pretty boy send her running.

Pat and Kegan embraced, Pat looking at Kegan like a son. "Been a long time since I've seen you in here."

"I hope you checked her ID." Kegan sat next to Sarah while Pat poured him a drink without him ordering.

Sarah rolled her eyes, which Kegan missed when his attention turned toward the commotion at the door. A small crowd stepped inside, and Pat wiped his hands off. "I need to settle some bar tabs with Sal and Joe." He playfully punched Kegan on the shoulder. "Good to see you, kid. Holler if you need anything."

"Thanks, Pat."

Kegan reached for his glass, fingering the edges before looking at Sarah. "Hi."

Sarah ignored him, sipping from her drink and staring at the mirror across the back of the bar.

"Oh, I see," Kegan said, nodding as he cupped his drink on either side with both hands. "You wanted to keep up your loner profile. I get it." He sipped from his drink, facing forward. "Must be a lonely way to live."

"You always talk this much at a bar?" Sarah tapped her cigarette, adding to the pile of ash in the tray nearby.

"People come for conversations," Kegan answered. "Otherwise they'd just drink alone at home."

"I should give that a try." Sarah took another long drag on

her smoke, and then snuffed it out in the ashtray. She reached for the whiskey and drank a large gulp.

"Might want to take it easy on that," Kegan replied. "Don't you have work tomorrow?"

Sarah tilted the glass toward her lips, staring at the liquid. "You going to rat me out?"

Kegan shrugged. "Depends on what you have to offer."

Sarah held up her hand, signaling for him to wait a minute, and then reached into her pocket. When she pulled it out, she flashed him the bird. "And that's my final offer."

Kegan laughed and took a sip of the whiskey. "Some guy must have burned you pretty bad."

Without even realizing it, Sarah reached for her scarf and gently prodded the bruises underneath. "Bad isn't the right word."

"What was that?" Kegan asked, leaning over.

Sarah quickly shook her head, drained the rest of her whiskey, and set the glass down hard.

"You leaving?" Kegan asked.

"Yeah." Sarah walked past him quickly before he could stop her and ignored the locals by the door as she burst outside and into the frigid night air.

The combination of the warmth from the bar and the liquor rushing through her veins harshened the cold in the air.

Sarah stood on the roadside, arms crossed, feeling lost. She turned toward the mansion on the hill, the structure a shadow against the darkened night sky. It seemed that no matter how far she ran, or how old she grew, she couldn't escape foreign homes filled with strangers she didn't like.

Twenty years she'd been searching for a real home. She thought she'd finally found that in New York, but it turned out to be just another shattered dream in the long trail of broken memories that had brought Sarah here.

She never wanted this life. She didn't ask for it. She was three when her parents were killed in a car crash. She knew it wasn't their fault, but a part of her had always been bitter about their death, and none more so than now.

Her eyes grew red and wet as she reached for her shoulder, unable to feel the scars beneath the thick fabric of her jacket. She had spent her entire life fighting for the right to live, and every time she thought she'd earned the right to happiness, the rug was pulled out from beneath her feet.

"Ma'am?"

Sarah jumped and then turned to find a man nearby.

"Is everything all right?"

"Yes, I'm—" And then Sarah noticed the uniform, the gun on his hip, and the badge on his chest.

"Ma'am?" The deputy stepped forward, and Sarah mirrored his motion in retreat.

"I'm fine." Sarah blurt the words in a stutter and quickly turned away, keeping a brisk pace toward the mansion.

"All right," the deputy said. "Have a good night!"

Sarah's heart hammered wildly in her chest, and she hugged herself tight. She didn't turn around; she didn't look back. The last thing she needed was to be ID'd by the police.

* * *

DEPUTY DELL PARKER lingered in the cold, watching the young woman walk back up toward the Bell Mansion. When she finally disappeared into the darkness, Dell shrugged and then turned toward Pat's for his regular end-of-shift drink.

The ruckus was already in full swing when Dell swung the door open, and he gave a friendly wave to the regulars in their corner, who were in the throes of an argument over the damned stuffed bear on the wall.

"Fifteen feet, I'm telling you!" Sal reached his arms high above his head. "Biggest damn thing I'd ever seen."

"The damn bear gets bigger every time you tell the story," Joe said, waving a dismissive hand toward Sal.

Sal plopped back into his seat, grabbing the handle of his half-full mug of beer. "Well, your wife has a few stories to tell about you in the bedroom, and they get smaaaaaaller every time she tells it."

The other fellas busted a gut laughing, and Joe slunk back into his seat, red-faced and sipping his beer.

Dell smirked and then wandered over to the bar where he saw Pat talking to someone. "Hey, Pat, I'll have a Coors—"

The stranger turned around, raising a glass and flashing a crooked smile. "Hiya, Dell." Kegan sipped from the whiskey and then set the glass down."

"Kegan," Dell said, stunned. "I didn't realize you were back in town."

"Came in the other day." Kegan widened his grin, giving Dell a look up and down. "Well look at you. Officer Dell from Bell!"

"It's Deputy, actually." Dell took a seat at the bar, keeping one open stool between him and Kegan as Pat handed him his beer. "Thanks, Pat."

Kegan chuckled to himself. "Giving me the cold shoulder, huh? Seems to be going around tonight."

Dell set his beer down. "I'm not sure what you expected, Kegan."

"Yeah, I guess you're right." Kegan spread his legs wide on the stool and then drummed his fingers on the bar. "I was just hoping we could put all of that behind us. Start fresh. After all, we have our reunion next year."

"I'll probably skip that," Dell said.

"Are you kidding?" Kegan asked. "Look at you! All of those girls that wouldn't sleep with you back then would be dying to get in the backseat of your cruiser now!" He leaned over, dropping his voice to a whisper. "All you have to do is flash those handcuffs." He cackled then retreated to his own section of the bar.

"I'm not going to have any trouble tonight am I, boys?" Pat flashed his eyes between the pair.

"Oh, c'mon, Pat!" Kegan waved a hand. "We're just catching up. We'll be fine."

Dell nodded. "We're good, Pat."

"All right." Pat disappeared, leaving the pair alone, aside from the raucous group still debating the bear's size.

"How long you in town for?" Dell kept his tone polite, but kept his attention on the beer.

"Not sure," Kegan answered. "Depends on how long Grandmother lasts." Kegan's voice trailed off.

Dell looked over. "I didn't know she wasn't doing well. I'm sorry."

"Yeah, well, she's old." Kegan shrugged, the playfulness gone as he took another sip of his drink.

While Dell had never been fond of the old woman—she had used to treat him like roadkill she'd found on the side of the road—he knew that she had a lot to do in raising Kegan. She was more mother than grandmother. He raised his glass. "To Iris Bell."

Kegan turned and raised his own glass. "The coldest witch this mountainside has ever known." He tapped his glass against Dell's and then drained the rest of the whiskey.

Dell took a more modest drink and then set his beer down while Kegan reached behind the bar and grabbed the bottle of whiskey to refill his glass. "Might want to take it easy there."

"Relax, I'm not driving." The glass overflowed, spilling liquor onto the bar. "I'll leave Pat a good tip. He won't mind." He tossed the double shot back and then slapped the glass down hard on the counter. "Well, I better get back." He reached into his pocket and then tossed a wad of bills next to the empty glass. "Don't want to keep Grandma waiting for her nightly pills." He slapped Dell on the shoulder and leaned in awkwardly close. "Always good to see you, buddy." Two more pats and he walked away.

"Yeah, you too." Dell watched Kegan leave and then returned to his beer. By the time he finished it, Pat stepped out from the back and wiped down the mess that Kegan had made. Pat peeled apart the wad of cash, and Dell noticed a fifty amongst the tens and fives. "He never had a problem flaunting his money."

"It was the only thing he had," Pat said. "You bragged about your mom a lot, but you don't hear anyone else complaining about it."

"That's because my mother was a saint." Dell aimed his thumb at the door. "He's a clown with a trust fund."

Pat was quiet for a minute and then looked at Dell. "You know Iris is sick."

"He told me." Dell pushed the glass toward Pat, which was their signal for a refill. "Think he'll sell the place?"

Pat shrugged. "I don't know. He grew up here, just like you and me, and that's not something any amount of money or distance can get rid of."

Dell knew it was true. Anyone who grew up in Bell and lived to tell the tale did so with a certain level of pride. It wasn't easy growing up in a decaying little town in the most northern, coldest part of the country.

Still, having Kegan back in town made Dell uneasy. Iris was hard enough to deal with on her own, but having two Bells back in town put the rest of them on their heels. But if the old woman was on her way out, Dell realized it could mean the same thing for the town.

6

*S*arah tried sneaking in through the side door on the east wing when she arrived back from Pat's Tavern, but found that it was locked. She grunted in frustration and then headed around toward the front entrance.

Unlike the side doors, the front doors were unlocked. Sarah chuckled as she shook her head, unable to comprehend the old woman's logic of security. She shut the doors behind her and then made her way up the grand staircase.

Sarah kept to the left side of the staircase, avoiding the red carpet and tracking boot prints over it. She didn't want to add more work for herself tomorrow.

The house was quiet on her ascent, and Sarah glanced around, realizing just how many rooms this place had. She suspected that people could go weeks without seeing each other so long as their schedules were skewed.

But when she passed the second floor, she heard muffled voices. She tilted her head toward the noise but was unable to make sense of the conversation. She crept down the hall and saw light through a crack in a door with shadows moving inside.

The closer Sarah moved, the clearer the conversation became.

"Keep them hidden, Dennis. Do you understand?" It was Iris.

"Yes, I understand."

"It's more valuable than anything in the house."

Sarah arched her eyebrows, her interest piqued. She might not have to stick around as long as she thought.

"But don't tell anyone. Not even Kegan."

"Yes, ma'am."

"Good."

Footsteps shuffled toward the door, and Sarah darted soundlessly back toward the staircase before Iris could spy her. She meandered back up the steps, wondering what they were talking about. Money? Jewels? Old crows like her always kept cash stashed nearby for emergencies. She just needed to narrow down where it might be.

Once Sarah reached the third floor, she turned from the staircase and toward her room. Her eyelids had grown heavy, and her thoughts turned to bed as she desperately hoped for a full night's rest.

"Hi."

Sarah spun around, too tired and slow to be startled, but her heart jumped. It was the girl she'd seen from her first night. She was dressed in the same maid uniform, but this time she faced her, though she had positioned her hair to cover most of her face.

"What is with people sneaking up on me?" Sarah asked. "Do I have a sign on my back or something?"

"I need to show you something," she said. "Something that can help."

Sarah exhaled and then looked back toward her room.

"It won't take long," she said.

"All right." Sarah reluctantly trudged along, following the woman toward the west-end staircase.

The air grew colder the higher she ascended, and she was shivering by the time she reached the fifth floor. "I didn't think we're allowed to be up here."

"It's okay if you're with me," she said.

At the top, Sarah peered out the small window in the stairwell. Below, she saw the woods that stretched to the horizon beyond the mansion's perfectly landscaped property. She pressed her hand against the window, the glass freezing, and quickly pulled it away, leaving behind a handprint.

"This way," the woman said.

Sarah wiped her print clean with her left sleeve, erasing any sign of her presence, and then faced the fifth-floor door, finding the woman gone. "Hello?" She glanced down the stairs, finding them empty. Had the woman already gone through?

Cobwebs dangled from the ceiling and covered the cracks of the door frame. The door itself was weathered, the wood grayed and cracked. The brass of the knob and the hinges had lost their shine and had rusted to the point of disintegration.

Confident that the door would be locked, Sarah reached for the knob. A light turn to the left, and it opened.

The hinges groaned, and dust drifted from the top of the door as it opened inward. Pushing it open, Sarah let go, letting it drift into the adjacent wall, where it thumped to a stop.

The wooden floors were in the same worn and tattered shape as the door, and they complained with Sarah's every step. She checked behind her, making sure the noise hadn't triggered any attention to herself upstairs. She knew that Iris's room was somewhere on the fourth floor, and the last thing she needed was the old bag of bones finding her up here, despite what the night maid said.

The entire floor looked as if it hadn't been inhabited since the house was built. Paintings in dirty golden frames hung from the walls, and Sarah took a closer look at the name etched at the bottom of the first one she passed.

Allister Bell – 1844

The man in the portrait wore no smile and sat on a gold-colored chair with a high back that was lined with red velvet cushions. While the painting had weathered over time, the focused expression of Allister Bell had not.

It was as if he was there in the wall, transported through time and staring Sarah directly in the face. He looked angry, as if her presence in the house he built offended him from the grave. But from her experiences with interacting with Bells, Sarah figured the expression was genetic.

Scattered between the paintings of the Bell family's lineage were tables with small pictures and candlestick holders, dripping with long, hard strands of old wax. More dust, more cobwebs, more relics from a past that refused to die.

"Down here."

Sarah looked toward the end of the hall, finding the woman at the window near the last door on the left, which was open.

Sarah left Allister to his brooding and continued her trek down the hall. Doors lined either side, the layout similar to that of her own floor.

The woman gestured inside the room, but Sarah hesitated. "What are we doing?"

The woman kept her head bowed and her face concealed behind the thick, straight strands of hair. "You must know why we're here. It will help us."

"You keep saying us," Sarah said, her tone becoming acerbated. "Are we in some kind of danger working here?"

The woman barely tilted her head up and exposed her left eye. "Please. Just look in the room."

Sarah remembered girls like her in the foster system. They were quiet and shy, beat down by the environment. She had always tried to help protect those girls, but she didn't always succeed.

Finally, Sarah approached the door. Inside, the room was darker than the hallway. She crossed the door's threshold and groped the wall for a light switch.

A chandelier that hung from the center of the room brightened, and Sarah arched her brows in confusion.

Unlike in the hall or even the rest of the house, everything inside the room was clean and new. From the floorboards beneath her feet to the paint on the walls and ceiling, there wasn't a speck of dirt or dust.

The deeper Sarah penetrated the room, the colder it became. She rubbed her arms, shivering as she placed her hand on the bedsheets. When she turned around, the woman was in the doorway.

"The nightstand," she said, pointing toward it. "Open it."

Sarah reached for the drawer and pulled. At first glance, it looked empty, but the drawer was deep, and Sarah reached all the way toward the back. And while she didn't find anything, the weight of her hand made the bottom of the drawer buckle. Sarah removed her hand from the drawer and then pressed down on the inside corner. It was a false bottom.

She wedged her fingernails into the side and lifted the bottom from the drawer, exposing clusters of old papers.

She removed the pages, the paper brittle and worn, and placed them on the table. She unfolded the top paper and discovered that it was a letter.

Much of the ink had faded, but the date was still legible. Still, Sarah had to read it twice before she was confident her mind wasn't playing tricks on her. It had been written in 1882.

"The truth lies within those pages," the woman said.

Sarah shuffled the papers in her hands. "What truth? What am I looking for—"

Before she could start on the first line, a door slammed down the hall. She looked back toward the door and found the woman gone, but heavy footsteps heading toward her.

Sarah quickly shut the drawer, keeping the letters in her hand, and then ducked under the bed, knowing it was too late to try and run.

The bottom of the mattress scraped against her back as she crawled, and she covered her mouth with her hand to quiet her breathing. She craned her head toward the door and watched a pair of dirty work boots enter the room. It was Dennis.

He walked all the way to the center of the room and then stopped. He said nothing and didn't move. Finally, he walked to the closet and lingered there for a moment. Then he sat on the bed, the mattress buckling from his weight.

"I didn't think you'd be awake already," Dennis said.

A quick jolt of fear pumped through Sarah's heart as it beat fast and hard against the floorboards. Unsure who he was talking to, she kept quiet and still.

"I'm almost done," Dennis said, a pleading desperation to his voice. "But it's hard." His voice grew thick with phlegm.

Sarah looked around, scanning the room for other people, but it was just the two of them.

"Help me," Dennis said. "Guide me."

The lights flickered, and the door slammed shut.

"Yes," Dennis said, his voice a breathless whisper. "Show me the way."

The mattress buckled as Dennis lay down, his legs still dangling off the side.

The bed rattled, and the room darkened. The air grew so cold that it burned Sarah's lungs with every breath. Vibrations hummed through her body, and she shut her eyes. Dennis wailed as the entire room trembled. The rumbling reached a crescendo until it sounded as if a freight train were tearing through the room.

And then it stopped.

Sarah opened her eyes, expecting to find the room destroyed, but nothing had changed.

The lights flicked on, and the mattress springs squeaked as Dennis climbed off the bed. He stood quiet and motionless for a minute and then whispered, "I will not fail you."

Sarah followed his boots out of the room and then watched the door close behind him. She waited until the boot steps faded and she was positive that Dennis was gone before she shimmied out from beneath the bed.

She brushed the dust from her chest, stomach, and legs and carefully scanned the room. Whoever Dennis had been speaking to was gone. And whatever had happened when she was under the bed seemed to have had no effect on the rest of the room. Was he just crazy? Did he have some kind of seizure that made the bed shake like that?

"He's one of them."

Sarah jumped, the woman appearing out of nowhere in front of her, and backpedaled into the wall. "What the hell is going on? Who are you?" She glanced down at the letters in her hand and then tossed them back onto the nightstand. "I don't want any part of this, understand? I don't have time for this shit."

Trembling, Sarah stormed forward, but the woman blocked her path.

"Move, or I will go through you."

"It's time to wake up, Sarah." The woman kept her head down, her face still concealed behind her long black hair.

"What?"

"Time. To. Wake. Up!" The woman lunged for Sarah's throat, and an icy burn accompanied her touch, freezing Sarah in place. The world turned black.

* * *

SARAH SHOT up and out of bed, clutching her neck as she gasped for breath. She patted the bed and sheets, her eyes frantically scanning the room.

Morning light spilled through the cracks in the curtains, and she saw her backpack on the floor near the foot of her bed. She was back in her room, still dressed in her clothes from the night before, complete with her jacket.

Sarah relaxed, but frowned, recounting the dream, though it had felt nothing like her usual ones.

She swung her legs off the side of the bed and hunched forward, glad to see that she had the good sense to at least take her boots off. Her stomach grumbled, and she checked the time.

"Shit!" Sarah flung off the covers, quickly dressed, and hurried downstairs. But instead of finding an angry Iris Bell, she found Kegan pacing near the front door.

"Morning, sleepyhead," Kegan said.

"Where's Iris?" Sarah asked.

Kegan approached the steps, going so far as to set his foot on the bottom stair as he gripped the newel post. "She's not doing well this morning. She asked me to show you the next room. And while she didn't explicitly say you did a good job with the drawing room on the third floor..." He paused, shrugging as he tilted his head to the side, the slightest inkling of charm leaking through. "When it comes to Iris Bell, no news is good news."

Sarah kept the flight of stairs between them, refusing to come down to him. "So where am I working today?"

Kegan trudged up the stairs, and Sarah followed him back to the third floor. She noticed that he carried Iris's silver key. It must have been the master key to the entire house, including Sarah's room. The fact that he had access to her room and could enter anytime he wanted triggered a small eruption of bile into her mouth that she forced back down to her stomach.

"It's small," Kegan said, stepping into the bedroom. "Shouldn't take you too long."

Sarah waited until Kegan was out of the doorway before she entered, finding that he was right.

"Wish you would have stayed last night," Kegan said. "We could have had some fun together."

Sarah walked toward him, and placed her hand on the door. She tilted her head to the side and smiled. "I doubt it." She shut the door, forcing Kegan to move before it slammed in his face.

Once Sarah was sure Kegan was gone, she returned downstairs to grab the cleaning supplies and then got to work. She followed the same method she had yesterday, starting from the top and working her way down, thankful to fall into the numbing rhythm of mundane manual labor.

Dust, dead insects, more dust, grime, cobwebs, and years of neglect layered over and over across the room. Moths had gotten into the curtains, eating big holes in the dusty red velvet. She tore them down, adding them to the trash pile of old clothes she had pulled from the closet.

Along the way, like she had done with the other rooms, Sarah scoured the drawers and nooks and crannies for anything that looked valuable, but again came up empty.

Lunchtime came and went, and when three o'clock rolled around, she used her last fifteen-minute break for a smoke.

She avoided the garden and instead walked out to the front steps and watched the still town below.

The end of her cigarette glowed red, and she closed her eyes on her first deep inhalation, letting the smoke warm her innards.

Sarah smoked the stick all the way down to the nub and then snuffed it out on the concrete. It was her act of defiance for the day. She knew Iris would see it. She smiled, picturing the old woman snarling and huffing her way up the steps, angry about the world that had shoved that stick up her ass.

With the high from the nicotine, Sarah leapt up the stairs quickly, knowing that she'd be able to take her time with the rest of the room until five o'clock arrived.

Sarah grabbed the sponge from the bucket, dripping a trail of soapy water toward the headboard.

Sarah slowly worked her way down, unearthing the faded paint beneath the filth. The grime from the walls ran down in thick, watery streams, making the house look as if it was bleeding tar.

Once she reached the baseboard, she was forced to move the bed's headboard away from the wall, which revealed an outline of the headboard's edges, but then she stopped when she noticed something carved into the baseboard.

Sarah dropped to her knees and squinted. Some dust had collected over the engraving, but it looked recent. Sarah swiped at the writing with her sponge, erasing the dust that covered the carved letters, and then cleared away the soap with her apron. The letters were small, but the words were clear.

In the shed.

The letters were hurried, jagged and frantic. They had been written by someone who couldn't keep their hand still, which meant that they were either angry or scared. Sarah was betting that it was the latter.

Then her thoughts turned to the conversation she overheard the night before between Dennis and Iris. If the groundskeeper were going to hide something, then the shed would make sense.

Maybe that other girl had found it. Maybe that's the help she was talking about.

"Sarah."

She dropped the sponge and then shimmied out of the tight space. Kegan was at the door, leaning his head inside. "Listen, I have to head out for the night. I need you to bring my grandmother some dinner. There's some chicken noodle in the cabinets. She'll eat that."

"All right."

"She eats early, so I'd go and get it ready now. You know where her room is?"

"Fourth floor."

"Good, and don't worry, she's not contagious." Kegan lightly knocked on the doorframe and then disappeared.

Sarah looked back down at the words scribbled on the baseboard. And she thought of the dream she had last night, and the woman that had been pestering her, and Dennis, and Iris, and the whole damn house.

"Just a few more weeks," Sarah whispered to herself. "Just get the money, and then run."

Sarah headed down to the kitchen, prepared the soup, and then located a tray to carry it up to Iris's room. She was careful up the stairs, making sure not to spill, knowing that she'd get an earful for making a mess.

The fourth floor had the same setup and structure as the others, but the furniture had been polished, the vases filled with fresh flowers, and the runner down the hall was new.

Sarah walked along the runner in the hall and toward the third room on the left, which was cracked open. She knew it was Iris's from the horrible coughing and hacking coming from inside.

Gripping the tray with both hands, she shouldered the door open and poked her head inside. Iris lay in a white gown, tucked beneath a pile of blankets, with a stack of pillows keeping her upright.

"What are you doing here?" Iris snarled, but the expression disappeared when she viciously hacked into a napkin.

"Kegan had to leave." Sarah set the tray down on the nightstand next to Iris's bed. "He asked me to bring you some soup."

"What a chivalrous gesture." Iris cleared her throat and shut her eyes.

Sarah took a moment to examine the room, which was surprisingly small considering the old woman's ego. There was a vanity, the bed, a nightstand, and then a side table which was lined with pictures.

All of them were old, most in black and white, and Sarah suspected that it was Iris's family. But in three of the family pictures, she noticed that one of the faces had been scratched out. And it looked to be the same face every time.

"That'll be all."

Sarah turned back to Iris, who was staring at her, twisting the wooden sphere of jewelry that still hung from her neck. And while Iris tried to maintain her intimidating glare, the intensity was lost in the frailty of the body beneath the covers. She was just an old woman, and from the stained red cloth that Sarah had seen in the trash can, she was also dying.

Without another word, Sarah left the room, closing the door behind her and muffling Iris's coughs as she returned to her work.

The sponge had leaked a puddle of soapy water onto the floor where she'd left it, right beneath the phrase that had been carved into the room.

A brief thought of heading to the police entered her mind, but she snuffed it out quickly. Talking to the cops would only expose her, and she didn't need to cause any more trouble for herself.

Sarah grabbed the sponge and returned to work, doing her best to ignore the words on the baseboard and the woman's request for help. She was an adult. If she needed help that bad, then she could do it herself.

7

_____

*S*arah stashed the cleaning supplies back in the kitchen and then made herself a ham sandwich on wheat, complete with lettuce, tomato, muenster cheese, and a generous helping of mayonnaise. She grabbed a bottle of water and then returned to her room.

Sarah opened the curtains, letting the evening light bathe the room in oranges and gold, and then sat cross-legged on the bed, where she ate her sandwich. She gazed out the window, finishing her meal, and wondered how far she'd have to run before she was finally safe.

Eventually he'd give up, right? She thought maybe a year from now she'd be able to relax.

With enough cash, she could buy a new identity. Time and distance were her best friends right now. She just had to ride it out.

Once she finished her sandwich, Sarah got the itch for a smoke. She reached for her backpack on the floor and stuck her arm inside, then froze.

Sarah's hand groped something foreign, and she trembled

when she removed her arm and found herself holding the stack of letters from her dream.

She dropped them, the letters unfolding and spreading over the floor. She rolled off the bed in the opposite direction and kept her distance as she circled around the foot of the bed.

It wasn't possible. It was a dream. It wasn't real. She'd woken up immediately after the woman had touched her throat.

Sarah reached up and grazed her neck, remembering the icy chill. Her heart rate increased, and her breathing shortened into quick, hyperventilated gasps.

Slowly, she crept around the foot of the bed, hoping to find the letters on the floor vanished as mysteriously as they appeared. But as she rounded the corner, she saw one of the folded pages.

Sarah stared down at the pages, trying to rationalize what happened. Either it hadn't been a dream, and she didn't remember going to bed, or someone had placed the letters in her backpack while she was out of the room.

The latter was possible. She didn't have the ability to lock her own room when she was gone, so anyone could have come and gone as they pleased. But why had the woman left the pages in her pack? What was she trying to accomplish?

Sarah carefully picked up one of the letters from the floor. She walked to the window and the dying light to help her read.

The ink was faded so badly that it had practically disappeared. She set it down and then reached for another one, but it was just as bad.

Sarah crouched down on the floor and spread the letters out and found a legible one near the middle of the stack. She leaned toward the light from the window and read.

My dearest Iris,

Our situation in Bell has deteriorated. I'm afraid that we won't last much longer without any aid from the outside world.

I know that you moved away because you no longer wanted to be a part of our family, but you should know that when I die here, it will be you who is held responsible, along with your family.

With no heirs of my own, your descendants will become the last of the Bell name, and while you may not have had a decision in departing our town, I can tell you that your distance from our home will have no impact on the effects our ancestor will have in reaching you.

There is nowhere else to hide, Iris. There is nowhere that you can run. If you choose that road, I sincerely wish you the best of luck. But if you want to give yourself and your family a fighting chance, then I beg you to come home. It is the only way.

Jameson Bell

Sarah lowered the letter, unsure of its meaning. The author of the note wanted Iris to come back, and it had obviously worked. But Sarah was under the impression that Iris had always lived here.

But the talk of ancestry caused Sarah to remember her conversation with Pat. He had mentioned that the first Bell had made a pact with a witch, and after he died the town went to shit.

"No." Sarah pushed the thought out of her head and dropped the letter back into the pile with the others. It was foolish. All of it. Nothing but fairy tales and ghost stories meant to frighten tourists.

Sarah crossed her arms, staring out the window until her eyes fell upon the shed on the outskirts of the property near the forest.

In the shed.

She eyed the worn-down structure curiously, returning to her ideas of where the groundskeeper would hide something valuable. If it was enough cash or jewels, then she'd bounce and head as far south and west as she could go on her remaining cash. Iris had never asked for her ID, and Sarah had never filled out any paperwork. They didn't know who she was, and they wouldn't have a clue on how to find her.

Sarah scooped up the letters and then piled them back into her backpack, which she zipped up and slid under the bed. She changed out of her uniform and into her jeans and shirt, donned her jacket, and bolted from the room toward the house's west-end staircase. Everything ready to go in case she needed to leave after a successful discovery.

Outside, Sarah kept her head on a swivel, making sure she wasn't being watched or followed. She spotted the shed past the green and kempt garden, nestled on the edge of the field just before the forest began.

Like the house, it was run-down. The windows were foggy and dirty, the roof sagging, weeds crawling up the sides. It looked as if it hadn't been touched or used in years.

Sarah marched over and then lifted the rusted chain and lock over the door. "Shit." She circled around the back of the shed and found a busted four-paned window covered with a tarp.

Sarah turned around, making sure the coast was clear, and then started to peel the tape holding the tarp in place. The work was slow, but she managed to make a hole big enough for her to stick her head inside.

It was dark inside, but she was able to see an old bench with some tools scattered on it.

Feeling pressured to hurry, Sarah widened the hole and jumped through the open window, landing awkwardly on the floor inside.

The wooden floorboards were dirty and warped. She stood and brushed herself off, noticing a tear in her shirt from the window, and then started her search.

Three benches lining the walls of the shed were stacked with a variety of tools and machine parts.

Sarah opened toolboxes, finding screws, bolts, washers, and nuts but nothing out of the ordinary.

Sarah scanned the shed one last time, walking the interior perimeter. Just when she was about to give up, the ground shifted beneath her feet. She poked the spot again with her toe and saw a section of the floor move.

Quickly, Sarah dropped to her knees, trying to wedge her fingers into the tight cracks of the cutout in the floor, but the space was too small. She snatched a flathead screwdriver from a nearby toolbox and used it to pry the wooden floor-board up.

The piece of wood sent dust and dirt flying when Sarah removed it, and she dropped the screwdriver, staring into the dark space below. She reached her hand inside and removed a shoebox.

The lid was dusty and weathered and so old that it no longer sat flush on the rectangular box. Her heart hammering with excitement, she lifted the lid, sending dust twirling through the air, and found rows of cards crammed inside.

Sarah frowned, then plucked one of the cards from the middle and flipped it over in her hand. It was a driver's license. An old one. The girl in the picture had been born in 1977 according to the birth date listed, and she didn't look older than twenty in the photo. Sarah set it aside and then reached for another one.

It was another driver's license, this one more recent. She quickly scanned the cards and found that they were all some form of identification. There were hundreds of them all piled up in this little box.

Sarah cycled through them quickly but then stopped when one picture caught her eye. It was a newer license, handed out no more than a few years ago. The girl in the picture was a little younger than herself, but there was something familiar about her.

It was the woman's hair. It was long, black, and straight, just like the girl who worked the night shift.

Sarah didn't understand. Why would they bury the IDs of the people who worked at the house? Why keep it a secret? Why—

Movement caught Sarah's attention outside, someone traipsing through the woods. Sarah pocketed the ID in her hand and then placed the box back in the shoebox, and then quickly scurried toward the window as someone fiddled with the lock on the door.

Sarah quickly flattened the tarp and held it down by the edges as she heard the door open inside.

Boots scuffed against the floor, and something heavy landed on one of the tables. Sarah held her breath, praying that they didn't notice the tarp was loose.

Grumblings echoed inside, and time slowed to a crawl. Sarah's muscles trembled from the concentrated effort to keep the tarp up. Finally, the door slammed shut, and the click of the lock and the rattle of the chain signaled that Sarah could let go.

She peered her head around from the back of the shed and saw Dennis marching back up toward the house. She turned toward the forest behind her, and squinted through the trees.

In the fading evening light Sarah saw something amongst the foliage. She checked the field one last time to find Dennis gone, and then stepped into the forest.

The thick brush and rocky terrain slowed her progress, but the deeper she penetrated the trees the more she realized that there was a clearing up ahead.

The space was man-made, evident from the clear

rectangular shape and level surface. But scattered around the clearing were piles of rocks, each of them the same size, and all of them spaced out in a grid.

Something about the tidiness of the area made Sarah uneasy. She carefully walked between the spots, her eyes on a hole up ahead. She trembled on her approach, a part of her already knowing what this place was. But still, she was drawn to it, the rational part of her mind in need of the proof.

And as Sarah approached the edge and looked down into the hole, she thought of all of those ID cards in that shoebox. She thought of the woman who worked at night that kept telling Sarah that they needed help. And when she saw the outline of a body wrapped in a tarp at the bottom of the hole, Sarah covered her mouth to stifle the scream.

8

No longer caring about whether someone saw her, Sarah sprinted back to the house, running to her room as quickly and as quietly as she could muster. She grabbed her bag from beneath the bed and quickly slid the straps over her shoulders. She did one last scan of the room, making sure that she had everything she needed, and then checked her pocket for the picture.

But when she patted her pants, she also found the ID she'd taken with her. If there was a chance that she might be alive, then Sarah had to let someone know.

She thought of Pat and decided the friendly bartender would be the best person to let someone know. She could give him the ID and let him contact the authorities. And then she'd get as far away from this place as she possibly could.

Outside, the golden shimmer of evening had given way to the dark of night. A stiff wind blew down from the northeast. Sarah adjusted her beanie and flipped the collar of her jacket up then shoved her hands into her pockets.

Sarah hurried toward the entrance to Pat's Tavern and yanked at the handle, but it didn't budge. "Shit." She pressed her face against a nearby window and saw that the chairs were still up and the lights were off.

"They don't open for another hour."

Sarah turned toward the voice and found the deputy sitting behind the wheel of a sedan, a steaming mug in his hand as he chewed something. She must have been staring at him for longer than she realized, because he set the mug down and wiped his mouth, eyeing her curiously.

"You were the girl I saw here the other night," he said.

"Yeah." Sarah's voice was breathless. A nervous sweat had broken out under her shirt, and she remained by the door.

"I heard you were working up at the Bell house," he said. "How are you liking it so far?"

Nerves tied her tongue. Despite the deputy's friendly demeanor, she knew that cops had a code.

"Are you all right?" he asked.

All she had to do was give him the ID, tell him that something was off, and then leave. "No, I mean, I'm fine, but…" She stepped closer, removing the driver's license from her pocket. "I think there might be another girl up in that house, and she's in trouble." She extended the card to him, keeping an arm's length between them, and forced Dell to step out of the car to grab it.

When he took the ID, flashing a light on top of it to get a better look, Sarah saw the name on his uniform: Deputy Dell Parker. "Where did you find this?"

"In a box buried in the shed on the back edge of the property. There were a lot of other cards in the box too." She hesitated to tell him about the body, knowing that it would only prompt him to follow her, or even take her into the station. But if he found the box, then she figured that would be enough.

Dell flipped the license over and then finally looked up at her. "What kind of cards?"

"Driver's licenses, like that one." Sarah took a step back. "Some of them were pretty old."

"And did you see this girl up at the house?"

Sarah hesitated. "I saw someone. Or something." She frowned, the commitment in her statement waning.

"What do you mean 'something'?" Dell asked.

"Listen, I just wanted to give you that." Sarah retreated. "I have to go."

"If you just want to come over to the station in Redford and make a statement, I can—"

"I can't. I'm sorry. Good luck."

"Hey, wait!"

Sarah broke out into a jog. She knew that she wouldn't have many options if the deputy decided to chase her. But she didn't think he would. After all, she hadn't done anything wrong, at least not that he knew of.

* * *

DEPUTY DELL PARKER retreated into the warmth of his car when the girl disappeared. He tapped the card against the steering wheel, wondering if she was just pulling his chain.

The Bells had employed quite a few interesting characters over the years, and growing up in the small town had afforded Dell an up-close-and-personal look at the family itself.

Personally, he had never liked them. They were cold people, distant and unforgiving in their disdain for the collapse of the town named after their ancestor who had founded it all those years ago.

Using the laptop in his passenger seat, Dell accessed the Bangor Police Department database. Maine was filled with so many tiny little towns that local police used a lot of the capital's resources.

Bell was so small that Dell's office wasn't even in town. It was just part of his daily route, and he happened to enjoy Pat's company at the bar. Pat was practically the only person in Bell who smiled, and he had been kind to Dell and his mother when he was growing up.

Like most small towns, Bell thrived on gossip. And when Dell's dad walked out on him and his mother when he was five, it was all people could talk about until Patsy Stevens found out her husband was having an affair with her sister.

Waiting for the search field to populate on his computer, Dell saw Pat walk up, bundled in a coat with a scarf covering his neck and chin. He waved quickly at Dell, who reciprocated the gesture, then unlocked the bar and went inside to get ready for the evening rush.

It was always the same people every night, and Dell was always surprised that Pat had been able to stay in business for all of these years when things in Bell got really bad. Even Dell's mother had moved away once he'd saved up enough to find her a little spot outside of Bangor when he established himself on the force. She kept trying to get him to transfer, but as dead as this stretch of Maine seemed to be, he couldn't work up the courage to leave.

A force he couldn't explain kept him tethered to this patch of northern wilderness. Maybe it was the hope that the town would find its footing again. Or it could have been the fact that he had made good friends with the three other deputies that were assigned to this territory. But past all of those thoughts, as Dell grabbed hold of the root of his reasoning, he knew the truth. He hadn't seen his dad since he was nine. And maybe he came here to this tavern because it gave him a good view of anyone coming into town. And maybe he'd be sitting here one night and a rusted green Ford pickup with only one working headlight would pull off the highway and find its way back to Bell, its driver searching for the son he'd left behind. For the son he'd never even said goodbye to.

The computer dinged, and Dell examined the search results. He'd found a match in the system, which confirmed the license's authenticity. He glanced to the north, spotting the hulking Bell mansion high up on the hill.

He thought about heading up there to have a chat with Iris, but he knew that with Kegan back in town he wouldn't get any answers.

The two men had a history that stretched back to when they were kids. He had been poor, Kegan rich; his dad left, Kegan's dad died. When boys were ten years old, that was all the ammunition they needed to tear each other down.

If this Maggie Swillford was working at the house, then there might be a paper trail that he could trace back to employee filings, which he could access at the station in Redford.

Dell put the cruiser in reverse and then headed back toward the highway, keeping his eyes peeled for the girl who'd handed him the ID, but she was nowhere to be seen.

The drive from Bell to Redford was less than ten miles south. Dell had an apartment there, and it was about as big a city as he wanted to live in.

Traffic was surprisingly busy as he wove his way around shoppers getting ready for the winter season. He wasn't sure how the folks down south handled winter, but up here, everyone turned into squirrels after fall ended. Folks packed as much food and supplies into their homes as they could afford and accommodate. Which reminded Dell that he needed to stock up on extra heaters.

Dell turned into the station, parked, and then hurried from the car to the building, a bell chiming at his entrance, but Faye didn't even bother looking up as he hung his jacket on the rack. "Any calls while I was out?"

"Ms. Furtter was complaining about a noise she heard in her attic, but after spending a few minutes on the phone with us, she realized it was just one of her cats that had gotten up there." Faye turned the page of the newspaper. She was still wearing her gloves and scarf as if she were sitting outside, but as she sat so close to the door, he didn't say anything.

"How many of those things does she have now?" Dell asked, grabbing a mint from the bowl on Faye's desk.

Faye lowered the paper, staring at Dell as he unwrapped the peppermint candy and popped it into his mouth. "What are you doing here? You don't have a shift tonight."

Dell leaned on the counter, his weight pressed into his forearms as he pushed the mint around his mouth with his tongue. "The Bell house uses contract workers, right?"

"I think so. Why?" Faye asked.

"Maine law states that employers need to perform background checks on any hired employees," Dell said then smiled. "I was hoping you could get them for me."

Faye grunted in frustration, kicking her legs off the desk, and then rocked out of her chair. "You only flirt with me when you want something." She turned around, hips swaying back and forth as she headed toward the file room. "If a rat bites me when I'm down in that hellhole, you're going to have sex with me on your desk to make up for it."

Dell laughed and then skirted the reception area and sat at his desk. He stared at Maggie Swillford's ID, waiting for his desktop computer to turn on. It took about fifteen minutes for the hulking beast to warm up. It would probably be faster for him to just go out and grab the laptop from the car, but he liked using the quiet time to think.

The computer finally booted up, and Dell logged into the crime database to see if Ms. Swillford had had any legal trouble. She'd had a drunken and disorderly charge, but he found that it was the weekend after her twenty-first birthday. He found another charge of underage drinking when she was nineteen. Her rap sheet stretched a little bit longer from speeding tickets and parking violations, but it was ordinary as far as civilians went.

Dell drummed his fingers on the keyboard and then swiveled in his chair toward the hallway down which Faye had disappeared. "Faye? You all right down there?" After a minute of silence, he got up to investigate but then stopped at the slamming of a door and her feet thumping down the hallway.

Faye stopped at the end of the hallway just before stepping into the small office space where Dell and his two coworkers resided. "A rat bit me."

"It'll take a few minutes to clear off my desk," Dell replied. "I wouldn't want to break the computer."

She smirked, hips swaying wildly on her return to the reception desk. "There weren't any background checks on file, though I could have told you that if the captain would just upgrade us to a digital system so I didn't have to root around in that musty rat trap of a file room."

Dell frowned. "They've never requested any background checks or filed any paperwork? What about that groundskeeper? He was there when I was a kid."

"Nothing." Faye returned to her reclined position and picked up the newspaper again.

Dell looked at the ID card again, examining the young woman's picture. She was around the same age as the woman who had given him the license, which hinted at a pattern, albeit a blurred one. But if the Bells never filed any background checks for their workers, that meant he had cause to go to the house and poke around. Which was exactly what he intended to do.

9

*O*nce out of the town, Sarah darted off the road and into the woods but stayed close enough to the road to help guide her to the highway.

Headlights pulled her attention back to Bell, and Sarah watched the deputy's sedan drive toward the highway.

And despite having done what she thought was right, Sarah stopped, the crunch of leaves under her boots ending as she finally turned around.

The forest blocked the view of the mansion, but she knew it was there, sitting high on that hill. When she had first seen it when she entered town, she'd thought it was a sign of what was possible, but now a cancerous tumor came to mind.

Shame reddened her cheeks. Shame from not telling the deputy about the body, about not doing more to help someone else, but she had enough on her plate to worry about. It wasn't her fault other people couldn't take care of themselves.

The forest was full of rustling leaves, and the darkness made its depths that much more sinister. Sarah jerked from any sudden movement or noise. She'd gotten used to being jumpy, and for better or worse, she'd grown used to being hunted.

Nothing was so soul crushing as helplessness. She had fought so hard and so long to earn independence that when she finally had it, she cherished it. No one to answer to, no one to tell her how to live her life.

But after a while, she had discovered that while the world had its freedoms, it also had its limitations. And those limitations would beat you down into a pulp if you let them.

The forest ended, and Sarah stepped from the trees and onto the highway. There were no light posts, and clouds blanketed the moon and stars, casting the road into pitch black.

Sarah turned south, staying on the shoulder, her eyes peeled for any potential rides that she could bum.

It didn't take long for the cold to eat through her clothes, reaching all the way to her bones. Sarah kept her arms pinned at her sides in a feeble attempt to trap what little body heat remained to her.

After the first few miles, she lost all feeling in her face, and the tip of her nose became so cold it burned. Every exhalation puffed icy clouds from her lips and chattered her teeth. And the longer she walked, the heavier her backpack became.

The faint hum of an engine turned Sarah's attention to the north, and she saw a pair of headlights growing brighter and closer in the distance. She stuck her thumb out, walking backward and hoping that the driver would stop.

The truck slowed then completely stopped in the middle of the road. The engine idled, and Sarah squinted in confusion at the yellow headlights.

"What the hell?" Sarah asked, her voice trembling from her shivers.

The truck engine revved, roaring with an anger that shattered the night. Sarah dropped her thumb and began a slow retreat.

Sarah kept her eyes locked onto the headlights while the truck idled. And then, just as quickly as it slowed, the truck charged forward, and Sarah sprinted into the forest.

The moment she broke through the trees, her foot smacked a fallen branch, and she was hurled forward. She thrust her arms out in front of her as she skidded across the cold dirt and dead leaves.

The headlights illuminated the forest ahead as the truck veered off the road, screeching to a stop before hitting the ditch. Sarah turned her head around, eyes open wide in terror, as Dennis stepped out of the truck's cabin.

When Dennis stepped down the embankment from the road, Sarah scrambled to her feet, continuing her blind sprint into the forest.

Tears squeezed from her eyes as she ran, arms flailing as she smacked away tree limbs. A few small branches scratched her cheeks, the pain worsened by the cold.

She moved in a serpentine pattern, hoping to lose Dennis in the darkness or find someplace to hide.

Every strike of Sarah's heel against the uneven earth sent a stabbing pain into the backs of her knees. The boots she wore were meant for hiking not running, and their inadequacies were exacerbated by the rough terrain.

The cold burned like fire in her lungs, and she hacked and coughed. All those cigarettes had caught up with her, and the pain eventually forced her to stop. She ducked behind a tree and tried to quiet her breathing as she listened for Dennis.

While Sarah listened, she remembered the pepper spray in her backpack's side pouch. Her fingers wouldn't stop shaking as she retrieved it from the tiny pocket and then removed the cap.

Finally armed, Sarah returned her attention to the forest,

which remained silent. She couldn't even hear the hum of the truck's engine anymore. Sarah pressed her fingers against the rough bark of the tree and slowly stepped to its side, scanning the forest behind her. She squinted, spotting the truck's headlights.

But there were no signs of Dennis, not a sound, and the silence made it worse. It was as if the man had evaporated, floating through the treetops, just waiting to swoop down and snatch her up.

Sarah waited another minute, and then after still hearing and seeing nothing, she continued her trek forward. She moved quickly but no longer ran, and she kept her head on a swivel.

Leaves crunched to her left. Sarah froze. She turned toward the noise, but everything had been consumed into a pit of darkness.

After another minute of waiting and no more noise, Sarah stepped forward, exposing herself to the forest. She trembled, searching the darkness. And then hands grabbed her neck.

"NO!" Sarah tried to sprint forward, but she was lifted from the ground and then slammed onto her back, losing her grip on the pepper spray. The pack provided a little cushion to break her fall, but the awkward shape buckled her painfully.

Sarah gasped, and then those hands were around her throat again, choking the life from her, stealing her voice and breath.

"You shouldn't have gone snooping around," Dennis said, saliva dripping from his lips. "And you shouldn't have tried to leave." He inched closer, and some of his spit dripped on Sarah's cheek. His breath was hot and wretched. "I came to bring you back. I came to take you home."

Sarah smacked at his arms and kicked her legs, but her

defiance was useless against Dennis's size and strength. But as she squirmed, she kept reaching blindly for the pepper spray, raking the dead leaves and dirt with her fingers.

"Hey," Dennis said, his voice angry. "I don't want to hurt you."

And then Sarah's fingers scraped something plastic. She froze and then nodded, hoping to buy herself some time.

Dennis smiled. "Good girl." Still keeping on top of her, he reached around to his own pocket and removed a rag. "I'm going to gag you." He leaned in closer. "Do you like that?"

Sarah nodded, hoping to prod his ego a little bit longer as she prodded her fingers closer toward the tiny bottle of spray.

"I liked watching you at the house. You've been one of my favorites. So pretty in that little uniform. I think I'll have you put it on for me when we get back."

Sarah finally wrapped her forefinger and thumb around the base of the bottle and positioned it so she could spray.

Dennis stuffed the rag in her mouth and then removed a roll of duct tape from his pocket. "We're going to have so much fun."

Sarah shimmied the bottle closer to her hand, and then when he used both hands to loosen a strip of tape, Sarah shoved the pepper spray close to his face and pressed down.

"AHHH!" Dennis swiped at the hot chemical burst and rolled to his left, clawing at his eyes. "You fucking bitch!"

The cloud of spray lingered in the air, and Sarah was close enough to feel the effects. She coughed and hacked, a burning sensation in her eyes and throat, as she scrambled to her hands and knees.

Muscles trembling, she managed to push herself off of all fours but only made three steps before crashing back down in a fit of coughing, her eyes stinging as she tried to escape the cloud of pepper spray that had enveloped them both.

Tears and snot oozed from her orifices, and she tried to wipe away the residue with her thick jacket sleeve.

Something knocked against her foot and then clamped down on her ankle. Still blind, Sarah glanced behind her as the pair of meaty hands pulled her back.

"You shouldn't have done that!" Dennis backhanded Sarah's face, and the harsh slap briefly replaced the pain of the pepper spray.

Sarah cracked open her eyes, and through blurry, tear-soaked slits, she saw Dennis reach for something in his pocket, which he then jammed into her arm.

The tiny pinprick was followed by a dull, numbing sensation. The pain faded and she sunk deep into unconsciousness, the world black and empty.

* * *

IT WAS the burning that awoke Sarah from the drugged slumber, residue from the pepper spray. She gagged, tasting the gritty fabric of the dirty rag taped over her mouth. Disoriented and groggy from whatever Dennis had fed her, the world around her was still slightly blurred. But it wasn't until she tried to lift her arm and remove the gag that she realized she was tied down.

Restraints kept her hands tied behind her back, and her legs were bound at the ankles. And when she glanced down at her own body, she found that Dennis had stripped her down to her shirt and underwear.

With the lingering burn from the pepper spray still in her eyes, she glanced around to try and get her bearings. It was dark, no lights on, and at first she saw only oddly shaped silhouettes that lined the walls. As her eyes adjusted, she saw that she was in a room with no windows, and a single door to her left.

Having found the one exit point, Sarah scanned the room once more in search of anything that could help her escape and found a few boxes in the far back left corner of the room.

The chair itself wasn't tied down, and the surface was smooth enough to scoot across.

Sarah pressed her toes onto the cold concrete floor and pushed. The chair wobbled, but she didn't move forward. She tried again, this time rocking the chair harder, and nearly crashed to the concrete, but she remained upright and found that she had moved forward an inch.

Hope swelled in her chest, and she repeated the motion, the progress slow but steady. By the time she passed the halfway mark, she had worked herself into a rhythm, and all her focus was on the boxes. Every inch gained added to the momentum for the next push.

The slow progression toward freedom reflected her life for the past week. All of that time on the road, all of those nights she had gone to sleep unsure of if Brent would find her in the darkness to kill her had transformed into a rage that burned like fire.

Every aspect of her life, every memory she could recall, had been born from some type of struggle. It was as if she had always been tied to that chair, forced to crawl forward one inch at a time until she could reach the box that offered her freedom. Whether it was a job, a car, or an apartment, there was always something that she eyed on the horizon. Something just out of reach.

Less than a foot separated Sarah from the box. And then she heard the echo of footsteps. She froze, turning back around toward the door, and then hastened her approach toward the box.

Keys jangled outside the door and then scraped into the

lock. Before Sarah could reach the box, the hinges groaned as the door opened.

"Hey!" Three quick steps and hands pulled Sarah back from the boxes, erasing all of her effort in seconds.

Sarah screamed into the gag, the hope deflating with her dying voice. Even when Dennis stepped around to face Sarah, she kept her eyes fixated on the boxes.

Dennis laughed as he shook his head. "You trying to escape?" He straightened up and walked over to the corner. He picked it up the box in front effortlessly and then flipped it upside down, sending balled-up pieces of paper to the floor.

Sarah went numb.

Dennis tossed the box aside and flattened the paper balls as he walked back over to Sarah. He leaned over with his hands on his knees and brought his face within inches of hers. "You're here to stay, Sarah. Don't you understand that?" Slowly, he lifted his hand and ran his finger along her cheek. The tip was callused and rough, scratching a bright-red line from her cheekbone to jawline. "You're so important." A tone of childlike wonder returned, and he lingered close to her face.

Finally, he backed away and then reached into his pockets, a light jingle sounding, no doubt from the keys he carried around, and she wondered how many times the creep had been into her room.

"You found something that you weren't supposed to see," Dennis said. "If you had just done your job and kept your nose out of business that doesn't concern you, then you could have had a little more freedom before the ceremony, but now I'll have to keep you down here."

Sarah pinched her eyebrows together, unsure what "ceremony" meant to the cretin staring down at her.

"I'll bring you food and water," Dennis said, addressing

Sarah like a mongrel dog. "And try not to mess yourself until I can figure out an arrangement for you to go to the bathroom. But don't worry." He smiled and ran his fingers through her hair. "It won't be much longer now."

Dennis slammed the door shut and locked it behind him, his footsteps fading.

Sarah shivered, pulling her body inward and keeping her legs squeezed shut tight. She glanced down at the crushed paper balls, goose bumps spreading over her bare arms and legs, and she cried.

The sobs were muffled by the gag, and her falling tears reignited the residue of the pepper spray on her cheeks, but the chemical had dulled, and the reaction was only a mild burn.

She had gotten so far and survived for so long, but it all crumbled with the dull sound of paper balls spilling onto concrete. Her hope was dashed, and all that was left was to wait for the inevitable death by whatever ceremony Dennis had planned. After everything she'd done, she was still going to be killed by a man she'd angered.

With all her fight gone, Sarah sat motionless, her head hanging lazily to the side. She had stopped shivering from the cold, which meant that hypothermia was starting to set in, which explained the cloudy, foggy nature of her thoughts.

She faded in and out of consciousness, and each time she came to, it took her a minute to remember where she was. Her lips had turned a light shade of blue, and her skin had transformed from porcelain to almost translucent.

"Help us."

The words were whispered in Sarah's ear, and she jolted awake, the hairs on the back of her neck standing up as she expected to find Dennis had returned.

But when she scanned the darkened corners of the room,

she was alone. She shook her head, trying to shake off the madness that was creeping into her mind.

"Help us."

The whisper lingered in her ear and echoed in her head. She shut her eyes, trying to force it to be quiet, but it wouldn't obey.

"Stop it," Sarah said, her words rolling off a numb and lazy tongue. She twitched in random spasms. "Leave me alone."

"It will kill you."

Sarah lifted her head, and the shivers returned as she found herself staring at a woman dressed in a maid uniform. But this time she had her hair pulled back, exposing what she'd been hiding.

The left side of the girl's face was completely smashed, half of her skull flattened, which crammed what features remained on the left side into unproportioned clumps. Brain matter and blood dripped freely down the mangled portion of her face, and one unblinking eye stared down at Sarah.

Sarah's lips trembled, but she forced the word out of her mouth. "Maggie."

Maggie nodded, the woman's one good eye staring at Sarah. And the longer they maintained eye contact, the colder Sarah became.

"You must save us," Maggie said, her voice a crackling whisper. "He feeds on us every day." The first signs of fear broke along Maggie's battered face, and the one good eye produced a single tear that quickly froze to her cheek like an icicle.

"I-I can't," Sarah said, desperation clinging to her voice like the sweat and grime that covered her skin. But then she remembered the deputy. "The police. I told the police." The fact that there was someone on the outside that could help fanned the flames of hope.

"The police can't save us." Maggie stared at Sarah then pointed at her.

Sarah's frustration bubbled to the surface. "I told you I can't—" And just when Sarah was about to scream more, the restraints around her wrists and ankles dropped to the floor. Her back and knees popped as she stood. She rubbed the red marks the rope had burned into her skin, frowning in disbelief. "How did you—"

Maggie was suddenly in front of her again, teleporting in the blink of an eye. Sarah turned away, unable to stomach the gore and the stench of the woman who had granted her freedom. But Maggie grabbed Sarah by the shoulders and spun her around, sending a shock like fire and ice speeding through her veins.

Maggie distorted her face with mixed expressions of fear and anger. "It's always hungry! It always wants to eat!"

"What are you talking—"

"Find the orb! Break the curse! Set us free!"

A breeze blasted Sarah's back, and she clamped her hands over her ears as Maggie screamed. The eardrum-shattering cry brought Sarah to her knees. She shivered on the concrete floor, and the side of her face ached, the pain transforming into a splitting headache. Just when she didn't think she could take any more, the noise and the wind ended just as quickly as they had started.

Sarah slowly lifted her head, breathing heavily, and lowered her hands from her ears. Something warm formed on her upper lip, and she swiped at it with the back of her hand. A red blood smear appeared when she examined the liquid. She stared at it for a moment and then checked to see if her nose was still bleeding but found it had stopped.

She scanned the room, searching for Maggie, but found that she was gone.

So what had Sarah seen? A ghost? She knew she hadn't

imagined it, but if what she had seen was real, she thought she might be losing her mind.

Slowly, Sarah got her feet under her and then hobbled toward the door. The knob was as cold as ice, but she barely felt the difference since her own skin was nearly frozen over.

The door buckled as she tugged on the knob, but any attempt at turning it left or right only ended with stiff resistance. It was locked.

Sarah was one step closer to escape but somehow just as far away as she had been when she was tied to that chair. She knew she didn't have the build to knock the door down. She'd break her arm before that happened. She turned around, pressing her back against the door, knowing it was just a matter of time before Dennis returned, making the help she had received pointless.

Tears in her eyes, Sarah lifted her head, finding the crumpled-up balls of paper that Dennis had dumped from the box. But then she looked toward the wall near the door, finding more junk in the corner.

Sarah crawled over to the piles of junk like a desert wanderer stumbling upon an oasis. She ripped open the top of the first box she came across, thrusting her hands inside and finding nothing but old rags. She dumped them out onto the floor and moved onto the next box.

Rusted silverware and a few old pots rattled inside. Sarah set aside one of the rusted forks, thinking it could come in handy. She considered trying to smash the doorknob with one of the pots, but she knew that breaking it would just keep her locked inside, though it'd make it harder for Dennis to get back in.

Every box that she came across was an opportunity for escape, but as she neared the end of her search, that hope again started to dwindle. But as she searched her last box, she heard the heavy clank of metal inside. And when she opened the top, her heart beat faster.

Sarah grabbed the rusted handle of the toolbox inside and flipped the latch, the hinges squeaking as she opened the top. A hammer, nails, wrench, and screwdriver rested inside. The tools were old, and when Sarah picked up the screwdriver, she found the handle to be smooth old wood. She gently ran her fingers over the sharp tip and then looked to the exit.

The door was built to swing inward, the hinges on her side of the room. Sarah hurried to the door and jammed the rusted screwdriver into the bottom of the bolt in the hinges, trying to work them out.

Like the movement in her chair, the progress was slow, and it was noisier. Every whack of the rusted metal spear sparked a thud that ran through the room and most likely out into whatever hall or part of the house she was trapped inside.

But when no one came down the hallway and burst down the door, she kept going, slowly working the brass pegs from their holes to create a crack big enough for her to squeeze through. It wouldn't need to be big. She was small. And as that plug worked its way through the halfway mark, Sarah forwent the screw driver and pulled on the rusted brass.

The pegs were stubborn, and Sarah picked and prodded until her fingers bled, the red streaks crawling down her forearm as she finally removed the first hinge from its holder.

Hands shaking, she dropped it to the floor and then moved to the next. She fell into a rhythm, ignoring the pain and focusing on the task.

Sarah pried the middle peg from its hinge and then tried to wedge the door open. The crack to her freedom had widened another two inches, but it still wasn't wide enough to squeeze through. She pulled back, getting scratches along her stomach, back, and shoulder as her shirt ripped.

She reached for the screwdriver, jamming it up at the highest hinge. Even with her arm all the way extended, she couldn't reach. She quickly brought the chair over, using it to reach all the way to the top hinge.

Exhaustion skewed her aim, and Sarah only hit the bottom of the hinge every third try. The blood from her fingers crawled down her forearm in veiny lines. The pain in her body was screaming for her to stop, but the urge to survive, the spark of finding freedom, pushed her past the pain.

Sarah repeatedly smacked the end of the screwdriver with her palm, the cold accentuating the pain with every hit.

She hammered out the last few inches of the brass peg. Finally, it sprang from the hinge, and Sarah had her hands in the crack of open space before the brass peg even hit the floor.

Sarah pushed the door open as far as it would go, then thrust her head through the tight space.

Sarah harnessed her remaining strength and jumped, her legs smacking against the door and the frame as she landed hard on the hallway floor.

"You have to hurry." Maggie stood over her in the hallway, pointing toward a door that Sarah prayed was to freedom. "He'll be back soon."

Sarah pushed herself to her feet and was consumed by the thought of freedom, but as she stared down at her nearly naked body, she thought of her backpack, and her clothes, and then she remembered her photograph.

Sarah spun around, staring at the mangled woman in the hall. "My bag. Where is my bag?"

Maggie pointed up. "The fifth floor in the room I showed you."

"Shit." Sarah wiped the snot dripping from her nose, smearing some blood from her hand and onto her upper lip. She couldn't stop shaking. She saw the screwdriver that she'd dropped to the floor. She picked it up then headed for the door at the end of the hall.

With the mixture of cold and adrenaline, Sarah wasn't sure how much noise she was making on her ascent, but she made it to the fifth floor without incident.

She burst through the door, running toward the room at the end of the hall, the door open like it had been before, and then found her backpack on the bed. Still gripping the screwdriver, Sarah slung the pack over her shoulders, and then pivoted toward the exit.

The door slammed shut, and Sarah flung her body against it, tugging at the doorknob that refused to open.

And then the room darkened, as if all light had been sucked from inside. The temperature plummeted, and her entire body broke out in gooseflesh from the frigid, painful cold. Her bones ached, and her muscles seized up.

"Sarah."

Slowly, she turned toward the voice, which spoke her name in a throaty hiss, that originated from the darkest corner on the opposite side of the room.

The figure had no shape, no physical form, but Sarah knew it was there. She thought of the spirit that Maggie had spoken of, and how it was hungry.

The darkness spread across the room, the voice reaching deep into her thoughts. She examined the screwdriver in her hand, and she suddenly remembered all of the pain from her time in the foster care system.

The lonely nights in foster homes, the abuse from foster parents, the pranks from other kids, the loss, the fear, the pain, all of it assimilated into one motivating thought that was front and center in her mind, and the only way to get it out was to ram the screwdriver in and fish it out.

Sarah smiled. It would be easy. One quick thrust through the eye and it would all be over.

No more cold. No more pain. No more nightmares.

She gripped the wooden handle with both hands and positioned it over her eye, aiming it directly over all of those bad thoughts. Her smiled widened.

"Sarah, no!"

Sarah's paralysis broke. She turned away from the screwdriver, and she saw Maggie paralyzed in the darkness, her skin slowly icing over.

"Go," Maggie whispered. Then her voice jumped in pitchy screams, the ice continuing to crawl over her entire body. "GO!"

The shrill cry triggered Sarah into action, and she crammed the screwdriver into the hinge. Maggie's shrieks and cries of pain grew louder, and the room shook.

She turned around and screamed as she found Maggie had turned to nothing but ice—and then her frozen figure dropped to the floor, shattering into a thousand shards that spread over the floorboards.

The door opened, but Sarah only made it one step before a hot pain struck her heel, and she turned to find the dark void wrapped around her ankle. Color drained from her porcelain skin, which then turned an icy blue.

With what remained of her strength, Sarah yanked her leg free and then scrambled on all fours until she gained enough momentum to push herself up and into a sprint.

Sarah turned around, finding that pitch black creeping toward her, turning the walls and the floor and the ceiling black, void of any light. She hurried down the stairs, the floorboards creaking and groaning with every step.

Moonlight guided her path, and while she still felt cold

and sick, she didn't stop running.

At the bottom of the staircase, Sarah shoulder-checked the door open and ran down the first-floor hallway and toward the foyer. Toward freedom.

Still gripping the screwdriver, she hobbled forward, exhaustion creeping its cold fingers around her body.

The exaltation and relief of escape was so close that Sarah started to sob. But when she turned the corner, she froze, quickly hiding the screwdriver behind her leg so Dennis couldn't see it.

Dennis stood in front of the double doors, the features of his face darkened, though Sarah could still tell that he wasn't smiling. "He was hungry tonight." He stepped to the side, exposing the glass in the doors and the freedom that rested on the other side.

Sarah watched him strike a match and then light a candle on the table. The flame flickered, illuminating the grimace on his face. He turned toward her, the light shifting the shadows beneath his eyes, nose, and mouth. The fire made him look hollow, as if he was only a skull.

"You're one of the more willful people we've had come through," Dennis said, and then he smiled. "I've always liked a woman who made it hard."

"People will find out what you did," Sarah said, unable to keep her voice from trembling. "You can't keep killing people."

"I don't kill people," Dennis said, taking slow steps toward Sarah, the candle still in his hand. "Surely you saw it."

Sarah didn't retreat, and she readjusted her grip on the screwdriver behind her back. She shook her head. "I don't know what the hell I saw."

"You saw the face of a god," Dennis said, his voice an awed whisper. "You saw an eternal being that will take human form again, and when he does, he will reshape this world in his image, and those that have been faithful to him will be rewarded."

"Count me out," Sarah said.

Dennis erased the amusement from his face. "I can't let you leave."

"I'm not giving you a choice."

Dennis stopped, only a few feet separating the two of them in the foyer. Nothing but the flickering flame moved, illuminating their stoic silence. Sarah had to be quick whenever Dennis made his move. She'd only get one shot at getting out of this alive, and she intended to do it any way she could.

Dennis finally lunged, his massive fist reaching for her throat, but Sarah darted left then launched forward herself, leading with the rusted screwdriver, and jammed it into Dennis's arm.

"GAAH!"

The candle crashed to the floor as Dennis reached for the wound and the rusted tool standing straight up on its own. But Sarah never turned around to see what happened next.

She slammed into the double doors, finding them locked, then sprinted up the grand staircase. Dennis's scream followed her up the stairs, but she never stopped moving her feet.

The moment she reached the second floor, she pivoted toward the closest door, which she slammed shut and jammed with a nearby chair. Dennis's footsteps grew louder outside in the hall as Sarah scanned the room, looking for an exit and finding only windows.

Dennis pounded on the other side of the door. "Open up, Sarah!" And then there was the jangling of the keys that he always had on his person. "There isn't anywhere for you to go."

A second chair sat in the middle of the room, and Sarah

picked it up. Once she had it in her hands, she hurried toward the window, heaving all of the weight and strength that she had left into the chair.

One of the legs cracked into the glass just as the lock on the door broke. She ripped the chair free and then heaved it again, this time shattering the window panes and sending the chair through the open window.

Sarah approached the exit, turning briefly to look behind her to find Dennis heaving his weight behind the door in his attempt to break down the barricade that Sarah had erected.

Toes sticking over the window ledge, Sarah glanced down at the concrete below. She inched toward the outer walls, looking for any grips or crevices that could help guide her path down, but they were few and far between.

The door broke, and Dennis burst inside, stomping toward Sarah. She quickly lowered herself from the window, fingers hanging off the edge as she tried to lower herself to another ledge.

"NO!" Dennis appeared above, reaching down for her hand, but Sarah shimmied out of reach, the movement costing her grip as she dangled from one arm. "You don't understand what you could become! You don't understand what you can do!"

Sarah quickly reached for the worn head of a nearby gargoyle and carefully placed her free hand around the smooth, weathered surface.

She glanced back up to the window and found Dennis gone. Bushes lined the ground below, and knowing she was running out of time Sarah let go, dropping fast and landing hard into the shrubs.

Legs and ass aching from the fall, Sarah forced herself up and sprinted away, her heels smacking against the pavement of the walkway.

The front doors of the house groaned and opened.

Dennis screamed, his voice echoing through the night air.

"You can't leave! STOP!"

Despite her fatigue and her attire, Sarah ran straight through the middle of the street. And when she no longer heard Dennis's voice, she finally turned around.

The mansion on the hill was still there, still looming over the town. And now Sarah could finally see it, the true essence of what that house was to the town. It was a sickness, a plague that had dried everything up, claiming the lives of anyone who stayed with a fate worse than death.

Headlights flashed ahead, accompanied by blue and red lights, and Sarah lifted her hand to shield her eyes from the brightness.

Car brakes squealed, and then a door opened. "Hey, are you all right?"

Sarah lowered her hand, her eyes slowly adjusting to the sharp contrast of light, and she saw the deputy she had spoken to earlier was reaching into the backseat and then walking toward her.

"We have to go." Sarah met him halfway and then grabbed hold of his arms, feeling her own legs finally giving way. She half collapsed, but Dell scooped her up in his arms as if she was a child.

"Christ, you're freezing." Dell carried her to the back of the car and laid her down on the seat.

The warmth from the heater and the blanket Dell had draped over her helped ease the pain, but it made her sleepy, and she started to drift off as he climbed into the driver's seat.

"Just hang on," Dell said. "I'll get you some help."

Sarah's eyelids fluttered, and she drifted between consciousness and unconsciousness. "They're killing them… They're… Killing…"

"Hey! Stay with me!"

10

The dreams came all at once, and they were vivid. Too vivid. Sarah was back in the basement, but she was only there as a bystander. She saw herself in the chair, and she saw her interaction with Dennis and Maggie.

All of the same feelings returned, the rush of adrenaline, the fear, the anger, but she was watching it all unfold from outside her body, and she stayed in the corner, unable to speak or intervene. She started to think that she wasn't supposed to.

Suddenly, Sarah was transported to the bedroom on the fifth floor.

The cold returned, and the terror was the same, but this time, the room didn't darken. This time, she saw a figure appear where she hadn't seen one before. And it wasn't the devil or some evil deity. It was a man. His hair was long, thick, and black, and his hands were pale white, almost the color of the ice she had watched Maggie transform into. He was dressed in old clothes from another era, probably more than one hundred years ago. And suddenly Sarah realized who it was. It was Allister Bell.

"You must return." Allister spoke louder, his tone throaty and his cadence slow, almost as if it were painful to speak. "You must find the orb."

"I don't understand," Sarah said.

Allister wore a sad smile. "I cannot stop what has been started, but I will send you another to help. But you must hurry, Sarah. The orb moves but is always in the same place. There isn't much time. Hurry!"

Sarah woke, gasping for breath.

Sweat beaded on her forehead, and she glanced down at her body, finding it covered in a hospital gown. Wires and tubes ran up her arm and down her chest. The room was empty save for the beeping hospital machinery, the rhythm growing faster and faster as she hyperventilated on the bed.

The door opened, and a nurse and doctor stepped inside, both of them with their hands up in a passive stance. "Ma'am, everything is all right. You just need to lie back down—ma'am, please!"

Sarah had flung the sheets off her and ripped off the wires that connected to her chest and arm, along with the tubes sticking into her veins, causing her to bleed. "I need to get out of here." She made it three steps before the doctor and nurse caught her and kept her still.

"We need you to stay here," the nurse said, her large, meaty hands easily wrapping around Sarah's thin arm. "You're safe now."

"Let me go!" Sarah tossed her elbows, but she found that her strength still hadn't returned, and she was lifted back onto the bed, legs kicking in protest.

"Everything all right in here?" Dell stepped into the room, and Sarah stopped her squirming. Dell took the doctor's place at her bedside. "Hey, there isn't any need for that, really."

"You said she couldn't leave," the nurse said.

"Why can't I leave?" Sarah asked.

"It's fine. Please, if I could just have a minute to talk with her alone?"

The medical team plugged Sarah's IV back into her, and then put sensors back on her fingers before stepping out of the door.

Sarah backed up to the head of the bed, pulling her knees into her chest as she formed a small, defensive ball. "What do you want? And why can't I leave?" The words came out like those of a defiant child wanting to leave her room.

"I just have some questions," Dell said, pulling up a chair next to her bedside. When he sat, he folded his hands in his lap. "Do you remember what happened before I found you?"

Sarah wasn't sure she should tell him the truth, and even if she did, she wasn't sure he'd believe her. After all, what had she seen? Ghosts? Demons? Some madman trying to sacrifice her to an evil spirit? And then she remembered the bodies.

"Are you all right? Do I need to bring the doctor back—"

"I'm fine," Sarah said, head still down. "I just want to leave."

Dell leaned back in his chair, unable to get comfortable. "Well, before you leave, I need to know what happened. I ran the license you gave me, and it turns out Maggie Swillford is a real person who hasn't been seen by any of her friends for over a month. I need to know what you saw, Sarah."

Sarah went cold, and her heart monitor spiked. "How do you know my name?" The words escaped her lips in a whisper.

Dell gestured to the table by the door. "Your backpack. Found your ID inside. The doctors wanted to check to see if you had any medical history they needed to be aware of."

The color drained from Sarah's face, and her stomach turned. "Oh, God, no." She shook her head, her expression pained. "No, no, no, no, please, no." She rocked from side to side.

"Sarah, what's wrong?" Dell asked.

Sarah's breaths grew shallow, and she looked at Dell. "Did you run my name through the DMV? Did you run my license?"

Dell fidgeted uneasily. "Well, yeah, but—"

"FUCK!" Sarah balled her fists by her head, the burst of fear and anger flushing her pale cheeks with color. "He's going to find me. He's going to fucking kill *me*."

"Who's going to find you? Who's going to kill you?"

The sobs rolled out of her, and she shrugged her shoulders, knowing that it didn't matter anymore. "My ex-boyfriend." She sniffled, wiping her nose and forcing herself to regain some composure. "He killed a woman. Probably killed a lot of people. But I saw him do it one time, and he gave me these to keep quiet." She pointed toward the bruises that still lingered on her neck, easily visible in her hospital gown.

"What was his name?" Dell asked.

"It doesn't matter," Sarah answered, her tone dismissive.

"Sarah, I can help. If he hurt you—"

"He's a cop!" Sarah threw the words in his face. "He's a detective, and he's got a whole fucking crew around him. He's got people everywhere. The DA's office, Internal Affairs —he's like a mob boss." She turned away, looking toward her backpack on the table.

"Sarah, I can help you." Dell reached out and placed his hand on her arm. "If this guy is a cop, I can protect you. I promise."

Sarah scoffed, her eyes bloodshot from the tears, and from the exhaustion, and from spending an entire life fighting off trouble. "No. You can't."

Dell let her go and then leaned back in his chair. "Listen. I need to make a call. Just, hang on a second, okay?"

Dell left, and Sarah's company dwindled to the beeping machines that were hooked up to her body. She lifted the blanket and peered down to examine her foot then grimaced at what she found.

The flesh was blue and icy, almost as if it were frosted. She lowered the blanket and shut her eyes, wondering what in the hell she was going to do next, but knew one thing that could help.

Slowly, Sarah crawled out of bed, wheeling the machines with her to avoid another attack from the nurses, and reached for her backpack. She removed her jeans from inside and sighed relief when she found the photograph still folded in the left pocket.

Sarah carefully unfolded the picture along the well-worn creases and smiled. It was the last picture taken of her parents. She didn't know when or where it was taken, but her father had Sarah on his shoulders, and her mother was clutching his arm, looking up at Sarah.

All of them were smiling, even Sarah. It was a moment frozen in time, and it was proof that she could have had a better life if she'd never been orphaned. Never in her fifteen years in the system was she able to recreate the happiness that was in the photo.

As she grew older she noticed which physical features she'd inherited from her parents. She had her mother's nose and eyes, but she had her dad's smile and ears. It was the only connection that she had to them. She didn't know if they smoked, or drank, or what foods they liked. She didn't know if she got her love of music from either of them, or her irrational fear spiders. She knew nothing about them save for what the photograph offered.

Sarah folded the picture back up and then kissed it before

sliding it back into the false bottom of her backpack, and then tell stepped back inside.

"All right," Dell said, reaching into his pocket and removing a pen and paper. He returned to his chair and looked up at her. "Are you ready to tell me what happened?"

She doubted that he would really be able to keep her safe. He didn't understand what was chasing her. And now, with whatever happened to her at the Bell Mansion, she had an entirely new stack of problems.

And whenever Sarah had faced these types of odds before, she always did the one thing that she knew best. She ran.

* * *

IRIS BELL SAT in her room on the fifth floor at her makeup table, running her brush through her white and silver hair. Some of her strength had returned, and she was finally able to climb out of bed.

Like Iris herself, the mirror had faded, losing most of its shine over the decades, but she could still catch her reflection, not that there was much to look at anymore.

The makeup she applied every morning had been wiped away, leaving a wrinkly old face and sagging skin that looked ready to drip from her skull. She was an old hag, and what was worse, she knew it. But things could change. She just had to right the ship that was her family's destiny.

The knock at her door was expected. She'd heard the commotion downstairs and chosen to stay out of it. She was nearly ninety years old, and by the time she tried to make it down the stairs, the commotion would have been over with. But judging from the glass shattering and the sheepish knock on the door, Iris figured that whatever news was coming was bad.

"It's open," Iris said.

The doorknob turned, the latch disengaged, and the hinges groaned slowly as Iris caught Dennis's reflection in the mirror. He kept his head down, shoulders slumped, like a child who knew the punishment for his failure. A bloodied bandage covered his arm, and crimson stained his clothes.

"She's gone," Dennis said.

Iris set the brush down and then turned, her old bones creaking like the hinges and the frame of her family's house. "Has she been marked?"

Dennis nodded.

"Then she has nowhere else to go." Iris returned to the mirror, the cloudy reflection scarred with black marks from chipped-away flecks of the mirror. "He'll call her back to the house, and then it will be done."

Dennis raised his head. "There's something else." He flexed his fingers nervously and shuffled another step toward her. "The letters are gone."

The confidence from Iris's face vanished, and the old woman forced her creaking joints up and out of her chair. "I told you to burn those."

As Iris walked closer, Dennis refused to look her in the eye. "He wouldn't have liked it."

"I don't care!" Iris thundered, the anger and violence in her voice mismatched against the frail body that spoke. "You've exposed us! Do you know what is in those letters? Do you have any idea what could happen if she shows those letters to anyone? Everything could be undone!" She grabbed hold of his chin, and Dennis finally looked her in the eye.

"I'm sorry." Dennis's eyes watered and reddened.

Iris calmed herself then patted his cheek with three hard slaps. "It won't matter." She returned to her seat and the mirror, picking up the brush again and continuing her grooming ritual. "We're too close now. We only require one more. And he will make sure that she comes back to us."

Dennis wiped his eyes, moving deeper into the room. "You really think that this will finish it? That this is the end?"

Iris gently grazed her weathered and aged cheek and then turned toward the family pictures on the table, her attention on a photograph that had one of the faces scratched off. "It will be. One way or the other."

$\mathcal{T}$he late hour didn't lessen the lights and sounds of the big city. From the air, New York's skyline was beautiful, and the city was peaceful, the lights twinkling in the darkness and creating a brilliant brightness that challenged the night. But closer toward the city's surface, the beauty faded.

The cracks and stains and smell of human shit and piss ran rampant along the streets. Homeless people begged for change and slept on the streets. Gangs roamed in small packs, defacing any piece of property they didn't own.

Sirens screamed in the night, alerting the city to the crime that plagued the poor and broken neighborhoods on the island. Gunshots accentuated the anger behind the hands and people that wielded them, violence the only expression in their repertoire.

Authorities struggled with the violence and masses that flocked to the island of Manhattan every single day. The city was a living, breathing entity that required constant attention lest it choke on its own spit and die, killing the millions that clung to its back for survival.

And tonight, among the many that reveled in dark deeds, Brent Alvarez walked down the sidewalk, hands in the pockets of his black leather jacket, the bright silver zipper pulled all the way to the top, and his jet-black hair slicked back with gel.

He moved quickly and deliberately, his dark-brown eyes trained on the run-down apartment building ahead. Steam rose from the sewer grates behind him, and he exhaled his own icy breaths. He'd always loved the cold, ever since he was a kid. Winter brought death.

While everyone else grew weak in the cold, he grew stronger. He was drawn to death and violence like a fly to shit. Few other things gave him as much joy and excitement.

Brent ascended the front steps of the apartment building quickly, removed his gloved hand from his pocket, and twisted the doorknob, which he found locked.

He checked the street, ensuring he was alone, and then removed a small lock-pick set from his other pocket. He inserted the tiny metal prongs, blindly guiding them around the four-tumbler lock. Thirty seconds later, he was granted entrance at the sound of a light click.

Television chatter and screams penetrated the paper-thin apartment walls as he moved through the foyer. Keeping one hand in his pocket, Brent ascended the steps, the stairs groaning from the weight, but aside from the old wood giving its protest, he moved toward the third floor quietly and skillfully.

It had taken him a long time to obtain his status, and at thirty-five, he was finally captain of his own fate. No man or law could prevent him from accomplishing a goal. If he wanted something, he simply took it. He even had his own crew.

They had carved out their own section of the city, and

nothing happened without their approval. But last week they had to make an unsavory, and unexpected visit. It should have been routine. His crew were well versed in shutting people up. But during the job an unforeseen complication had arisen, and it had been Brent who'd caused it.

He had tried to take care of the problem quickly, but in doing so, he had broken his one and only rule: don't hesitate.

Brent examined the apartment numbers on the left that ended in odd numbers and stopped in front of door 417. He checked behind him, again finding himself alone in the hall, and then kicked the door down.

The door frame shattered, splinters of wood flying as the door swung inward, denting the adjacent drywall of the narrowed hallway entrance. Brent charged forward, gun already drawn and aimed at the man and woman on the living room couch, their arms in the air.

Brent passed the kitchen, finding it empty save for dirty dishes and trash. With the pair on the couch paralyzed in fear, Brent backtracked, keeping his attention on the couple, and shut the door.

Drug paraphernalia littered the coffee table. Needles, coke, pills, weed—it was a pharmaceutical smorgasbord. However, the pair on the couch looked more like dealers than like users.

Brent remained silent, gun still aimed at the couple, then pressed the barrel of his pistol against the man's temple. The woman started to cry.

"Where did she go?" Brent asked.

The man was young, mid-twenties at the oldest, and had long blonde hair that had been crimped in what Brent assumed was an effort to detract attention from the large mole that clung to the side of his nose and his harelip. He wore a jacket, but Brent knew that underneath the clothes was nothing more than a skeleton covered in skin, and the bag of bones couldn't stop shaking.

"I-I don't know." He shut his eyes, hands still in the air. "She just said she was leaving, man! I didn't get a forward fucking address!"

The woman next to the skeleton had curled up into the fetal position. She was small like Sarah, though not as pretty.

Brent removed the gun from the skeleton's head and then aimed it at the woman, which transformed her moaning sobs into a full-blown hysteria.

"NO! PLEASE!" She thrust her arms out as if she could block bullets with her hands. Tears streamed down her cheeks, and she pushed herself backward until she hit the couch's armrest. "I don't know what happened to her. Please, she didn't tell us. She just wanted to be left alone."

Brent tilted his head to the side. "Alone?" He stepped around the skeleton, the little shit too much of a pussy to protect the woman, as he cowered in his seat.

Brent's shadow engulfed the tiny woman, her tremors of fear shaking the pistol in his hand as he pressed it against her temple. "Why would she want to be alone?" He arched his eyebrows in surprise. "Because of me?"

The woman shook her head.

Brent lingered for a moment but then removed the pistol. He circled the coffee table and examined the drugs and needles, holding the weapon casually at his side. Large multi-colored stains hardened the carpet that crunched beneath his boots.

The place was a dump. Hell, the whole neighborhood was a dump. And despite all his resources and all the eyes and ears he had working the streets, he still hadn't been able to find her. One fucking woman had eluded him. He had tracked down every lead, spoken to all of her friends, and none of them knew where she'd gone. He was positive they were telling the truth. He needed to make sure that the bums in front of him were telling the truth too.

"So you don't know where she went, huh?" Brent asked. "And you're sure you don't have anything else to tell me? Nothing you want to share before I leave?"

Skeleton shook his head, and the woman only trembled. "N-no. W-we don't know. I-I promise."

Brent smiled, revealing white but crooked teeth. "Well, then. I guess I don't have anything left to worry about." He paused for a minute and then raised the pistol, aimed it at the woman, and squeezed the trigger.

The bullet went straight through her head, spraying her skull and brains onto the back of the sofa, and sending a few bits onto the skeleton, who'd frozen in shock.

Brent aimed his pistol at the skeleton. "You know how long it'll take for anyone to come and check on this apartment after that gunshot?" He stepped closer. "Thirty minutes, minimum. And do you want to know why?" He bent over at the waist, shoving his face close to the skeleton's, where he caught a scent of the warm brain matter speckled on his cheek. "Because no one gives a shit what happens with the people around here, because people like you die in these fucking slums every single day. One more dead body is one less person the city has to support."

"Jesus Christ, man." These were the only words that the skeleton could spit out, and he repeated them in the same hysterical laughter that only a person on the edge of madness could utter. He turned toward Brent, looking past the gun pointed at his head, his eyes bulging from his skull. "You fucking killed her, man!"

"I did," Brent answered, his tone calm. "And I will kill you if you can't tell me where she went. I'll give you to the count of three."

"I told you I don't know where she is!" His cheeks

reddened, and the muscles along his neck and throat strained as he struggled to tell Brent what he wanted to hear. "I'm not lying, man!"

"Two."

The skeleton slipped from the couch and landed on his knees, clutching his hands together. "Please." He worked his mouth to try and form words but found none. His knuckles turned white from the pressure, and the skeleton bowed his head and pressed his forehead against the dirty carpet. "I don't want to die. Don't kill me, please. I won't tell anyone you were here." He grabbed Brent's ankles, his voice muffled against the floor.

Brent looked down at the cockroach next to his boot, gun still aimed at its head, and then looked to the dead woman on the couch. Her eyes were still open, staring upward to some point on the ceiling, her lips slightly parted.

The dead were always still and quiet, and they never slobbered over your brand-new shoes. Brent kicked the skeleton's hands off his feet and then stepped backward.

The skeleton looked up at Brent, snot and tears dribbling from his orifices, his cheeks bright red, his eyes narrow slits. "Please."

"Three."

The skeleton screamed. Brent squeezed the trigger. Another stain was added to the carpet.

Smoke drifted from the pistol's barrel, and Brent lingered in the living room, staring at the growing puddle of blood engulfing the dead man's head. After a minute, he picked up the two shell casings and shoved them in his pocket. They jingled on his walk to the door, where he stopped and turned back toward the dead. He smiled.

As he suspected, no one came out of their apartments, and no one stopped to question him as he stepped outside the building and returned to the street. If Sarah wasn't here, then he was beginning to think that she wasn't in the city at all.

Brent opened the door of his black 1968 Pontiac GTO Judge and climbed inside. The leather was cold, but it smelled wonderful. He'd rebuilt and refurbished the vintage car himself. It was a labor of love, and he had ended up dumping more than sixty grand into the damn thing. But holy fuck, did he love that car.

It was a beast of a machine and one of the most recognizable cars in the city. He loved watching the little street junkies and wannabe thugs scatter at the sound of his throaty four-hundred-twenty-horsepower V8 engine. The car was power. And Brent loved power.

Brent tapped his finger on the steering wheel and noticed a bloodstain on the fitted leather glove. He grimaced and removed a packet of wet wipes from the glove box. He vigorously scrubbed at the stain, the leather darkening under the moist cloth.

Finished, Brent threw the dirty cloth onto the pavement. His phone rang. He answered, still examining the glove. "Yeah."

"We got a hit," the voice said. "Northern Maine in a town called Redford. Local PD ran her license through the DMV."

"Text me the address." Brent hung up and then placed the phone in his cup holder, his eyes still locked on the vanished bloodstain.

So Sarah had decided to try her chances up north in the middle of nowhere. It was a bold move, especially with winter on its way and barely a penny to her name.

Brent smiled at the thought of her wandering through the woods like a hermit, hitchhiking all the way to the Canadian border. Was that her end game? He laughed. The dumb bitch had imagination, he'd give her that. But she had finally run out of rope.

Brent revved the GTO to life and took one last glance at the apartment building where he'd left two bodies. Then he started his journey north, where he would take one more.

12

Sarah had pulled the hospital blankets up to her chest. The gown they'd put her in was thin, and made her feel exposed. She picked at the corner of the thinnest sheet, the fabric scratchy beneath her fingernail as the deputy in the seat next to her tapped the pen against his notepad, examining his notes.

"You said you found a box of IDs in a shoebox hidden beneath a loose board in the shed." Deputy Dell Parker read the statement, underlining the section with his pen, then looked up at Sarah. "And that was when you ran."

"Yes." Sarah kept her answers short.

"And then Dennis, the Bells' groundskeeper, chased you down, drugged you, and then brought you back to the house for a—" He flipped to a previous page of his notes. "Ceremony."

"That's what he told me." Sarah ended her assault on the corner of the bedsheet and started to pick the chipped turquoise nail polish on her finger. Her hands had been wrapped with gauze, injuries from her escape out of the house, the details of which she embellished to the deputy.

"So you woke up in the basement, broke out of the room, had the sense of mind to grab your backpack," he looked to the bag on the table by the door, then returned to his notes, "and then ran out of the house, escaping through a second-story window." Dell removed his gaze from the notepad and looked at Sarah. "Am I missing anything?"

Sarah shook her head, knowing full well that there was more to the story. She had avoided telling him about the body and the ghost because she knew divulging that information would only lengthen their chat and make it harder for her to leave.

The deputy tapped his pen onto the notepad, staring at Sarah for a long time, and then finally stood. "All right, Ms. Pembrooke. I'm going to head over to the Bell house now and have a conversation with the family and question the groundskeeper. In the meantime I have a deputy outside and down the hall to keep an eye on you. I'll also put an inquiry into," he returned to his notes, "Brent Alvarez." He closed the notebook and placed it inside his jacket. "See if what he has to say matches up with your story about him."

Sarah nodded, knowing that her ex would deny whatever allegations she said about him.

"You just get some rest." The deputy smiled, and then left.

Sarah exhaled relief once he was gone, and waited until the sound of his footsteps faded and there was only the slow cadence of beeps from the machines monitoring her vitals.

Sarah flung the sheets off her, climbed off the bed, and rolled the machines toward the table and her backpack. Her hospital gown flowed behind her as she opened her backpack and removed her clothes, planning to dress quickly.

Naked, Sarah examined her pale flesh. Up till an hour ago, she had been freezing, but now, even with her bare feet against tile, there was nothing. No cold. No goosebumps.

Sarah paused when she slid on her socks, gently touching

the icy scales that shimmered on her heel, which had transformed her pale flesh to a frost blue. It was the only proof of her supernatural experience at the Bell mansion, but the doctors had dismissed it as frostbite.

Ghosts, demons, spirits, curses. The words swirled in her head and consumed her thoughts. She had run this far north to avoid trouble, not be caught smack in the middle of it. She ran her fingers through her blonde pixie cut and shut her eyes.

She hadn't asked for this life. She had been born and then thrust into a situation in which she was forced to fight for her life every day. Growing up, she'd always hated the kids with two parents and a stable home. She hated them because she envied them. She would have paid any price to have that security, to feel loved, to lay her head down at night in her own bed and not have to worry about whether she was going to eat the next day or if her foster parents would beat her.

The past week on the road had been exhausting, but they were nothing compared to the past few days. Sarah wanted nothing more than to stop and rest, but she knew that if the cops had run her license through the system, then Brent would find out about it. The bastard had people everywhere, and he wasn't someone who let things go. She needed to leave before he was able to track her down.

Before donning her shirt and pants, Sarah shut off the machines monitoring her vitals, and then plucked the sensors off her chest and fingers. She'd tried ripping them off before, but the devices beeped in alarm and brought the nurses to her room. Turning them off completely might raise some internal flag, but for the time being she was in the clear.

Dressed in her Carhartt jacket, jeans, and boots, Sarah reached for her backpack and positioned its straps over her shoulders.

"Sarah."

The whisper tickled her ear, and the hairs on the back of her neck stood up as she spun around, but the room was empty.

Disoriented, Sarah blinked a few times, shaking the voice from her thoughts. She had already watched the woman die, killed by that... thing. It couldn't have followed her here, could it?

Sarah shut her eyes and whispered to herself. "It's nothing. Just walk out the door and leave." She nodded a few times to affirm her resolve and then spun around.

She opened her eyes on the turn and gasped as she stumbled backward into the foot of the bed. Blocking the doorway was a woman dressed in an old white gown that covered her skin from neck to ankle.

The woman pressed a slender finger to her pale lips, her skin whiter than Sarah's but her cheeks dotted with clusters of freckles. She smiled, her thin lip drawn tight and nearly disappearing from her face. She was pretty, but it was the bright-red hair that flowed behind her in long, wavy strands that made her beautiful.

Sarah frowned, slowly gathering her nerves. She swallowed, finding her mouth dry. "Who the hell are you?"

"I was sent to help you." The woman smiled. She was tall, close to six feet. She was lanky too, her arms and legs too large for her frame. "So you can help us."

Sarah shook her head. "No. I'm not going back to that house. I'm done, you hear me?"

"You've been marked, Sarah." The redhead glanced down to the foot with the icy scales. "He won't let you leave now."

"Look, I'm sorry to whatever happened to you, but I have my own problems," Sarah said.

"You've always run, Sarah." The redhead's voice began to fade. "That's all you've ever done since you were a little girl.

But if you want to survive this, if you want to make it out alive, then you must face it. You must find the orb in the house."

"I told you I'm done." Sarah spun around and headed toward the door.

"She's sacrificed herself to save you."

Sarah stopped abruptly. Her stomach soured as she slowly turned around.

"Maggie sacrificed her soul so you could escape the house, so you could save those that have been damned." The redhead slowly floated toward Sarah. "Can you really just walk away from that responsibility?"

Sarah grimaced. "People have walked away from me my whole life. It's just how it is."

Saddened, the redhead faded with her voice. "You're the last soul he needs. Save us, and you save yourself. It's… the… on…ly……" And then she was gone, disappearing as quickly and mysteriously as she had arrived.

Sarah reached into the space where the ghost had been but felt nothing. She rubbed her fingertips together, contemplating the redhead's words. But the Bell mansion wasn't her problem anymore. She needed to move.

But before she left, Sarah remembered the letters in her backpack, the ones she found on the forbidden fifth floor. She removed them from her backpack and set them on the table. Maybe the cops could use them in their investigation. She didn't want to have anything to do with that house again.

At the doorway, Sarah slowly craned her neck around the doorframe. The authorities had stationed a deputy to guard her room, but Sarah spotted him at the end of the hall with his back turned, flirting with a woman at the nurse's station.

With the pair distracted, Sarah hurried in the opposite direction and followed the emergency exit signs to a stairwell that dumped her out onto the side of the building and into the cold night air.

Thick woods backed up against the hospital, and Sarah followed the narrow strip of concrete that separated the two until it fed her out into the front parking lot.

She adjusted the straps of her pack and then flipped the collar of her Carhartt jacket, keeping a sharp eye out for anyone in the lot. But the late hour and small town offered little traffic. With some distance between herself and the hospital, Sarah stopped to catch her breath.

Between the week on the road and the events of the last couple of days, her energy reserves were running low. She turned around, looking back to the hospital, and the sudden urge to head back flooded her thoughts.

Leaving meant an endless journey for the rest of her life, one void of any peace and rest. She'd be looking over her shoulder until she was six feet under. Just the thought of it was daunting. But what if Dell could make good on his promise and keep her safe? A chance of success was slim but possible.

Sarah dismissed it quickly. If a life in foster care and orphanages had taught her one thing, it was that the only person she could count on was herself. Eventually, everyone else would always let her down. And because of that, Sarah left the town of Redford behind.

When she reached the highway, she turned south, knowing that trying to cross into Canada would cause more problems than it would fix. Her best shot was to head south and then make a hard right toward the west.

Two miles and three cars into Sarah's retreat, one car finally slowed to offer a ride. It was a sedan, sporty, which lowered the chances of finding a woman behind the wheel. The majority of drivers that picked her up on the journey here were men. And while she had avoided any incidents, she knew that the law of averages would fix that soon enough.

The passenger window rolled down before she approached, and sure enough, she found a guy behind the wheel, alone. "Need a lift?"

"Yeah," Sarah answered, making sure to keep her coat closed. The bulkiness of her winter attire did a good job of hiding her figure. The less they could see the less tempted they'd be to touch.

"Well, hop in," he said.

With no alarm bells ringing in her head and the road growing longer, Sarah opened the passenger door.

The driver reentered the highway, speeding up quickly, and then slowed back to the speed limit.

"How long have you been walking out there?" he asked.

"Too long." Sarah did her best to keep conversation to a minimum during all her rides. The less people knew about her, the better.

The driver looked Sarah's age, early twenties. He was clean-shaven, but awkward looking, his head to big for his body, and didn't act like the frat boys that she'd typically seen drive this type of car.

"Well, uh, there's a blanket," he gestured to the backseat, "buried under some of my clothes if you're cold. But I'll warn you in advance that the clothes on top are dirty, so grab at your own risk." He smiled, flashing a wide grin with small teeth.

"I'm all right, thanks," Sarah said, pocketing her hands again and inching closer toward the door. The last thing she wanted to do was send any false signals. An exterior of cold hard bitch seemed to be the only way to keep guys from wanting to try their luck.

"You heading down for the break?" he asked.

"What?"

"Winter break, for school." He gestured to the backpack. "You go to Redford Community College, right?"

"Oh, no." Sarah cleared her throat.

"Wow." He laughed. "So what the hell are you doing all the way up in Redford, Maine, at the start of winter? Do you just like to be cold?"

"Not really." In fact, Sarah realized that during her walk she hadn't noticed the temperature outside at all.

"Well, I've lived in Redford my whole life, which I am desperately trying to change. It hasn't been easy, but I know it'll be worth it once I've got set up in a new place. You ever been to New York?"

"I visited once."

"Well, I've never been. Always wanted to go, though. One day I'll have a penthouse apartment and throw crazy parties, and the girls! Well—" Lost in his own fantasy, he looked over to Sarah, slightly embarrassed, and cleared his throat. "I'd be incredibly respectful to them, of course, and—"

Sarah laughed. It surprised her at first, the emotion bubbling up so quickly and so easily. "It's fine." She waved her hand at him, her cheeks tightening from the smile. "I hope you get all those fine honeys in the city."

He laughed. "Well, I'd settle for having one honey." He kept as much eye contact with Sarah as he could while still paying attention to the road. "My name is Tye."

"I'm—GAH!" Sarah buckled forward as a burning sensation flared in her left heel and crawled up her leg. She reached down, furiously swiping at her pant leg, the pain growing. It was crippling, tossing her backward into her seat.

"What's wrong?" Tye leaned back and slowed down, pulling off to the side of the road, growing more panicked as Sarah continued to buck and thrash in her seat. "Are you okay?"

A scorching, burning sensation crawled up from her heel.

She gasped for breath as it felt like her skin was being torn from her body, the pain so intense it left her speechless.

"Just hold on." Tye unbuckled his seatbelt and fished his phone out of his pocket. "I-I'm going to get you some help!" He placed the phone to his ear, and while Sarah screamed in pain, she still knew what would happen if the police came and found her on the run.

"No!" Sarah reached for Tye's phone and tossed it into the backseat.

"What the hell?"

With enough presence of mind to grab her pack, Sarah opened the car door and collapsed onto the pavement of the highway's shoulder. With the pain in her leg spreading, she scrambled toward the woods that lined the highway, half crawling, half limping toward the tree line.

"Wait!" Tye exited the car but didn't follow. "You need help!"

Leaves and branches crunched underfoot as Sarah traveled deep into the woods. Tye continued to call out to her, but instincts and pain propelled her forward. She sprinted through the forest like a wounded animal, searching for safety but unsure of where she could find it.

Finally, her muscles growing exhausted, Sarah collapsed to the dirt, wheezing. She lay still for a long time before she managed to gather enough strength to lift her head. Slowly and carefully, she peeled her pant leg up. "Shit."

The frost-blue scales had crawled from her ankle halfway up her calf. She reached down and touched one of them and found the scales hardened. Exhausted, she collapsed onto her back.

She had no idea how far she'd run, and she had no idea in which direction. The pain and the panic had disoriented her. Finally, she pushed herself up and spun around a few times, trying to get her bearings.

Directionless, Sarah started walking. Periodically, she glanced down at her left leg. She thought of Maggie, who she'd watched transform into ice and then shatter.

Puffing icy breaths and still unable to feel the frigid temperature, Sarah emerged from behind a large maple and stopped. She squinted at something on the horizon, but the thick brush and the darkness masked the image.

Sarah hurried forward, the object growing larger and closer. She noticed a clearing past the trees, and she prayed it was the embankment to the road. At a full sprint, Sarah broke through the forest and then skidded to a stop, paralyzed.

The Bell mansion stood towering in the distance.

Sarah shook her head. "That's not possible." She spun around, seeing the town below. At the realization she had returned to the one place she was trying to avoid, she broke down into tears. "This isn't happening." Sarah dropped to her knees, sobbing.

Had she knowingly run here? Had the redheaded girl been right about her not being able to leave? Sarah peeled back her jeans. The icy scales shimmered beneath the moonlight. If running away from Bell made the scales spread, then she was stuck. And if she couldn't run, then she was dead.

* * *

DEPUTY DELL PARKER had left the hospital with more questions than answers after the interview with his tightlipped victim. He reached for the radio and contacted dispatch. "Faye, this is Dell, I need you to run a name for me."

"Go ahead, honey," Faye answered.

"Brent Alvarez. Traditional spelling. He's a detective with the seventy-eighth precinct in New York. I need to get in contact with him."

"Got it. Anything else?"

"Not yet. I'm heading back to the Bell house now to question the groundskeeper."

"Do we need to call the sheriff?"

"I don't want to wake him up just yet."

"Copy that."

Dell's headlights flashed over the sign for Bell as he turned off the highway and onto the two-lane road into town. It was a path he was familiar with, having grown up in Bell. And he also knew the family the victim had worked for, which had made all of this even more strange.

Dell parked at the foot of the hill the Bell mansion topped and got out of his car. He looked up at the house, which presided over the entire town. Growing up here, it was impossible to try and get out of the shadow of that house. And while he had his own bone to pick with the family that resided inside, he needed to make sure those old feelings didn't interfere with the investigation.

It was a long walk from the gate and up the steps to the front door, and Dell was short of breath by the time he reached the top. With his head tilted back, catching his breath, he noticed a window boarded up on the second floor. He walked over to get a better look and crunched something beneath his boot.

Glass shimmered beneath his foot, and he squatted to examine the pieces. He picked up a shard, rotated it in his hand, then tossed it back onto the concrete.

Dell knocked on the door, and after five minutes passed Dell had raised his fist to knock again when the door opened.

"Dell? What the hell do you want?" Kegan was red-eyed and covered in a long black robe, the hem hovering near his slippers.

"I need to speak to Dennis," Dell said, retaining the even-keeled tone that he'd honed after five years on the police force.

Kegan crossed his arms, positioning himself in the middle of the doorway, purposefully blocking the entrance. "Why?"

"There was an incident reported, and he was named as the prime suspect."

"If you want to talk to anyone in this house, I suggest you provide a warrant or a subpoena or have enough for an arrest, but judging by the lack of documents, I'm going to assume you have neither." Kegan smirked. "Tell me I'm wrong."

It took every ounce of Dell's willpower to not throw a pair of cuffs on him at that very moment.

"Kegan?" Iris Bell's voice echoed inside, and the weathered old woman appeared at his side in the doorway. She was dressed in a nightgown, her skin wrinkled like a raisin. "What's this all about?"

"It's fine, Grandma," Kegan answered. "I'm handling it. Go back to bed."

"It doesn't look fine," Iris said. "What do you want, Dell?"

"I need to speak with Dennis." He tried looking inside, but Kegan blocked his view. "Do you know if he's here?"

"I already told you that unless you have a warrant, you're not getting anything from us," Kegan answered.

"Oh, Kegan, stop it." Iris gently slapped her grandson's arm and then pushed him off to the side. "Dell, if you need to speak with him to sort out whatever is happening, then come in. It's ungodly cold outside. And I need my beauty rest."

Kegan eventually moved out of the way, and Dell stepped inside. "Thank you, Mrs. Bell."

"Dennis!" Iris leaned on the bottom newel post and hollered up the steps. "Get down here, now!" She turned around, smiling at Dell. "It'll just be a minute. The man usually sleeps with his shoes on, so he's always ready to go."

Dell nodded, forced to linger in the awkwardness of the family squabble, and then watched Dennis descend the staircase.

"Dennis, Dell wants to ask you a few questions," Iris said, guiding the groundskeeper from the steps and across the foyer. "Just be honest with him, all right?"

"Yes, Mrs. Bell." Dennis nodded quickly, refusing to look Dell in the eye.

Dell regarded the aging groundskeeper, and noticed an odd lump beneath the arm of his left shirtsleeve. "What happened there?"

"Got stabbed in the thorn bushes," Dennis answered, keeping his head down.

"That's quite the bandage for thorns." Dell squinted. "Have you had any interaction with Sarah since she started working here?"

"If this is about Sarah, then why don't we just call her down?" Iris asked.

"Yeah," Kegan echoed.

"Because Sarah was the person who made the report." Dell watched the reactions of both Kegan and Iris, and while they played the part of shocked and confused, Dell was most concerned with Dennis, who didn't react at all. "Do you have a shed out back, Dennis?"

"Sure." Dennis shifted back and forth on his feet, eyeing his toes.

Dell stepped closer, and Dennis took a step back. "Mind if I take a look?"

Dennis immediately looked to Iris, and Kegan stepped between them.

"No." Kegan stomped his foot. "There no way I'm letting you a step farther without a warrant. If you think you can—"

"It's fine, Kegan," Iris said.

"No, it's not!" Kegan spun around, but the moment he caught the flash of anger that spread over Iris's face, he deflated. "Fine." He flapped his arms at his sides. "Do whatever the hell you want." He stormed off, muttering to himself as he trudged up the stairs.

"Dennis, why don't you show Dell where you keep your tools?" Iris asked, providing Dennis the needed push to head out the back. "You'll excuse me if I don't join you, but I don't like the cold. I'll make some tea, though, and have it ready for both of you when you come back into the kitchen."

"Thank you, Mrs. Bell," Dell said and then followed Dennis, who shuffled forward along the tile, dragging his feet, his head down.

Dell kept an eye out for anything peculiar on his trek through the old mansion, but he didn't spot anything out of the ordinary. It had been a long time since he'd been inside this house. And even with all of those years behind him, traversing these halls still gave him the creeps.

Despite the family's attempt to keep the grounds neat and tidy, they couldn't fight crippling effects of age and time. Like Iris Bell, the old structure looked one stiff breeze from falling apart.

Dell had been invited to the house once when he and Kegan were kids. There were enough rooms for everyone who lived in the town, and while they explored every nook and cranny, the fifth floor was off-limits. Kegan never told him what was up there, but now he had the sudden urge to find out.

Secrets clung to the walls of the house, its history written on pages as brittle as the old woman who lived here.

Dennis used a flashlight to guide them out to the shed, which he unlocked with a set of keys from his pocket. The walls of the shed leaned to the left, and the tiny pitched roof was caved in on the right side. Dell was surprised it hadn't collapsed on itself yet.

Dennis stepped aside after he opened the door, and Dell approached, flashing his light inside. The walls were lined with various garden tools: picks, shovels, hoes, and clippers. He stepped inside, finding the floor covered in wood, and he immediately started feeling around for any loose boards.

A couple had some give, but it was mostly just due to age and frailty. It wasn't until Dell reached the rear of the shed that a plank finally gave way. Dell dropped to a knee and pried away the loose board, finding the box that Sarah had spoken of. He removed it and set it on the floor, looking back to find Dennis still standing there in the doorway, watching him.

Dell returned his attention to the shoebox and then opened it, and he frowned.

"I don't trust banks," Dennis said.

Crumpled bills and change filled the box. Dell dumped the money onto the floor, looking for the IDs that Sarah had seen, but the box was empty save for the cash. Dell walked around the place for a little longer, looking for any other signs of loose boards, but he did so haphazardly. He was at a dead end.

Finished with the shed, Dell followed Dennis back to the kitchen, where Iris had the tea ready for him to drink.

"Find anything, Deputy?" Iris smiled from behind her cup then gingerly sipped her tea.

"I appreciate the time, Ms. Bell, and the cooperation. I'd like to take Dennis down to the station for some more questioning." He didn't think Sarah had lied, and if he could get the groundskeeper alone and out of the house, he might be able to work some information out of him. It was apparent that Dennis had been instructed to do whatever was asked of him, and it had been well rehearsed.

Iris looked a little surprised. "Did you find something to warrant more questioning? Did Dennis not comply with everything you've asked?"

"Just some due diligence, ma'am. I think we both agree that making sure we get the facts right here is what's most important."

The smile vanished from Iris's face as she set the tea on the table and stood. "If it'll end whatever nonsense you're chasing, then so be it." She turned to leave, chin up, but then stopped just before she reached the kitchen's exit. "But make sure you don't keep him all night. Dennis has work in the morning." She looked past Dell toward Dennis, glared, and then disappeared.

"Do I need to bring anything?" Dennis asked.

"No," Dell answered. "This won't take long."

Dell escorted Dennis down to his squad car, rehashing the conversation with Sarah. He didn't think she was lying, but he knew that he wasn't getting the whole truth on what happened at the house, and what happened with that detective in New York. But he would.

13

*S*arah kept her pant leg rolled up, keeping an eye on the icy scales that had progressed to just below her knee. She'd tried every direction—south, east, west, and finally north. Their only commonality was that they led her away from Bell, and the farther she walked from Bell in each direction, the more the scales spread.

Sarah touched one of the scales, the hard edges thick and dull. And the more they spread, the harder they became. Her foot was like an alligator's hide. She turned back to the north and returned to Bell, nursing the headache that had plagued her whenever she tried to distance herself from the town.

It was the house, and whatever… thing lived inside it.

But aside from what that thing was doing to her, Sarah didn't know anything about it, and if she wanted to fix whatever the hell was wrong with her, then she needed to learn more about the house and the family that lived there. And during her time in Bell she had met one man who knowledgeable about the town's history, and that's where she went.

The lights in Pat's Tavern had gone out, the bar already

closed for the night. Sarah circled around to the back of the building and found the small shack that acted as Pat's studio. A light shone through the shack's only window, and Sarah was glad to know he was awake.

Sarah knocked on the door quickly and then listened for any movement inside. When she heard nothing, she knocked harder. She descended the short staircase and then waited as the sound of footsteps headed toward the door.

"Sarah? Jesus, what are you doing out here at this hour?" Pat was dressed in jeans, shoes, and a long-sleeved shirt. He looked outside, checking to see if anyone was with her.

"I need to talk to you," Sarah answered.

Pat stepped aside and then motioned for her to enter. "You must be freezing. Come in, come in."

Sarah paced the small area, examining Pat's living quarters. It was a simple setup: bed along one wall, a two-person table with only one chair along another, and a small kitchenette near the door. No television. No technology of any kind that she could see.

"It's like a hermit's hut in here," Sarah said, noting the lack of fire in the wood-burning stove.

"It's better than sleeping outside." Pat reached for his only chair and then gestured for Sarah to sit. "What's going on?"

Sarah's legs groaned in relief when the pressure from her knees disappeared. She felt safe here. And after she took a minute to gather her thoughts and figure out what she wanted to say, she cleared her throat and looked Pat in the eye. "Those stories you told me about. The ones about the town and the deal that Allister Bell had made with that witch..." She watched him closely, studying his expression. "Are they real?"

Pat narrowed his eyes, tilting his head to the side. The hint of a smile crept up his cheeks. He laughed, more nervous than excited. "Are you serious?"

Sarah lowered her head and pinched the bridge of her nose. "I know it sounds crazy, but..." And before she could talk herself out of it, Sarah rolled up her pant leg, exposing the icy scales.

"Oh my god," Pat said, his voice a harsh whisper, then bent down to take a closer look. He grimaced, but amid the horror, there was fascination. "What is that?"

"I don't know," Sarah answered. "The doctors at the hospital thought that it might be frostbite, but it's not like any frostbite that I've ever seen."

"No," Pat said, that sense of awe still in his voice. He raised his eyes to meet Sarah's. "And you think this has something to do with the Bell house?"

Sarah nodded and then rolled her pant leg back down. "When I was there I saw a woman at night, but she was... hurt." She couldn't bring herself to say "dead" because it still sounded like nonsense in her own mind. "I found a box of driver's licenses and IDs, including the license of the girl I saw. I think all of them used to work at the mansion." She swallowed. "And I saw a body."

"Christ." Pat rubbed his face until his cheeks turned red and then crossed his arms. He stared at the floor a while, shaking his head. "Did you tell the police?"

"I told the deputy about the IDs," Sarah answered. "I didn't mention the body."

"What? Why?" Pat stood. "Sarah, you need to report this."

"Because the Bell house isn't the only thing I'm running from."

Pat frowned. "Sarah the police—"

"I can't!" Sarah blurted out. "I can't talk to the fucking police!" She felt control slipping away, and the desire to tell someone, the need to purge herself of what had happened in New York and why she had run here in the first place tipped the scales and became overwhelming. Her breathing quickened, and Pat kept his distance. Sarah prowled back and forth like a wounded animal.

"What did you do that was so bad?" Pat asked.

Tears broke through despite her anger, and Sarah smeared them away with the sleeve of her jacket. "It wasn't something I did." Her lip quivered. "It was something I didn't do." She sat on Pat's bed and sobbed.

Sarah could see the girl now, could see her screaming for help, begging for them to stop, but all she had been able to think of in the moment was saving herself. Because that was how she had grown up, and that instinct for survival was all she knew. She looked at Pat.

Pat walked over and placed his hand on her shoulder. "What happened, Sarah?"

Sarah shook her head, clasping her hands together so tightly that her knuckles whitened, and she walked over to Pat's bed. "I just watched her die." She froze, feeling as empty as the ghosts that had visited her over the past few days. "I watched them put a gun to her head, pull the trigger, and I didn't tell anyone. I just ran." She turned around and saw Pat by the door.

"So this person you saw murdered, was she a friend?" Pat asked.

Sarah sat down on the edge of the bed, picking away what remained of her nail polish. "No. But I knew the guy that killed her. He was my ex." She looked back up at Pat. "And he was a cop."

Pat exhaled and then ran his hand through his pepper-and-salt hair. "Shit."

Sarah chuckled. "Yeah." She crossed her arms, retreating inward. "He ran a little gang of crooked cops on the city's north side. I didn't find out until it was too late." She leaned back against the wall. "We were heading out for drinks one night when he said he needed to make a stop. I didn't think anything of it when he told me to wait in the car. But when he took a long time, I got out to go find him, and that's when…" She finally looked to Pat. "He killed her. And it wasn't just him, but it was a group of people… his gang."

"A gang of crooked cops," Pat replied, muttering the words to himself. "No wonder you ran."

The memories replayed in Sarah's head and became clearer the more she thought about them. "He found me the next day and tried to explain it wasn't what it looked like. When I told him I didn't want to see him anymore, he didn't think that was a viable option. Told me that if I wanted to live I should keep him warm in bed at night until he was tired of me." She squeezed herself a little tighter, the large jacket engulfing most of her body. "So I grabbed what I could carry and took off."

Pat nodded and then walked over, joining her on the bed. "Listen, Sarah. Whatever guilt you're feeling for running, I'm sure it's misplaced. You were just trying to survive." He put his hand on her knee. "I've seen a lot of bad people during my years as a barkeep." He leaned close. "You're not bad."

"I've always considered bad to be more of a spectrum than black and white." Sarah rubbed her forehead. "And I've been in enough foster homes to know that much."

"You were an orphan?" Pat asked.

"My parents died when I was three." Sarah reached for the photo of her parents in her jean pocket but didn't unfold it. "I don't have any real memories of them. They're more… feelings, I guess." She shook her head, shaking off the nostalgia.

Pat was quiet for a while and then slapped his palms on his thighs and stood. "I think the only option you have on the table right now is to get Dell to help you."

"He can't—"

"I've known Dell since he was little, and that boy has

more gumption than you give him credit for," Pat said, pointing at Sarah accusingly. "And the best way for you to help him is to tell him what we know."

"We?" Sarah asked.

Pat stood and smiled. "You don't expect me to sit out after hearing all of that, do you? This is the most excitement this town has seen since we were told Redford was getting a McDonald's. And that's not even in our town."

"Let me go into the tavern and give Dell a call, let him know you're here." Pat walked toward the door. "I'll be right back."

"Pat," Sarah said, causing him to stop. "Listen, I, um." She cleared her throat. "Thank you. For helping me."

Pat smiled, the same friendly grin he gave her when they first met. "Just sit tight."

The door swung shut, and Sarah was alone.

Sarah stood and paced the room. She nervously chewed on her lower lip, the skin chapped and rough against her tongue.

So far, everything the redheaded girl had said was true. Sarah hadn't been able to leave, and any attempt at escape from the town's vicinity was met with more pain and icy frost that crawled up her leg. And she had a good idea of what would happen to her if it spread to the rest of her body.

With the room growing hotter, Sarah needed air. She stepped out into the night, her boots crunching the hard frozen grass beneath, and puffed icy clouds with labored breaths. She looked toward the north and saw the Bell mansion, and the anxiety worsened. Her muscles seized up, and she collapsed to her hands and knees.

Sarah thrust her palms out to catch herself, her bare skin slamming into the frozen ground, pain shooting up her arms and into her shoulders. She tried to ball her hands up, raking her fingers across the ground, and then pounded her right fist into the dead chunk of earth.

"This isn't happening," Sarah said, shutting her eyes and struggling to regain control of her breathing. "Wake up. Wake up." She clenched her jaw, grinding her teeth until her head started to hurt. She pounded the ground again. "Wake up!"

"You're awake."

Sarah opened her eyes and looked up to find the redheaded woman floating in front of her. Startled, Sarah scurried backward and away from the floating apparition. But as the shock from the scare subsided, Sarah realized that she was no longer outside.

Sarah leapt to her feet, and the redhead floated toward her. "How did—" She spun around, examining the bedroom she was inside, then her excitement slowed, and she frowned. The floor, the ceiling, the windows. She was in a room at the Bell mansion. Finishing her spin, she landed on the ghost again. "How is this possible?"

"You're connected to this place." The redhead floated, circling Sarah. "You've been marked by the evil inside. It calls to you."

Sarah reached for the door handle then grunted in frustration when she found it locked. She spun around and faced the redhead again. "Why did you bring me here?"

"You're free to leave whenever you want." The redhead shrugged with casual indifference and then floated over to hover above the nearby bed.

Sarah tossed her hands in the air. "What are you talking about?"

The redhead shook her head. "Your mind put you here. Right now, you're just a projection. Like me." She motioned her thumb toward the window. "Your body is still on its hands and knees on the frozen dirt outside the tavern."

Sarah eyed the girl skeptically. "Bullshit."

The redhead laughed, and Sarah noted its charm. She shook her head, tossing the long, curly locks of red back and forth. "Put your hand on the doorknob and see for yourself."

Sarah turned, eyeing the doorknob, and then glanced back at the redhead to see if she was smirking, but she wasn't. Slowly, Sarah made her way toward the door, and she suddenly felt lighter. It was as if she had just smoked pot without getting high.

Sarah stretched out her arm, afraid to touch the doorknob if the redhead was trying to play a trick on her. Less than an inch away, Sarah lunged forward, her hand going right through the door as if it wasn't there at all.

Startled, Sarah jumped backward and landed hard on her ass. But instead of wincing in pain, she only winced out of reflex. She relaxed and then stood, staring at her body. She hadn't felt a thing. "Whoa."

Sarah wiggled her fingers, trying to find some missing detail on her hands to prove that this was just an illusion or a dream, but every line, freckle, and hair was accounted for. Even the chipped paint of her turquoise nail polish. She dropped her hands to her side and smiled. "Can I fly?"

Redhead arched an eyebrow. "Let's not get ahead of ourselves. C'mon." She floated toward the door and then through it, leaving Sarah alone.

Sarah walked toward the door, noticing that her footsteps were soundless against the normally fidgety wooden boards. She stopped just short of the door and then stuck her arm out. It went straight through the door. She moved it around and then pulled it back. She giggled to herself again and shook her head. "Fucking nuts." She gulped and then took a breath before shutting her eyes and stepping through the door.

Slowly, Sarah opened her eyes and found herself on the

first floor in the middle of the hallway. But it was different, newer. The walls weren't chipped and cracked, and the tables and chairs that lined the hall glimmered under the lights.

Sarah spun to her left and saw the sun shining through the window. "That's impossible."

"The afterlife here is reflective of when we died," the redhead answered, already sensing the question on the tip of Sarah's tongue.

"So it's always like this for you?" Sarah asked, walking toward the nearest chair and tracing her fingers along the golden square pattern imprinted on the evergreen velvet cushion. She knew that chair. She'd seen it when she had worked here, and the tear along the seat cushion had vanished. "What year is it?"

"I don't know," the redhead answered, a hint of sadness in her voice. "We don't remember much."

Sarah peeled her eyes from the cushion and toward the redhead, who looked pale even by ghost standards. "You don't know your name?"

"All I remember is being here when I died." She frowned, floating back and forth through the air as if she were pacing, and then stopped cold. "And I remember who killed me." Her eyes grew big and wide, and her mouth went slack, her entire body sagging. But then she perked up. "But you can save me. You can save us."

"Yeah, you keep saying that."

The redhead circled Sarah, glancing around the house. "The orb is hidden in this house. It moves, but it's always in the same place."

"How can something be in the same place, but always moving?" Sarah asked.

The redhead shrugged. "That's all I can remember."

Sarah sighed. "Right." She looked around. "So you're the only person that can see or hear me?"

"Yes."

"And I can go anywhere in the house?"

"Yes."

After spending her time here in the house, Sarah knew at least one place she wanted to start looking, and that was the fifth floor. If the Bells were going to hide something anywhere, it was going to be up there. After all, it was where she found those letters.

Without a word, Sarah sprinted toward the staircase at the west end of the building and then leapt up the steps two and three at a time. While she couldn't fly, she was light on her feet.

They ascended to the fifth floor, but when Sarah burst through the closed door, she found that the fifth floor was exactly how she had found it, in the same rotten condition it had been during her stay.

The floors were worn, cracked, and stained. Dust covered the paintings and candlesticks along the walls and furniture. The blinds at the other end of the hall were sealed shut, casting the hallway in darkness. It was just as barren and cold and deserted as she remembered.

Sarah made it one step forward before the redhead shot up through the floor with her arms jutting out and to block her path.

"You can't be up here," the redhead said, terror in her voice. "You need to leave."

"You said I can go anywhere," Sarah said. "And there's something up here."

Before the redhead could protest further, Sarah stepped through the woman and marched toward the door at the end of the hall.

The redhead sped up to catch her, trailing along her side. "Please, don't go inside."

"You said you wanted help," Sarah replied, getting closer. "Let me help."

The redhead continued to retreat until her back was flush against the door but not touching it. "I'm begging you to stop!"

But Sarah ignored the girl, ready to charge ahead, ready to end whatever was on the other side. She reached out her hand, prepared to go right through the girl, when all of a sudden the redhead belted an eardrum-shattering scream.

The pain split through the middle of Sarah's head and forced her to stop. She shut her eyes and dropped to her knees. The ringing faded slowly, and then the pain stopped. But when she opened her eyes, she found herself back on her hands and knees outside of Pat's house.

An immediate feeling of nausea overtook her, and Sarah vomited onto the grass. The hot bile was sour on her tongue, and she wiped her mouth with a shaking left hand. She looked around, finding the redhead gone, but she glanced back up to the mansion.

Quick as her legs would take her, Sarah sprinted toward Pat's Tavern, finding the old barkeep with the phone to his ear.

"Tell Dell to bring the letters," Sarah said, blurting out the words in a single breath. "I think they can help."

14

The ride back to the station was quiet. Dell stole glances at Dennis in the backseat, who smiled vacantly through the window and at the woods they drove past. Each time Dell looked, it gave him the creeps.

The headlights illuminated the Redford Sheriff's Department sign in front of a small building the city had graciously designated as their police headquarters. It had been previously used as an auxiliary building for the post office. But after they closed due to competition from UPS and FedEx, the city had allocated the building to the Sheriff's Department. It was a definite upgrade from the basement in the city hall building, which flooded every time it rained.

Dell removed Dennis from the back of his squad car and ushered him through the front door, where a very surprised Faye lowered her magazine and removed her feet from the counter.

"Faye, will you grab me the keys to the interrogation room?" Dell asked, moving quickly through the office. He'd never really conducted an interrogation before, but Dennis didn't know that, and he could tell the man was already starting to sweat.

"Um, yeah." Faye retrieved the keys from her drawer and tossed them to Dell on his walk past, waiting until Dennis wasn't looking her way to mouth, "What are you doing?" which Dell ignored.

Dell flicked on the lights and gave Dennis a little push toward the chair. "Sit down."

"You're not going to take the cuffs off?"

The steel bracelets clamped around his wrists were uncomfortable, and the longer Dennis wore them, the tighter they became. It wore on a person, both physically and mentally, to not have the simple freedom to scratch one's nose when it itched. It was enough to drive most petty criminals to a confession.

"No," Dell answered. "Sit."

Dennis did as he was told and was forced to maneuver himself to the end of the chair's seat to make room for his arms pinned behind his back.

Dell took a seat opposite Dennis and rested his arms on the table between them. Heat pumped through the vents, banishing the cold they had walked through outside, and Dell removed his jacket and laid it on the table off to the side. He took his time, letting Dennis sweat it out.

Finally, Dennis showed his first signs of cracking. "Well? What do you want to ask me?"

Dell repressed a smile and shrugged. "Whatever you feel like talking to me about, Dennis."

"You said you wanted to ask me questions about Sarah," Dennis replied, a hint of irritation in his voice. "That's why you brought me here, right?"

Dell hadn't had a lot of experience with interrogations, but from what he recalled with his training, he remembered that once a suspect started talking, it was best to let them work themselves into a corner. You did it by plucking at the threads that they gave you while maintaining control of the narrative. "You said that you and Sarah talked a few times. What did you talk about?"

Dennis cast his eyes down at the table and shrugged. "We talked about the chores and the different responsibilities of taking care of the house."

"Why?" Dell asked.

The follow-up threw Dennis into confusion. "Wh-What do you mean, why?"

"Why didn't you talk about other stuff? Didn't she like you?"

Dennis frowned. "I don't know. I guess we didn't have a lot to talk about."

"But you said you did talk, right?"

"Yeah."

"And you never talked about anything other than work?"

Dennis hesitated a moment then answered more slowly, unsure of himself. "Yeah—I mean no."

"So you lied to me?"

Dennis's eyes widened in trepidation, and he shifted in his seat, rotating his shoulders. "No!" Dennis shouted. "I didn't lie, I was just telling you what… What…"

"What Mrs. Bell and Kegan told you to tell me?" Dell asked, pushing it further.

Dennis shut his eyes, muttering something to himself, and then lifted his face, snarling. The anger streaming off Dennis was like that of a child that wasn't getting his way.

Dell stoked the anger. "Is that what happened? Did Mrs. Bell and Kegan make you lie?"

Slowly, Dennis produced a smile followed by a giddy laugh that escaped tight lips. It went on for some time, and then tears leaked from his eyes. "You can't stop it."

Dell leaned forward, trying to remain calm despite his

eagerness. "Stop what?"

"He's almost here," Dennis answered, relaxing as if the burden of secrecy had been lifted. "And he's going to reward those that have been faithful to him." Another spate of giddy laughter spewed from his lips. He lowered his face slowly, all the while his eyes locked on Dell. "I have been faithful." He leaned forward. "And I will continue to be faithful."

Dell's heart rate spiked. "And who is this man you've been faithful to?"

"My master is no man," Dennis answered. "And when he arrives he shall embrace the world to his bosom and let us suckle from his nurturing strength. The dark lord will be freed from his prison of hell and walk the earth for all eternity."

If Dell understood what Dennis was saying, then —"You're talking about Satan?"

Dennis smiled, exposing his yellowed teeth, and then stood, leaning over the table with his hands still locked behind his back. "People will burn, consumed in the eternal flames of the damned. Millions, no, billions!" The shadows beneath his face darkened as he maneuvered himself directly under the light in the center of the room. "They will burn forever."

Confusion had been replaced with anger, and Dell stood, towering to the same height as Dennis, who backed down. "A lot of talk for a man who hides behind a big house and an old lady." Dell leaned forward, and Dennis turned his face away. "What was the plan, Dennis? What did you do to Sarah?"

"She was being difficult!" Dennis said, the muscles along his neck flexing as he screamed, "She didn't understand what she was! She didn't understand that she was the last!"

"The last what, Dennis?" Dell asked, matching Dennis's intensity as he invaded the groundskeeper's personal space. "The last what?"

"Sacrifice!" Dennis answered. "But she will come back." He smiled and produced another giddy laugh. "It is her destiny."

After that outburst, the only words that Dell was able to get out of Dennis were: the last sacrifice. It was like something in the man's mind had finally snapped, and he just paced back and forth, repeatedly muttering the same phrase over and over.

Finally, Dell stepped out of the room and stared at Dennis through the viewing window.

It was almost too fantastical for Dell to imagine that the family he'd grown up with had been killing people right beneath his nose. But if he was going to make any kind of charges stick, he needed an official statement from Sarah, and that meant convincing her to go on the record. And judging from their last encounter, he wasn't confident he could be successful.

Dell removed Maggie's ID from his pocket. If they had killed her or any of the other people that they had employed at the house, then he was willing to bet there was a mass grave somewhere on the property. But getting a survey team up here from Bangor could take a while.

"Faye!" Dell returned to the reception desk, head down as he walked, thinking. "Get Sheriff Nettles on the phone for me."

Faye sat behind the desk with her nose buried in one of those fashion and glamour magazines. "You sure you want to do that?" She peeled her eyes away from the text. "He's not going to be happy about it."

"He'll be even less happy when he finds out what I have to tell him." Dell grabbed his jacket from the coatrack and put it on. "I'm running to the hospital real quick. Keep an eye on Dennis for me."

"You're leaving me here with that weirdo?" Faye asked. "What happens if he breaks out?"

Dell buttoned his jacket and then reached for the door. "I still have him in his cuffs, and the door's locked. If he starts to give you any trouble, just radio. And let me know when you've got the sheriff."

The drive from the station to the hospital was short. While Redford was bigger than Bell, it was still small. He pulled into the parking lot and then marched up to Sarah's room, riding the elevator with a pair of nurses.

One of them smiled at him, and Dell blushed in return. The elevator dinged, and the doors opened for his floor. "Excuse me." He stepped between them, and then caught their giggles before the doors closed again.

At the end of the hall, Dell spied George down at the nurse's station, chatting it up with Margaret instead of manning his post. "Don't forget you're on the clock, Deputy."

George spun around, and gave a friendly wave before returning to his conversation.

"Well, Sarah, I think you might have been on to something at the house—" Dell stopped in the doorway, finding the bed empty. "Shit." He spun around, finding only a stack of papers on the table near the door. He picked them up, frowning as he flipped through the brittle pages, then stepped back out into the hall and marched down to George, overhearing his conversation with Margaret.

"So, this guy is swerving all over the place," George was saying, leaning in closer as the nurse did the same. "Finally, he stops, the car still halfway on the road, and I tell him to get out of the car and place his hands on the hood, which he does… and he's completely naked."

"Oh my god, no," Margaret said, covering her mouth with excited surprise then breaking out into a fit of giggles.

"And let's just say it was quite a cold night to be out and driving around—"

"George." Dell pulled on the deputy's shoulder. "Where is she?"

"Who?" George asked.

Dell pointed down to the room. "Sarah! The woman you're supposed to be watching." He shoved George in the chest a little too hard to be considered playful.

"Whoa, hey, I dunno. She was just in there."

Dell groaned and reached for his radio. "Faye, this is Dell. Have you gotten ahold of the sheriff yet?"

"No, but I did just get a call for you," Faye answered. "It's Pat."

"Tell him I don't have time to deal with any of his drunks right now." Dell returned to the room, and saw that Sarah had taken her backpack too. But he walked over to the table, finding a cluster of papers.

"He says he has Sarah over at his place and they need to talk to you. And to bring… letters? I don't know what that means."

Dell rotated the old pieces of paper in his hand. "Tell him I'm on my way."

* * *

DELL REMAINED STANDING while Sarah told him about the bodies, the ghosts, the visions, the icy scales that had spread when she tried to leave, everything. And all the while unable to gauge from his stoic expression whether he believed her or not.

"And that's all I know," Sarah said, keeping her seat on the edge of the bed. "I should have told you about the body sooner."

"Yeah," Dell said, his tone irritated. "You should have."

"It's a lot for anyone to take in," Pat said, trying to be the voice of reason.

"We'll have to get a warrant to search the grounds," Dell said. "We might be able to wake up Judge Warner, but it's a long shot." He grunted in a long sigh. "In the meantime I want you to come back to the station in Redford."

Sarah frowned. "Didn't you hear what I just said?"

"Yeah, and the safest place for you to be is back in the station," Dell answered.

"Dell, you heard her, if she tried to leave the town that stuff gets worse," Pat replied.

"I'm not going anywhere," Sarah said, shaking her head in defiance.

"You just told me there is a dirty cop trying to hunt you down. If he's been watching the DMV databases, and he's as well-connected as you say, then there's no reason why he couldn't follow you here." Dell pointed to the floor. "This isn't up for discussion."

"Then I'm not signing any official statement," Sarah said.

"What?" Dell asked, his tone in disbelief. "Why the hell not?"

Sarah frowned, agitated at having been put on the defensive. "You don't know those people, Dell. They kill anyone they want, whenever they want. It's like they're judge, jury, and executioner all rolled into one. And it's not just cops he has in his pocket. I've seen him meet with judges and district attorneys. Whatever shit he's involved in has some serious power behind it, so you'll have to excuse me if I don't have much faith in your criminal justice system!" She shot up from the chair and paced to room's back wall, opposite Dell.

"And what does that mean for the person you watched that cop murder?" Dell asked. "What does it mean to all the other people he's probably hurt? You know this is bigger than just you, Sarah."

"Easy for you to say when your head isn't the one on the chopping block," Sarah muttered.

Dell remained quiet for a minute, but Sarah noticed the twitch of his left nostril. "Murder is a crime, and the fact that it was done by a cop makes it even worse." He tapped the badge on his chest and stepped toward the middle of the room. "This means something to me, and anyone that disrespects it or takes advantage of the power that it wields doesn't deserve to wear it."

Sarah walked toward him, arms still crossed, meeting him in the middle, their faces so close that their noses nearly touched. "And where were those badges when I was getting the shit beat out of me when I was seven years old at a foster home? Where were those badges when I was thirteen and was felt up by my foster father? Or how about when I was sixteen and I had to fend off a rape from three older boys that were in the same orphanage as me? You wear that badge, and it makes you what?" Sarah shrugged, laughing sadly as her eyes watered. "You're some kind of hero? That all cops are heroes and people will always do the right thing, because if they don't there are consequences?" She bared her teeth like a rabid dog. "Those fuckers that hurt me, beat me, abused me in those homes never saw jail time. Hell, the system gave them even more kids! I don't give a shit about your badge, I don't give a shit about some woman that got herself killed by some crooked cops, and I don't give a shit about how it makes *you* feel. You want to help?" She stepped back, the laughter rolling off her tongue angry and forced. "You really want to be the hero in this story? Then track that dirty cop down and put a fucking bullet in his head, because that's the only justice that he'll ever get, and it's the only justice he deserves."

Sarah retreated to the rear wall, no longer caring about the tears streaming down her face and whether he saw.

It was quiet for a while, neither Sarah or Dell speaking, and it wasn't until Pat walked over and stood directly between them that he broke the silence.

"We can point fingers all day long," Pat said. "But the bottom line is we don't fully understand what's happening." He walked over to the table where Dell had dropped the letters. "But these might give us some insight. Plus—" Pat held up his finger and hurried toward his bed.

Both Sarah and Dell frowned as Pat dropped to a knee and reached beneath his bed. "I've been collecting history on this town ever since I was little." A harsh scraping sounded, and Pat removed an old, worn chest from underneath. "There was a newspaper that operated out of Redford back when Allister Bell founded this town, and they documented a lot of what happened after he died." He flipped the latches of the chest, opened the top, and then reached inside. "And being the amateur sleuth I am, I started collecting the articles." He pulled a thick notebook out and then held it up for Sarah and Dell to see. "Between this, and those letters over there, I think we've got something we can work with."

Dell was quiet for a minute and then shook his head. "I still think the best thing for us to do is take you back to the station. But—" He sighed, and then looked at Sarah. "It's your life that's on the line."

Sarah nodded, thankful for Dell's acknowledgement. "I want to help you, Dell. But I'm with Pat on this one. We need to learn more about the house and what is happening to me. And if you help me do this, then I will go on record with telling you everything."

"Perfect." Pat walked between them and dropped the heavy notebook on his table, then spun around to face them. "I'll start the coffee."

* * *

EMPTY STYROFOAM CUPS were littered at feet twitching from the buzz of coffee. Pat, Dell, and Sarah all sat in different areas of Pat's tiny studio shack. Sarah managed to snag the bed, Pat sat cross-legged on the floor, and Dell resigned himself to the tiny table, which teetered to the right.

The letters provided a variety of challenges, not the least of which was the difficulty in trying to read them. Time and faded ink had transformed the letters among the Bell family members into a mundane version of wheel of fortune.

"I'd like to buy a vowel," Pat said, grinning.

"It stopped being funny after the seventh time, Pat," Dell said.

Any letters that were considered completely illegible were discarded into a separate pile over in the far back left corner of the room. The rest were divvied up between the three of them, each taking notes on what they read.

Sarah shook the cramp in her hand, finishing up her last letter. "I haven't done this much writing since high school."

"How are we looking, guys?" Pat asked, finishing a scribble, and then tossed his pencil on the floor. "I'm all done."

"Nearly there," Dell answered, his focus on the papers.

Sarah had watched him for a little bit, and smiled every time he furrowed his brow in concentration, which was often. She returned to her last letter, and she and Dell finished at the same time.

"So," Pat asked. "What do we have?"

"The earliest letter I have was marked in 1898," Dell answered, reading from his notes. "It was from a cousin of the Bells who had written to Allister's children about their parent's death." He looked up. "That was a common theme in all the letters I read. Notifications of deceased family members."

"Me too," Sarah replied.

"And me three." Pat scribbled another note on his pad. "So that's a commonality. Anything else?"

"All of the letters were marked with the same three numbers," Sarah answered. "Six-six-six."

"Mine too," Dell replied.

"Again, me three," Pat said. "It's a sign of the devil. And since all of these letters are dated after Allister's death, then we could assume that was part of the witch's curse."

"She started killing anyone named Bell?" Sarah asked.

"Anyone with their bloodline, maybe," Pat answered.

"But that doesn't explain Sarah," Dell replied, frowning. "Or the girl Sarah said she saw."

"Wait." Sarah reached for her stack of letters and then plucked one out from the pile. "I found one that was addressed to Iris." She got up and walked toward Dell, Pat getting up off the floor to join them. Sarah flattened the letter on the table and let them read.

My dearest Iris,

Our situation in Bell has deteriorated. I'm afraid that we won't last much longer without any aid from the outside world.

I know that you moved away because you no longer wanted to be a part of our family, but you should know that when I die here, it will be you who is held responsible, along with your family.

With no heirs of my own, your descendants will become the last of the Bell name, and while you may not have had a decision in departing our town, I can tell you that your distance from our home will have no impact on the effects our ancestor will have in reaching you.

There is nowhere else to hide, Iris. There is nowhere that you can run. If you choose that road, I sincerely wish you the best of luck. But if you want to give yourself and your family a fighting chance, then I beg you to come home. It is the only way."

Jameson Bell

They all pulled back from the letter, Dell frowning and

Pat scratching his head. Sarah tapped her finger against the brittle paper. "So Iris came back because she thought it would stop her family from dying?" She looked to Pat.

"But it didn't," Dell said. "Both of Kegan's parents died." Dell got up and paced the floor, following the thought. "And our theory only makes sense if they all died the same way, right?" He gestured to Sarah's leg. "Maybe they all had the same condition like you?"

Pat gasped, drawing both of their attention toward him. "Disease." Without another word he grabbed his notebook and slammed it on top of the letters on the table. "Here, look at this."

Sarah and Dell walked over and stood on either side of Pat. The page he'd turned to all had the same headlines. "Plague" and "Cursed" and "Witch strikes again" were a few of their favorites. Most of the actual articles played up the sensationalism of what was occurring, no doubt using fear to sell more newspapers.

"The medical community described the physical symptoms as being similar to shingles or frostbite," Pat said. "And all of the individuals that came down with the affliction were descendants of Allister Bell. And here, look, here."

Sarah leaned closer to the line that Pat had highlighted and read aloud. "Any patient that was transported from Bell to Redford was immediately returned due to making the conditions worse. While most patients didn't survive, one local doctor managed to save a woman's life."

Pat pounded his fist on the table. "It can be fixed!"

Hope swelled in Sarah's chest.

"Who was the doctor?" Dell asked.

Pat turned a few more pages and then stopped on an article taped to the center of the page. "Dr. Henry Nash."

"Oh my god, look at the patient that was cured," Sarah said, reading farther down the article.

Dell leaned closer and read. "Iris Bell."

"How old is this article?" Sarah asked, searching for the date.

"Thirty years," Pat answered.

Dell raised his eyebrows. "The doctor might still might be alive. I can make a call to dispatch and look up his address." He headed for the door, already on the radio.

Sarah watched him go. "Do you think that doctor is still alive?" Her voice was small and tired like that of a little girl grasping for a piece of hope she wasn't sure she'd be able to obtain.

Pat's expression softened, and he walked over and gently placed his hand on her shoulder. "I do."

"How can you be sure?" Sarah asked. "How do you know he hasn't died or—"

Pat squeezed her shoulder. "We'll find him."

And when Pat smiled, despite Sarah's reservations, she let herself believe him.

It had been a while since she'd had a friend to help her and even longer since she'd had someone she could trust. It was a feeling she missed. Foster homes and orphanages tended to kill trust at a very early age. Sarah remembered when it had broken for her.

She had been six, and she had just moved into a foster home that would be shut down three months later, social workers citing unlivable conditions and neglect. Sarah lived in a room with nine other kids, and between them they shared three pillows and two blankets and zero beds. The house had had no heat and hardly any insulation, so they would all huddle together in the middle of the floor like a pack of dogs.

When Sarah had first arrived at the house, her foster father had made a big deal about her birthday, and when asked if she'd ever gotten a cake and a present, she said no.

Chuck—foster parents always had the sleaziest names— told her that they'd get her a cake and whatever present she wanted.

Unsure of what to ask for, she decided to go with something simple. For food, she requested a strawberry cake because she remembered having one at a church event the previous Thanksgiving, and it had been the best food she'd ever tasted. And for a toy, she wanted a ballerina skirt. The few bits of television she'd seen had been a PBS special on the ballet. After watching those dancers float across the stage to music, it was all she wanted to do.

The night before her birthday, Sarah didn't sleep a wink. She lay huddled on the floor, imagining herself as one of the ballerinas she had seen on television. And when the first rays of sunlight finally pierced the window, she sprinted into the kitchen, where Chuck was passed out on the table.

"Chuck!" Sarah tugged at his sleeve, jumping up and down as she smiled. "Chuck, it's my birthday!"

But no matter how hard she tugged, he wouldn't stir, so with her guardian indisposed (drunk, as she would later understand), she went to the fridge in hopes of finding the cake. But the only thing inside was beer.

Sarah turned back to Chuck, still asleep on the kitchen table. She looked down at his feet and saw a dozen crushed beer cans littering the floor. She had seen foster parents like him before. She understood that they got mean and angry when they drank that stuff. And even though she was scared, she had built up the excitement about the day in her head so much that her disappointment outweighed the fear of repercussions.

"You promised!" Sarah slapped Chuck's arm, but he still didn't wake. She hit him again, repeatedly, each time harder than the one before. "You promised me!" Her voice rose to a shriek, and it finally stirred the drunk awake.

"Wha—?" Chuck lifted his face, struggling to open his eyes as Sarah continued to beat him with her tiny little fists. "Hey, stop that!" He shoved Sarah, and her butt smacked the dirty black-and-white-checkered tile.

Chuck pressed his hands against his temples and burped a few times, while Sarah cried silently on the floor. After another minute, he looked down at her, almost as if he didn't even recognize her. "What are you crying about?" He dismissed her. "Go back to bed."

"It's my birthday," Sarah replied, her voice shaking from the tears.

"Yeah, well, happy birthday." Chuck provided no sincerity or fanfare as he stood.

The dismissal boiled Sarah's rage, and she pushed herself up from the floor. He was just like all the other foster fathers she'd been with, all talk and no action. They made promises that were never kept, and she had finally grown sick of it.

Sarah flung herself against Chuck's leg, kicking, punching, flinging all her strength behind every blow, which to Chuck was only an annoyance.

"Knock it off, kid." Chuck shook his leg and sent her flying backward, crashing against the tile.

But the abuse failed to deter her spirit, and Sarah sprang back to her feet and attacked again. Her voice had risen to an ear-shattering scream as she pounded against his leg, beating her little fists as fiercely as she could. "You promised! You promised! You promise—"

The backhand that knocked Sarah from Chuck's leg and beat her into the floor also paralyzed her body. A white flash blinded her, and it was quickly followed by a crushing defeat of pain as her vision adjusted to black-and-white-checkered tile.

"What the fuck is the matter with you?" Chuck towered over her, his face beet red as he screamed. "You think I wanted to do that? You think I wanted to hit you?" He raised his hand high to hit her again, but when Sarah winced, he lowered it. "If you're gonna be a stupid fucking bitch, then I might as well send you back to the orphanage." He stomped off, still muttering to himself, while Sarah remained on the ground. "You ain't worth the fucking trouble!"

Blood trickled down from the corner of her left eyebrow, the red a brilliant streak of color against her pale skin, and as it mixed with her tears, she looked as if she was crying blood. Sarah remained there on the tile until one of the older kids came from the room and picked her up, carrying her back to the safety of their tiny room.

That was the first of thousands of other scenarios that Sarah had experienced as an orphan, and it was the foundation of the callus that had formed over the past two decades of her life.

It was the start of every mistrust she'd ever had with a man and the basis for every failed relationship she'd ever experienced.

But the man next to her wasn't Chuck, or any of the foster father's she'd known.

"You know, you remind of Mr. Westbrook," Sarah said.

"Who's that?" Pat asked.

"He was one of the social workers assigned to my case file over the years." Sarah drifted into the past. "One of the really good ones. He was the only one who actually made sure I was pulled out of bad situations. He went the extra mile. Like you."

Pat grinned. "Just trying to help."

Sarah held his hand and gave it a squeeze. "Thank you."

"Don't thank me yet," Pat said. "It's not over till it's over."

And while Sarah understood that all of this was a long shot, it still felt good to find some light at the end of the tunnel.

Dell returned, stepping back inside, and Sarah quickly stood.

"Did you find him?" Sarah asked.

Dell grinned. "He lives off a dirt road just west of Redford. It's a bit of a drive, and he's in the middle of nowhere, even by northern Maine standards, but he's alive."

Sarah threw her arms around Dell, hugging him tightly, happy tears rolling down her cheeks. She then pushed him back and punched his arm in a fit of joy.

"Ow," Dell said, rubbing his arm. "You have a funny way of saying thank you."

Sarah laughed again and then spun around and flung herself into Pat's arms, squeezing him tightly as well. "Thank you, Pat." She peeled her cheek off of his chest and stared up at the man with the greying hair with white patches, the tan face, and the weathered wrinkles around his eyes and mouth. "Thank you so much."

"I'll run and talk to him." Dell backtracked toward the door and reached for his radio. "And I'll call for a deputy to come over to keep an eye on things."

"We'll be fine," Pat said. "I've got a shotgun in the closet. Plus I have Sarah to protect me."

"I'm still calling the deputy." Dell headed toward the door and then stopped and turned around once the pair were close. "Just stay put. But if something happens before my guy arrives, then I want you to head to Redford and talk with Faye. You can trust her. She'll keep you safe."

The door swung shut, and Sarah sat on the bed. Patience had never been Sarah's strong suit, and it grew thinner every time she stared down at her leg. She tugged up her jeans, the icy scales shimmering beneath the yellow light of Pat's lamps.

"You all right?" Pat asked.

"Fine, just—" Sarah paused. "Anxious."

"I've known Dell for a long time," Pat said. "He's not someone who quits when it gets hard."

Sarah dropped her pant leg, and then picked at the fading nail polish on her fingers. "Most people aren't like that."

"No," Pat said. "They're usually not as good-looking as he is either."

Sarah tossed a teenage-like glare, and Pat raised his hands in defense as he walked toward the door.

"I'm just saying." Pat laughed and then turned back to Sarah. "I'm heading into the bar for a drink. You want anything?"

"No, I'm fine."

But after Pat left, Sarah decided that she did need something, air.

Outside, the night sky was clear, and Sarah gazed up at the stars. It was a beautiful night. But when she lowered her gaze, it fell upon the Bell mansion, and her smile turned to a frown.

Despite having more answers than she did an hour ago, Sarah still had questions. She wanted to know why Iris returned to this place. She wanted to know why she had started killing people. And most importantly, she wanted to know how to stop it.

She remembered what the redhead had told her about the cure being inside the house. It moves, but is always in the same place. She glanced down at her palms and wiggled her fingers, then lifted her gaze toward the mansion.

Sarah looked back at Pat's Tavern, making sure the coast was clear, and then faced the mansion on the hill again. She pumped her hands into fists a few times and then tried to recreate the exact conditions she'd experienced before when she was projected into the house. She dropped to her knees, pressed her hands against the ground, and tried to do it again.

he black GTO blended in well in the darkness off the side of the highway. Brent had pulled over past the shoulder and onto the slope of the ditch that spread into the edge of the forest. The angle kept him leaned against his driver-side door as he listened to the police scanner.

There hadn't been much chatter since Brent pulled over, but he hadn't been there long. Still he fidgeted. The drive up had made him antsy and stiff. But he didn't want to barge into town without knowing what the cops knew. There was no telling what Sarah had said after the police ran her license through the system.

He hoped that she had the good sense to keep her mouth shut, but that all depended on how desperate she'd grown.

Brent turned his head out the window and stared into the woods. It was pitch-black between the trees, and the darkness looked to stretch forever.

The speaker on the scanner crackled, and a woman's voice broke through. "Dell, it's Faye."

Brent perked up, and his lower back popped as he leaned closer toward the scanner and turned up the volume.

"This is Dell."

"I've got the sheriff on the line for you. Patching through now."

"Dell?" The voice was gruff and agitated. "What in the same hell is going on out there?"

"Sheriff, I need you to call the state troopers in and get Judge Warner to sign a warrant to search the Bell house. I think we have a multiple homicide situation on our hands."

"Dell, what in the hell are you talking about?"

"I have a witness, former employee over at the Bell house, who says that she saw a body on the property, buried somewhere out back. I think we should call the forensic team up from Bangor."

"Hold on, now, just hold on." The sheriff cleared his throat. "You're saying that Iris Bell has bodies buried in her backyard and that you have a witness?"

"Yes, sir."

"Jesus Christ." The sheriff sighed. "All right. You have Faye get the paperwork ready and make sure your witness understands that she will have to testify, and then I'll call the judge. I'm sure he'll be as happy about the call at this hour as I was."

"Thank you, Sheriff. Faye, did you get all of that?"

"Copy," Faye said.

"Where are we at with Brent Alvarez?"

Brent balled his fists in anger.

"I called the precinct and spoke to the shift supervisor, but they told me he's not on duty, but they'll try and reach out to him."

"Keep pestering them. I want to know where this guy is."

"Copy."

The chatter ended, and Brent turned the volume back down to lessen the static. "Shit." He knocked his head against the window and then snarled.

Those Andy Griffith Show cops up here could call his

precinct all they wanted. Nobody was going to rat him out, but since the bitch had already talked, it meant that Brent had to approach this from a different angle, and that meant keeping Sarah alive. If he could do that then he would just have the DA file so many charges and forge so many documents against her that it would make whatever Sarah told these idiots look like a desperate attempt to clear her own name.

Defeated, Brent tilted his head back, shutting his eyes. He should have killed Sarah when he'd had the chance. But when he had arrived at her apartment and saw her standing there in her shirt and jeans, staring up at him with those big blue eyes, it was the first time that beauty had changed his mind.

No, not beauty. He had been with other beautiful women whom he never would have left in that apartment alive.

Sarah had something else. It was innocence. But it wasn't naïve or inexperienced. She possessed an innocence that allowed her to be free and, in turn, free the people that she was with. Brent had never been with anyone like that. And he suspected he wouldn't be with anyone like that again.

Brent chuckled, the grin stretching wider as his laughter grew and then died down, fading with each shake of his head until his expression became stoic. "The things we do for a good fuck."

He removed his phone and found the town of Bell on his GPS. It was close. He started the engine and the four hundred horses roared to life, vibrating the steering wheel and seat. He pulled back onto the highway and continued his journey north.

The sign for Bell appeared quickly, and Brent hit the brakes hard, nearly missing the turn. His tires screeched, and he was forced to slow his pace on the dark, winding, two-lane road.

Trees lined either side of the road, and Brent cast a few quick glances about, wondering if the bitch was hiding in the cold.

The road and forest eventually opened into an even smaller town than Redford. The sad excuse for its main street boasted buildings that looked one day away from demolition. But Brent's eyes widened as he took in the massive mansion high on the hill above the town. "Talk about propping up the one percent."

Brent made it past the buildings on the right and parked the GTO behind a diner, making sure it was hidden from view of the road. The last thing he wanted was Sarah or the cops spotting him. He cut the engine, quieting the rumbling GTO with a turn of his key.

Brent opened the glove compartment and removed his .38 special. The serial number had been scratched off, making the weapon untraceable. He pocketed the weapon and stepped out of the car.

Bell wasn't much of a town to look at. It only had seven buildings and what looked like a burned-down church across the street. He walked the storefronts, casing the joints with a practiced eye.

Once he cleared the right side of the street, he meandered over to the left, his attention focused on the large, bold lettering of Pat's Tavern. He smiled and decided that he could use a drink.

The front door lock was an easy pick, and thirty seconds later he was greeted with the scent of stale beer and smoke. He weaved between the tables and made his way to the bar. He stepped behind it, perused the tequila selection, and settled on Patron, which had always been his favorite ever since he was a kid.

Brent found a clean glass and then gave himself a generous pour. He sipped at first and then downed the rest quickly. He worked his mouth into a large "O" shape and shook his head. "That'll put some hair on your balls." He chuckled and then poured himself another drink, when the back door opened.

Quickly, Brent returned the bottle and skirted back around the bar, taking his glass with him, and darted into the adjacent room, ducking behind a pool table.

Crouched low, Brent removed the revolver from his pocket and listened to footsteps back over by the bar. Glasses clinked together, but the lights never came on. A few grumbles floated through the air, and from the deep tone it sounded to Brent like a man. Probably Pat, seeing as how the place was closed.

But then the grumbles faded and the footsteps sounded like they were coming for the room. Brent looked at his drink, downed it, and then popped up from behind the pool table with the gun aimed at a startled, grey-haired man.

"Who are you?" the man asked.

"Wrong question, asshole," Brent answered. "The right question would be, why shouldn't I blow your brains out right now?"

The man frowned. "What?"

"Yeah," Brent answered, walking closer. "Because I want to know what you can do for me."

The man stared at the revolver. "W-what do you want?"

Brent smiled and placed the end of the revolver barrel against the man's forehead. "I'm looking for a girl."

* * *

KEGAN WAS ALREADY on his third glass of bourbon by the time Iris found him back in his room. He had never been one to handle the family business well. It was the main reason he had left in the first place. But it wasn't something Iris had

169

ever held against him. She had left once too. But the Bells always came home, lest they suffer the consequences.

"Dell knows something," Kegan said, his speech slightly slurred.

Iris walked over and removed the glass from her grandson's hand.

"That blonde bitch saw the IDs. She has the letters." Kegan extended fingers from his fist, one at a time. "Who knows what else she's seen, and what she's told the police!"

"Stop fidgeting." Iris set the glass down on a table and reclined in a nearby chair. "You're going to wear a hole in our floor."

"Dennis has been gone too long." Kegan continued his pacing, though he dropped his hand from his mouth, but he twisted his fingers back and forth in exchange for the biting. "The idiot is going to tell him something, and it'll just be a matter of time before they march back to the house with an entire army of—"

"I will not have you come unraveled when we are nearly done," Iris said.

"No one has ever left before!" Kegan's voice was strained. "This wasn't part of the plan!"

"The plan stays the same," Iris said. "She cannot leave, and the curse will bring her back."

"That doesn't help us with the police," Kegan said.

"We'll deal with that when the time comes!" Iris wheeled on her grandson, hissing through her teeth. "Right now, all we have to do is stick to our story. You and I both know she can't leave, not unless she wants to die. He'll call her back, and when he does, we need to be ready."

Kegan stood, wobbling a bit on two feet, and then snagged the bottle and took a swig. "There are bodies buried on our property. When the cops start taking a closer look, it won't matter what story we tell, *Grandmother*."

Iris slapped Kegan across the cheek, and while she left a mark, she suspected that her hand hurt worse than his face did. "Our family's future is at stake. There is no one left but us, and you and I both know what will happen if we fail."

With the bottle still in one hand, he gently raised his cheek.

Iris slouched. "I'm sorry, my dear." She reached for his hand and gave it a peck with her thin lips. "It's my head. Help me get my medicine."

Kegan nodded, leaving the bottle as he helped guide Iris back to her room. Her grandson was very much like his father, who had worried himself to an early grave. The heart attack had been massive, but it was also quick. She was thankful that he wasn't meant to suffer. But despite the good-natured grandson who came from a good-natured father who came from a good-natured husband, Iris had discovered her husband's family secret too late.

Iris was not a true Bell, and when she had learned the truth, she'd wanted to disappear. She had even gone as far as having an attorney write up divorce papers.

But the day before she had been about to file for divorce, she received a letter in the mail. It was from her husband's brother, who had stayed in Bell to look after the house even though he had been the second born. Her husband had forsaken the duties that nature and honor had bestowed upon him as the first-born son and heir and also the burden of their bloody past.

Kegan guided Iris into her room and helped her onto the bed. "I'll be right back, Grandmother."

But Iris didn't hear him, or see him leave. Her attention was on the dresser where that letter was stored. She must have read it a dozen times and rewritten her response a dozen more. She had returned to that letter throughout the years as a reminder of what would happen should she fail.

But it was only in times of dire desperation. Times in which she began to doubt herself, the future, her choices. Times like now.

Wearily, Iris walked toward her dresser. Her old bones groaned, the gusto of her youth long since faded. She had felt old for a long time, but none more than the past few weeks. The last few steps were always the hardest.

Iris gripped the edge of the worn oak to help keep herself upright, her knees aching to the point of breaking. The pain was sharp, and she shut her eyes, squeezing the wood tighter, which only made her hands ache.

After the pain eased, Iris opened the top drawer and pushed aside the nightgowns and undergarments until the letter was exposed. It was folded into thirds, the creases in the paper well defined from its life in the drawer.

Iris collapsed in the nearby chair of her vanity, the letter clasped in her hand. She kept it in her lap for a while, reluctant to read it. There was always trepidation when traveling into the past. It was like reopening a wound, knowing that she'd bleed when she did.

Slowly, Iris flipped open the first fold then the second, flattening out the paper as best she could. The words along the creases had become distorted, but she knew those lines by heart.

My Dearest Iris,

I'm afraid my attempts to reconcile with my brother have failed. He no longer wishes to have any contact from me, and I believe that the last few letters I've written have been either thrown away or burned before they were even opened.

I tried phoning a few times, as you know, but Christopher has hardened his resolve to deny me even a few words or a hello. But my time is running short, and if I am unable to convince him to come home then he will die.

As you know, I was never able to have children, and now I'm afraid of the future of my family and my soul.

I know now that you are in full knowledge of the Bell family history, and the shame that comes with it. And I also know that you understand what happens should I die and no one else is here to manage our family's situation.

It will come for Christopher, Iris. Despite his attempts at renouncing his name and his titles, he cannot renounce his blood. Your husband will die, painfully, and then it will attack your children, who share his blood too. It won't stop until we've all died. But if you can convince Christopher to come home, I've developed a plan. A way to save our family, to save our children. To save our souls.

If you love him, bring him back. Do whatever is necessary. I know what I ask is difficult, but his life, and the lives of your children, will depend upon it.

Sincerely,

Tobias Bell

Iris reread the letter a few times, and as she did, she was transported back to the small kitchen table at her and Christopher's home in Virginia. And just like the first time she'd read it, purpose flooded through her veins. Because she knew that if she failed, the souls of her children, her grandchildren, and her husband would be lost; consumed by the devil himself.

"Grandmother?"

"Huh?"

Kegan stood in front of her, the medication gripped in his outstretched hand. He lowered the medication and then dropped to one knee, taking Iris's hand into his own. "What's wrong?"

Unable to hold back the tears any longer, Iris let them fall. "You look so much like your mother, you know?" She smiled and then placed her hand on his cheek. It was warm, smooth.

"But you've always acted more like your father." The thought of her daughter triggered another round of tears. "They would have been so proud of you."

Kegan's face softened, his expression worried, as he placed his hand on top of his grandmother's. "What's wrong?"

"Nothing, my dear," Iris answered, drawing in a breath that helped revive her strength. She took the pills from him and then reached for the glass of water on the table beside her. She plucked two pills from the bottle and washed them down. Finished, she patted Kegan on the shoulder. "Everything is perfectly fine."

"All right." Kegan still looked worried but offered Iris's hand a reassuring squeeze and suddenly looked tired. "I'm going to bed to try and catch a few hours of sleep before morning. If Dennis comes back or something happens, will you wake me?"

Iris smiled, her face wrinkling into a raisin. "Of course."

And with the reassurances from the matriarch, Iris watched Kegan relax as he left the room. He did look tired. She knew he was worried. It had been the reason he'd come back home in the first place. That and because she had asked him to.

While Iris was confident in her ability to finally end this terror that had torn apart her family and taken the life of her daughter and husband, she couldn't be sure that her own life wouldn't give out before it was finished. And if she died, it would fall to Kegan to finish it. But she hoped it wouldn't come to that. Because as much as she loved her grandson, he knew that he wasn't like her. He wasn't a murderer.

Iris fidgeted in the chair uncomfortably, her old bones tired. She was always tired. Sleep eluded her, and most of the night was spent tossing and turning in her bed, hoping to avoid the nightmares just waiting for her on the other side of consciousness.

No, not nightmares. They implied that the images she saw weren't real. They were premonitions, visions of the future, past, and present. And they were gruesome sights.

She relived that violence and death had been her family's legacy since Allister Bell settled this land and built this house.

The puppet strings that had controlled her family for generations had left Iris with little wiggle room. But she was so close to the scissors that would cut her and her family free. She just had to keep pushing toward the light at the end of the tunnel.

Iris had never been proud of the Bell family, but like most children who had grown up in her era, she believed a sense of duty was rooted in family, because before the age of high-speed internet and cell phones, people had been forced to get to know the people they spent most of their time around, which was family.

And while she took no joy in luring the unsuspecting souls into her home, there was no other way for her to save her family. Besides, they were loners, drifters with no other place to go. At least here their lives and deaths served a purpose.

The pain in her right leg returned, and Iris winced as she gingerly massaged her calf. A vicious spat of hacking and coughing came next, and she wiped away the bloody phlegm on a nearby white doily that she clenched in her fist. It was rare that she went more than a few hours without some ailment flaring up, and at her age, there was no shortage of options for her body to pick.

It was duty that kept her going, and the knowledge of what would happen to her should she die before the curse was lifted. Still, the void beyond called to her every day, taunting her to let go.

And every day, she was forced to tell the void no. Because as much as she loved Kegan, she knew that he wouldn't be able to finish the job. The boy lacked that malicious instinct that so many Bells had possessed. Iris hadn't been born with it either, but she had adopted it, and it had consumed her life.

Family, Iris thought. She turned to the picture frames on the table, three of the photographs of her family with one face scratched out.

Iris straightened in her chair and opened her eyes, blinking to try and rid herself of the fog of sleep. After a few moments of concentrated effort, a ray of clarity returned, and those doubts disappeared.

"One more," Iris said, repeating it to herself like a mantra.

She had known that this last girl would be difficult, but she had failed to calculate just how troublesome she would become.

The farther Sarah wandered from Bell, the worse her condition would become. The outside world would start its assault on her body and her senses and her soul. It would drive her mad, willing her to return to the house, where she would find peace. And in that peace, her death would grant Iris's family their freedom.

16

_____

*S*arah kept her eyes shut tight. She focused all of her attention on the mansion, on being inside. She took slow, deep breaths, breathing in through her nose and out through her mouth.

After a minute, her mind calmed, and she heard the chatter of the forest to her left. The wind blew quickly across the surface of her ears, whistling as it passed. The muscles along her arms and shoulders relaxed. Her palms no longer stung from the cold of the ground.

Sarah envisioned the room she had been in before. She detailed the paintings on the wall, the yellow bedspread, and the crocheted lilies on the pillows on the bed. She suddenly felt warmer, and she knew she was getting close.

She recreated the floorboards, the wood stiff and warm against her skin. Candlelight flickered against the thin skin of her closed eyelids, the flames wiggling back and forth and shifting the shadows along the room.

A quick tug at her waist and Sarah gasped, but when she opened her eyes, she was no longer outside. She'd done it. She'd projected herself into the house.

She smiled, pushing herself off the floor, and glanced around at the room. It was exactly how it had been before, every detail. She paused, waiting for the redhead to return, but after a few moments in the room alone, Sarah knew that she wasn't going to come.

But then as Sarah stepped toward the door, ready to press through the walls, she realized that there was something different.

The candles. The last time she had been transported into the house, it had been daylight outside, which meant... what? She was in a different time period? The redhead had told her that all of the souls were stuck in the time during which they had been killed, so they only saw the house as it had been when they lived.

So since it was night outside, this couldn't have been the redhead's version of the house. But if it wasn't hers, then whose was it?

Sarah stepped into the hallway, finding more candles lit along the hall, though the light did little to improve the dreary nature of the surroundings. And just as Sarah was about to head down the hall to the staircase, she stopped herself.

The chair she'd seen in the hallway was no longer vibrant and new. The green and gold had faded, and the tear was visible down the middle of the seat. She reached out her hand, tracing her fingertip over the cut, hovering just above the cloth so her hand didn't pass through it.

Sarah frowned and then examined the rest of the hall, noticing details she remembered from working here. If the first time she had projected herself was among the company of one of the dead, then she must have been a part of their world. But since she had projected alone this time, that meant that she was in her version of the house.

Unsure of how much time she had, Sarah hurried toward

the stairs, rocketing up toward the fifth floor, remembering the orb that the redhead had told her was hidden in the house. And after Iris's lecture to never go on the fifth floor, Sarah was betting that was where it was hidden.

Sarah reached the top of the stairs quickly, then glided through the door and toward the last room on the left where she again passed through, smiling at her own efficiency.

The room was just how she remembered it, and she started her search. While she scoured the room, she found that the only downside to her projection powers were her inability to pick anything up. If a picture or letter or object was face down, she couldn't turn it over.

But after searching the room top to bottom, Sarah found nothing.

She checked every other room on the floor, peering through every wall and door. She checked closets and bathrooms. She poked her head through cabinets and chests and drawers. And after her methodical, grid-like check of the fifth floor, she was still empty-handed.

Sarah descended to the fourth floor to begin her search of the rest of the house. She passed through the rooms, looking for anything orb like, but finding nothing of the like aside from a few marbles in bowls.

She passed through room after room after room, and then finally stopped, gasping and covering her mouth from the noise.

Iris sat asleep in a chair near her vanity. Void of any make-up, she looked incredibly frail.

Circling the room, Sarah eventually made it to the vanity where Iris slept, and behind her Sarah saw the opened letter. She leaned closer, examining the letter beneath the candlelight that still flickered nearby.

When she finished, Sarah looked back at the old woman and frowned. "So you did come back to try and save your family." But then Sarah remembered about what happened to Kegan's parents, how they died. So what did the old woman do? Just save herself? The thought angered her.

What kind of a mother saved herself over her own children? But Sarah knew the answer to that question. She had experienced it repeatedly in the foster system. Women collecting children for the check, for tax deductions, to fill some void in their life.

In all of Sarah's experiences with foster mothers, Sarah never felt like she was there to be helped. It always felt like she was there to help the women. And despite her efforts, Sarah failed every single time.

Knowing that the old woman couldn't hear her, Sarah leaned close to Iris's ear, her lips just a breath away from touching Iris's skin.

"I want you to know that you deserve everything that happens to you," Sarah said. "For all the people you hurt, and tried to hurt, just to save your own skin."

But when Sarah leaned back, she wasn't sure if she was really addressing the old woman, or if she was talking to herself.

After all, Sarah had went on the run to save her own skin. And she wasn't searching for the orb to save the redhead, or avenge Maggie's sacrifice. She was here for one reason only: to save herself.

The thought sickened her, and Sarah turned to leave, but then stopped when she reached the door. She spun back around and looked at Iris, her eyes falling to the wooden sphere around her neck.

Iris always wore it, and the longer Sarah stared at it the more she frowned. "It moves, but is always in the same place." Her eyes widened in shock. "The orb!"

But just as Sarah lunged for Iris, stretching out her hand, she felt a tug at her waist, and everything went black.

After a moment of being lost in the darkness, Sarah suddenly realized that she was outside, her head aching as she lay on her back on the grass. She blinked, trying to rid herself of the black spots that plagued her vision. She propped herself up on her elbow and caught a glimpse of the mansion just before she turned around to find Brent hovering over her.

"Hello, sweetheart. Did you miss me?" Brent smiled.

A scream began to crawl from the back of her throat, but it was cut short by the harsh crack of a pistol against her face.

The pain was sharp and hot. Blood trickled down from the wound, casting a brilliant streak of red against her pale skin. Hands groped her neck and shoulders, and she was yanked from the ground, too disoriented to fight back but still conscious enough to see Pat lying motionless on his back.

"Pat? Oh my god, Pat?" Sarah wiggled herself free, scrambling toward the old barkeep who lay lifeless on the ground.

Pat had pressed both hands to his bloodied stomach, his body trembling. Blood pooled in his mouth and he locked eyes with Sarah before he spoke, his voice raspy and tired. "Sarah."

"It's okay," Sarah said, starting to cry. "Everything's going to be all right."

Sarah pressed her ear to his nose to check his breathing, but it was so cold outside that she couldn't feel if there were any breaths or not. Pat grabbed hold of her arm, transferring bloody prints to her jacket. His eyes were wide, the white turning the same shade of red as the blood welling up from his gut.

"I didn't know you two were so well acquainted," Brent said, walking over to hover over Sarah's back. "Well, say goodbye."

Sarah turned. "No, wait!"

The gunshot cut through the night air fast and hard. A high-pitched whine in Sarah's ears deafened her to her own screams as she turned back around to find Pat's face blown away.

"Get up!" Brent yanked her by the collar, lifting her completely off the ground with one hand, and dragged her, kicking and screaming, toward the road.

"NO!" Sarah wriggled and punched at Brent's arm, but the defiance ended when he placed the end of his pistol against her forehead.

"Move again and I'll blow your brains out across the snow," Brent said, his voice spitting anger against her cheek. "And then you can be just like your little friend over there."

With her face still turned in the opposite direction, Sarah glanced at Brent from the corner of her eye. She hated that she couldn't stop shaking, she hated that he had found her, but what she hated even more was the hope that she had allowed herself to believe that she could escape his reach.

"You didn't have to come here," Sarah said, this time forcing her gaze into Brent's eyes. "I'm not a threat."

Brent laughed. "Not in the way you think, sweetheart, no." He readjusted the grip on his pistol and flicked the end of it toward the road. "Get moving, honey."

Sarah turned back to Pat one last time.

Brent raised the pistol and pressed it against her forehead with his finger on the trigger. But she didn't turn away this time. She faced him, stiffening in courage.

"You want to kill me?" Sarah asked. "Then just fucking do it. C'mon." She taunted him, leaning into the revolver's barrel. "Do it!"

He paused as if he was going to pull the trigger, but he only laughed. "Son of a bitch." He lowered the revolver. "I really wish I could, sweetheart, but I can't. You've made a lot of trouble for me, and now I'm going to have to take you back to New York, so let's go."

Brent picked her up by force, and Sarah screamed, crying and fighting back as hard as she could, but it was no use. He was too big, and she was too tired. He tossed her into the GTO like a rag doll, and was cried out by the time he zip-tied her wrists together, then put on her seatbelt.

He climbed into the driver's seat and started the car. "You know, you had me fooled." Brent laughed, shaking his head. "But you're all kinds of fucked up in the head, aren't you?" He nodded. "Yeah, you are." He leaned closer, his lips barely touching her ear, his voice tickling her skin. "And I know that from all that crazy shit you liked to do in bed."

Brent kissed her ear, and Sarah slammed the side of her skull into his face. The harsh crack of bone against bone caused both of them to wince, and Sarah opened her eyes just in time to see the backhand coming toward her face.

Brent's heavy knuckles pounded her mouth, smashing the thin cushion of her lips against her teeth and knocking her entire body toward the window.

"Dumb bitch!"

The curse was followed by the pressure of a pistol to the back of her skull, and Brent used it to jam her face up against the window.

"I told you no funny business!"

Sarah struggled for breath with her face pressed against the glass, her mouth numb. More pressure was applied to the back of her head, and then with one final push, it ended. Brent settled behind the wheel, and Bell faded into the rearview mirror.

Head throbbing, Sarah gently sat back in the seat. The GTO's engine hummed loudly, the pistons firing on all cylinders as the muscle car's tires chewed up the road ahead on their way back to New York City.

"I won't make it," Sarah said, her head gently swaying left and right with the curves of the highway. She stared at the exit for Redford, watching the sign grow smaller in the rearview mirror until it was completely gone.

"Bit of a pessimistic outlook, don't you think?" Brent asked, smiling. "I'm not gonna kill you, Sarah. If I wanted to that, I would have just done it back in town." He shook his head. "No, I need you alive to take the fall for me."

"I'm not going to do that," Sarah said.

"If you want what's left of your friends in New York to survive, you will," Brent replied, his tongue sharp and forceful. "How many deaths do you want on your conscience, huh? Three? Four?" He shook his head. "I can keep piling them up for you, Sarah. Stack 'em as high as the fuckin' Empire State Building."

Sarah's eyes watered as she wondered who he'd already killed. At least half a dozen names scrolled through her mind, all of them good people. She had no doubt that he'd killed at least one of them, probably Moss or Cassie. She hoped they hadn't suffered.

When the first tear fell, Sarah turned her face away so Brent wouldn't see, but she couldn't hide her reflection in the mirror.

Brent started laughing. "Oh, don't be sad, sweetheart. Listen, I'll tell you what." He inched closer, keeping his left hand on the wheel while he rested his elbow on the center console. "When we get back to the city, I'll arrange a quick little meet for you at the graveyard so you can say your good-byes before they lock you away and throw away the key."

More gut-bursting laughter rolled off of Brent's tongue, lashing her ears with a wicked laugh that echoed through her mind. But the laughter faded, and Sarah's stomach churned sourly. Beads of sweat broke out on her forehead. It was happening.

Sarah flung her back against the car seat and shut her eyes, her muscles starting to tremble as she gritted her teeth in pain. "GRAAAHHHHH!"

"Hey!" Brent said, ending his laughter and leaning away from Sarah. "Knock it off!" He placed one hand on his pistol. "I said—"

But Sarah thrashed back and forth, the pain reemerging in her leg as she reached for her jeans with her bound hands. The burning sensation crawled up her thigh, the pain growing more intense with every passing second.

"Calm down!" Brent backhanded Sarah once more, this time striking the center of her nose.

The force of the blow should have knocked her into unconsciousness, but the pain crawling up her leg made the blow feel like nothing more than a light breeze against her cheek.

In retaliation, Sarah flung herself into Brent, grabbing hold of the wheel and turning it hard.

The world immediately spun, tires screeching, and centrifugal force flung Sarah back into her seat. She cracked her head against the glass, which shattered, and the last thing that Sarah remembered before she blacked out was watching the road pass beneath her, the world upside down, and a loud crunch when the car rolled into the ditch on the side of the road.

17

The moment Dell was out of Bell, he floored the gas pedal. The cruiser sped down the two-lane highway, lights flashing red and blue against the backdrop of the forest.

Dell gripped the steering wheel tightly, his vision focused on only the road ahead. A sense of urgency flooded through him, and while the consequences of failing to obtain a cure for Sarah had gone unsaid, he understood them perfectly clear. If the doctor couldn't cure her, she'd die. But when that would happen and how long it would take, Dell had no idea.

And what was more was how the idea of Sarah's death affected him. It was a thought he refused to let fester in his consciousness. But despite his efforts, he couldn't shake it. And he wasn't sure what to make of that.

Sarah wasn't exactly his type. She was pretty, of course, but there was a reckless danger to her that clashed against his own ideals. Not to mention she was stubborn and seemed to find trouble wherever she went. Not exactly a "bring her home to Mom" kind of girl.

And still, Dell couldn't get her out of his mind.

Once he was west of Redford and onto the mountainous dirt roads, Dell's GPS lost its signal. Luckily, he had a vague remembrance of the doctor's location. There was a lookout point in the same area where high school kids would go on dates. It was a popular destination for kids to lose their virginity. It was where Dell had taken his high school girlfriend. He was sixteen and she was fifteen. It was hard to believe he was ever that young. And even harder to believe he was ever that scared.

Maybe it was the fact that he was returning to a place where innocence was lost, but those same nerves returned to him on the dirt road, and it didn't take long for a layer of cold sweat to accumulate beneath his uniform.

The cruiser's shocks were tested on the rocky road, and Dell was tossed left and right behind the wheel like a rag doll as he kept his eyes peeled for any sudden turns. Northern Maine's back roads had claimed more tourists than Dell could count, and a few drunk locals. The moon and stars being covered by a thick blanket of clouds only made the night darker.

Headlights flashed on a small road sign, barely two feet off the ground, and Dell slammed on his brakes, the cruiser sliding forward in the gravel. Dell leaned across his center console and squinted to make out the sign's text.

Black paint had been used in the lettering, and the wooden plank that it had been written on had faded to a dull gray, making it unreadable from inside the car. So Dell unbuckled his seatbelt and stepped out.

With the headlights from the cruiser illuminating his path, Dell dropped to a knee in front of the sign and wiped away some of the crud that had collected over the wood's surface. Beneath it, he found the doctor's address.

Dell looked down the road that the sign marked and found that its path was even narrower and less maintained than the dirt road behind him.

Back in the car, Dell reversed a few feet and then carefully turned down the narrow path, which climbed upward on a steep incline. The cruiser's tires slipped multiple times on the way up, the seatbelt over Dell's chest tightening with every jerk, and twice the decline backward nearly resulted in contact with one of the thick maples that lined the road. But Dell maintained a slow and steady pace, and eventually the gravel gave way to more compacted dirt, which allowed for a smoother ride.

Maintaining a crawling pace forward, Dell kept his eyes peeled for any other signs or roads that veered off his path. But the longer he drove up the hillside and through the forest the more his confidence shrank.

The address Faye had pulled from the system was three years old, which meant that the doctor could have moved somewhere else. It wasn't uncommon for the elderly to flock south, selling off everything they owned, and disappear to warmer weather without notifying the appropriate agencies of their departure. It was an easy way for them to avoid certain tax payments.

A lot of them also rented out their houses through the winter and fall to tourists, which helped pay for their tiny beach condos down in Florida. So the possibility that Dell was about to walk into a winter-break holiday party with a house crammed full with wasted college kids was just as likely as waking up an old man from his bed in the dead of night.

The rough path continued for another mile, and just when Dell was about to find a spot to turn around, he saw a break in the path ahead, and beyond that break was a shimmer of taillights.

Dell breathed a sigh of relief when he saw that the truck was parked at the end of a long drive, blocking the path toward a small cottage nestled quaintly in a grove of trees.

With no sign of a family or college kids inhabiting the place, Dell parked his cruiser directly behind the truck in the long drive.

Dell's vision adjusted to the darkness, the features of the forest taking shape as he scanned his surroundings on the walk toward the front door.

Leaves rustled from a steady breeze coming down from the northwest. The cold stiffened Dell's movements. He kept one hand on his service pistol, the strap over the handle already unbuckled in case he needed to draw quickly.

The windows of the cottage were darkened, and the closer Dell moved toward the house, the more he saw its age and imperfections. The rain gutters were clogged and overflowing with leaves, and the small plot of land that had been cleared in the trees was overgrown with grass and weeds.

A three-foot-high, rusted iron fence surrounded the house, a lattice with dying ivy leaves crawling over it acting as a sort of bridged entrance. The gate's hinges groaned as Dell entered, and a few critters scattered from the untouched landscape.

The grass was so overgrown that there wasn't even a worn path from the gate to the front door. He approached warily and checked the window to the left of the door. The view was limited, the interior even darker than outside.

Unsure if anyone was even home, Dell pounded his fist on the door, rattling the old wood and ending the quaint silence of the forest. "Doctor Wagner, Redford Police Department. Open up!"

Dell waited for a response or the flick of a light but saw no movement inside the house. He peered through the window again, hoping to see an elderly figure heading his way, but there was nothing. He pounded on the door again.

"Doctor Wagner, this is Deputy Dell Parker with the Redford Sheriff's Department!" With his hand still on the handle of his service pistol, he stepped back, examining the sides of the house, and then looked back toward the truck down the worn drive.

Dell pounded again. "Doctor Wag—"

A light flicked on, and mumbled groans penetrated the sleepy, sagging walls of the cottage, followed by the noisy turn of the lock. The door opened only a crack, and Dell stepped back when he saw that he was staring down the barrel of a twelve-gauge shotgun, held by an old man with a walker standing in front of him.

"What do you want?" Doctor Wagner asked, his expression a snarl ensnared by hundreds of wrinkles that puckered his face like a raisin.

Dell slowly raised his hands, knowing the old man's bark was worse than his bite. "I'm Deputy Dell—"

"I already heard that," Doctor Wagner spat from behind the crack of his door. "I'm old and immobile, not deaf and dumb. What do you want?"

Dell stared at the shotgun. "Do you mind lowering the weapon, sir?"

Wagner grunted and reluctantly complied with the request. He opened the door and set the shotgun in the corner near the entrance, both hands now gripping a silver walker that looked as fragile as the man who used it for support.

"Thank you," Dell answered. "May I come inside?"

"Fine." Wagner spun around, shuffling toward the kitchen as Dell entered the foyer. "I was finally drifting off to sleep when you started pounding on my door!" He flicked on a light as he entered the kitchen, Dell watching him through the tiny cutout in the wall overlooking the sink. "You know how difficult it is to get rest at my age? Might as well try and run up this mountain in my bare feet, that's how impossible. So whatever ended my chance at some peace and rest better be good."

Dell shut the door behind him, examining the bare-bones interior of the living room. A single reclining chair with a tabletop next to it was positioned directly in front of a television that had to have been more than thirty years old. The face of the box still had dials on it, and a pair of rabbit ears stuck out the back, sagging like everything else in the house.

A few pictures lined the walls, and Dell spotted one of a young woman, the picture black and white, but even the lack of color couldn't hide her beauty.

"My wife," Wagner said, reappearing from the kitchen without a sound, his tone gentler than his earlier greeting. "God rest her soul. Passed away for nearly ten years now, and I still can't figure out what the hell the bastard is keeping us apart for. I was ready to go when she did, but—" He shrugged and shuffled toward the recliner. "Here I am."

Wagner transitioned from the walker to the recliner with a practiced motion, though it still took some time. Dell nearly asked if the old man needed help but thought better of it. The elderly didn't need reminding of their own frailty. They lived with it every day.

"Doctor Wagner—"

"I haven't practiced medicine for over thirty years," he said. "Mister will do just fine."

"Mister Wagner," Dell said. "I'm here because of a patient you treated back in the early eighties."

Wagner laughed, folding his swollen, arthritic, liver-spotted hands. "Deputy, do you have any idea how many patients I've had over the years?"

Without any other place to sit, Dell stood, arms crossed. "But you only had one case that made headlines."

Wagner sank deeper into the back of his chair, the already sagging features of his face slackening. He nodded, his jowls wobbling like a turkey neck. "No, I don't remember that." He worked his fingers over one another, wincing from the arthritis, and lowered his head, the lamp to his right illuminating half his face while casting the rest into darkness.

"The patient was Iris Bell," Dell continued, knowing that the doctor was lying. "She had a rare infection spreading up her leg." He stepped closer. "You were reported as saying that it was a new disease."

"Which the Maine medical board denied and nearly voted to suspend my license to practice medicine," Wagner replied.

"So you do remember the case," Dell said.

Wagner kept his head down, still fumbling with his fingers as he fidgeted uncomfortably in his seat. "I have always prided myself on being a man of science and reason. I've never believed in legends and myths, though I must concede that I am not above the fear of evil." He lifted his eyes to meet Dell's. "Of true evil."

"That infection you treated," Dell said. "Another person has come down with it, and she needs your help."

Wagner remained seated, staring at Dell with curiosity and a healthy dose of skepticism. A smile crept up the left side of his face, triggering a ripple of wrinkles that faded into his balding scalp. "That's not possible."

"It is." Dell reached into his jacket and removed the article they'd found in Pat's trunk. "Everything that you describe in that article is happening to another woman."

Wagner examined the article, the paper as brittle as the trembling pair of hands that held it. After a moment, he set it aside, head still down, and only nodded to himself but said nothing.

"Doctor Wagner," Dell said, his tone growing impatient. "I need you to come with me so you can fix this woman like you did Iris Bell."

Wagner shook his head, finally looking up from his lap. "You don't understand, boy." He tightened his hands into fists and pounded the armrests of his chair. "Whatever's happened to this woman is beyond my help."

Dell shook his head. "But you said in the article—"

"I know what I said." Wagner dismissively waved his hands toward Dell, the gesture meant to shoo him away. "I was there. I think I would remember what I said." He rolled his eyes around, which were the only sharp thing left about him besides perhaps his mind. "The article doesn't tell the whole story."

Dell snatched the article from his lap then shoved it in the old man's face. "You said you cured it! You even brought it to the Maine medical board!"

"To advance my career!" Wagner barked back. "Do you have any idea what the mundane life of a family physician in this tiny little town was like? I studied at Johns Hopkins under some of the best minds in the field. I could have gone anywhere, but I got a woman pregnant who happened to live in this godforsaken town, and back in my day, when you did something like that you had to take responsibility!"

Spittle fell onto his chin, and he hastily wiped it away.

"Why did you lie?"

"The kind of attention a new disease receives can put its discoverer on the map." Wagner held out his hand, extending an arthritic finger for every disease that he ticked off. "Polio, malaria, hepatitis, all of them global killers with the potential to bring humanity to its knees. And each of them with a mind behind the cure that made them famous. Rich." He pressed his finger into his chest. "I could have been one of those people. But I stayed here to be with my wife and my son. Instead of greatness, I had a family." He grimaced as if something sour had touched his tongue.

"Then how is Iris Bell still alive?" Dell asked.

Wagner shrugged and exhaled a breath that rattled his bones. "She cured herself."

Dell stepped backward, the uniform growing tight beneath his chest and constricting his movements. "Oh my god."

"You and I both know the extraordinary circumstances that have surrounded that family over the years. And I know most of it is hearsay, but you can't deny the number of Bells that have succumbed to early graves. When I saw those… scales crawling up Iris Bell's leg, I was sure I'd found the truth behind the myths. But I ran every test available to me at the time, and I can tell you without a trace of doubt in my head that there was nothing medically wrong with that woman. Blood work, heart rate, all her vitals were normal, and yet there were those things just staring me in the face, taunting me." He scoffed, shaking his head. "The board said I was trying to make trouble over a bad case of the shingles. But you and I both know better, don't we, Deputy?"

"How did she do it?" Dell asked. "How did she cure herself?"

Wagner smiled as he stared at Dell. "You'd have to ask Iris Bell."

The moment Dell was out of the woods and off the dirt road, he hit the lights and the siren. He knew both were redundant, but he needed something to help focus the rush of adrenaline coursing through his veins.

Both hands on the wheel, Dell tightened his grip until his knuckles flashed white and he thought he was going to break the steering wheel in half. The engine roared, the speedometer ticking up past seventy, eighty, and then ninety miles an hour.

"Dell, you there?"

Dell picked up the receiver. "I'm here, Faye."

"Listen, the sheriff just called me and told me that the judge approved the warrant, and that the troopers are on their way to Bell, probably thirty minutes out."

"Perfect," Dell said, relieved at the good news.

"I also got some more information about those Bell family members."

"Go ahead."

"Turns out their medical records all listed the same type of death as hypothermia or frostbite. There were even a few special notes about how odd the afflictions were, but they all occurred during the winter."

Dell kept his thumb off the receiver. "Son of a bitch."

"I also got some information back on that Brent Alvarez. He's mid-thirties, black hair, brown eyes, around six feet tall. He has a 1968 Pontiac GTO Judge registered with New York State. Still haven't been able to track him down though."

Dell hugged the curves of the highway, his headlights illuminating a clear path ahead. When he came around a left-leaning bend, he saw the two beams of light shooting up from the ditch on the right side of the road, penetrating the darkness.

Dell slowed, pulling his cruiser off to the side of the road, eyes widening in horror as he gazed upon the wreckage of the smashed GTO in the ditch. He flung the door open before he even put the cruiser in park. "Shit. He's here, Faye."

"What?"

Dell quickly fiddled with his seatbelt. "Send backup to a wreck heading southbound on the highway one mile past Redford. Suspect is a one Brent Alvarez."

"Copy that," Faye replied.

The blue and red lights from the cruiser highlighted the twisted and crumpled metal chassis of the muscle car. The roof and side doors had been caved inward, most likely from a roll down the berm. The windows had shattered, turning the clear glass into frosty panes of white.

Dell removed his flashlight and then his weapon, unsure of what he would be walking into. The driver's side door was open, so he flashed his light into the cabin but found it empty.

He was just about to turn away when his light caught a jacket in the passenger seat. The light green was familiar, and he grabbed it. It was a Carhartt jacket. Sarah's jacket.

"Sarah!" Dell shouted then stepped toward the tree line, raising his gun and flashlight. The beam of light passed over a group of trees, illuminating the broken paths that led into the forest.

Dell dropped the beam to the ground, heading toward the trunk of the flipped GTO. He searched the ground, hoping to find footprints. A flash of red caught his attention as he passed over the grass. He jerked the light back over the area and knelt.

Blood droplets lingered on the dead blades of grass like dew. Slowly, Dell followed the droplets along the ground, using the flashlight to help guide him through the forest. He switched between flashing the light on the ground and up ahead. He grew more worried as the bloodstains grew larger, becoming red streaks smearing across the ground.

Dell hastened his pace, weaving between the trees, sweat collecting beneath his uniform. And just when he thought he'd taken a wrong turn, a gunshot echoed through the forest. Dell scurried for cover, the bullet zipping past his head and splintering the tree trunk.

He flicked off his light and ducked behind the fattest tree trunk that he could find. Both hands clasped on the pistol, and when the barrage of gunfire ended, Dell slowly craned his head around the trunk.

A high-pitched whine deafened him to the breeze drifting through what leaves remained on the trees above. He squinted, spotting no movement ahead, and then tucked himself back behind the tree. "If you're heading west, you'll find nothing but forest all the way to Quebec." He inched closer back toward the tree's edge. "And it's only going to get colder, so unless you're carrying shelter with you, you'll freeze to death." Still no movement in the darkness from the gunshot's origins, not even a sound. "Put the gun down, come out with your hands in the air."

The ringing in Dell's ears slowly faded, and he spun around to the other side of the tree, trying to get a different perspective, but still saw nothing ahead but darkness.

"I think you're forgetting about the ace I have up my sleeve," a voice said, his voice sounding more distant than the previous gunshots. "She's unconscious right now, so I think putting a bullet through her skull wouldn't be very sporting of me. But all those big words sound a lot like a threat to me, so I'd be remiss if I didn't make my own."

Dell shut his eyes, cursing under his breath. He shouldn't have left them alone at the tavern. He should have waited for a highway trooper for backup or gotten George's ass out of bed or—

"So this is what's going to happen," he said, his voice a little closer now, which meant that he was moving toward Dell. If Sarah was unconscious, he'd left her alone somewhere. No way he could be moving that quietly while carrying her. "You're going to toss that gun on the ground, and you're going to come out with your hands in the air, and then we're going to talk like the pair of upstanding law enforcement officers we are. What do you think about that?"

The voice was coming from Dell's right, so he worked his way to the opposite side of the tree, standing straight up, the pistol still in his hands. "I say no."

The voice paused. "Well now, that's a real shame."

The air, the trees, time itself stopped cold as Dell waited for movement, for a sign of the man's position, all the while struggling to keep his thoughts in the present moment and not on Sarah's status.

A branch snapped to his left, and Dell spun in position to fire, only to be pushed backward by three gunshots that missed wide left and right, sending him running to the safety of another tree.

The man followed, the gunfire relentless, as Dell huddled behind the trunk. He waited for any break in the barrage of bullets, but they only grew more frequent.

A brief pause triggered Dell to spin around the opposite side of the tree, quick as he could, gun raised. When he cleared the tree trunk, Brent collided into Dell, knocking both men to the ground.

Their pistols were flung from their hands, the pair transforming into a blurred ball of hands, elbows, and legs as they rolled over the frozen and rocky terrain.

Dell was to his feet first and lunged, but Brent quickly spun around, arm reaching for his left hip, from where he drew a knife that he slashed with wildly. Dell pulled his hips back, watching the blade nearly skim across his uniform.

Brent stabbed forward, forcing Dell to retreat, his boots scraping against the frozen ground, until Dell's heel hit something metal. When Brent dropped his eyes, Dell did as well, and both spotted the pistol in the grass.

Brent stumbled back, and Dell charged. He worked the body, two quick punches to both sides of the ribs, and then delivered a thundering right cross to Brent's face that spun him around and knocked him to the ground.

Both men rolled, hands clamoring through the frozen and dead foliage, fingers twisting over the deadly weapon. Shoulder to shoulder, their cheeks reddened. Dell had his fingers on the handle, while Brent had his fingers wrapped over the barrel and a portion of the trigger.

Dell head butted Brent, loosening the detective's grip. Dell yanked the weapon free and then jumped to his feet, his vision blurred and his forehead bleeding from the fight. "Don't move." He wobbled on two feet, gun aimed at Brent's head. "Where is she?" He panted, watching Brent rise to his knees, blood streaming down his smiling face, which only made Dell's anger boil over. He lunged forward, pressing the gun against Brent's forehead and gripping the collar of his shirt. "I said, where is she!?"

"What happens when you find out she's already dead?" Brent asked, a smile creeping up his face. "You wander out into the darkness, and your foot catches on her arm, and you find her face down in the frozen dirt, blood already congealed around the body and the life drained from those pretty little eyes." He wobbled back and forth, clearly disoriented from the blows. "You know how many guys she's made have that same look on their face that you're wearing right now?" He laughed. "She managed to wrap you around her little finger, and you couldn't care less."

Dell pulled the hammer back on the pistol, and all of that rage and adrenaline and fear focused to the pinpoint accuracy of the sight on the gun. "You didn't kill her. You wouldn't have run out here if you had, so where is she?"

"Your guess is as good as mine, amigo," Brent said. "I woke up in the ditch back there with my car wrecked, and I saw blood traces leading into the forest."

Dell grimaced and then let go of Brent's collar and reached around for his handcuffs, keeping the pistol trained on Brent's head. "Turn around."

The cuffs clicked into place, and Brent winced when Dell tightened them and then shoved him toward the road.

The red and blue of the flashing lights acted as a lighthouse of sorts, a beacon guiding him home. Dell shoved Brent into the back of the squad car and put the guy's revolver in his glove box, then took one last look at the wrecked GTO and the darkened forest. "Where did you go?"

18

*S*arah stumbled through the woods like a zombie, nothing on her mind but getting back to Bell. It was a primal instinct, one that she knew was fed by the icy scales on her leg.

It was in the darkness that filled the night. It was an inaudible whisper that tickled the hairs on the back of her neck. All of it was leading her back to Bell, back to the house.

In a fit of exhaustion, she collapsed to the ground, rolling to her side, her breaths shallow and quick as she stared up at the night sky.

Barren tree branches twisted up and outward against the starry night sky. She caught her breath and thought how beautiful the night would have been if it weren't for the circumstances. But that had been the story of Sarah's life. A series of unfortunate events, that had accumulated to bring her life to an end before she had ever had an opportunity for real happiness. For real peace.

Sarah closed her eyes, her arms spread out at awkward angles, and all she wanted to do was sleep, to just melt into the earth where she lay. But she couldn't.

Sarah stood and, like before, the farther she walked and the closer she drew herself to the town, the better she felt. Twice she stopped to check her waistline to see if the scales had started to spread and watched the frost blue shimmer beneath the moonlight.

"It's getting worse."

Sarah spun around, finding the redhead floating nearby. "I don't have time for you." She trudged forward, traveling through the maze of trees. She figured she was close to the house now that the redhead had returned.

"You're running out of time," the redhead replied, floating next to her.

"I know." Sarah kept her tone short, but the frustration mounted, and she whirled on the ghost. "Where the hell have you been?" The redheaded girl cringed as she backed away. "Do you have any idea what's happening? Pat's dead!"

"I'm sorry." The apparition lowered her head and turned away. "I was afraid to show you."

Sarah stomped around to the girl's left and saw what looked like tears running down her cheeks. But with the translucent nature of her body, the tears looked like crystals that sparkled in the darkness. Never had grief looked so beautiful.

The redhead wiped away the diamonds from her eyes and straightened her posture. "It's time for you to see."

"See what?"

"To see why this all started."

Sarah frowned, and then that familiar tug yanked at her waist, and the world around her went dark. The floating sensation returned, and after a moment, Sarah blinked, her surroundings transformed back to the same room and time she had been in before.

But this time, after Sarah dropped to her knees and

cradled her head, a cramp formed in the pit of her stomach. "What's… happening?"

Redhead appeared through the floor beneath Sarah's face and stared straight into her eyes. "The spirit's control over you is growing." She pointed to the leg on which the scales had crawled up past her waist and onto her stomach. "It can feel you getting closer."

Slowly, Sarah lowered her hands and stood, trying to focus on anything but the splitting pain running down the center of her skull. "Christ." A few deep breaths and the sickness became more manageable.

When Sarah felt a little better, she found the redhead at the door and then followed her upstairs, doing her best to stay upright on the upward spiral path.

"I won't be able to go inside with you once we're upstairs," the ghost said, keeping a few feet of distance between the two of them.

"Why?" Sarah asked, reaching for the rail as another bout of dizziness struck her. When her hand went straight through the wood, she nearly tumbled downward before quickly correcting herself.

Redhead frowned. "It's like the door is locked, and whatever… Happened inside—" She stopped abruptly and then turned around. "The thing that killed me, it doesn't want me to see it. And since I'm living in its house, I'm forced to follow its rules."

Once the pair passed through the door on the fifth floor, Redhead allowed Sarah to walk ahead, and when they reached the halfway point, she stopped completely. Sarah looked back at the girl, whose gaze was locked on the door at the end of the hall.

"You don't have to listen to it," Sarah said. "It doesn't have to control everything you do."

Redhead's mouth went slack, and she gently shook her

head. "No, whatever's on the other side of that door—" She swallowed. "I just can't see."

Sarah stepped closer. "Show it that you're not afraid. Show it that it can't frighten you."

The sunlight breaking through the window at the end of the hall dimmed, and Redhead floated backward, shaking her head. "I'm sorry, Sarah." Her voice trembled with fear, and she looked at Sarah one last time before disappearing through the door. "Good luck."

And just like that, she was gone, leaving Sarah alone in the hallway. She turned to face the end of the hall, the light fading as if it were being sucked from the sky itself.

The darkness swallowed shadows from the furniture and paintings as Sarah neared the door. She reached out her hand and her heart hammered in her chest. The closer she drew to crossing the barrier, the louder the noises grew on the other side.

They were muffled at first, but then they started to sound like sobbing, and just before her face went through the door, she was greeted with a shrieking cry of pain.

"AHHHHH!"

It was the redhead, except she was in bed, sheets up to her chest and wearing the nightgown that Sarah had seen her floating around in. And much like the ghost's, her living cheeks were a pale white, the color gone from her lips. But her hair was even more striking in person, the red so vibrant against the white of her skin and nightgown that it looked to be on fire.

Two people were in the room with her, a man on the left side of the bed and a woman on the right. At first glance, Sarah would have thought it was the girl's mother and father, but then the man removed a stethoscope from a briefcase, and she noticed the long white coat. He was a doctor.

"Mary, you need to keep still," the doctor said.

But the expressions of pain etched on redheaded woman's face shifted and squirmed with the rest of her.

"Keep her still!" The doctor barked the order across the bed to the woman, who sprang into action, grabbing the girl by the shoulders and pinning her back into the pillows.

"Mamma, make it stop!" Redhead—Mary—screamed, bucking her hips up and kicking her legs while her mother kept her upper body pinned to the sheets.

"We're trying, but you have to try and keep still!" The mother had a frantic anger to her words, the struggle of trying to maintain empathy while giving orders. And Sarah couldn't help but notice how familiar the tone sounded. The mother turned back to the doctor, her daughter continuing to flail. "Isn't there something you can give her?"

"I don't even know what's wrong with her." The doctor placed the stethoscope against the girl's chest and shook his head. "Her heart is racing. Mary, you need to calm down."

Sarah inched toward the bed, wanting a closer look, as the doctor and the mother continued to try and calm her down, and Sarah noticed that the girl was covered from the neck down, even wearing gloves. As she stared at the girl, she finally saw the first frosted scale appear on her neck.

"Oh my god," the mother said. She released her daughter and lunged across the bed and gripped the doctor by the throat. "Do something!"

But the doctor only shrugged, lifting his hands impotently in self-defense. "I don't know what's wrong with her. I'm sorry."

"Mother!" the redhead shrieked, stretching out her hand, which her mother quickly took. "I can feel it! I can feel all of it!" She yanked her mother closer to her face, the pair only inches apart, the frosted blue scales crawling up the girl's cheeks. "I'm so scared."

The mother cupped the scales forming around her

daughter's face, her voice thick with grief. "It's okay, baby, everything is going to be okay. I'll bring you back, okay? I'll find a way to bring you back!"

"Mamma?" Mary's eyes were covered, and the scales consumed the rest of her face as she belted out another piercing scream before the ice shattered into thousands of icy shards.

The doctor retreated against the wall, his cheeks ghostly pale, and the mother had her hands pressed into the sheets on the mattress.

"Iris?" the doctor asked, his voice sheepish as he kept his distance against the wall.

And then Sarah saw it as Iris fisted a handful of the sheets and slowly turned her head toward the doctor, her cheeks glowing a bright red. It was that same expression of disdain with which Iris had greeted Sarah upon her arrival to Bell.

"Get out," Iris answered, her voice a seething whisper.

The doctor pressed himself harder against the wall and started to shake, but he remained glued to the spot, frozen by fear and a mother's wrath.

"GET OUT!" Iris roared the order, and the doctor snapped into action, quickly grabbing his bag. He sprinted past Sarah and then out into the living room, his footsteps disappearing down the hall.

With the doctor gone, it was just Sarah and Iris alone in the room, and Iris returned her gaze to the bed where her daughter had just been. Sarah walked around to the other side of the bed so she could get a better look at Iris's face.

The old woman that Sarah had known had yet to arrive, but the pain and anger and bitterness were evident in her expression.

"You did this," Iris said, again producing that seething whisper. She lifted her face toward the ceiling and then stomped around the room, shaking her fists in the air. "I don't care how long it takes, and I don't care what I have to do, but I will get my daughter back from you." Her cheeks reddened, and that first shade of bitterness spread over her face. "Do you hear me?"

Iris ended the rant with a heavy stamp of her foot, and in the same motion, Sarah felt a tug at her chest that yanked her from the room and thrust her back outside as she collapsed to her hands and knees.

Sarah gasped for air, like she'd been choking. She hacked and coughed, and the pain in her head forced her to her side, but it was also accompanied by a queasiness in her stomach.

Bile crawled up her throat, and Sarah managed to turn her head just in time to vomit across the frozen ground. She heaved two more times before it stopped, and even then her stomach remained uneasy. She rolled to her back, too tired to put any distance between herself and the stench of her dissolved dinner from the day before.

"You saw me."

Sarah spun around, finding Mary. "You're Iris's daughter."

Mary scrunched her face in confusion as if Sarah had just spoken another language. "I think... I know that name." She nodded but still looked confused. "But I can't—" She shut her eyes hard, shaking her head, and then terror spread across her face. "I remember. The evil, consuming me." She shivered, and the red in her hair started to fade. "It's still calling me." She looked at Sarah. "My mother. She can help you."

"How?" Sarah asked.

"Tell her—GAH." Mary winced, her body trembling. She took a few breaths and regained her composure. "Tell her that the moon still shines." Another spout of pain crippled Mary, and in a panicked frenzy she gripped Sarah by the shoulders, her fingernails like ice picks digging into Sarah's flesh. "Help me!"

Sarah winced. "Mary, you're hurting me."

But Mary didn't let up the pressure; in fact, she pressed harder. "You have to help me!" she screamed, and Sarah shut her eyes, the noise more painful than the nails digging into her skin, and then Mary was gone.

Sarah spun around, but saw nothing but the night air, then felt a warm drizzle run from her nose. She swiped at her upper lip, and when she examined it under the moonlight, she found blood. She was rubbing it between her fingers when a flash of twirling red and blue lights through the trees caught her attention.

Sarah sprinted toward it and burst through the tree line to find the town of Bell. She spotted Dell's cruiser as it screeched to a stop outside of Pat's Tavern, and she smiled.

"Dell!" Sarah ran to him, waving her arms, moving her legs as fast as they would carry her, and the only sound from their greeting was the light smack of their bodies as they embraced. Sarah clung tight, holding on a bit longer than she intended, and it was Dell who had to initiate the break. He looked her up and down, checking to see if she was injured.

"I saw the wreck and looked for you, but Brent—"

The only thing she could focus on was the icy clouds that formed close to his lips with every breath. "Where is he?" Sarah asked, the rush of fear returning at the mention of his name.

"It's fine." Dell turned around, pointing to the back of the squad car. "He's in cuffs and not going anywhere anytime soon."

It was hard for Sarah to see him through the tinted glass, but she was able to see the outline of his figure, those sloped shoulders and face made all the more ominous by the fact that she could only see his silhouette.

And then, like a lightning strike, Sarah remembered why Dell had left in the first place. She hopped up, grabbing hold of his arms in the same motion, her eyes growing as big as saucers. "The doctor! Did you—"

Sarah cut herself off after the expression formed on Dell's face, and when he shook his head, all the hope she had allowed herself to feel on the way through the woods, that turning point that she was so desperate to embrace, completely shattered.

"He didn't know how to cure her, did he?" Sarah asked, still keeping her hold on Dell's arms, though now it was just to keep her knees from buckling.

"No," Dell answered, looking past her toward the house. "He said that Iris cured herself."

Sarah finally released Dell, spinning around and shuffling a few paces toward the Bell mansion high on the hill, her eyes falling on the one window in which a light flickered to life.

Dell appeared on her right-hand side, looking at her now instead of the house. "Sarah, going back up there is a gamble. If we can wait until I can get a few highway troopers up here, just so there are more witnesses, I think that's the safest way to go." He gestured back to the cruiser with his thumb. "We wait for them to back us up, and then we go in and find the cure."

"You really think she's just going to hand it over like that?" Sarah asked. "We both know that she's been involved with whatever's happening and has been involved for a very long time." She shook her head. "There isn't any amount of backup or people that are going to stop that." She placed her hand on her left leg, squeezing it gently. "And if we bring more people into this, I think it's only going to increase the likelihood of more casualties. We need to go inside, and we need to go in quickly."

And as if whatever demon entity was causing all of this trouble had heard her, the pain in her leg spiked. She collapsed to the ground, clutching at the leg, eyes shut, but still able to see. The vision took her inside the house, up to the fifth floor, back into that room. Iris was there, sitting on the edge of the bed, dressed in a white gown, that perfectly combed white hair flowing down her back. She looked tired and weak and disarmed.

She didn't notice Sarah at first, but then she turned her head slowly and smiled. "Come inside, dear, and warm yourself. It'll be over quickly."

Sarah gasped, suddenly thrust from the vision back onto the road with Dell staring down at her, holding her hand to his chest.

"Sarah? Are you all right?" Dell asked.

A tug in her chest sucked her backward, and the last thing she saw before darkness descended upon her was Dell reaching out, his mouth opening in a scream, though she couldn't hear anything. Not even her own screams.

19

The darkness lingered for a while, and Sarah felt as if she was floating, suspended between the world she had been taken from and whatever world she was being transported to. And then, just as quickly and mysteriously as the darkness had descended over her, it was lifted.

Sarah was back in the Bell mansion, on the fifth floor, in Allister Bell's room. And just like she's seen in her vision before she was pulled in, Iris sat on the bed, dressed in that white gown that ran all the way to her ankles, and matched the color of the sheets she sat on.

"I had you pegged the moment you walked into town." Iris stared at the wall, smiling, not yet acknowledging Sarah's presence, twirling the wooden sphere that dangled from her necklace between her fingers. "A little girl from the big city, on the run from a past that she desperately wanted to forget, looking for a place to start fresh, to start over."

Iris turned, chuckling, and finally looked at Sarah. "I've been on this earth for eighty-seven years, Sarah. And I can tell you from my experience that you can never start over.

You can never start fresh, because the past remains imprinted on you like dirty fingerprints that never wash off."

"I know about the witch," Sarah said, still keeping her distance. "I know about the others that you've pulled into this mess, but it's all over." She swallowed, the confidence she'd felt before waning. "The police know, and they're on their way. It's over, Iris. You've lost."

Iris stood and walked to the end of the bed. She dropped her gaze to Sarah's leg and then smiled. "I'm sure it's spread to most of your body by now." She squinted, frowning. "I'm sure the voices have told you all sorts of things." She raised her eyebrows. "That feeling never goes away, though some of the scars remain." Iris lifted the hem of her gown, exposing scars in the same shape of the pattern of scales that were currently consuming Sarah's leg.

Sarah shook her head. "Why? I saw what happened with your family. I know all of the Bells have died. So why are you helping that thing kill people? How can you just lead someone to slaughter?"

"Because she made a deal with the devil."

When Sarah spun around, her senses numbed, and her jaw dropped in disbelief. "Pat?"

Pat spread his arms wide, that same warm grin on display that had first greeted her when she'd arrived in the town alone and afraid. The deeper he penetrated into the room, the larger he seemed to grow. "I knew you wouldn't let me down, Sarah." He laughed, rubbing his hands together slowly.

"I thought you were—"

"Dead?" Pat shook his head, slowly walking around the room, examining it as if he'd been here before, gently running his fingertips over the comforter on the bed and then along the baseboard at the end of the bed frame. "It'll take more than a bullet in the gut to kill me. Something more..." He swayed side to side. "Holy." He smiled.

Sarah turned her attention back to Iris, who had kept her head down the entire time. Sarah noticed that the old woman was trembling, silent tears streaming down her cheeks and dripping onto the hardwood.

"Don't mind her," Pat said. "We have a bit of a history with one another." He casually walked over to her and pulled back the bangs that hid her face. "I'm afraid it's not a very pleasant one though."

Iris turned away, but Pat caught her chin with his right hand and pulled it back toward him.

"This should be a happy day for you," Pat said. "Why the tears?"

"Just keep your end of the bargain. You get her, you get your revelation, and I get my daughter back."

Pat laughed and released Iris, who retreated toward the door but didn't leave. "Oh, you'll get much more than that, my dear. Everyone will." He lifted his hands triumphantly into the air. "I have waited centuries for this day, and it tastes just as sweet as I thought it would." He closed his eyes and ran his tongue over his lips.

But Sarah's confused and surprised gaze hadn't disappeared. "You were a part of this? But... why did you help me?"

"I wasn't just a part of this, sweetheart. I started it all!" Pat laughed, swinging his hips forward before leaning against the bedpost for support. "That witch that made a pact with Allister Bell over one hundred and fifty years ago?" He spread his arms wide, stretching that smile even wider.

"You?" Sarah asked.

"In the flesh," Pat answered and then looked down at his form. "Well, not exactly. But this body has served its purpose over the past few decades." He looked up. "I try on something new every now and again, but now that the jig is up, I suppose I don't have to put on the front anymore, do I?"

Pat suddenly shrank, the clothes he wore growing smaller as his limbs retracted, the bones just beneath the surface of his skin shifting and reshaping themselves. The features along his face morphed and grew more slender. His hair lengthened, switching from the salt-and-pepper gray to a silky jet black. Eventually the clothes slid right off, and once it was all said and done, there was nothing save a naked woman standing in front of Sarah, wavy locks of hair cascading down her shoulders and clashing against her porcelain skin.

She smiled, wrinkling her nose as she sauntered toward Sarah. "I've always been vain, ever since I was little, but damn, do I love this body." She glanced down at herself, running her hands up and down her smooth skin, and then slightly tilted her head up toward Sarah. One eye was covered by her bangs, while the other one stared at Sarah seductively, the hazel color so bright it was almost amber. "If you've got it, flaunt it, right?"

"What are you?" Sarah asked, still gawking at the woman.

"I'm a woman who made a pact with the dark lord centuries ago." She circled Sarah and outstretched her hand, trailing her finger along Sarah's shoulder then the top of her back, all the way around to her collarbone. "I've seen enough through the years to know that it's better to be beautiful and powerful than ugly and weak, so I found a man who could give me both."

"This can't be possible." Sarah shook her head, the flesh beneath her eyes hollowing out as she suddenly felt tired. "But you tried to—"

"Help you?" the witch asked, finishing the sentence. "I just needed to keep an eye on you, make sure you didn't leave Bell. I couldn't have you sniffing around for the actual cure to your ailment. And I knew that once the curse had consumed more than half of you I could control you and do what I want." She smiled. "Which is how I got you here now."

"You were just buying time," Sarah said, feeling sick at the realization.

"Though I must say I didn't expect Allister to find a way to send the souls back through the orb to speak to you," the witch said. "He was more clever than I thought." She walked to Iris, plucked the wooden sphere from the necklace, and smiled. "It moves, but is always in the same place." She crushed the wood and exposed a crystal sphere that was the same color as the frost slowly covering Sarah's body.

The sphere gleamed and reflected in the witch's eyes. "You're the last soul I need, Sarah. Number six-six-six." She cackled, the tone high-pitched. "You see the idea was to keep the Bell's breeding until I obtained the number of souls needed to be sacrificed until the portal could be opened. But before we reached the halfway mark I realized the number of Bell's were growing short, so Iris made a pact with me. In exchange for luring unsuspecting victims to her house and offering them to the dark lord, she would save her daughter's soul." She turned to Iris. "Feels good doesn't it?"

Iris trembled. "I didn't want to have those people killed, but I didn't have a choice. It was the only way to save them."

"It's not too late," Sarah said. "Iris, please…" She walked closer to Iris and gently placed her hand on the old woman's back. "I know what happened to your daughter. But this isn't what she would want." Sarah felt how weak Iris had grown, and it seemed that all it would take to kill Iris would be to apply the slightest amount of pressure. "There has to be another way." And then she remembered what Mary had said. "The moon still shines."

Iris gawked at Sarah, as if she were stuck in some trance. Only the slightest twitches around her mouth and eyes broke the stoic expression. "Hand in hand with the stars." She clasped her hands together, clutching them tightly. "You spoke to Mary?"

"She doesn't want you to do this," Sarah said. "Help me end all of this."

The witch laughed, that cackle filling the room. "Stupid girl. You think you can sway her now?" The witch held out her hand. "Give me the orb, Iris. And you will have your daughter back."

Iris fingered the smooth crystal still attached to the necklace, and smiled sadly as she looked at Sarah. "My late husband thought the same thing you did. He couldn't understand how his own family could make a pact with the devil. He didn't understand that it would take our children, that it would take my daughter!" Iris stepped from Sarah's reach. "I understood what my husband couldn't." She plucked the orb from her neck. "The devil gets his due."

When Iris dropped the orb into the witch's palm, Sarah lunged for it, but was suddenly squashed to the floor, unable to move her body.

The pain returned, but it was different this time. It felt closer, more intimate, and when Sarah clawed at her shirt, she felt the scales spreading up her stomach. The pain reached her chest, and she grew short of breath and then lost her voice as she felt the vibrations of her screams in her throat.

"It's going to hurt," the witch said, walking closer, her hips swaying and that coy little smile still spread across her stunningly beautiful face. "And I know it's in your nature to fight and resist, but the more you try and put this off, the more it's going to hurt. You're going to die, Sarah. Your soul will vanish, and you will cease to exist. The scary part is knowing that beforehand, but I can tell you that when it happens…"

She leaned close, and Sarah caught the faint stench of decay on her breath. "You won't even remember what it was that you were afraid of."

* * *

"Sarah!" Dell stumbled forward, but before he even made it a step and had a chance to reach out his hands to grab her, she was gone.

Dell waved his arms around in the spot where she had disappeared, but he touched nothing but air. Spinning in circles, he looked back up at the house.

Dell sprinted back to the squad car, reaching for the radio inside and ignoring Brent's pestering questions. "Faye! Tell the state troopers that I'm going to the Bell house, and tell them that our situation has changed to involve hostages." He tossed the radio receiver onto the dash and popped the trunk.

"Dell? What the hell is going on out there?" Faye's voice crackled through the radio, and Dell scooped the dashboard receiver one last time before he left.

"Just tell them that I'm going to the house and that the kidnappers involved are Iris and Kegan Bell. Both should be considered armed and dangerous. If I don't make it out, I need you to take care of Sarah, all right?"

With Faye still screaming questions, Dell opened the trunk and grabbed the shotgun and started loading shells. His nerves started to fray as he loaded the weapon, and he could hear Brent screaming through the back window.

"You're going to get yourself killed, man!" Brent's voice sounded throaty and hoarse. "That's what she does. It's all just a game for her to try and make herself feel better. Don't get caught up in it!"

With the shotgun loaded, Dell shoved another handful of shells into his pocket and then slammed the trunk closed, revealing Brent staring at him through the back window, still shaking his head.

"Don't go!"

But Dell wasn't going to lie down. He sprinted toward the mansion, the butt of the shotgun shoved into the crook of his shoulder, and his gaze focused on the weapon's sights.

The Bell family had sunk its teeth and claws into his town for too long, and now they had taken nearly everything. Dell knew that they weren't going to stop until it was done. But he couldn't let them win, not now. He was going to put a stop to it, and he was going to do it by any means necessary.

Dell leapt up the steps to the Bells' front door two at a time, winded by the time he reached the top, and slowed as he approached the doors. He gripped the shotgun with both hands and then flung the doors open.

Dell kept the shotgun poised to shoot but after a quick sweep of the foyer, he found it empty save for the candles that wiggled flames, moving the shadows inside, bringing the house to life.

Shadows and light danced in a tango of mystery and defiance. Despite the cold inside, Dell was sweating. He stood there in the foyer for a moment, unsure of where to go.

"Sheriff's Department!" Dell shouted, his training taking over and forcing him to identify himself. "I want everyone inside to come out and identify yourselves, now!" But his voice only echoed off the walls and bounced off the high ceiling. No one exited. No one left.

Dell turned toward the grand staircase, lifting the barrel of his gun up the winding steps to the second floor. If Sarah was here, he was betting that she'd be on the fifth floor. He approached the stairs carefully and then made his way up, leading with the shotgun.

He passed the second floor and then the third. Halfway up to the fourth floor, Dell heard a blood-curdling scream that propelled him up the stairs in a sprint, sacrificing the steadiness of his aim as the shotgun wobbled back and forth from his increased pace.

The screams worsened when he reached the fourth floor, and just before he reached the steps leading up to the fifth, a heavy thud whacked the back of his skull, sending him sprawling out onto the floor and sending the shotgun from his hands and skidding across the boards.

"You know it's not polite to enter without knocking first."

Dell turned his head at the voice, the back of his skull throbbing in a dull ache, and before his eyes had an opportunity to adjust, a fist rammed his nose, drawing blood from his nostrils and flinging back his head.

Still disoriented, Dell felt hands picking him up by the Kevlar vest beneath his uniform.

"You should have just stayed out of it, Dell," Kegan said, dragging Dell's body along the hardwood, struggling with the man's size and weight. "All you had to do was stay in Redford, but you just couldn't stay away from this house, could you?" He laughed. "You never could."

A quick flood of adrenaline helped pull Dell from the throes of confusion, and he swung his arms, forcing Kegan to wrap him in a chokehold on the floor. His airway tightened, and pressure started to build in his head.

"You want to do this the hard way?" Kegan asked, his voice strained from the effort of having to choke him out. "You want to travel back in time to grade school when I kicked your ass up and down these halls?"

With his cheeks turning purple, Dell clawed at Kegan's arm, the pressure in his head causing his eyes to bulge from their sockets. He choked, and his vision blurred.

"You never could get the girl, Dell," Kegan said, a joyful

malice to his voice. "I bet it's been frustrating for you to never have been the guy, the dude, the man who had it all figured out." He leaned closer to Dell's ear, dropping his voice to a whisper. "You're just a bastard whose daddy left because he couldn't hack it. I guess it runs in the family."

Dell grimaced, then steadied his legs, squared up his hips, and lifted them both into the air and slammed Kegan hard on his back.

After the harsh crack of contact between Kegan's back and the floor, the pressure and tightness around Dell's neck loosened, and he flung Kegan's arm off him and scrambled toward the shotgun that lay nearby.

Fingers clasped Dell's ankle, and he looked back to find Kegan latched onto his leg. Dell kicked, the heel of his boot missing the first two strikes but connecting against Kegan's forehead on the third, which again released him.

Dell crawled again toward the weapon. Just when he had his hands around the stock of the shotgun, he was flattened to the ground, his chest atop the weapon he had been reaching for.

"You stupid fuck!" Kegan had wrestled his way on top of him, punching Dell's back and sides with quick, heavy strikes. "You just don't know when to quit, do you?"

The Kevlar around Dell's torso helped lessen Kegan's punches, and Dell managed to twist himself around and then wrap his legs over Kegan in a scissor hold, choking him out with his knees.

"And you never knew when to shut up." Dell tightened his hold, and Kegan pounded impotently at his leg, the motions growing weaker and weaker until finally he passed out.

Dell released him, his own muscles trembling from the exertion, and then stood, picking up the shotgun off the ground. He removed a pair of zip ties from his belt and restrained both Kegan's wrists and ankles.

Once he was tied up, Dell flipped Kegan the bird, but his victory was cut short with another scream from upstairs. "Sarah." Her name left his lips in a breathless whisper, and he hurried up the steps and toward the commotion. He prayed that he wasn't too late and that whatever Sarah had gotten herself into he would be able to get her out of.

2 0

---

*E*ven though Sarah could no longer hear herself screaming, she still felt her throat grow raw. Terrified, she forced herself to look down at the horrid transformation of her body. The icy scales had crawled to her neck and covered everything but her head.

The witch stood off to the side, watching as Sarah struggled with the evil that was taking control. "The darkness is inevitable, Sarah. Why fight it?" She stepped closer. "Soon, you will join all of these souls, and yours will be the final key to unlock Satan's wrath upon this earth. Your meaningless life and soul will have purpose, which is what all people search for their entire lives, and it's right here in front of you. Just imagine!"

And Sarah could imagine. Because she felt the fire and smelled the death. Destruction was barreling toward them like a freight train. The sum of all her fears had accumulated into a single entity, and it was breathing down her neck.

But it wasn't just her own fears. No, it was an entire world full of hate and confusion. It was a spectrum of humanity's suffering that stretched from its conception to its end. It replayed over and over in her mind, and Sarah finally felt the levy break. A few frosted blue scales appeared on her neck.

"You can't stop it," the witch said. "You've struggled for so long, and you've suffered so much, why not just give in? Why prolong the torture of a life that has never had any meaning?"

Sarah spied the orb on the bed. She could hear the screams of the souls inside, and the light on the orb grew brighter and brighter. If it weren't for the cries of pain, it would have looked beautiful.

"All of those people who let you down," the witch said, now close to Sarah's ear. "All of those people who cast you aside and told you that you weren't worth the time, those are the people you're helping right now. Those are the individuals you're saving. And why? They hurt you, cast you out, amplified the pain and loss of a little girl who couldn't defend herself."

A few more scales appeared on her neck, inching toward Sarah's throat, and she started to feel the last of her resolve slip away. The witch's words were stoking the flames of hate and resentment in Sarah's own heart. It was a fire that had always been there, and though she had tried to douse it with hope and love over the years, it was too strong to die.

"I can feel it," the witch said, her tone laced with sympathy and longing. "I see all of your pain and confusion, and I'm here to tell you that it's fine to let go. That's all he wants. He wants to release you from the heartache that no one else has been able to ease. He wants to cradle you in the warming embrace of a father. Touch with the gentle caress of a mother."

Three more scales appeared, and the blue in Sarah's eyes started to fade, and her striking blonde hair greyed.

The witch shut her eyes, her lips pressed against Sarah's ear now. "Just. Give. In."

Sarah screamed, that fiery pit of hatred blazing to life in a horrible nightmare of pain. The control had slipped away. And she couldn't fight the flames anymore. She couldn't fight the hate. She couldn't ignore the pain.

The witch was right. Why should she struggle to save lives in a world that had never cared anything for her? Why should she try and save the souls of people who never paid her any mind or helped her when she cried for help. She'd always been on her own. And it was time for the rest of the world to feel what she'd gone through her whole life.

But then she felt something. It was like a cool summer breeze after finding a shady spot in the grass in the park. She turned her head toward the door, looking past Iris, who stood there with a twisted expression of pain and excitement on her face. Her features had grown exaggerated, and she looked to have aged another twenty years in the past minute they'd been in the room.

But past Iris and the door was the source of the breeze. A ray of light penetrated the dark shroud that had encompassed her body, mind, and soul. It was someone she knew. One of those souls out of millions that was coming for her. And then she felt him.

"Dell." She whispered his name in her mind, and the hate and pain started to fade. She remembered meeting him, remembered the touch of his hand and the warmth of his smile. She had liked him. And he had made her a promise. A promise that she let herself believe would not be broken because of the man that had given it.

She felt him close, in the house, coming for her. All she had to do was hold on now. All she had to do was keep the faith that she'd survive and that the pain would end. Because there was light at the end of the tunnel, but it was still far away. So Sarah shut her eyes, returning to her fight against the cold darkness spreading over her soul, and tried to hang on for just a little bit longer.

* * *

DELL REACHED THE FIFTH FLOOR, his breathing still wild and uncontrollable, and the door slammed shut. He grabbed the handle, finding it locked. He shoulder checked the door, the screams louder and more frightening than before.

"Sarah!" He pounded on the door, and sweat poured off him in buckets. Heat penetrated the wood of the door. It was as if the house had caught fire, but there were no flames.

Dell stepped back, aimed the shotgun at the doorknob, and squeezed the trigger. The slug blasted through the door, leaving a hole in the doorknob's space. The recoil of the blast knocked the butt of the shotgun hard against Dell's shoulder. When he pushed the door open moments later, it was like opening the door of an oven that had been turned all the way up to broil.

Dell turned his face away, the heat so strong it felt as if his skin was melting off his face. But he pressed forward.

The screams grew louder and stronger at the other end of the hall, and Dell staggered toward the door, all the while the heat growing hotter and hotter. "Christ." The weapon's stock burst into flames, and Dell was forced to drop it to the ground. His eyes widened in terror as the flames were quickly snuffed out and the metal of the barrel melted to the floor.

Another scream brought Dell's attention back toward the door at the end of the hall. "Sarah." He stumbled forward, the soles of his shoes melting toward the floor, and he was forced to abandon them and walk barefoot.

Pain and heat and exhaustion clouded Dell's senses, and

his concentration waned. He couldn't think anymore. He couldn't remember why he'd even come up here, and he couldn't remember who he was trying to save.

Slowly, his thoughts turned to his own survival. He wanted to leave. It was as if the heat had gotten inside of him, where it was trapped and burning him from the inside out.

"Help me."

The voice penetrated the screams and the heat and his doubts, and Dell turned back toward the door. He knew that voice. "Sarah." Dell pushed forward, his body growing heavy, as if the gravity of the house had increased and was trying to push him through the floor.

His very will was being stripped from him with every step, but Sarah's voice fueled his drive. He could hear the pain in her voice and what remained of her hope beginning to fade. She couldn't hold on much longer.

Dell was forced to crawl toward the door, but the closer he came to it the farther away it seemed to feel, and his own hope started to dwindle. His body had frozen, and that pressure, that monumental weight that had been crushing him for the past few minutes had finally done its work and flattened him to the floor, which was as hot as a stovetop.

His skin burned, searing itself to the wooden floorboards, and while Dell felt every excruciating minute of the pain, he couldn't scream. All he could think of was that Sarah was on the other side of that door, and she was hurting. But he couldn't hear her anymore. He couldn't feel her anymore. The moment had passed, and he had failed.

And so Dell lay there, his body fused to the floor, the pain reaching such a crescendo that he finally opened his mouth to scream but couldn't even hear it himself. It grew so intense that he broke into hallucinations.

"We're so close, Dell." Tears streamed from Sarah's eyes but then caught fire as they dripped from her chin and hit the floor, exploding into small plumes of fire flowers before dissipating into nothing. "Don't give up."

Dell screamed, writhing on the floor, but the anger and shame grew so strong that he broke free and pushed himself off. He felt his cheek, expecting to find nothing but jagged flesh, exposed muscle, and bone. But when his finger hesitantly grazed his skin, it was smooth and even a little cold. It was wet, though, from the sweat.

He looked to the door, the waves of heat causing the entrance to the room to ripple like a desert mirage. She was just on the other side of that door. It wasn't too late. He could save her. He just had to push a little farther.

* * *

THE SCALES HAD CRAWLED up Sarah's cheeks and rested just below her eyes. Her mouth had been sealed shut, and she couldn't move anything save for her pupils. She looked back to the orb on the bed, knowing that if there was any opportunity at stopping this, it was through that.

"Almost done, my dear," the witch said, circling Sarah like a shark, sniffing the blood-soaked air that Sarah had bled from her body and her soul. She grazed Sarah with her fingertips, her nails scraping against the blue scales that had nearly consumed her. "The last soul. The last flame of hope snuffed out like that." She snapped her fingers. "And to replace the flames of hope will be the fires of the damned, the resurrection of the rightful ruler of this realm, and the fulfillment of a prophecy that cannot be denied."

The orb on the bed had grown brighter, and the souls trapped inside swirled around in frenzy. With every second that passed, Sarah's connection with them grew stronger.

"I open the portal!" The witch said. "And with the flesh of

the last damned soul connects to the orb, our dark lord will rise!"

All of those memories from her past and her childhood flooded back like a tsunami, the pressure from the push so intense that it consumed all of her senses. She heard only the curses and verbal abuse from her foster parents, she felt only the rough and drunken hands that bruised her body, and she tasted only blood from the fights with the other kids. She was transported back into a world of hunger, pain, and discomfort. And that was all that she would know until the very end.

The witch raised her hands, smiling as she lifted her face toward the ceiling. "There is nothing that his power cannot restore. There is nothing that his fortune cannot buy. He is the end and the beginning, and he will shape this earth to its true image!" She lowered her face, her eyes burning as she stared straight into Sarah's soul. "Death."

The scales crawling up her face covered Sarah's eyes and blinded her to the room. And with the last of her senses gone, finality set in. She was deaf, mute, blind, and numb to the material world. This was how her life was going to end. This was how she would die.

But then a shape started to form in the darkness. The pitch black broke apart, fading into a dull gray, like dirt swirling in water, dissolving and sinking toward the bottom.

The legs formed first, walking closer toward her, the swirl rising to the waist and then the chest and arms and finally the head. And when the features filled into place, Sarah found Allister Bell standing in front of her.

"Hello, Sarah." The accent had a faint British tone to it, and a massive mustache covered most of his lips, making it look as if he was speaking without moving his mouth.

Half expecting to have no voice, Sarah was surprised when she had the ability to answer. "You're dead."

"I made a choice a long time ago that has haunted my family and others for nearly two hundred years." Allister's already pale cheeks lightened even more, and the dim light in his eyes grew lifeless as he lowered his head in shame. "I do not have the ability to end this curse." He lifted his eyes. "But you can."

Another spasm of fear-induced pain pulled Sarah toward the darkness, and she struggled to stay in the moment. It was nearly over. Even though she couldn't see what was happening anymore, she still felt it. "It's too late."

"Someone else is coming," Allister said. "A life to be sacrificed for yours. It will buy us some time."

"I'm not letting anyone else die," Sarah said. "I'm not letting anyone else take the fall for something that I got myself into."

Anger flushed Allister's cheeks, and he took one large and quick step toward her. "Then anyone that is left out there in the world that you care about will burn the moment the dark prince steps from his realm and into this one." A flicker of life returned to his eyes, and for an even shorter moment, so did his humanity. "I will fight it as long as I can, but if you aren't able to break the curse that binds me to this evil realm, then it won't matter. He's coming, Sarah." Allister's tone became grave. "And there isn't any convincing him otherwise. So you can either do something once you're free to save his soul or spoil what little time you'll have left on this rock before the world burns and you burn with it."

Sarah had wanted a chance at redemption, and she had wanted an opportunity to do something good, and this was her shot to help all of the women she'd seen in her visions.

"How much time can you give me?" Sarah asked.

"I can make it last a day," Allister answered. And even now, Sarah noticed the sweat breaking out on his face and the flashes of pain and anguish. "But don't dawdle—GAH!"

He buckled forward at the waist, clutching his stomach and dropping to his knees. He trembled, the ends of his mustache shaking as he lifted his head to look at Sarah. "You know all the players in this game. All you have to do is put the pieces in order." Anger flashed over his face again, but this time it darkened his features, and the flicker of life in his eyes turned yellow and hot. "Run, Sarah. RUN!"

Just like the transportation into the house, a harsh tug at her waist yanked Sarah backward and pulled her from the darkness.

* * *

THE MOMENT DELL had his hands on the door, the gravity that had kept him pinned down was suddenly lifted. With his strength restored, he shouldered open the door, stumbling inside as if he was running downhill.

Everyone turned toward him upon his entrance, but Dell's gaze fell onto Sarah. The scales had crawled all the way to the top of her head, but they hadn't completely covered her yet. But he spied the orb on the bed. With the witch about to make a move and Iris screaming bloody murder either from pain or from shock, he lunged toward the object.

He couldn't explain what propelled him toward the orb, but it consumed his thoughts. The rest of the world faded around him, and he clutched at the orb's surface just as the witch reached for his arm. But while she tried to pull him back, it was too late.

With his hand on the orb, Dell looked back toward Sarah just in time to watch the scales crumble from her face. He wasn't sure if she saw him before she disappeared, but the only thing that mattered to him was the fact that she was safe.

21

*T*he brief flash of Dell's face was seared into her mind as she suddenly found herself cold and alone out in the middle of Bell's main street, staring at the mansion high on the hill overlooking the town. After a minute of shock, she shivered, realizing the cold for the first time since she had been taken, and squeezed her arms around her shoulders. She stared up at the monstrous building on the hill, where Dell was now trapped, forced into whatever hell he had freed Sarah from joining.

And while it was a welcome reprieve, Sarah knew it was only temporary. The clock was ticking, and the longer Sarah waited to get started, the less time she had to figure out how in the hell she was going to save Dell and stop that family from ending the world. With her grit returned, Sarah spun around and marched toward Dell's cruiser, knowing that he had radioed for help but unsure of how long it was going to take for them to arrive. But what she hadn't realized was who was sitting in the back of his squad car, handcuffs still binding his wrists.

Brent stared at Sarah through the tinted back windows of

the cruiser, and she blinked a few times before the realization of who it was finally sank in. It was a surreal moment, looking at him in the back of a squad car. She imagined the irony wasn't lost on him now that she was free and he was not.

Sarah had envisioned this moment for a long time and had replayed the meeting repeatedly. But now that it was here and she finally had a taste of the justice that she had longed for so much, she discovered that she didn't care.

The only thing that mattered now was getting Dell back and ending whatever shit storm the Bell family was trying to set upon the world.

Sarah opened the driver's side door, tossing only the briefest glance toward Brent, who pressed his face against the steel mesh backing that separated the backseat from the front. She reached for the radio blaring loudly from beneath the center of the console.

Never having used a police radio before, Sarah fumbled the receiver awkwardly in her hands before finally squeezing the side and sending her voice echoing via radio waves. "This is Dell Parker's cruiser. Is anyone there? I repeat, this is—"

"Who the hell is this?" A woman's voice blared from the speakers.

"My name is Sarah Pembrooke," she answered. "I'm outside Pat's Tavern in Bell, and I need backup to this location immediately." Sarah released the radio.

"Been a while since you wanted the cops to show, sweetheart," Brent said, his face still pressed up against the mesh.

"Fuck you," Sarah replied, snapping back at him.

Brent laughed, more chatter spilling over the radio. He shook his head and then leaned back in his seat. "For a woman who prides herself on being worldly, you sure don't know shit about the way the justice system works in this world, sweetheart. It's all about perception and clout, and

I've got both in spades. What do you have, huh? You're just some shitty little street urchin that I happened to bed a few times due to boredom." He nodded to the house. "You think Dudley Doright up there is going to be able to pull you out of trouble? Hell, I bet he's already dead judging by the fact that you magically appeared in the center of the street, because whatever you're dealing with seems more dangerous than anything I've done."

It was true. What she'd experienced over the past few days was more evil than the man cuffed in the backseat. And it was because of the evil that she'd experienced in that time frame that she was even able to look the man wearing those cuffs in the eye without dissolving into a puddle of fear. There were bigger fish to fry out there, and if she was going to save Dell, she'd need one hell of a frying pan.

"Sarah?" The woman's voice brought her attention back to the radio. "Sarah, are you still there?"

"I'm here," Sarah answered.

"State troopers are en route," she said. "Just stay put until they arrive, okay?"

But as Sarah was about to respond, she let her finger off the talk box. It was the phrase "stay put" that triggered the wheels in her mind to turn.

If the troopers arrived and detained her for questioning, it would cost valuable time she needed to figure out how to help Dell, and that wasn't time that she could afford. There was no training manual for this, no instruction booklet. And she doubted there was anyone that she could turn to now for help, because the only person who would believe her was currently being tortured on the fifth floor of the house of the family that had started all of this.

No, the best thing for Sarah to do was to try and finish this herself. There wouldn't be any strings attached to hold her back, no red tape for her to cut through. It would be her brains and will and cunning against the worst evil the world had ever known. And in order for her to defeat that evil, she needed to understand it.

The door to Pat's—no, she thought. It had never been Pat's place. It had belonged to the witch who had orchestrated this entire ordeal. Pat was nothing more than a shell, a ghost that had tricked her into friendship and then left her out in the cold to die.

Either way, Sarah shouldered open the witch's house, surprised to find it open and empty but knowing that it wouldn't remain that way for much longer. She hurried to the bed, dropping to her knees, skidding toward the edge, and reached beneath the bedsprings for the chest she knew was there.

Catching hold of the old piece of wood, Sarah pulled, her muscles straining as the big chest scraped against the floor.

It was still unlocked from their previous tries, and Sarah flung the top open, immediately rummaging through the clippings the witch had saved. "C'mon, c'mon, c'mon. I know you're here. I know you're—"

Sarah froze when her fingers scraped against something hard, and she pushed aside the articles stacked on top of the notebook until she found the edges and heaved it out of the chest.

After that she scrambled for the letters that they'd studied, and then found a spare bag and chucked everything inside. She headed for the door, but then stopped.

Sarah turned back to the opened chest, and she walked back over, and searched inside. There might be something else inside that could help her, something that the witch didn't want her to see, something—

Sarah's fingers scraped against something hard, and she lifted a book from the random junk inside the chest. It was old, and worn, and holding it brought a mixture of awe, fear, and excitement that made her heart thud heavily against her chest.

"Codex Gigas." Sarah ran her fingers over the title as she read it aloud, and a spine-tingling chill ran up her back.

She stuffed it in the bag, and then did one last scan of the chest before running out of the house and headed toward the forest. What came next wasn't just a fight for her life anymore, it was a fight for the survival of humanity.

She was in the realm of good and evil, the lines clearly drawn. She only hoped that she had enough good in her to win the battle.

* * *

THE CUFFS around Brent's wrists had caused both his shoulders to go numb, and his back was horribly stiff and tight. When he watched Sarah appear out of nowhere in the middle of the road and make her way over to the car, he couldn't help but laugh at the situation.

But when she left, disappearing back behind the tavern without a word, leaving him locked up in the car, it was tough to stomach. A spasm of anger rippled through his body, and he slammed his back against the cushion, rocking the squad car back and forth.

"Fucking bullshit," Brent whispered angrily to himself even though he was alone. Out of all the ways for his career and life to come to a screeching halt, he never would have thought it was going to end like this.

Despite the big talk he spit in front of Sarah, he knew that no matter how he came out of this, the investigation into his work and personal life would yield some unflattering results. He wasn't going to walk out of this unscathed.

"Gah, dammit." Brent stared down at his foot. Ever since he'd been shoved into the back of the squad car, he hadn't been able to shake the cold, tingling sensation at the bottom of his heel. It was a perpetual itch that he hadn't been able to scratch, though with his hands tied behind his back, the metaphor had turned into a reality.

And with his attention turned to the heel of his foot, he missed how the woman to his right got into the car without opening the door.

"Hello, Brent."

"Shit!" Brent leapt, slamming his head into the roof before retreating to the driver's side door. Hyperventilated breaths escaped his lips, and a cold sweat broke out all over his body. That little itch in the heel of his foot had ignited into a searing pain that seemed to be on fire and freezing at the same time.

The woman wore a tight red dress. Her face was done up with minimal makeup, her jet-black hair flowing down in curls, her hair the same color as the dark shade of lipstick she wore. She giggled and wrinkled her nose, and Brent couldn't shake the primal urges aching in his loins in a swirling combination of fear and lust.

The woman smiled coyly and then inched closer toward Brent, who remained glued to the car door. "Relax, sweetheart." A hint of mockery riddled her tone, and she walked her hand over the seats, her nails digging into the cushions until they pressed into the stiff fabric of his jeans. "I'm only here to help."

"How did you—" Brent licked his lips, his mouth suddenly dry, and shook his head again in disbelief. "What the hell are you?"

Gentle laughter rolled off the woman's tongue as she reclined against the passenger-side door, lifting her legs and poking the pegs of her stiletto heels into the seat cushions, her legs spread open and inviting. "I'm your salvation. I'm the girl who's going to get you out of this car before backup arrives. How does that sound?"

Brent couldn't keep his eyes from staring between the woman's legs, and while his cheeks glowered red with shame, he couldn't shift his gaze. "Like it's too good to be true."

"Clever boy," she said, her tongue rolling in pleasure in her mouth. "I only want the tiniest little favor from you in exchange for your freedom." She placed her hands on her knees and tugged at her dress, pulling it up her knees slowly, exposing the pale, toned, and supple skin along her inner thighs.

Brent's mouth hung open, his mind as slack as his jaw. "What?"

"That girl," she said, still hiking the skirt up. "The one you've been looking for. I want you to find her, and I want you to bring her to me." The hem of her skirt reached her waist, and she leaned forward, digging her nail beneath Brent's chin and lifting his gaze to meet her own. "Think you can do that for me, big boy?"

Brent blinked a few times, a dull ache forming beneath his chin and in his groin. "Why... Why can't you go and get her yourself? Why do you need me?"

The woman showed her first signs of anger and displayed her displeasure by digging her fingernail deeper into Brent's skin, hard enough to draw blood that trickled down her finger. "Because she's being protected by something that I can't get through." She flashed a hint of doubt. "Something I can't see." Then she turned her attention back to him. "But you can get her, which is something I know you want." She closed her eyes, sniffing the air around him. "You're like a dog in heat." When she opened her eyes again, the smile returned to her face. "So, what do you say, sweetheart?"

"And what do I get out of this deal?" Brent asked.

"Your freedom," the woman answered. "All of these problems with the girl and the cops will go away." She snapped her fingers. "Just like that."

And while Brent wanted to answer, he found his tongue tied. But after rolling it around in his mouth a few times, he nodded. "All right."

"Good." The woman gestured behind her, flinging her head toward the mansion. "I'll be in the house." She leaned forward and then kissed his lips. "Don't keep me waiting."

Brent closed his eyes at the touch of her lips on his, and when he opened them again, he found the woman gone, and he was alone in the car. But just when he thought he'd been swindled, he lifted his hands to run his fingers through his hair.

The cuffs were gone. He rubbed his wrists, the flesh tender where the zip ties had been, and he stared at the imprints with a certain level of wonder and awe. "What in the hell did I just get myself into?"

The radio crackled, that woman, Faye, coming through the radio waves. "Sarah? Are you there? The troopers are turning off the highway now. Sarah?"

And before the hint of red and blue lights could appear down the road, bathing the small town in color, Brent opened the car door and stepped out into the frigid night air. He discovered two surprising elements. The first was that his heel no longer itched. The second was that, despite knowing how cold it was and how he'd been shivering for the past hour in the back of that car, he wasn't cold anymore. And he knew that he had the lady in the red dress to thank for that, though he figured both would come back to bite him in the ass.

But the only thing that concerned him for the moment was the fact that Sarah was still out there, and it was his job to bring her back. He was glad the woman had not specified whether she preferred her dead or alive.

22

*D*arkness washed over Dell quickly. Blind and disoriented, he lost all sense of time. He floated aimlessly, unable to determine for how long. Eventually his feet scraped a hard surface, and the sensation of gravity returned. But when the world around him finally came into view, he wished for that darkness to return.

The foreign landscape that stretched to the horizon was a far cry from the Bell house he had just been inside. Walls, ceilings, floors, and furniture had been replaced with rock and ash and floating embers. No water, no grass, or trees, nothing but red and black, jagged rocks. It was like standing on the inside of a volcano.

The air was thick with smoke, and an unforgiving heat baked his skin. Every breath was a struggle, but each inhale provided enough oxygen to wheeze until the next breath came. If there was a hell, then Dell Parker was positive that he'd found it.

"That was a brave thing you did."

Dell spun around, startled enough to fall backwards onto

the hard rocks. "Gah!" A sharp pain ran from his tailbone and up his spine to the base of his skull, where it lingered.

Dell leaned forward, shoving his head between his knees to ease the pain, but it did nothing. Like the darkness that covered him, the pain was content on making him wait, pushing him to the point of collapse before finally offering a reprieve.

"I wish I could say that you get used to this place, but that's just not true."

Dell looked up and found an old man standing nearby. He pushed himself to his feet. He cradled his lower back and then grimaced. He gave the old timer the once over, shaking his head. The old man wore clothes from another era, and his thick white beard concealed most of his face. "Who are you?"

"Allister Bell," he said.

Dell narrowed his eyes in disbelief. "Allister Bell died over a century ago," Dell answered. "And if you're dead, then—" Dell examined his body, looking for bullet holes or knife wounds, any sign of his demise.

"You're not dead," Allister Bell said, walking over and placing a heavy hand on Dell's shoulder. "At least not yet."

But Dell shrugged Allister's hand off his shoulder. "No." He took quick, shallow breaths, and his heartrate accelerated. "No, I can't— This isn't real." He retreated from Allister, spinning around in circles to get his bearings. "This isn't—"

And then Dell heard it, and he felt it. A heavy bass thudded through his chest. The vibration started from his core and spread outward to his limbs and toes and fingertips.

The beats grew stronger, and then suddenly they weren't coming from inside of him anymore. Dell looked to the horizon where a high-rise of boulders and rocks blocked the commotion beyond it.

"They're ready to leave," Allister said, appearing alongside

Dell. "They've been in a frenzy lately, and it's only going to get worse. For everyone."

A heavy gong silenced the world and cracked the molten sky above, bringing a rain of fire and ash, and if Allister hadn't grabbed him and pulled him away, he would have been smothered by the rain of molten rock.

The uneven ground cracked and shook beneath Dell's feet as Allister pulled him toward the ridge of rocks where those drums echoed beyond.

Eventually the hell rain from the sky ended, and the quaking of the ground subsided, and Allister flung Dell against the side of the high ridge. He shut his eyes as he collapsed to his side, hacking and coughing. His innards had caught fire, and when he opened his eyes, he saw that he was coughing streams of black smoke.

Dell shook his head, unable to shake the panic washing over him. "How is this possible?"

"Listen to me," Allister said, taking hold of Dell's hand. "Look over the ridge. And be quiet, and careful."

After a moment, Dell acquiesced, but as he crawled forward, Allister shuffled backward, remaining hidden beneath the cover of the rocks. Dell watched the deep lines of fear carve out Allister's expression. It was the type of fear that was a product of decades of neglect and suffering, someone who had grown to fear the rod.

Despite the sheer horror that Dell saw on the old man's face, Dell couldn't stop himself from peeking over the ridge. He needed to see it. He needed to know where he was, and what in the hell was going on.

The drums returned, the bass vibrating through Dell's body as he flattened his stomach against the rocks, then slowly crawled toward the top. He only went as far as it took for his eyes to see, and when he saw, he understood Allister's fear.

Beings of fire and rock swarmed the valley below, spewing lava and acidic smoke and gas from their bodies. They had no eyes, but carved into their heads were large mouths filled with jagged and razor-sharp teeth.

Their craze was magnified by the hastening pace of the drums. They turned on one another, killing and tearing apart rocks with their claws and teeth, spilling their molten innards on the ground, which they drank from thirstily.

But for every demon that was killed, two more took its place, and the violence spread to the horizon. There were millions of them. Hundreds of millions.

Slowly, Dell lowered himself back behind the ridge and turned around to find the old man staring at him with a knowing glance.

"It's the devil's army," Allister said, moving his eyes about as if even speaking the name would cause Satan to appear like a version of Bloody Mary. "They were created to destroy; to transform life into death."

Dell examined the barren landscape, the rocks and the fire and ash. He tried to envision Redford or Bell like this, the beautiful Maine wilderness destroyed, the life sucked from the world and replaced with only death.

"How do we stop it?" Dell asked.

Allister smiled sadly. He shook his head. "My dear boy. I've been here for a long time, and until you showed up, those things remained with the dark lord behind the gates of hell." He returned his gaze to Dell. "You were the last soul that the dark lord required. You were the key. And yet..." Allister touched Dell's shoulder, as if he was still unsure if Dell was real, or only a figment of his imagination.

And then Dell remembered the curse, the witch, and Sarah. "Six-six-six." He looked to Allister. "There are others down here, aren't there?"

"Yes."

Dell jumped again, scrambling to his left and away from the redhead that had appeared out of nowhere. She wore a white gown that was dirtied from streaks of black and grey, and the gown blended seamlessly with her pale skin. The only color on her was the fire red of her hair, which matched the same brilliance of the embers that surrounded them.

"I'm Mary Bell." The redhead smiled, breaking the sadness that had seemed to overpower the rest of her features. She extended her hand, and Dell took it warily. "It's nice to meet you."

"Mary Bell?" Dell asked. "You're Iris's daughter. And Kegan's mother."

Mary nodded. "We all saw what you did to save Sarah, and that might give us a fighting chance."

"Us?" Dell asked.

They appeared from thin air. Hundreds of them, each of them dressed in the same clothes that they died in, and Dell was surprised to discover many of them in maid's uniforms, which meant that Sarah was right. The Bells had been luring women into the house to kill them.

Dell stood, his eyes peeling away from the hundreds of people that surrounded him, and turned his attention back to Allister and Mary, who stood side by side. "So we're dead?"

Allister frowned. "Well, that's what's so strange. We're dead." He gestured to the circled ghosts. "But you're not."

Dell blinked, his brain growing foggy with confusion. "How is that possible?" He pointed back toward Satan's army in the valley. "Those are—"

"Demons, yes," Allister said. "But as I mentioned before, we're not in hell. It's possible that this… purgatory, is able to consume living tissue."

"So what does that mean?" Dell asked.

Allister and Mary both slowly lowered their eyes.

"What are all of you—GAH!" Dell's ankle gave out and he

collapsed to the rocks. He reached for the hem of his jeans and pulled up the pant leg and then widened his eyes in terror.

Icy scales appeared just above his shoe and slowly crawled up his leg. He reached down and touched one, and it multiplied under his finger. He quickly retracted his hand and rolled down his jeans.

Suddenly, Dell's body sickened. And it wasn't just a physical pain. The poison spreading up his leg and coursing through his veins also affected his mind, exposing the darkest corners and unearthing the worst memories of his mind.

He saw his father leaving, and he relived the ridicule from his classmates, the embarrassments of his youth. The images flashed in his mind like a vile highlight reel, the moments passing quickly and slowly at the same time, forced to relive his shame.

It was an endless pit that he was cast into, and Dell thought he would fall forever. But it was the touch of a gentle hand against his cheek that pulled him from the darkness, and when he looked toward the light, he saw only one face: Sarah.

The darkness faded, and when Dell came to, he realized he was holding Mary Bell's cheek, and she was holding his. Dell quickly let go and retreated, embarrassed.

"You saved her," Mary said.

"Sarah's alive?" Dell asked.

"Yes," Allister answered. "You took her place. And now she has a chance to end this."

Dell frowned. "How?"

"The orb," Allister answered. "It is the key to opening the portal and unleashing the armies of hell onto Earth." He looked to the horizon and the valley of demons that surrounded them. "When the gate reopens, the dark lord will use the energy from our souls to propel his army onto Earth. That's why we were collected. That is our purpose."

Dell deflated, unable to comprehend the insanity of his situation. He kept waiting to wake from the dream, but the images that surrounded him did not fade. He was stuck between hell and Earth, surrounded by the dead and demons, and on his way to becoming one himself before vanishing into nothing as hell was released upon the mortal world.

---

23

*D*awn pierced the horizon, the first rays of light breaking through the barren trees. Winter's breath had stripped them of vegetation, transforming them into sticks that stretched toward the early grey blue of morning.

Sarah had sprinted into the woods, churning her legs as fast as they would carry her while her heels smacked the uneven earth covered in dead grass and leaves. Her muscles and lungs burned, but she didn't slow down. She didn't stop. Because while she had escaped the clutches of the Bell family, she still felt the shadow of their reach clawing at the back of her neck.

Eventually the cold, exhaustion, and fatigue overrode the fear propelling her forward, and Sarah slowed, then collapsed to her hands and knees, dropping the sack she'd carried from Pat's house. She sucked wind, her lungs burning with every breath.

It was the first time she'd stopped since leaving Pat's place. No, she thought. There never was a Pat, just a witch who managed to trick her. Whatever idea of Pat she thought existed, she had to push from her mind.

Sarah tilted her head up, catching the silhouettes of a few trees that blocked the sun struggling to gain momentum over the mountains. There was no wind, no rustling of dead leaves, no chirp of birds or animals, nothing but silence and Sarah and the still earth beneath her.

She wiped the sweat from her forehead, smearing some of the dirt across her skin, and then shifted to her side, sitting on her hip. She was trembling and freezing. Sarah frantically reached for her pant leg and rolled up her jeans, finding the pale flesh of her legs. Not icy scales, her own skin.

Sarah carefully ran her fingertips along her skin. She laughed, choking on the excitement, then quickly examined the other leg, finding it bare of any frosted blue scales as well. She checked her arms and hands and lifted the shirt to examine her stomach. They were gone. She was cured.

Sarah collapsed on her back. Tears of joy leaked from her face, but she wiped them away, knowing that if she was alive, it was only because of what Dell had done.

Sarah turned to look at the sack on the ground. She stared at it, hesitant to once again open Pandora's box. But it was the only lead she had, and Sarah wasn't sure how much time she had to figure it all out.

Sarah grabbed the bag and dumped its contents onto the cold soil, then opened the first page of the notebook the witch had put together. She flipped through the pages, having already looked through most of the articles, but found nothing useful. She tossed the notebook aside and then reached for the letters.

After straining to re-read the faded ink of the Bell family letters, Sarah found nothing that was useful to her situation or anything that she didn't already know. But then she remembered what the redhead had told her, about the orb being the key. But even if she was able to retrieve the orb, Sarah had no way of knowing how to destroy it.

And then Sarah's eyes fell to the mysterious book that she had lifted from Pat's house. It was an old book, the spine and cover weathered, the pages along the side browned from age. She reached for the book hesitantly, struggling to lift its weight and set it in her lap.

Sarah ran her fingers over the cover, tracing the title with her fingers, which spelled *Codex Gigas*. Slowly, she opened to the first page and grunted in frustration when she saw it was written in a foreign language. She flipped through a few more pages and confirmed that the entire book was unreadable.

Frustrated, Sarah tossed the book aside and then hugged herself, rubbing her arms to try and stay warm. Since she found the book among the witch's things, Sarah figured it might contain something useful, but if she couldn't read anything inside, then it wouldn't do her any good.

What she needed was someone she could talk to, someone she could trust, but the first person that she'd chosen to trust when she came to Bell ended up being the very thing that was trying to kill her, and the second person she trusted was gone.

She sat in the dirt, staring at the book she'd stolen, and then reached for it again. She opened the cover and turned to the table of contents. It looked as though each of the chapters were a name instead of a number.

She scrolled down the page, the words unfamiliar, but then stopped. She squinted at the name, reciting it. "Ecclesiastes."

It was a name she recognized. Most of the orphanages that Sarah had lived in growing up were extremely religious, and every Sunday she was forced to go to church. She didn't much care for the sermons, but she did like the fact that they served donut holes after the service. She'd stuff as many as she could in her pocket and snack on them the rest of the day.

Ecclesiastes was a book in the bible, but why the hell a witch would have something like this, Sarah had no idea. But it brought another thought to mind. If she was going to try and fight the devil, then she might benefit from a little holy intervention.

Bell didn't have a church, at least not anymore after it was burned down, but she remembered seeing one when she was passing through Redford. It was as good a place to start as any, and seeing how she didn't have any other leads, it was her best option.

Sarah shut the book and then scooped it off the ground. She shoved it back inside the bag along with the letters and the notebook and then turned south toward Redford.

* * *

BRENT ALVAREZ LINGERED in the back of the squad car after the woman disappeared, still in shock over how she'd vanished into thin air, just like the handcuffs that had been around his wrists. He wiggled his fingers, smiling at his freedom.

Brent reached for the door handle of the cop car, and then laughed when it opened and he stepped out into the cold.

The difference in temperature between the back of the squad car and outside was minimal. But he didn't complain about the cold. He'd lived in New York City his entire life, but the cold had eaten through his leather jacket and jeans after being stuck in the back of the fucking cruiser for the past few hours. And the more irritated he became, the more he wanted to shove the barrel of his pistol down that podunk cop's throat.

Brent reached into the front compartment of the dash and grabbed his wallet and badge that Dell had confiscated upon his arrest, along with the revolver. He flicked the barrel open and found it empty, remembering that he'd fired all of his shots in the forest.

Brent popped the trunk and searched the back, but the only thing he found were a few road flares, a spare Kevlar jacket, and a box of twelve-gauge shotgun shells. He angrily tossed the box back inside and then slammed the trunk shut. "Shit."

There were more bullets for the .38 special in the glove box of his GTO, though his precious car was currently flipped upside down in a ditch off the highway heading south. He could head there and check it out, but he wasn't sure if the troopers hadn't already arrived to confiscate it.

Hands on his hips, Brent glanced around the town until his eyes landed on the tavern. He was willing to bet the old bastard had a shotgun or rifle stashed beneath the bar and decided to go inside and check it out.

No longer concerned about keeping up with appearances, Brent smashed the front door window with his elbow, littering the inside with glass. He reached for the lock, gave it a twist, and granted himself entry.

The place reeked of stale booze and dirty dish rags, and Brent wrinkled his nose in defiance as he headed for the bar, feeling beneath the cash register, but to his surprise, he found nothing but counter. "You're kidding me." Brent ducked underneath and checked all along the inside of the bar, but there was no firearm to be found. "Dammit!" He pounded his fist against the bar and then reached for a bottle of tequila.

The liquor was warmer than the air outside, and Brent

poured it straight into his mouth, spilling some of it down his chin and the front of his jacket. He poured for five seconds before finally setting the bottle down.

Brent shut his eyes, letting the liquor burn and calm his nerves. Tequila had always been his drink of choice. He caught a lot of shit because of it when he was growing up because everyone in his neighborhood drank whiskey.

"Don't be one of those wetbacks, Brent!"

He could still hear their voices now, twenty years later. But the torment of his heritage was at the bottom of his concerns. He knew that Dell had radioed the troopers, and he knew that he told them about what happened, but that didn't mean they knew every detail. And if the woman who set him free was as good at helping him escape as she was covering up murders, then he had some wiggle room. But that meant finding Sarah and killing her.

Outside, a siren wailed in the distance, and Brent hurried out the door. The harsh din of the sirens preceded the flashing lights that bathed the town in blues and reds.

Before the cop were even in the town, Brent sprinted for the woods. He'd feel better with a few bullets in his empty chamber.

24

*I*ris wasn't sure what she had expected when it was done. She had hoped that the weight of doubt and pain that she'd experienced over the past several decades would be lifted. She was tired of feeling so hollow and empty. She wanted it to be done, but when she saw Dell disappear into that orb and the witch claiming its last soul, there was no sweet moment of release, no light that guided her from the darkness. She only felt weaker.

A cold hand lightly grabbed her shoulder, and Iris turned to find the witch circling from behind. "My dear Iris, you don't look well."

The witch had chosen to remain unclothed in the house, though her long black hair covered her breasts, and Iris found it difficult to look the woman in the eye. She was so bold in her body. Iris had never had that confidence, even as a younger woman, at least not in the company of strangers.

"Where is my daughter?" Iris kept her head down, and she couldn't stop shivering. "You promised me I could have Mary."

The witch slowly peeled her fingers off Iris's shoulder

and then stepped toward the bed where Sarah had been confined. "She is still needed." The witch gripped the nearest bed post and then looked back, half her face covered by her bangs. "But the dark lord will give you what you seek. He can provide everything."

Iris finally looked up from her feet. She clenched her fists by her sides and then took an aggressive step forward. "You told me that if I gave you the souls you needed that I would get my daughter back!" She thrust a curved and swollen finger, crooked from arthritis, and aimed it at the witch.

The witch kept her back to Iris, the threat repelled off of her porcelain skin. "You know you're very much like Allister Bell." She turned, holding one of the picture frames that contained a photo of her daughter that had been scratched out as she walked back toward Iris. "When his family was in trouble, he did whatever was necessary to save them. No matter the cost." She smiled, handing the picture over to Iris. "Love is dangerous, Iris. Love kills more people than any war or disease. It clings to people like a parasite and sucks them dry till there's nothing left. Love leaves you hollow." She placed her long red nail against Iris's cheek and then traced her jawline with the gentlest of strokes. "You put all of your blame into the dark lord for how you feel. But you are the one in control of your emotions, Iris Bell. Not him. You."

Tears welled up in Iris's eyes and then fell along her wrinkled cheek, catching in the lines of her skin that distorted its path. She traced the scratched-out features of Mary's face in the picture, trying to remember her daughter's face. She had always been so beautiful, even as a baby. That fire-red hair was so striking it caught glances everywhere she went. There wasn't a man in town that didn't want to marry her, though none of them, not even the one she'd say yes to, was good enough for her.

"So pure," Iris said, remembering her daughter. "Fresh as

a brand-new morning." But while she wanted to smile, and while she wanted the words leaving her lips to taste sweet on her tongue, Iris frowned, and the words tasted sour.

"Let go, Iris," the witch said, grabbing hold of her arm. "That sadness, that uncertainty, it can all fade away. You can make it disappear in the blink of an eye."

She wanted to let go, she wanted to feel that sweet release of apathy and drift into nothing. Her hands ached from holding on for so long, but she wasn't even sure if she knew how to do that anymore.

"Allister didn't have the opportunity that you have right now," the witch whispered in her ear. "You could reshape your future. You could be young again, and strong, and desirable."

The last word pricked at her soul. She wanted to feel that way. She wanted men to look at her the way she'd seen people look at the witch, the way Iris was looking at her right now.

"All you have to do is let go," the witch said, continuing her seductive whispers.

And just when Iris was about to do it and feel her fingers slip from the ledge so she could fall, she lowered her gaze to the picture frame, and she kept hold.

"Fine," the witch said, displeased. "Have it your way, hag."

The witch stormed out of the room, leaving Iris alone with the picture held in her arthritic hands that curved around the silver frame. A tear splashed over the glass, and Iris leaned up against the wall to help keep herself from falling.

Grief spilled out of her in waves, and she dropped the frame from her hands, covering her face, smearing the tears along her cheeks, and then collapsed to the floor. How did she get here? How did all of this happen?

"Grandma?" Kegan froze in the doorway and then immediately dropped to his knees, gently placing his hands on her shoulders. "Are you all right?"

Iris leaned her head back, eyes red and glassy. "It was wrong." She turned to Kegan, locking eyes with him, and then grabbed his arm before he could pull away. He was like his father. He always had a problem staring difficulties in the face. He ran from them. But unlike his father, Kegan could be swayed. He could be convinced of another way. "Kegan, I—"

Sirens blared beyond the walls, and both turned to the door. The noise grew louder, and both of them knew what the police had come here for.

"C'mon, Grandma," Kegan said, gently lifting Iris off the floor. "We need to get you to bed."

"No," Iris replied. "I need to see."

Kegan opened his mouth to protest, but then stopped himself and only nodded as he helped her out of the room and down the hall.

The going was slow, and before they even reached the first floor, they heard officers banging on the door. No doubt Dell had called for backup when he arrived. But there was no Dell here, no bodies, nothing to incriminate them. The witch would see to that because she still needed to perform the ceremony.

"Wait." Iris held up her hand for Kegan to stop as they reached the second floor. She gestured toward the nearest room and then walked to the window. She pulled back the curtain and saw half a dozen highway trooper vehicles parked along the end of the main street, which dead-ended into the circular drive of the mansion's property.

"They'll press us hard," Kegan said. "Dell's car is still down there, and I don't think they're going to just go away if we pretend not to know anything."

"The wolves at the door," Iris said, her voice a breathless whisper. "Scratching, clawing to get inside. They never stop."

The pounding continued, and Kegan tried to pull her away from the window. "The longer it takes for us to answer, the longer they're going to stick around because they think something's wrong."

But Iris just kept staring out of the window, ignoring Kegan's pleas for heading downstairs, and then her gaze turned toward the town. Even from far away, it looked like it had deteriorated into nothing. "We made it. We can destroy it."

Kegan pulled Iris from the window, forcing his face into hers. "What are you talking about? Grandma, we need to head down there and talk to them."

And Iris wasn't sure she understood what she was saying herself. But there was something growing deep within her thoughts, an idea that wanted to break free. She couldn't live like this anymore. She couldn't put her family through this anymore. The witch was right. She could make a different decision than Allister made. She could set what was left of her family on a different path. Because she was starting to realize that the road she'd chosen had a dead end, and it was coming up. Quickly.

25

*A*fter battling the woods again for the hundredth time, Sarah broke from the trees and saw Redford stretched at the bottom of the hill where she stood. The sun had risen higher in the sky, and Sarah figured it was somewhere around mid-morning; late enough to where people had already commuted to work, leaving the roads below barren.

The chapel was on the west side of town, and Sarah spotted the cross rising from the sharply-pitched roof. The sun was still low enough for the tip of the cross to scrape the bottom of it, which cast a shadow that stretched into the road and covered the building to the north.

Sarah adjusted the book in her bag over her shoulder, looking up to check her distance from the church, and then lowered her eyes.

The closer she moved toward the church, the more her stomach soured. And despite the cold, beads of sweat appeared on her forehead and dripped from her underarms and down her ribs.

When she was a kid, either in the orphanages or in a

foster home, there were always people that came from the church to help volunteer their time or donate clothes or toys. And while Sarah accepted their hand-me-downs, she never enjoyed the transaction.

The volunteers always looked down on her and the other kids like they were disease-ridden. But it was the looks of pity that she hated most.

The people that gave all of those donations weren't giving orphans all of those toys and clothes because they wanted to make the kids feel better, they were doing it because it made themselves feel better.

It was like some kind of moral 'taking out the garbage' that involved dropping off toys and clothes that their kids had outgrown. A yearly purge of do-good that came and went quickly.

But where were the church goers when she had gone two days without food? Where were the priests and pastors when her foster father was beating the shit out of her? Where was God when she was scared and alone and cold in the middle of the night during winter because her foster mother had gone on another bender and didn't have enough money to turn the power on?

Those memories swirled to the forefront of Sarah's thoughts, and by the time she reached the front chapel, she was seething with anger. She no longer cared for seeking answers, she just wanted something to yell at.

Sarah burst inside, finding rows of long pews empty with a red carpet that ran through the middle of it, which led toward the pulpit. Light shone through the stained-glass windows that sat high on the walls to her left and right, breaking up the sunlight into different shades of colors that brightened the empty pews.

And at the front of the church, nailed to a cross that sat

high on the front wall, lording over anyone that came to visit, was a statue of Jesus Christ.

Sarah walked all the way down the red carpet, her eyes locked onto Christ's downturned face, wearing that crown of thorns the Romans had placed on his head to mock him. He looked weak, tired, and hungry. But Sarah had no sympathy for him. Why should she? She had gone her entire life weak, tired, hungry, and afraid. He experienced it for only a few days.

"Hello."

With a snarl etched on her face, Sarah turned and found the priest dressed in black, hands behind his back with a coy smile on his face. He faced the sunlight, and the glasses he wore reflected the rays that penetrated the windows.

When Sarah didn't say anything, the priest stepped closer, and the smile faded to concern. She watched him examine her and her haggard state. "Do you need help?"

Sarah laughed, but it had no joy. It was mocking the priest's question, and she looked back up to Christ on the cross. "Isn't that what he's for?" She smirked and then looked back to the priest, though his expression of concern hadn't faded.

"Would you like to sit down?" The priest gestured to the front pew and took a seat before she agreed to join him.

Sarah walked toward him but didn't sit down. She figured she wouldn't be here that long. She had never found church useful before, and she was confident that wouldn't change now. He'd tell her that she needed to be saved, and that the only way to break Satan's hold on her heart and soul was to accept the love of their lord and savior.

The priest raised his eyebrows at Sarah's glaring silence. "This may come as a surprise, but I don't read minds."

Sarah unzipped her jacket and removed the Codex Gigas, making sure the cover was facing the priest. She set it on the pew next to the priest and then stepped back and crossed her arms. "Do you know what that is?"

The priest simply looked at the book, picked it up, and flipped it over in his hands as he nodded. "I do."

Sarah waited for more, but the priest didn't budge. "And?"

The priest set the book back down on the seat. "This is the bible of Satan."

Sarah frowned, shifting her consternation toward the book on the pew. "It's what?"

The priest pointed to each word of the title. "Codex Gigas. The Devil's Bible."

Sarah stole glances between the bible and the priest, then eventually sat down, leaving the book between them. "There is something coming, and I need to know how to stop it."

"What do you think is coming, and why do you think you need to stop it?" the priest asked.

Sarah shook her head, taken aback by the question. "Because it's the end of the world." She pointed to the book. "The devil is coming, and he's bringing hell with him."

"You're referring to the end of days?" the priest asked, furrowing his brow.

Sarah gritted her teeth. "I'm serious."

The priest looked Sarah up and down and nodded. "I can see that. And I can also see that you don't want to be here." He gestured toward the doors at the back. "No one's stopping you from leaving."

It was the priest's aggressiveness that threw her off guard. She squinted at him, the pair in a standoff. Finally, Sarah walked to the pew and sat down, keeping her posture stiff and rigid. She pressed her finger against the book's cover. "The guy who wrote this is on his way unless I can figure out a way to stop it."

"The apostles are coming?" the priest asked.

"The Devil." Sarah pointed to Christ. "You know, the guy who did that to your friend up there."

"Satan didn't do that," the priest said, and then he picked up the book. "And he didn't write this. You know who did?"

"Who?"

"People."

Sarah deflated. "People wrote this book and killed Jesus."

The priest nodded. "That's right." He smiled, but this time Sarah didn't feel belittled or degraded, it was the smile she suspected an older brother would have given a younger sister if she'd ever known what that was like.

"God is real," the priest said. "Satan is also real. But neither really play a large role in our day-to-day lives. They whisper to us." He held up a finger. "But they don't make our decisions for us, they don't put us in predicaments, and neither of them can save you from yourself in this world."

"So I guess I came to the wrong place?" Sarah asked.

The priest chuckled and then shifted in the pew to more of a relaxed position. "People come in here all the time, looking for answers. They're convinced beyond a shadow of a doubt that Satan is responsible for everything bad that's happening in their life, and they want to know why God isn't doing anything to stop him. But what people don't understand is that they're the ones making bad decisions. They want an excuse for the choices that they've made in their life, and all of them had the same look on their faces that you do right now when I tell them that God can't help them. You have to help yourself."

Sarah rubbed her temples, trying to stem the headache forming. "Look, I know that you might get a lot of people coming in here with a lot of bullshit problems, but when I tell you that the devil is coming, and that I need to know how to stop it, I'm not fucking around."

"And you think the answer is in this book?" The priest asked.

"I don't know, genius, that's why I came to talk to you."

The priest laughed. "Fair enough." He picked up the devil's bible, the motion quick and agile, which surprised Sarah. He flipped through the pages, too quickly to actually be reading them. "Did you know that the first portion of this book is actually the bible?"

"The bible that you read?" Sarah asked.

"Word for word." The priest stopped halfway through the book and pressed his finger against the page. "It was around the fifteenth century that a group of monks decided to add their own books to the bible. They had a different idea of the teachings of Satan along with a different version of the book of Revelations."

"Revelations," Sarah said, a few more memories of her childhood Sunday school resurfacing. "That's when the rapture is supposed to happen."

The priest leaned forward, resting his left forearm on the back of the pew. "The bible speaks of the second coming of God as an apocalyptic event, and that only those that are true to God and have followed His word will be rescued from the earth, and the rest will be forced to suffer after God takes His children to heaven and the devil takes control of the earth. The monks from the medieval ages had a different take that it would be Satan who returns in Revelations, rescuing humans of earth from the wrath of God."

"So people just wrote the sides they wanted to win." Sarah lowered her eyes to the book between them. "That's the way it always is." She stood and walked closer to the pulpit and glanced up at Christ. "Everyone has their own version of what they want to happen, and the people pulling the strings at the top don't care so long as they win, and everyone else is an afterthought."

"Is that what happened to you?" the priest asked.

Sarah chuckled, the laughter hopeless and exhausted. She turned toward the priest. "You want to know what happened to me? You want to know the story of my life?" She reached for the collar of her shirt and exposed the scars on her back to the priest. "And that's just the ones that left a mark." She let go of her shirt. "Do you know how many kids I knew that never made it out of the system alive? I lost count. And all you can do is sit there and tell me that it has nothing to do with your boss or his enemy? You're going to sit here, in this place, in a fucking church, and tell me that God can't do anything? Why?" Desperation rose with her anger, and her cheeks flushed red. "I want to know! Why? WHY!" She screamed, her voice echoing off the walls, and the shriek burned her throat as the priest only stared at her while she caught her breath and wiped the saliva dripping off of her chin.

"God wants to help," the priest said. "So does the devil. But the moment they choose to decide for us, what's left?" He stood and walked toward her, his movements steady and calm. "I believe in heaven, and I believe in hell, and I also believe that God gives us strength to handle whatever life throws at us, and if we can't?" He shrugs. "Then we get to meet Him at the gates of heaven, and our struggle is no more."

Helplessness flooded through Sarah's veins. She wanted to hit him, she wanted to scream, but instead she only returned to the pew and sat down, where she buried her face in her hands. There was no grief, no tears, only emptiness.

"It never changes, does it?" Sarah asked, staring at the floor. "It's the same people on top, and the same people at the bottom, every time. And hope just teases and tricks us into thinking that it will change one day." She looked up at the priest. "But it doesn't."

The priest's stoic expression softened, and then he walked to Sarah and knelt on one knee. He placed his hand on her leg, and it was the first time in her life where a stranger had touched her and she didn't flinch. She wasn't sure what that meant.

"It does," the priest said. "Because of people like you."

"You don't know who I am," Sarah said.

"Yes, I do." The priest smiled and then picked up the book she'd brought and placed it in her lap. "You're the girl who's going to stop the end of the world. Not because you were chosen, or it's your destiny, but because you want to help save people."

"But how?" Sarah asked.

The priest opened the book and turned to the pages toward the end. He searched for a minute, pinpointing the exact page that he was looking for, and then tapped it when he found it. "In order for the devil to return, it was said that he would need a portal. Some powerful object that would act as the gateway to hell so his demons could escape and he could bring the fires of hell to the earth."

Sarah nodded, reading the same scripture that the priest had pointed to. It was the orb. That's what the witch was going to use now that she had the souls she needed to accomplish it. "So if I destroy the gate, then they won't be able to get through."

"In theory, yes," the priest said. "But it will take a powerful force." He found another line and read. "Blood is the beginning. Blood is the end."

Sarah looked at the line, then at the priest. "What the hell does that mean?"

"I'm not sure." The priest kept his attention on the text. "But it is in the same section as the portal."

"Right," Sarah said, exhaling a sigh. "Which of course makes everything crystal clear now."

The priest smiled. "Come with me."

Sarah followed the priest back behind the wall where Jesus was nailed to the cross and they stepped into a small office, each of the walls lined from floor to ceiling with books, and at the center was a small desk that the priest stepped behind.

"There are a few things that can help you with demons." The priest opened the drawer and removed a wooden cross and two tubes of water. "Any sign of Christ and agents of the devil will be repelled. The two biggest weapons you have in that regard are crosses and holy water."

Sarah walked over and picked one of the tubes up, running her thumb over the corked top. It was cold, nearly freezing.

"But this is your most important weapon." The priest reached deep within the drawer and removed a bible that he placed next to Sarah's hands. "Nothing causes the devil to sweat more than the words written on those pages."

The bible was small, only about the size of Sarah's hand. The cover was leather, and she ran her fingertips over the little bumps along the front, then traced the gold lettering.

"Satan's connection with this world is strongest at the witching hour," the priest said.

"When is that?" Sarah asked, rotating the tube of holy water between her fingers.

"It starts at 3am.

The priest grabbed her arm, and she looked up. "Whatever you're facing, even if it feels like you're alone, I promise you one thing. You won't be."

Sarah nodded, gathered up her things, and left without a word. Outside, she kept looking back at the church, waiting for the priest to run outside and join her, or for her to run back and tell him thank you for listening, thank you for giving her what she needed, and telling her what she needed to hear.

If by some miracle she actually made it out of this alive, then she would go back to that church and thank him properly. She nodded, liking the idea of returning as a triumphant hero and handing the bible back over to him, smiling.

Sarah held onto that moment and savored the future. It was the same thing she used to do when she was little. She would see some great thing in the distance and focus on that until whatever bad shit she was going through had ended.

It was a method she used throughout her entire life, looking ahead for tomorrow and a new day. But as often as she used it growing up, by the time she reached adulthood, there wasn't much left for her to look forward to on the horizon, so she filled her days with things to make her forget.

Booze, drugs, cigarettes, sex, anything to up those endorphins and push down the bad thoughts. But now all of those bad thoughts had come to a head, and Sarah had to focus on today. Because if she couldn't do that, then there wouldn't be a tomorrow.

26

*A*n officer descended the grand staircase, and Iris watched him give a light shake of his head to the troopers that occupied the foyer. When he made it to the bottom, he followed up his glance with a few whispers and they then stepped outside into the cold morning.

The doors had remained open, and from her spot in the foyer, Iris could still see the police vehicles down below, but what had occupied most of her attention was the decay in her own home. She'd always been able to look past it, but now she found her eyes lingering on the blemishes.

One of the tiles in the foyer was chipped, exposing a black mark against the brilliant white of the marble flooring. A strip of wallpaper had curled and broken free from the wall to her left along the corner. Her eyes traveled over the room, finding stains, holes, and decay everywhere, hidden amongst the grandeur of the home.

And her critical eye bled from the house and to herself.

The stitching at the end of the sleeve on her nightgown had come loose, dangling freely from the rest of the cuff. The nail polish of her left hand had chipped, exposing the age and frailty that lay beneath.

Spots and wrinkles crawled over her body. She had never been so aware of her own age as she did in that moment. And she didn't just feel it in her body, it was her mind as well. The years had battered her memory.

The curse, the witch, her devotion in trying to free her family of the wretched damnation that her husband's ancestor had led them toward, it had consumed her life. It was all she could focus on for the past thirty years.

Thirty years gone in the blink of an eye.

"Mrs. Bell?"

Iris looked up from the floor and into the gaze of the young highway trooper taking her statement. She frowned, wondering how long she'd been dazed and how long he'd been repeating the same question. "I'm sorry, what did you say?"

"I said, when was the last time you saw Dell Parker?" the trooper replied.

"Oh, um, he came yesterday morning to speak with our groundskeeper, Dennis." Iris cleared her throat and shifted her weight on her feet. "After he looked around, he left and took Dennis with him, and said that he wanted to ask him some more questions. I thought he'd be back by now, but he never returned."

"And can you tell me what Pat Landon was doing here?" The trooper pointed across the foyer where Pat was being interviewed by another trooper.

"Dennis usually comes in for a drink, but he didn't last night, so Pat came up to ask what was wrong." Iris recited the words like she was reading them from a script.

The witch had transformed back into Pat to confuse the trooper who Dell had said was shot. Finding him healthy and at the house punched a big hole in Dell's story. And with no evidence of any wrongdoing, the troopers had nothing on them but what Dell had reported. And Dell was nowhere to be found.

"We're going to head to Redford and speak with Dennis about Dell's investigation," the trooper said, jotting down notes as he spoke. "Which means that he'll most likely be in our custody for some amount of time. Does he have any family we can notify?"

"No," Iris answered. "We're Dennis's family."

"Thank you for your time, Mrs. Bell."

Iris watched the trooper return to the clustered pack of officers as they huddled to discuss their next steps.

They were probably discussing how Dell had misreported a crime. After all, he was just some small-town cop with nothing to do all day except to pick up the trash on the side of the road and rescue kittens from trees. The troopers didn't consider him a real cop, and they weren't going to treat him like one.

It was a shame. She'd always liked Dell. If she had a son like him, she suspected that she wouldn't have had to carry this kind of burden all by herself.

Kegan was called over by the troopers and brought into their huddle. He nodded, said a few words, and then shook their hands as they left.

The doors closed, shutting out the cold and the light, and Kegan lingered with his back turned after they left. Iris watched him as he lowered his head and then looked to Pat, who transformed back into her original form, quick as shedding a towel.

Kegan finally turned and walked toward Iris as the witch neared as well. The three of them huddled together in the foyer, but Iris was still looking at the doors.

"They're going to leave a unit here in case Dell comes back," Kegan said. "And they've requested that if we hear from anyone, or remember anything, to give them a call." He reached into his pocket and removed one of the trooper's cards.

The witch laughed, the high-pitched squeal growing louder until it faded with a quick breath as she inhaled. "I suppose it helps to have a person that's immortal to help tip the scales in your favor." She walked toward the staircase and ascended the steps. "I'll be in the room, preparing for tonight." She turned back and cast them a glare with a flash of fire and brimstone in her eyes. "I hope you can hold on for that long at the least." Then she disappeared beyond their sight.

Kegan waited until they couldn't hear her steps anymore before he finally looked down and spoke. "How are you holding up, Grandma?"

But Iris was still focused on the closed doors. They were sealed tight, blocking out the light and casting the interior of the foyer in darkness. She looked to the closed drapes and curtains that covered the windows. It was daylight outside, yet it felt like night in here. It was always dark in here, and she had been the one to close the blinds.

"Grandma?" Kegan asked.

"I need to lie down." Iris exhaled and cradled her head as Kegan gently took her arm and helped her up to the room.

Whatever had been draining her energy had ratcheted up its efforts. Life was slipping away, sifting between Iris's fingers. It was moving quicker now, pricked by an integral vein that fed her life. And now that same vessel was killing her.

"Grandma?"

Iris was dizzy and she shuffled toward the bed before she fell over. She didn't bother pulling back the sheets, she just lay down on top of the white comforter and slowly rested her head on a pile of pillows that kept her propped up.

"What can I do?" Kegan's voice trembled, but when he gripped her hand, she felt strength.

"I thought I could change it," Iris said, opening her eyes and staring at a patch of the ceiling where she spotted the beginning of a water stain. One of the pipes had most likely burst, or at the very least was cracked. It wouldn't be long before the plaster and wood finally rotted and water broke through. "Holes in the boat. It's starting to leak." She frowned, remembering a time from her youth out west when she was out on a friend's boat on her father's lake. "My mother was furious because I ruined my new dress." She laughed.

"Grandma, listen to me," Kegan said and then pulled her face toward his own. "I'm going to call a doctor, okay? You're not well."

Iris placed her weathered palm against Kegan's cheek and then finally mustered a smile. "I'm fine." Though her voice was riddled with weakness, and she had to drop her hand after only being able to hold it up for a few seconds. She drew in a ragged breath. "I don't need a doctor."

Kegan stared at her, confused, and then turned sharply, but Iris snatched his wrist, the speed in which she grabbed him surprising to both of them. Iris zeroed in on that one quick moment of clarity and strength.

"I might not last much longer," Iris said. "And that means you have to fix my mistake."

Kegan gingerly took a seat on the edge of the bed, holding his grandmother's hand. "What are you talking about? If you're sick, then I can get help."

"It's too late for me, but it's not too late for you." Iris kept her voice at a whisper. "You can do what I didn't have the strength to do."

Kegan shook his head. "Grandma, you don't know what you're—"

Iris squeezed his arm tighter, and pulled him closer. "Listen to me. The girl will come back. And when she does, you need to help her, do you understand? Help her."

"Sarah? Why would she come back? How am I supposed to help her?"

Doubt seeped into her thoughts. "You will know when the time comes." She closed her eyes, and sleep started to take hold. She hadn't felt tired like this in a long time. It was a good tired, an aching tired, and she didn't want it to go to waste. She had a feeling that this would be her last sleep, and she wanted to make it to be a restful one.

27

*B*efore heading back to Bell, Sarah had decided to make a pit stop. If she was in Redford to collect information, then there was one spot heading out of town that she might be able to gain some additional insight into the house and the family trying to bring about the end of the world.

And it would be nice to know what the cops knew about the situation, assuming that Sarah could pry the information out of Faye over at the station. Judging from the conversation she'd overheard between her and Dell, she didn't expect for the girl to put up too much of a fight. And Dell had told her that if anything happened to him, then she should talk to Faye. That fact alone was enough.

Still keeping an eye out for the authorities, Sarah made her way to the Redford police station, snickering to herself over the fact that she was about to do the one thing that she'd been avoiding for the past week: talk to the cops.

The Redford police building stood alone near the front of the town, and as Sarah approached, the timer on the lights in the parking lot finally shut off, which was empty save for one car. It was a purple Nissan, the tires void of any hubcaps, and Sarah passed the windows of the car slowly.

The steering wheel was concealed beneath a leopard print cover, and a pair of pink fuzzy dice hung from the rearview mirror. The floors were littered with trash, mostly Starbucks Coffee cups, and the back seat had stacks of clothes in it.

A blast of warm air greeted Sarah upon stepping inside, and she closed her eyes, glad she was able to feel the heat again.

The entrance to the inside of the building was cramped, and Sarah found herself in a narrow hallway, with a coat rack to her right and a beige wall to her left. Ahead she could see a cut out, and even before Faye came into view, Sarah could hear the smacking of gum from Faye's mouth.

The woman Sarah saw was much like the one she'd expected. Faye was dolled up with too much make-up on her face that included blue eyeshadow, rouge, and red lipstick that would have given Iris Bell a heart attack.

But while Sarah stood silent and dumbstruck in the hallway, Faye continued to peruse the magazine clutched in her hands, which Sarah noticed was Glamour.

With Sarah gawking at Faye's long, acrylic nails that looked more like knives than actual nails, she didn't even notice that Faye had peeled her eyes off the page of the latest 'how to get a good man' article and stared her down.

"Can I help you?" Faye asked, her arched eyebrows matching the same accusing tone of her voice, and Sarah suddenly regretted coming here. It was stupid, foolish. She didn't even have an idea of what she was supposed to ask. And what would the woman tell her anyway? It wasn't like—

"Miss?"

Sarah snapped out of her daze and found that Faye had

dropped her magazine, all of her attention focused on Sarah. She chewed on her lower lip, and Faye gave her a look up and down.

"Do you need help?" Faye asked.

"My name is Sarah Pembrooke."

The gum smacking ended when Faye's jaw hung loose. "Oh my god." Faye placed her palm over her chest and she breathed heavily, her cheeks growing even brighter from the combination of her flush and the rouge. "You're the girl Dell told me about." She looked toward the door. "Is he with you? I haven't been able to reach him on the radio and—"

"Faye." Sarah slowly approached the counter, making sure she kept both hands up so Faye could see. Sarah wasn't sure what the receptionist might be packing behind the counter, and Sarah wasn't in the mood to have her day end with a chest full of lead. "I don't know what people told you. I don't know how I'm even alive, but I need to know what Dell knew, and I need to figure out what's happening at the Bell mansion. Dell told me that I could trust you."

Faye was quiet for a while and then nodded. "You can." She shuffled around a pile of notes on her desk, and then picked one up. "Uh, the state troopers arrived on scene a few hours ago, but I haven't gotten an update from them." She looked at Sarah, her face concerned. "Dell's desk is over there if you want to sit down. I'll be just a minute."

Sarah sat down in Dell's cracked leather chair. The bottom was well worn, and she thought she would fall straight through after she sat down.

From Dell's desk, Sarah could see Faye's back as she sat hunched over the desk, phone to her ear. She spoke quietly, but quickly. Sarah drifted her eyes from Faye's back to the rest of Dell's desk.

Aside from the monitor, keyboard, and mouse, there

wasn't much decoration. Not that she expected to find much personality. Dell never struck her as someone who had tons of flair. And while after her first encounter with Dell, she didn't want to know anything about him, Sarah found her curiosity piqued about the man who had sacrificed himself so Sarah could live.

"Hey," Faye said, walking over to the desk. "The troopers finished their scan at the house. They didn't find anything."

"What?" Sarah asked, standing. "That's impossible."

"Dell had called in a report that Pat was shot," Faye replied. "But when the troopers showed up, they said that Pat was there and completely fine. Do you know anything about that?"

Sarah shut her eyes, turning away from Faye. "Son of a bitch." The witch was clever. She must have returned to Pat's form, which meant that any evidence of wrongdoing on Brent's part had been erased. She spun back around at that thought. "Brent."

"The detective?" Faye glanced down at her notes. "Dell told me that he was in the back of his squad car, but the troopers said he wasn't in there either." She lifted her eyes. "And, um, the troopers are considering you a suspect."

"What?" Sarah asked.

"They think something is going on between you and Dell, and after Dell reported all of those things with Pat being shot, and bodies at the house, and nothing being true, it's not painting a pretty picture." She hesitated and then stiffened with courage. "Sarah, what happened?"

Three quick steps and Sarah was able to grab hold of Faye's shoulders. She was tall, made even taller by the heels she wore. "I need to speak with Dennis. I need to know what he knows about the house."

Faye hesitated. "Are you sure about that?" She looked down a hallway and shivered. "He gives me the creeps."

Sarah's cheeks went pale, and when she saw that Faye had noticed, they flushed red again from embarrassment. "Talking to the guy who stripped me down to my underwear and then tied me to a chair in a basement isn't exactly on the top of my list right now either. But I don't have a lot of options."

'"Right," Faye said.

Sarah followed Faye down the hallway and toward the interrogation room. Sarah remained three or four hesitant steps behind and crept up to the window that Faye was looking through.

Dennis lay across the table, feet hanging off the side, with his arms folded over his chest and his eyes closed. He looked like he was sleeping.

"You're positive you want to do this?" Faye asked, fiddling with the key in her hand.

"He might know something, and if the troopers think that me and Dell are working some kind of conspiracy, then I need all the information I can get. And besides, I might get lucky with something he knows." Something that could help him figure out how to get Dell back.

Faye walked over, fumbling with the keys in her hand, and slid the brass key into the lock. Before she turned it, she looked to Sarah. "Do you want a gun?"

Sarah spouted nervous laughter. "Maybe. No. No, I'll be fine."

"I'll stay out in the window to watch. If anything goes wrong, you come out, and I'll shoot him."

"That works for me."

Sarah's heart rate spiked at the turn of the lock, and when the door opened, Dennis lifted his head from the table, squinting as Sarah stepped inside, and the door quickly shut behind her.

Dennis just stared at her in silence, and Sarah remained

277

close by the door. She was glad to see that he was still wearing his cuffs, but she would have preferred to have him shackled to the floor.

"That's not possible." Dennis slowly sat up, shaking his head. It was like he was staring at a ghost. "You're supposed to be dead."

"Seems to be a popular opinion lately." Sarah skirted the front wall, tossing a quick glance to the one-way glass where she knew Faye was watching. The fact that she knew she wasn't alone boosted her confidence.

Sarah and Dennis circled the table, Sarah making sure the table remained a physical barrier between the two of them, and Dennis growing angrier in the silence.

"Why aren't you with Mrs. Bell? Why aren't you at the house!" Dennis screamed at her, spit dribbling down his chin, his cheeks flushing red.

Sarah did her best to remain calm. The last thing she wanted to do was trigger Dennis into an unstoppable rage. Even with the cuffs on, he was formidable, and Sarah wasn't in the mood to relive her previous encounter with the groundskeeper.

"It's not going to happen," Sarah said, keeping her voice calm, which only agitated Dennis. "Your sacrifice escaped, and she's not going back."

"You have no idea what you've done," Dennis said. "There will be a reckoning for this, oh, yes. You will know what it feels to be tortured by demons. You will finally see." He opened his eyes wide and exposed his yellow teeth as he smiled. "You will burn."

Sarah pivoted to the left as Dennis started to walk around the table, mirroring his movements. "And how did you think it was going to work? What did you expect to happen?" Sarah knew that trying to ask Dennis directly wouldn't get anywhere, but if she egged him on, tricked him into telling her what she wanted, then she might be able to pull some useful information out of him.

Dennis pulled his chin inward, and the crease of his lips grew thinner as the smile widened. "It would have been glorious. You would have been a piece of history, and your story would have been told through the ages." He closed his eyes and tilted his face toward the ceiling, slowly swaying back and forth as if there was a melody stuck in his head. "The screams. The pain. The fire."

It was like he was drunk on some sort of evil. Whatever poison that the Bells and that witch had funneled down his throat had rotted away reason and control, if he had any to begin with, but Sarah was hoping to use that to her advantage. "And this would have happened in the basement where you tied me up?"

"The house is sacred ground," Dennis said as he continued to circle the table. "It is destined to be the fortress of the unholy and the damned."

"What about the room?" Sarah asked, still mirroring Dennis's movements. "Allister's room."

Dennis inhaled quickly and deep, a breath of excitement. "He is the surrogate father of the children he has helped set free and will be honored for eternity as the man who set the foundation for this future. His room shall act as the throne for the dark lord's arrival."

Sarah stepped around the end of the table, watching the expressions of elation spread over Dennis's face. Just talking about the end of the world propelled him into euphoria. "And when does it happen? This opening of the portal?"

"When Satan's connection is strongest to this world," Dennis answered. "The Devil's hour." He stopped pacing, and so did Sarah. The joy ran from his face and his expression grew stoic as he slowly turned his head, that pair of dead eyes setting on Sarah and sending a piercing cold through her heart. "You have seen him."

"How do you protect the portal?" Sarah asked, hoping to learn a weakness through one of its strengths.

"Mrs. Bell protects it."

"What does the phrase 'Blood is the beginning. Blood is the end' mean to you?"

Dennis tilted his head to the side and then gave it a gentle shake. "You think you're clever, don't you?"

Sarah looked toward the glass window and then gestured toward the door. But before Sarah even had a chance to turn around, Dennis was up and over the table, and then he smashed her up against the wall.

Sarah's head knocked viciously against the wall, turning her vision black, and when it faded, Dennis was less than an inch from her face. She caught the stench of his breath as he snarled like a rabid animal.

"You haven't escaped," Dennis said, the words spilling out of him quickly as if a wound had opened and blood was pouring out of him and he had to speak his truth before he died. "You're tied to that house just like me, and you'll go back, and when you do, you'll burn like the rest of them. You will *die*." Excited laughter smacked Sarah in the face, and the door to the room opened and Faye burst inside, gun in hand, shaking as she tried to aim it at Dennis's body.

"Let her go!" Faye shouted, but kept her distance. "I will shoot you, Dennis, I swear to God."

Dennis peeled his gaze from Sarah and set his eyes on Faye, though he didn't move his body, which he used to pin Sarah down. But the distraction gave Sarah enough time and space to fight back.

Sarah thrust her knee up and connected with his crotch, which forced Dennis backward, and he smacked against the table. Sarah spun toward the door, following Faye on their escape outside, and then slammed the door shut before Dennis could make a move toward it.

"You can't escape it, Sarah!" Dennis positioned himself at the one-way glass, pressing his face and body up against it as he screamed and pounded his forehead against the glass. "It won't stop following you!"

Sarah struggled to catch her breath as Faye squeezed her shoulder, groping it and repeating the same question over and over.

"Are you okay?"

Sarah nodded, but while she managed to regain control of her breathing, she couldn't bring her heartrate down. It beat wildly in her chest and continued to pound faster as Dennis's outburst escalated.

"The fires are coming!" Dennis continued to pound his head against the glass, which buckled with every contact, until the skin broke and blood trickled down his forehead. "Blood, and fire, and death will consume you! It follows you like a shadow, Sarah! It won't stop! It'll never stop! You hear me? It'll come! He will come!"

Faye eventually forced Sarah out of the hall, nearly having to use the gun to get her along. But Dennis didn't stop screaming, and he repeated the last phrase over and over until Sarah was convinced that she was saying it herself.

"He will come," Sarah said, whispering softly to herself. "Can I borrow a jacket?"

"Um, yeah."

Sarah followed Faye toward the reception area, and Faye handed Sarah a lumpy black pullover.

"Listen, Sarah, I don't know what's going on, but I think we need to tell the troopers. I mean, this is getting out of hand."

"No," Sarah said, her answer quick. "It's beyond them."

She stared down at the gun in Faye's hand. "But there is one more thing that you can help me with."

28

On the trip back to Bell, Sarah again stayed to the woods, and she repeatedly rubbed her thumb over the cross, the motion like an addiction that soothed her nerves. She would have preferred a smoke, but she had to make do.

Sarah pocketed the cross and then removed one of the tubes of holy water, and she was surprised to find it still liquid. It had to have been below freezing, and yet the glass felt the same temperature as when she got it. She pulled the jacket she wore tighter, thankful that Faye let her borrow it, then pocketed the water.

But the pistol that Faye gave her provided the most confidence. It was a more tangible weapon, one that she knew would work. She hoped that she wouldn't have to use anything, but the tools provided security.

The lights from the police cars gave Sarah a check marker of how close she was getting to Bell, and it also alerted her to the authorities still in the area. She approached cautiously, her senses heightened. It was like sneaking around the houses when she was a little kid in foster care. Except if she got caught now, it would be a hell of a lot worse than being thrown back into the system.

Keeping to the tree line on the west side of Bell, Sarah struggled to keep her attention ahead with all of the commotion in the streets. She counted eight highway trooper vehicles, plus Dell's cruiser.

With the sun still high in the sky, Sarah knew she had time, but she didn't want to wait longer than she had to. The quicker that she could get in and destroy the orb, the faster all of this would be over. But she needed to wait until the place was cleared.

So Sarah lingered at the tree line and waited, remembering what Faye had said before she left. "Just stay alive, okay, girl?"

Sarah wanted nothing more than to oblige Faye's request, but this was uncharted territory. Had she previously foiled an apocalypse before all of this, she would have felt better about her chances. The advice was better than what most therapists had given her growing up.

During Sarah's journey through the system that was foster care in the United States, she had been questioned by hundreds of adults, all of them asking the same types of questions over and over, expecting some type of life-changing effect on a troubled young girl.

The counseling wasn't unwarranted. She had stolen a car and crashed it into a United States postal box before quickly fleeing the scene. She did some time in juvie, and part of her rehabilitation was weekly visits with a court-appointed therapist.

Sarah kept quiet for most of the sessions, just nodding and only answering questions when the therapist threatened to tell the judge that she wasn't cooperating. But she never truly opened up, and the therapist was smart enough to cut through the bullshit.

"You're weak, you know that?" The question had come after nearly three minutes of dead silence, and Sarah felt her cheeks redden from both anger and surprise.

"Excuse me?" Sarah straightened in her chair and resisted the sudden urge to strangle the bitch in front of her. "Well, why don't we step outside so you can find out for yourself."

The therapist raised her hand and worked it like a puppet. "Talk, talk, talk, talk, talk. That's all you do. And what little action you do perform is nothing more than a cry for help." She leaned forward, matching Sarah's intensity instead of shying away from it like every other adult that had tried to intervene in her life. "So you got hit a few times, and your parents are dead, and you had a really hard life growing up. You know who cares?" She leaned closer, so close that Sarah could see the hole from the nose piercing she had in her right nostril. "No one. Zero people give zero shits about you and your troubled past."

"Fuck you." Sarah retreated into her chair and crossed her arms. She bounced her leg nervously and impatiently, staring up at the clock and wishing that their thirty minutes would pass quicker. "I don't need to hear this shit from—"

"From someone who doesn't understand?" The therapist feigned sympathy and batted her eyelids as she puffed out her lip. "You've been giving that excuse since the day you figured out it worked." She pointed to the closed door of her office. "You know how many kids I see every month? Every year? Hundreds. And every single one of them has a sob story, sister, so don't sit in that chair where so many have sat and tell me that your story is worse than theirs."

Sarah lowered her head, picking at her fingernails, which she always did when she was nervous. "Maybe it is."

The therapist scoffed and shifted the papers on her legs as she fidgeted in her chair. "I can promise you that it's not." She huffed a little longer, and then finally settled down. "You keep heading down this path and it's going to cost you more than you think."

"And what's that?" Sarah focused in on her left index cuticle, scratching harder.

"Your life."

Sarah stopped her scratching and looked up.

"You could do a lot of things, Sarah." She flipped through the papers on her lap and lifted one up for Sarah to see. "You scored through the roof on your assessment test, which means that your failing grades aren't due to a lack of ability, it's due to a lack of effort."

"Where did you get those?" Sarah asked.

"And in my experience, kids with ability who choose not to flex them end up applying their time to more unsavory deeds, and that's not a road that I want to see you walk down." She set the test scores aside and folded her hands in her lap. "You can either come to these sessions and listen to what I have to say, which will help you, or you can just sit there like you have been for the past two weeks, do your time, and when you're released, go and fall into whatever routine that you want." She leaned forward and this time placed her hand on Sarah's knee, squeezing hard. "But if you don't change what you're doing, you won't be doing it for very long."

It could have been the fact that no one, in a position like the therapist had been in, had ever talked to Sarah like that before. Or it could have been the fact that Sarah was able to recognize the truth when she saw it, but when the session ended and Sarah was escorted back to her cell and she was forced to sit on her cot while her roommate yammered on about how she would cut Sarah if she tried any shit on her while she was asleep, Sarah decided that she did need to make a change, and the exclamation point was the heavy, metallic thud of the door closing and being locked in her cell.

And that's exactly what she did.

Sarah was seventeen when she made that choice, and she suspected that if she had chosen a different path or decided to ignore the woman's advice, that her future would have turned out exactly how the therapist had envisioned. Sarah had seen firsthand the future that the therapist described. She saw it in the homes that she was forced to live in and the people that were responsible for her care.

Sarah didn't understand it at the time, but that therapist saved Sarah's life. And sitting in the woods in some forgotten town in the northern-most portion of the country where it got so cold you could freeze to death, Sarah wondered if she had wasted the opportunity.

While she had been able to stay out of jail, she couldn't stay out of trouble. And that trouble had led her here, and she wasn't sure if she'd be able to escape.

Finally, after another few minutes, the lights on the trooper's car lit up and he peeled out of town, speeding toward the highway. Faye had come through. She had asked her to call in a report of a tip that they had spotted Dell twenty miles south. They said a young woman was with him.

Once the lights had disappeared and she couldn't hear the sirens anymore, Sarah darted from the woods and made her way toward the house.

From her position in the woods, she was able to see the side door that she had used frequently to walk out back and take her breaks for lunch. She remembered that the doors had never been locked when she stayed there, that was until they tried to kill her.

With daylight shining down and the sun acting as a spotlight, Sarah waited until a cloud passed overhead before she sprinted from the woods. She felt incredibly slow, but she figured that it was due to the fatigue and lack of sleep, which she'd gone without for nearly forty-eight hours.

Black dots peppered her vision when she reached the door. The short distance had winded her and left her legs shaking like bowls of jelly. She shut her eyes, keeping below the window line of the door, and concentrated.

She just had to keep it together for a little longer. She gritted her teeth, took a breath, and then opened her eyes. She slowly peeked her head above the window line in the door and peered inside.

The sunlight made it difficult to break through the contrast of the darkness inside, and Sarah's heart beat faster when she reached for the door handle. She gave it a quick turn, but it was locked.

"Shit," she muttered under her breath, then maneuvered her way toward the back. There were two other doors that she knew of that could grant her access. One was on the back side of the building that led into the kitchen, which was locked, and the other was on the mansion's east wing that faced the great north, which was also locked.

After the defeat of the last door, Sarah briefly considered checking the front entrance. The Bells were cocky enough to leave that unlocked, but it was also the entrance that they could see her coming from anywhere on the front side of the house.

Sarah stayed low, tapping her foot, trying to figure out her next move. She still wasn't pressed for time, but she also knew that the longer it took her to retrieve the orb, the less time she had to destroy it. The last thing she wanted was the clock ticking down to zero and pushing her luck.

She briefly contemplated trying to project herself back into the house, but she figured that since those icy scales were gone that those abilities had vanished, too.

Attempting to climb and try for a second-story entrance was out of the question since there weren't any scaffoldings or concrete ledges for her to try and climb, which left Sarah only one option. Break a window, rush inside, and pray that she could hide before one of the Bells heard her escape.

Sarah picked up a nearby rock, then crouched near the east wing door. It had a single window pane, which looked like single pane glass. She shut her eyes, visualizing where the lock was on the door, then smashed the rock into the glass. She thrust her hand through, the thick sleeve of her jacket protecting her from the shards, and grabbed hold of the lock before giving it a quick twist.

Glass crunched beneath Sarah's boot as she sprinted inside, and she immediately darted up the stairs and before she even made it to the second floor, she heard the commotion in the house.

With her heart pounding, disoriented from the rush of adrenaline and confusion that was flooding through her veins, Sarah broke away from the staircase and sprinted onto the second floor. A quick scan of the hall revealed that the coast was clear, but the thundering footsteps coming from above signaled that they were getting closer.

Sarah reached for a door handle, which ended up being the sixth door on the right, and she burst inside, shutting it quickly and quietly behind her.

The room was one of several that hadn't yet been cleaned, and Sarah tiptoed toward the closet and concealed herself in the darkness.

Old clothes lined the rack, their scent musty and damp, the wool coarse and scratchy as it grazed Sarah's cheek on her retreat deeper into the darkness. The hurried steps from Kegan were muffled by the walls, but it grew louder and when Sarah heard the quick opening and shutting of doors on the second floor, she struggled to quiet her breathing.

Every slam that drew closer made her heart skip a beat and pound faster. She leaned up against the back wall and removed the pistol from her waist, gripping it with both hands.

And Sarah waited, the door slams growing more frequent and closer, until she heard the quick rush of wind that accompanied her door opening. Sarah froze.

The wooden floorboards groaned with every step, and panting breaths accompanied Kegan's footsteps. Sarah aimed the pistol at the closet door, her palms sweaty against the pistol's handle despite her knuckles being frozen stiff from the cold.

The footsteps traveled around the room, and Sarah heard the ruffle of sheets as Kegan checked beneath couches, chairs, and the bed, until finally all that was left was the closet.

Two columns of shadows appeared at the crack at the bottom of the closet door, blocking out the limited light from the cracks along the closed curtains. Sarah's muscles tensed as she placed her finger on the trigger.

The door handle turned. Sarah held her breath, motionless as she waited for the reveal.

And quick as a snakebite, the door swung inward. Sarah rushed forward, blinded by the light behind Kegan, who was nothing more than a silhouette.

"Stop," Sarah said, her arms shaking as Kegan froze, hands lifted into the air. "Don't move."

"I can help." Kegan spoke the words slow and articulated his speech carefully. "I'm not going to hurt you, all right? But you have to be quiet. You have to be—"

"Did you find her?"

Both of them turned toward the voice, but when Kegan turned back to Sarah, he raised a finger to his lips and stepped out of the closet, greeting the voice at the door.

"No," Kegan said. "Nothing."

"She's here." It was the witch's voice. "I can smell her."

"I'll keep checking and work my way up. She has to be here for the orb."

"Or to kill you." Though Sarah couldn't see her, she knew that the witch had said the words with a smile. "When you find her, bring her to me."

"It'd be better to kill her quickly before she can cause any trouble."

"Smart boy."

The witch's laugh and Kegan's footsteps faded down the hall, and Sarah was left in the closet alone. She waited until they ascended the stairs before she stepped out of the closet, still dumbstruck over her encounter.

Kegan had just let her go. And what was more, he covered for her when the witch pressed him for questions. She finally lowered the weapon and leaned against one of the posts for support. It didn't make any sense, but as Sarah listened to their ascent to the other floor, she realized that whatever window that Kegan had given her to break free was rapidly closing.

If the orb was anywhere in the house, it was in one of two places: Iris's room or Allister's room. Since Iris's room was closest, Sarah sprinted up the stairs to the fourth floor, being mindful of the witch and Kegan, who were just one floor above, and kept the pistol in her hand.

Questions raced through Sarah's mind on her way to Iris's room. What would she do if Iris was inside? How would she react to the woman who had orchestrated her near-death experience?

Sarah swallowed, then paused outside of Iris's room before she slowly opened the door. The hinges gave a light groan, and when the crack in the door widened, Sarah found Iris on the bed, asleep. She entered and left the door cracked open, cautious on her approach.

Iris lay in her nightgown on top of the sheets, her frail

body fully exposed. The fire in the fireplace heated the room nicely and also illuminated the age and wrinkles along her exposed arms and legs. Her white hair flowed freely over her pillow, and while she resembled more of a skeleton than anything else, Sarah, for the first time since she'd met the old hag, found her gentle.

The harsh tongue had been silenced, and the scowl had been wiped from her face, though a few of the wrinkles remained in a permanently angered position. But with no make-up, Sarah was finally able to see the face underneath. If they had met under different circumstances, if things had changed...

With Iris asleep, Sarah searched the room, carefully opening drawers and checking beneath the bed and in the closet. But after searching the room as thoroughly as she could, she found nothing save for old clothes and jewelry and cash hidden beneath her socks.

"Sarah."

She spun at the sound of her name, Iris's voice so frail it reminded Sarah of the ghosts she'd heard when she first moved in the house. Iris had her eyes cracked open, but she hadn't moved a muscle beyond her eyelids. Sarah aimed the pistol at Iris. "Scream and I'll kill you."

Iris attempted to lift a finger to coax the girl forward, but struggled. "Come here."

Eventually, Sarah placed one foot in front of the other, moving all the way toward Iris until she was right next to her bed. She kept the pistol aimed right between the old woman's eyes, who resembled a dying animal on the side of the road. Disgust and sympathy fought for control over her current emotional state.

"The orb," Iris said, her voice so haggard that it sounded like it hurt to even speak. "You need the orb to stop this."

"I know," Sarah said, confused by the sudden change of heart by both Kegan and his grandmother. "Where is it?"

"Fifth floor," Iris said. "Allister—" She coughed, and it grew into a hacking spat that curled her body forward and then buckled her chest as she tried to regain control.

Iris took a few deep breaths, her lungs rattling with every inhale. "I'm sorry." She shook her head, and her mouth downturned in grief. "I made the wrong choice a long time ago, and I don't—" She winced as she swallowed, the grimace akin to someone with a sore throat. "I don't know how to fix it."

Sarah wanted to tell her that it was okay. She wanted to tell Iris that she would have done anything to have an opportunity to see her parents again when she was a kid. To have them here, and to grow up knowing their love and learning from their wisdom. But she couldn't even lower the pistol.

"I've known people like you my whole life." The pistol in Sarah's hand started to shake. "You think that you can do whatever you want because you're in a position of power. You think that taking advantage of people like me is okay, because there isn't anything I can do about it." Sarah hovered closer, her shadow engulfing Iris as she sank deeper into her pillow, and pressed the end of the barrel's pistol against Iris's forehead. "But you push someone far enough, you force them to show their hand." With her free hand, Sarah reached for Iris's throat, and she applied pressure, which caused Iris to bring her weathered and frail hands up to meet Sarah's. But the old woman was too weak and fragile to fight back. "You want a second chance, but you don't deserve one. You want to live a life that you think you're entitled to, but you're not. How much pain have you caused? How many lives have you ruined?" She squeezed tighter and Iris started to squirm. "You really want to atone? Then why don't you go and meet your maker."

Sarah clamped down tighter, and Iris thrashed wildly, her liver-spotted hands clawing at Sarah's chest and neck. Tears filled Sarah's eyes and rolled down her cheeks. But while the rage boiled in her heart, Sarah finally released Iris, who coughed and hacked and sucked down air greedily.

Sarah stumbled backward and landed in a chair where she examined her hands. Hands that couldn't kill no matter how much she wanted them too.

"I know what I did," Iris said, her voice still a horse whisper. "I know what I am." She cleared her throat. She gestured to the dresser. "Bottom drawer. All the way in the back."

Her breathing still escalated, Sarah frowned, but then she slowly walked toward the dresser. She opened the bottom drawer, finding old pajama pants, and felt something hard wrapped in cloth. She wrapped her fingers around it and then removed the bundled object from the drawer.

Sarah fingered the object, making sure it wasn't a gun, and then peeked inside. Surprised, she turned back to Iris.

"I wasn't always like this," Iris said.

Sarah wrapped the object back up, and then walked over to Iris and gently rested it on her chest, where the old woman clutched it with both hands. She turned to leave, but Iris grabbed her wrist.

"My daughter," Iris said, longing in her voice. "You saw her?"

Sarah faced Iris once more. "I did."

Tears fell from the old woman's eyes. "How was she?"

Sarah shook her head, unsure of how to describe it. "She wanted to help you. She wanted to make you understand that you didn't have to do this."

Iris nodded and wiped the tears away. "Thank you for doing this."

"I'm not doing it for you." Quickly, Sarah stood and returned to the door. She slipped out just as she heard more footsteps coming down the stairs. She darted into the room across from Iris's to hide just when Kegan and the witch stepped into the hall.

"She's still in the house," the witch said. "She has to be."

"She might be hiding until the ceremony tonight," Kegan said. "Maybe she thinks she can stop it."

"If she's waiting until the ceremony, then she'll be too late." The witch scoffed and headed farther down the hall. "I'll check downstairs again, and—" The witch's footsteps ended. "I shut your grandmother's door when I left her room."

Sarah held her breath, listening to the witch walk back toward Iris's room, which ended with the slow groan of the door opening. Their voices grew softer when the witch entered the room, and Sarah slowly opened the door to the room where she was hiding.

The hallway appeared in the slivered crack, and she saw Kegan's body in Iris's doorway. His back was turned to her, and she couldn't see beyond his shoulders or the back of his head. She knew that the west wing staircase was close, only two doors down. She might be able to make it without tipping off the witch, but that was only if Kegan and Iris chose to stay true in their change of hearts.

Sarah hesitated, her muscles flinching and spasming as she struggled to go or stay. It could be a trick, a ploy to lure her out when they were all together, but it just didn't make any sense. None of it made sense. But knowing that she was short on time, Sarah bolted from the door, her footsteps soundless as she passed Kegan and reached the stairwell, thankful that its door was still open.

She paused at the doorway, looking back for a split second. It happened quickly, but Sarah was confident that Kegan flicked his eyes at her from the door before disappearing into Iris's room and shutting the door behind him.

Still flabbergasted by the turn of events, Sarah ascended the stairs toward the fifth floor.

Sarah couldn't find the answers to the questions swirling in her mind, and she wasn't sure she would ever understand, but when she returned to the fifth floor, she pushed all of it from her mind.

The door was closed, the old wood and dust that comprised the entrance just as ugly and terrifying as she remembered from her first visit. She took three soft steps and then placed her hand on the faded brass knob. It was the first real moment of trepidation, because a part of her understood that this was the last real opportunity to run for it. Once she had the orb, there wasn't any going back.

But she couldn't abandon Dell. She couldn't allow him to suffer the same fate as she after he'd done so much to help her. And even if she did run, she knew she couldn't get far, because after everything she'd seen and experienced, she knew that the apocalypse was real, and if she didn't attempt to save one life now, then the rest of the world would burn.

Sarah shut her eyes, focusing on that one life. She could save one. That much she was sure of.

The old brass wiggled loosely against the rest of the door when Sarah opened it, and she looked behind her to ensure that she was still alone. The witch had a tendency to sneak up on folks, and she didn't want to find herself on the wrong side of a surprise.

But Sarah was still alone, and she walked on the balls of her feet down the hall, still able to hear Kegan and the witch's conversation below. It was nothing but muffled nonsense, though Sarah recognized the cadence of the conversation. They were arguing.

Realizing that she had stopped to listen, Sarah restarted the slow and methodical walk toward the door at the end of the hall. Her throat dried, and the closer she moved toward it, the more nervous she became. She didn't understand why, especially since everything looked to be going her way. But when she placed her hand on the door knob, she froze.

Never had she felt such trepidation for one room since she was an orphan, and that's when she realized that's what was bothering her so much.

Somehow, at twenty-three, Sarah had returned to the same state of mind as when she was an orphan. She was sneaking around a house where she wasn't welcome, with people she barely knew, and struggling to stay alive.

Despite her efforts, despite trying to claw her way out of a system that did nothing but try and keep her pressed down and weak, and after thinking that she had finally made it out, she discovered that she had never really left. She was still that lost little girl after her parents had died. She was stuck in a loop.

Sarah let go of the handle and moved toward the nearby hallway window. The warmth of the sun was amplified by the glass, and she caught the lightest reflection of herself in the window. She didn't realize it until she saw, but she was crying.

Tears rolled down her cheeks and dotted the floor with dark blotches that mixed with the dust and grime that the floorboards had collected over the years. She tried to remember what that juvenile therapist had told her when she was seventeen. She tried to tell herself that life wasn't fair, and that everyone had a sob story, and that her problems weren't that big in the grand scheme of things. But she didn't care.

"It's not fair." And Sarah knew it wasn't. How had this moment been thrust upon her? How did she become the goat for the future of the world? She didn't want to be here. She didn't want to do this.

"I know."

Sarah spun around, finding the redhead floating behind her, though she was different, more ghostly. The striking red hair that floated around her head had faded considerably, and the vibrant and curious eyes that had greeted her when they first met had become sad and depressed. She was more ghostly than she looked before, like her soul was dying.

"Know what?" Sarah asked, keeping her voice quiet, unsure of where the witch and Kegan had disappeared to. "Know that this is all bullshit? That I shouldn't even be here." She wiped the snot collecting on her upper lip and angrily glared at Mary, who remained unfazed by Sarah's grief. "I didn't create this mess."

"We know," Mary replied, her voice soft and quiet. "But if you don't save us, then everyone will die, including Dell, and I don't think that's what you want."

The sound of his name pulled Sarah closer to Mary. "He's alive?"

"For now," Mary answered. "But there isn't much time. The same curse that afflicted you is coursing through his body. And it's growing worse." Mary winced, showing her first signs of pain. "I don't know who much longer he's going to last." And then she faded, growing lighter and lighter. "Help us, Sarah. Save us. Save *him*."

Sarah reached out and tried to touch Mary's arm, but all that remained was a cold patch of air. She reclaimed her hand and then looked back toward the door. Like it or not, and whether she asked for it or not, this was her trial.

Sarah returned to the door and opened it quickly before she lost her nerve, then stepped inside. She was sure she'd have to hunt for the orb, but she hesitated when she found it lying on top of the bed comforter in front of a pile of pillows.

It was too perfect, and as Sarah approached, she expected to set off some booby trap. But her approach went unnoticed and when Sarah touched the orb, she quickly retracted her hand.

The surface was hot, scalding hot, like it had just been taken from the oven, and when Sarah examined her fingertips, she discovered that they were red with first-degree burns. She grabbed a pillow and stripped it of its cover, then rolled it into the sack. She was unsure if it would burn through the cloth, but when she pressed her finger against the bulge at the bottom of the sack, she realized that it was cool to the touch.

Sarah headed toward the door and quickly scurried down the hallway. She was mindful of her steps, which elicited only a few groans on her descent, but what worried her more was how quiet it had become.

No whispers, no movement, nothing.

Sarah paused at the bottom of the stairwell, peeking through the crack in the door and checking the hallway. It was empty and quiet like the rest of the house. With the pillow cover slung over her shoulder like a hobo's stick and sack, Sarah hurried toward the door on the other end, hoping to escape the same way she'd entered.

She glanced behind her just before she was about to pass the gap in the hallway that led to the foyer and the front entrance, and when she faced forward again, the witch was blocking her path.

"Look who decided to come home," the witch said.

Sarah skidded to a stop, her heels scuffing against the runner that cut down the middle of the hallway. She turned around to run, but Kegan appeared from the bottom of the stairs, his face set in the cold expression of granite.

"Oh, he can't help you anymore," the witch said.

Sarah's attention was split, and she tried to keep an eye on each of them as they slowly closed in. "What did you do?"

"Gave him a little dose of persuasion." The witch puckered her red lips and blew a kiss toward Kegan. "I had a feeling something fishy was going on, and I was right. Turns out the Bells do have a conscience. They just decided to grow one at the wrong time."

"Kegan!" Sarah screamed, but he continued his methodical pace toward her, those eyes set in a fit of rage. "Don't do this."

"He can't hear you, sweetheart," the witch said. "Drop the orb, and I promise I'll make your death quick." She laughed.

One hand still holding the pillow sack, Sarah aimed the gun at the witch, who only smiled.

"You think that will stop me?" The witch asked. "You foolish girl!"

The witch lunged, and Sarah squeezed the trigger. At first she thought the bullet missed, but as the witch slammed her up against the wall, Sarah saw the bullet wedged in the middle of the witch's forehead.

"Mortal weapons cannot kill me." With one hand on Sarah's throat, lifting her off the floor and pinning her against the wall, she used the other to yank the pistol out of Sarah's hand. She held it up so Sarah could see, then crumpled the weapon in her fist.

Sarah's eyes bulged as she struggled for breath, then reached into her pockets and fumbled around until her fingers grazed the cross.

"Goodbye, Sarah," the witch said.

Sarah grabbed hold of the cross, then quickly pulled it from her pocket. The witch hissed, releasing Sarah and retreating from the sight.

Sarah crumbled to the floor, coughing and gasping for air, but she had the good sense to keep the cross raised, keeping the witch at bay.

"You won't be able to stop it!" the witch screamed.

Sarah stood, adjusting her grip on the cross, checking

behind her for Kegan's progress, who seemed unfazed by the holy object. "We'll see about that." Sarah inched the cross closer, drawing more agitation from the witch.

"GAH!" The witch hastened her retreat, and Sarah was only a few steps from the foyer. She'd head out the front doors and then run as fast as she could for the woods.

The witch looked past Sarah and at Kegan, the beauty from her face faded and stretched into a murderous rage. "What are you doing? Kill her!"

Kegan lunged forward, sprinting toward Sarah, but she'd already turned the corner and headed for the door. She turned as she opened it and saw Kegan barreling toward her, the distance between them already cut in half.

Sarah thrust herself out into the cold, her feet smacking against the hardened concrete as she made a sharp right toward the woods. She churned her legs faster than they'd ever moved. Her lungs and muscles burned. She kept her eyes on the forest, not even daring to look behind her, knowing that giving in to the urge would mean her end.

Pavement transformed to grass, and before Sarah realized it, she was across the grass and in the forest. Her ankles shifted awkwardly from the harsh terrain of the forest floor, and she pivoted her hips and shoulders, weaving through the trees.

And still Sarah didn't look back. Because all she could think of was running, and the consequences of what would happen if she was caught.

*R*eality and fantasy had blurred. Dell was convinced that it was the power of the place he was trapped in. Never in his life had he experienced such pain at the hands of resurfaced memories and forgotten fears.

It was like the very air he breathed cultivated the terrors of his past and the uncharted fears of the future. And the longer he stayed, the more he inhaled, the worse the harvest of his mind became.

It started small at first. He'd black out for a minute, and images of his father's abandonment would flash in his mind. He never saw his father's face as he walked out the front door, suitcase in hand. But every clack of his heels against the floorboards pounded in rhythm with Dell's heartbeat.

Dell tried to chase his father, but his mother kept hold of his arm. Tears squeezed from his eyes, blurring the final images of his dad that he possessed, screaming for him to stay, begging his dad not to leave. He pulled harder against his mother's arm, and she finally let him go after he was out the door and had started the car.

Dell twitched in his sleep, bursting out into the sunlight, but there was no warmth that greeted his face as he leapt off the front porch and tumbled to his hands and knees on the grass.

Clouds of dust were kicked up from the tires of his father's truck, and Dell hacked and coughed as he inhaled the particles, unsure of why his father was leaving and where he was going, and angry that he never had a voice in his departure. But no matter how far he ran, or how fast he moved, he never caught up to the truck. The trail of dust kicked up swallowed him whole and choked him. And that's when he would wake.

Dell's eyes popped open as he drew in a ragged breath that hurt even worse than his nightmare. He pushed from his back to his side and struggled to breathe, his hands pressed against jagged rocks and its uneven surface that never allowed comfort.

"It's better if you stand," Allister said, appearing at his side.

"I can't," Dell said, his face grimacing in pain.

"It just feels like you can't. Come on, up you go."

With the old man's help, Dell rose to his feet, and despite the agonizing pain, he did feel better once he was off the ground. He brushed what looked like black coal dust from his arm and then winced from a sharp pain in his abdomen. He wearily lifted his shirt and found the scales had spread to the lower portion of his ribs.

"It's getting worse," Allister said, looking at the spreading disease.

Dell let go of his shirt and then stumbled a few steps, suddenly dizzy and lightheaded. "How much time do you think I have left?"

"Not much," Allister answered.

And as if to echo the impending doom, the drums for war

beat over the horizon. Dell turned toward the army of demons and the undead that grew restless in the valley. The sky had brightened with fire, though there were still dark blotches of black and harsh greys, as if the sky was nothing more than a smoldering piece of fresh coal.

"She's fighting for you, Dell," Mary said, appearing alongside Allister.

"Sarah?" Dell asked.

Mary nodded, smiling.

"I wasn't sure if she would." Guilt flooded Dell's veins, knowing that even after his sacrifice, she wasn't out of danger. "I can't fix it."

"Fix what?" Allister asked.

Tears formed in Dell's eyes, and he scuffed his heel against the jagged and rocky terrain. He thought of his mother, his father leaving, all of the kids that had teased him in school, the Bells, his work as a cop. None of it was good enough. Not even giving his own life.

Dell flapped his arms at his side, and a spurt of laughter dribbled from his lips. "No matter what I do, I just can't get it right. It's like I'm—"

"Broken on the inside," Mary said.

"Like your thoughts are twisted and rotten," Allister added.

One by one, more of the souls that were trapped in this purgatory emerged.

"Or something inside of you doesn't fit."

"Like you were born with a missing piece."

"Like you're different."

Everyone had a different way to say it, but the more that Dell heard, the more he realized that burdens were universal.

"There isn't a human that has walked this earth that hasn't felt the weight of their own doubt," Allister said. "But what those people forget is what we no longer have."

Dell turned to Allister like a man lost in the desert and searching for water. "What?"

"The promise of tomorrow," Augustus answered.

Dell nodded, walking toward the valley's edge, pushing his toes over the edge, gazing down into the hellfire below. Those bastards had a tomorrow, and if they were granted that tomorrow, then it would come at the price of everyone else's.

Dell turned back toward the other souls that were trapped. "Why don't we fight?" The question poured out of him like a geyser, the surprise on his face mirroring everyone else. "We can help the people on the other side."

"There is no fighting those things on this side," Allister said.

"Have you tried?" Dell asked, addressing the group that had amassed near the cliff's edge. While no one spoke, when faces looked away or down, Dell had his answer. "We might be able to buy ourselves some time."

Allister stepped from the crowd. "Dell, it's a noble thought, but you haven't been here for as long as we have."

Dell stepped closer, maintaining eye contact with Allister. "I know it hurts, but it's better to stand than to lie down."

While Allister's shoulders deflated, a hint of a smile curved up his left cheek. He turned, joining Dell at his side. "He's right! Whatever pain we've endured, the sins we've committed, all of us have yearned for the simple opportunity to fight back, and this is our chance!"

The crowd stepped forward, pulled in by Allister's speech.

"We have loved ones, friends, and family that are still alive, and if those monsters make it to their world, then they will be burned at the stake!" Allister pointed toward the demons, and when Dell pulled his gaze toward the creatures, he saw that they had quieted, heads slowly turning toward Allister, whose voice challenged the fires that surrounded them. "But we are here, and they are not, and if we are to be the line in the sand, then let them come through us!"

A low horn blew in the distance, far across the horizon, that pulled everyone's attention from Allister. It rattled Dell's bones, and though he knew the sound was meant to bring him to his knees, he refused to bend.

When the blare ended, the horn was replaced by a unified thunder; it was the demons. They stomped, each quake louder than the first, growing so powerful that it fractured the rocks beneath Dell's feet.

He curled his hands into fists and stepped all the way toward the ledge, followed by the other six hundred and sixty-five souls, looking down on the demons below. And while he exuded confidence and bravery, he whispered a silent prayer in his own thoughts.

Sarah, if you can hear me, then please, hurry.

* * *

WHILE IT WENT against every fiber in Brent's body, he stuck to the woods on his trek back toward the GTO, and every step reinforced his hatred of nature. He batted away the branches that scraped at his cheeks and kicked the shrubs that ruined and stained his nice shoes.

Blisters had already formed on the sides of his feet, and his cheeks were flushed from the exertion of the hike. And the longer he was forced to walk, hidden among the trees like an animal, the more rage that bubbled to the surface of his consciousness.

He imagined every possible way to kill Sarah. Guns, knives, fire, baseball bat, tree branch, rock, pencil, his bare hands, just a handful of thousands of murder weapons that could do the job, though it was the method of his attack that he wanted to iron out.

Variables such as pain and suffering were high on the list, and he wanted to ensure that he was able to prolong them before her death as much as possible. He would bring her right to the edge and have her look over the side to the skeletons that riddled the valley and then pull her back, wait until she regained some strength, and then start it all over again until she couldn't take it anymore.

Though, he had to remember that all of this would have to wait until after her trial for murder, but he smiled, knowing that it would only give him more time to figure out just exactly how he was going to enact his revenge.

The woman's voice echoed in his mind, and he couldn't rid himself of the image of her face. Though he couldn't quite remember the details of the woman who set him free. They shifted and morphed like sand after a windstorm in the desert.

But the one consistent quality was her beauty. The kind of looks a man like himself would kill to have in his bed, and one of the rare few that actually had the resolve to do it.

Lost in his own thoughts, Brent nearly passed the mangled remains of his GTO in the ditch. He approached wearily, on the lookout for any troopers or cops that might be camping out. From the looks of the wreck, it hadn't been touched by the cops yet. They were probably too busy searching for Sarah. And him.

Brent emerged from the trees, the rage that was simmering just below the surface now at a full-blown boil, looking at the sight of his car. It had taken him years to refurbish the GTO, and it all came undone in the blink of an eye.

The chassis had been twisted, the front and back were crumpled, and all of the windows were either broken or completely shattered. Three of the tires were flat, two of the rims bent, and one wheel was completely missing altogether.

Oil leaked down the driver side door, the black goo blending nicely with the dark paint job.

With the vehicle upside down, Brent had to get on his hands and knees to crawl inside through the window. He would have just opened the door, but the wreck had sealed the doors shut. Glass shards scraped against his jacket and jeans, and blood rushed to his head as he ducked his head into the cab.

He reached across the seat. The ceiling, now beneath his knees, buckled from his weight and he outstretched his arm, his fingertips grazing the handle of the glovebox. "Come on, you fucker." He inched forward again, only a single boot sticking out of the cab, when he noticed flashing red and blue lights back on the road. "Shit."

The sound of cars zoomed past, and Brent finally managed to open the glovebox, sending its contents spilling onto the ground, the extra case of ammunition among the droppings. He pushed aside the papers and opened the box just as he heard one of the cars slow down and stop near the wreck.

Quickly, Brent loaded the weapon, shutting the revolver's barrel and pocketing the weapon just as the trooper stepped out of his vehicle.

"Sir, I need you to exit the vehicle slowly and place your hands on top of your head, now!" The trooper had the high ground, service pistol already drawn and aimed at Brent's head by the time he turned around.

"I'm a cop! This is my car!" The last thing he wanted was to take a bullet to the head, so he placed his hands on his head as he turned around, but he didn't stop talking. "This is my car—"

"Get down on your knees!"

"I'm a detective with New York's—"

"I said get down on your knees!"

"Hey!" Brent briefly raised his hands off his head, which allowed his jacket to open and expose his badge. "Would you just look? See? My badge, on my right hip."

The trooper kept his eyes locked with Brent's, but then finally lowered his eyes toward the badge. After another moment, the trooper lowered his weapon. "You mind telling me what the hell you're doing in that car, Detective?"

Brent removed his hands from his head. "I told you it's mine. I was working a murder case that brought me north. An officer with the Redford department flagged a suspect I've been trying to hunt down." He stepped up the embankment, and the trooper extended a hand to help him up.

The trooper grabbed hold of Brent's arm and then heaved him up the last few steps, planting him close to his side.

"Thanks," Brent said, dusting off his jeans.

"You all right?" the trooper asked, giving Brent the once over before looking down at the wreck. "Looks like you went through quite the number."

"Brother, you have no idea." Brent laughed, and then slicked back his hair with his hands. "Listen, you think you could give me a ride back to Redford?" He gestured down to his shoes. "These boots ain't exactly made for walkin'."

"No can do," The trooper said. "We've got a report of two suspects we're looking for heading south. You can tag along and I can drop you off after if you want. Or you're welcome to wait it out here."

"I've had enough of the outdoors for one day," Brent answered. "I'll just tag along with you if that's all right."

"Hop in."

Brent slid his left hand into his pocket, wrapping his fingers around the revolver's pistol in the same motion as his right hand reached for the passenger side door. And when the trooper turned his back to Brent, he removed the pistol, aimed for the back of the trooper's skull, and then pulled the trigger.

The pop and the harsh snap of the trooper's head forward were simultaneous as his fall to the ground.

With the barrel still smoking, Brent lowered the weapon and quickly patted down the cop, taking his service pistol and extra ammunition. He pocketed both, and then dragged the trooper's body to the edge of the ditch and kicked him over, the trooper's arms and legs flailing wildly as he rolled down the hill and crashed into the car, landing face up.

The bullet went straight through, leaving a large hole in the middle of the trooper's forehead. His eyes had gone cross, but they were still open, and his mouth hung open with his jaw slack and mouth askew. His arms were tangled over his body, and the tendons in his knee had snapped from the fall, leaving it bent at a harsh ninety degrees. He looked like a rag doll that some kid had tossed in his room.

The radio chatter pulled Brent's attention from the trooper and back to the car. He checked down both lanes of the highway, finding it clear. There wasn't anyone in the area that would have heard that shot, and even if they did, Brent would be long gone by the time they came around.

Brent climbed behind the wheel, the cruiser still running, and he turned up the volume on the radio. If they had spotted Sarah and that dipshit cop heading south, then he needed to know.

"Dispatch, this is unit fifty-nine, we're about a mile north of Millington, and we haven't seen anybody on the road. Suspects might be using the woods as cover. We'll head a little farther, but we might need air support to assist."

"Copy that, fifty-nine, we'll get on air to—"

Brent turned it down and tapped his finger on the steering wheel. "Where would you go, Sarah?" He chewed the inside of his cheek. She already had several chances to leave, but she'd chosen to stick around. Which meant that there was something here that she wanted, or needed.

Brent's thoughts turned to the house. She had lived there during her stint in this godforsaken portion of the world.

Brent shifted into drive and turned north, heading back to Bell Mansion.

---

*D*espite Iris's attempts, she couldn't get out of bed. The invisible weight on her chest kept her pinned to the mattress. She wanted to speak, she wanted to scream, but her voice had been cut off. The only movement that she was able to muster was her eyes, which she used to scan the cracks and the water stains on the ceiling.

The door to Iris's room opened, and while she couldn't turn her head to see who entered, she didn't have to wait long to find out.

The witch hovered over her in bed and grabbed her jaw, forcing Iris's eyes to lock with her own. Anger flashed across her face, her upper lip curved in snarl, which was accentuated by the red of her lipstick. She was still naked, and the witch's long locks descended from her face like strands of moss, which brushed Iris's nose and cheek.

"I don't know what little game you're trying to play, but you can consider our deal dissolved," the witch said, hissing through her teeth. "Your daughter will be the first soul tortured in Satan's new world order. And I will ensure that you have a front row seat to her pain." She tightened her grip. "You will hear every scream, you will feel every ache, and the only relief from the flames of hell will be the splatters of her blood against flesh."

With one flick of her wrist, she tossed Iris's chin aside, the sudden motion twisting Iris's neck, which elicited a groan of pain.

The witch glided to the end of the bed, and with Iris's head propped up by the pillow, the pair again locked eyes.

"Perhaps you just need a reminder of what I can do," the witch said, then raised her hands and snapped her fingers. Kegan entered the room, his eyes rolled back into his sockets, exposing only white. He stopped once he reached the witch's side.

Iris wiggled her mouth, her voice trying to break through the wall holding her back, and it started to crack. She mumbled, her lips writhing with incredible effort. The witch laughed, tossing her head back with a reckless gaiety that only increased Iris's fury.

"Time finally caught up with you, Iris?" the witch asked, digging her claws into Kegan's shoulder, who remained motionless in his zombie-like state. "All those years rattling around this house, your bones and innards aching, all of those lives you took?" She removed her hand from Kegan and crawled onto the bed, her movements slow and seductive. "Have they finally caught up with you? Have they worn down that hardened resolve?"

Iris continued to move her lips, still unable to produce any sound other than primitive noises, and held the object that Sarah had retrieved from her dresser beneath the sheets.

"With the dark lord coming, my powers have grown." The witch was right on top of Iris, her hands planted on the outsides of each arm, her body naked and exposed. "I know you must envy me." She smiled seductively. "My youth. My body." She lowered her breasts and gently touched them against Iris's flattened chest. "Has desire completely left you?" She pushed her groin against Iris's and smiled, eyes rolling back into her eyes as she gave a seductive grind. "Oh, you must miss it." She sat up, shaking her head to and fro, sending her hair waving in locks back and forth, and laughed. "You're nothing but a dried-up hag, Iris. One breath away from joining your daughter." The playfulness ran from her face. "But I'll make sure you hold onto that one breath. I'll force you to live for the next few hours, because I want you to see it. I want you to feel your failure."

The door slammed on her exit and the fire extinguished in the hearth, ending the light and the warmth in the room.

Exhausted, Iris rested her head back down on her pillow, though she felt better.

As her eyes adjusted to the darkness, Iris noticed that Kegan was still in the room, standing at the foot of the bed, that zombie-like stare still plastered on his face.

"Kegan," Iris said, a strength returning to her voice. "I know you're in there, somewhere. You have to fight it, do you hear me? Whatever control she's cast over you, you have to fight it."

Kegan remained quiet and still, and Iris lay her head back onto the pillows, shifting her body from side to side. Joints cracked and bones ached from the limited motion, though the movement triggered a rush of endorphins, which elicited a groan of relief.

Iris turned her attention back to Kegan, who has moved from the foot of the bed and to her side in the blink of an eye. The sudden motion startled her and she retreated from Kegan's side of the bed.

It was the face where she noticed the most change. Despite his efforts, he'd always had a kind face, which lessened his physical appearance. But with those attributes gone, all that was left was size and muscle. And Kegan had both to spare.

"Kegan," Iris said, still whispering. "Kegan, you have to fight it."

He grunted, the noise primal and guttural, but it was the only response that he gave.

Iris covered her mouth, her lips trembling as the tears returned. She sobbed silently to herself, staring up at her grandson. The same man who she had pushed so hard, the young boy whose mother was taken away and his father sent to an early grave from the drink. He was so little when Mary died, he was still breastfeeding. She knew how much of an impact that Mary would have had on his life. She could have shown him what it took to be strong, and kind.

Iris never had that skillset. She was strong, but she was too calculated, too efficient. It was her husband who showed their children how to be sociable.

But Iris had been so hard on him, and she knew why. It was because he reminded her so much of Mary. It was the eyes. They both had the same inquisitive stare that could cut you down with one look. It undressed you until there was nothing left but your soul. And Iris had never handled vulnerability well. So she lashed back at him. And while he had grown strong, he had also grown weak.

Kegan was strong because he was afraid of the alternative. And that kind of strength always grew brittle over time. Now he was nearly gone, his mind and soul controlled by that devil woman, and soon to be consumed by the fires of hell, as would she.

Iris understood the consequences should Sarah fail, but what she couldn't comprehend was the level of pain and torture that was just around the corner. She had done that to him. She had done this to her family.

"I'm so sorry," Iris said, blurting out the words between

sobs. She inhaled quick, sharp breaths, trying to regain her composure, but unable to find the grit that made it necessary. "Forgive me. Please." She lifted her arm, her hand shaking as it stretched toward Kegan, who stared at it with no connection. "Please, Kegan."

Another guttural cry left his throat, and then he turned away and walked toward the door, leaving Iris to sob alone in the dark.

* * *

DESPITE THE PAIN and the heat, a rush of adrenaline still surged through Dell's veins on the sprint toward the demons. Wild screams erupted from the over six hundred souls at his back, and Dell was sure that this was the most alive the dead had been in years.

And while Dell's small band of rebels charged toward the demons with a focused intensity, their cries of war were quickly muted by the thunderous sounds of brass horns and drums that vibrated rocks that splintered beneath their feet.

Armed with sharp rocks that they scavenged from the hell that surrounded them, Dell leading the charge, the two forces clashed together in a symphonic climax that ended the haughty bellows of war on both sides.

The force that hammered against Dell felt the equivalent of a freight train, and while the first blast of contact stole his breath and thunder, the heat of battle forced him to swallow the pain.

Up close, the demons were even uglier than Dell could have imagined. Their features were carved out of stone with molten rock. Their only weapons were the sharp, jagged features of their limbs, which they swung in savage, quick motions on their attack.

Heat radiated off the demons and scorched Dell's flesh,

which only amplified his anger. He dodged the vicious swings and countered with his own, smashing the rock in his hand against the demon's skull, knocking it to the ground, and then moved on to the next.

A never-ending wave of molten rock swept over Dell and the other souls as they penetrated demon after demon. Dell worked himself into a rhythm but after the eighth demon that he attacked, his hand suddenly ached.

He examined it and discovered the rock that he'd been using had been destroyed.

While his attention was only diverted for a moment, it was enough to lower his guard and leave him vulnerable to attack. Dell managed to turn his eyes away from his hand just in time to see the heavy piece of granite slam into his face.

The contact flattened Dell to the ground, which delivered just a powerful a blow as the punch, and greeted him with another blast of scorching heat. His back took another vicious pounding, the crunch so hard that he could have sworn his spine had busted in two. But then the feeling was repeated, over and over like a broken record player that skipped the same beat.

And what was more, the intensity of the pain never wavered. It was fresh and new with every blow.

Finally, after a lull in the bashing, Dell stood, forced to dodge another blow before he even had his footing ready. He swung at the demon and cracked it across the side of its misshapen, geo-formed skull. And when he felt no pain from the contact, he smiled.

But then as his vision adjusted to the sight of his hand, the smile faded. The scales had spread, reaching up to his chest and already spreading down both arms. The scales shimmered against the orange and reds that shone off the demon's skulls, reflecting the same color. It gave the impression that Dell himself was on fire, smoldering into oblivion.

Dell double-timed his assault, his savagery reaching a crescendo as he plowed his way through the army of the damned. His scaled fists did more damage than any rock could do. It split open the sides of the demons, spilling molten lava and fire.

Their screams of pain were unearthly and even more horrendous than the physical pain that they inflicted with their heavy blows. And while he plowed through the endless sea of demons, his rage growing wilder with every spilled ounce of demon blood, he realized that he was one of them. This shell that was covering his soul was nothing more than the granite and rock and caliphates that stumbled around him, and... yes, they were running from him now.

Empty space had filled the area around Dell's body, rather than the waves of rock that had pummeled him earlier. He stopped and turned around, expecting to see Allister and the army of souls that had marched into battle with him there and accounted for.

But they weren't.

Instead, there was nothing but the endless horizon of demons, running away, running toward what remained of those that were still fighting back.

There were no triumphant shouts. No fists thrust to the skies in defiance of the hell they'd been imprisoned. Dell was alone, surrounded by a sea of fire and rock and pain. It was endless, and it was then that he realized that this was their eternity.

Dell could lead a rebellion until the end of time, and it still wouldn't be enough. They were just keeping themselves busy. Busy until the forces on the other side of their hell either succeeded or failed. Dell looked to his hand, wiggling his fingers, which still reflected the fires around him. He was suddenly finding it hard to remember what his hand had looked like before.

Memories of whatever life he'd had were clouded with the thick fog of hate and violence. His mind was covered in it, and he started to swing wildly, screaming at the top of his lungs.

'His fists connected with demons, spilling more fire and lava, triggering more screams of pain, and the longer that Dell fought, the worse the noises became. And there he fought, alone, against a sea of evil. An evil that he was slowly becoming.

rent didn't take his foot off the gas until he saw the sign off the highway for Bell. The trooper's cruiser had made the trip back much quicker than his departure from the town. He wrung his hands over the steering wheel on the tight bending turns of the two-lane road that cut through the forest and dumped onto Bell's main street.

He turned sharply off the road, parking the cruiser next to Pat's tavern, and opened the revolver's chamber, rechecking the bullets.

Brent flicked his wrist, and the barrel snapped back into place, the motion fueling his ego as he climbed out of the cruiser, choosing to take the keys with him, leaving the cruiser parked skewed near the tavern.

He walked up the back side of the building, his eyes on the house on the hill. And as he walked toward it, he realized that he couldn't take his eyes off it, no matter how hard he tried. Fascination took over, and before he reached the end of the row of buildings, he slowed to a stop.

Mouth slack, Brent widened his eyes, a tingling cold crawling up his back that was even harsher than the air that surrounded him. It was like ice was crystalizing his spine, which stiffened. His heart pounded heavy in his chest, and he grew short of breath.

He suddenly thought of the woman that had set him free from the back of the squad car. A tickling whisper entered his ear with the calmness of a light breeze. It was wordless, and yet Brent understood what was said, and the realization spread the ice from his spine and into the rest of his limbs and body.

The icy glaze reached into his mind and seeped into his thoughts and memories. The terrible, thunderous voice of his father echoed through his mind, and Brent shook in fear. He shut his eyes, fighting back tears, knowing how much his father had hated seeing that kind of weakness from his son.

He was back under his bed, but this time his father threw the mattress off and across the room, exposing Brent like a cockroach in the darkness. He still held a nearly empty bottle of whiskey in his hand, his eyes red and glossy. The front of his shirt was stained red, and the blood on his knuckles was still damp.

If he was done with Brent's mother and he was still thirsty for punishment, then Brent knew that it was going to be a walloping. A viral hate of his mother's weakness flooded through him, and he screamed as his father lifted him off the floor, bringing him front and center to his father's foul stench.

The drunkard's breath always smelled like shit, and the mix of booze and heat and sweat only amplified the sourness that, even now, churned Brent's stomach.

The fear grew so strong that Brent wet himself. His father berated him, beat him, and left him bloody and bruised and for dead in his room once he was finished.

And just as quickly as the whispered memory surfaced in

Brent's thoughts it was gone, and he gasped for air as if he'd been holding his breath.

Still trembling, he glanced down at the wet patch on his jeans, which was now freezing in the cold. He grimaced in anger and disgust and then looked back to the house. And when he did, there was another whisper, and this time he was able to make out the words.

"Find her and bring her to me." The woman's voice purred into his ear. "And I will give you everything you want. I will give you the power that you deserve."

Another warmth spread through his groin, but it was triggered by a more primal sensation. He wanted that power, but what was more was the fact that the voice he was listening to understood what he had always known. That he *deserved* it.

And why not?

The power that he wanted was a chance at safety. Because if you were all powerful, then there was nothing that could hurt you. Nothing that could harm you. Enough power in your possession and you were invincible.

Brent started up the house, not sure what was drawing him to it, but coming to the self-realization that it was where he needed to go. And as he started up the hill, he could see the front entrance of the house. He kept off to the side, choosing not to use the grand staircase that provided an easy path to the top, again drawn by the primitive instinct that it was where he needed to be.

And with his eyes locked on the door, Brent stopped when he heard a door slam up ahead. His gaze turned west, and from his position on the hill, he watched Sarah sprint from the house and dart into the woods.

At first, Brent remained motionless, the shock of being so close to his prey immobilizing him. He watched her fade into the woods, and then he smiled and reached for his revolver.

It was perfect, a final chase to lead to a confrontation between the hunter and the hunted. And the prize for Sarah's bounty was clear.

No longer would the past haunt him. No more would the memories of his childhood prevent him from becoming the man he was supposed to be. The future was there for the taking. And as Brent broke out into a jog and headed for the woods, a sudden, excited madness took over him. While he was so focused on the task at hand, his vision had become so tunneled that he couldn't see the strings being pulled by the witch above his head.

* * *

IT WASN'T until the muscles in Sarah's legs finally gave out and she skidded across the dirt, and rocks, and twigs that she stopped running.

Crouched on all fours, Sarah inhaled sharply, sucking wind as she glanced behind her to make sure that she was alone in the woods, and then her eyes fell to the orb and the pillowcase that had become dirtied from the ground.

Sarah rolled to her side and wiped the sweat that was trying to freeze to her forehead, smearing dirt along her skin in the process. Still huffing, but having better control over her breath, Sarah peeled back the pillow cover and revealed the orb, being mindful not to accidentally touch it.

What sunlight filtered through the clouds from the height of the afternoon made the orb sparkle as she rotated it in her hands, keeping the cloth of the pillowcase to cradle the orb. In the daylight it was beautiful, like a solid sphere of crystal with diamonds sprinkled between it.

Sarah stood, still cradling the orb with the pillowcase, and spied a rock cropping to her left. She hurried over and raised the orb high above her head, and then brought it down with all the force her arms and body could muster.

She shut her eyes when the orb left her hands and turned away so she wouldn't be struck by the shards that would be sent flying. She winced from the heavy thud of the contact, but the noise wasn't the cracking, crushing noise that she had anticipated.

Sarah craned her head around, her eyes widened in disbelief as she found the orb in perfect condition. She dropped to her knees and hovered over the orb to get a closer look, but as she searched the orb's surface, she found no fractures, no cracks, not even the slightest signs of a blemish.

With the pillowcase, Sarah picked it up and again heaved it high and slammed it down harder, this time not turning away. And like before, the orb cracked against the rock, and then rolled off into the dirt.

Sarah retrieved the orb and heaved it against another rock, and then a tree, and then the ground itself. But no matter the surface and no matter the force, the orb refused to crack. "Shit." She huffed under her breath and then kicked the orb, sending it rolling against a tree.

Hands on her hips, Sarah remembered the holy water and the crosses that the priest had given her. If they worked against the witch, then there wasn't any reason why they couldn't have an effect on the orb. After all, it was used by someone who was evil, so it stood to reason that it could help destroy a weapon of evil.

Sarah removed the cross first and thrust out her hand, inching it closer toward the orb. She tilted her head back, unsure of the reaction the pair would create.

Arm shaking, Sarah moved the cross within an inch of the orb, but it had no effect. She relaxed and gave the cross a quick tap against the surface. Nothing.

Defeated, Sarah slouched and twirled the cross between

her fingers. She stared at it then pocketed it before replacing it with one of the glass tubes of holy water. She shook her head, still amazed that the tiny sliver of water hadn't frozen.

Keeping the cork in it, Sarah squatted next to the orb and cocked her head to the side, looking for any dent that she might have missed from earlier. When she found nothing, she uncorked the bottle and hovered it over the top.

She tilted the tube slowly, knowing that she couldn't waste all of it, especially if she had another run-in with the witch. She suspected that the priest didn't have this kind of stuff on demand. A drop would be enough to test, and when the first bit trickled out, she snapped her wrist back and corked it.

The droplets splashed against the orb and trickled down the sides. But as the line of water curved all the way down and pooled at the earth beneath the orb, Sarah saw no effect.

She quickly stood, spinning around in a half circle, tightening her grip on the glass tube, her arms shaking in anger. She pocketed the holy water before she accidentally smashed it against the ground in a fit of rage and then kicked the orb, hard, sending it careening through the woods and disappearing into some low-lying shrubs.

"*Fuck.*"

Anger steamed off of her, and she paced the ground in quick turns, going over everything that the priest had told her, but when she couldn't find the answer herself, she collapsed in the dirt.

If she couldn't find the answer herself, then she needed to go and speak with someone who understood what to do. So she decided the best course of action was to return to the priest. If anyone could help, it would be him.

Sarah snatched the pillowcase off the dirt, not bothering to brush it off, and reached for the orb in the bushes, but stopped at the harsh snap of a twig.

The noise spiked her heartrate, and the adrenaline that had been missing flooded her veins. She snapped her head around toward the noise.

Barren trees, rocks, and soil greeted her view, but Sarah continued to scan the area. There had to be bears and such up here that she didn't know about, or mountain lions, though she was so tired she knew that pretty much anything could kill her.

Sarah paused, her body coiled in anticipation for a fight, but the wilderness around her remained quiet. The tension in her muscles relaxed and she turned to pick up the orb, stuffing it back in the pillowcase.

"Hello, Sarah."

Color drained from Sarah's face, and she nearly dropped the pillowcase from her hand, but she tightened her grip at the last second and prevented it from falling.

A wicked smile had spread over Brent's face. It wasn't his natural, sly, charming grin that had first made Sarah take him to bed, but instead was wild and violent. The corner of his left eye twitched, which only accentuated his madness.

"Bet you never thought you'd see me again, huh?" Brent asked, as if she should be impressed that the pair had reunited. He stepped toward her slowly, methodically, arm outstretched with the gun in his hand, his finger on the trigger. "You're my ticket out of here, Sarah." The smile widened even further, stretching Brent's face to an unnatural width.

Sarah remained still, either frozen by fear or fatigue. Her muscles were little more than jelly. She knew that she couldn't make a run for it. She'd get three feet before he put a bullet in the back of her head. She had to keep him coming toward her. She needed to get closer.

"No," Sarah said. "I didn't think we'd see each other." She flashed a smile. "Goes to show how much more you know than me, Brent."

"I tried to help you, Sarah." Brent continued his walk forward, and the smile waned. "I wanted you to be my right hand. We could have done whatever we wanted, we could have ruled the city."

"We can't go back?" Sarah asked, keeping her tone docile and attempting to flirt even though she wanted to vomit. "We can't give it another try?"

Brent wiggled his eyebrows, the conflict raging inside of him evident from his expression. His arm shook, wiggling the pistol as he stepped closer. "No. I can't—We can't."

"If you kill me, then they'll send you to jail, Brent," Sarah answered. "You need me to take the fall for that woman you killed."

"And the trooper." Brent looked away for a second, his voice a whisper, as if he had suddenly just remembered all of the terrible things he'd done over the course of his life. He shook his head, shaking the memory from his thoughts. "It's over, Sarah. No more running. No more games." He cocked the hammer back. "No more."

Sarah's heart hammered in her throat, and her nerves grew hot and flustered. Adrenaline had her blood pumping and set her body on fire. "Wait, just wait." She held up her hands, trying to buy herself some time and knowing the one thing that even madness couldn't steal from a man. His lust.

Sarah dropped the pillowcase. She stepped toward him, opening her jacket as she did. And despite the cold, she didn't shiver.

Brent kept the pistol aimed, but when she passed the barrel and was less than an arm's length away, he slightly lowered his arm, his eyes transfixed on Sarah's figure.

She approached him slowly, hesitantly, as if she were aroused and frightened by his prowess at the same time. It was a technique that she had discovered that most men enjoyed, but Brent most of all.

He dropped his eyes to her chest, his mouth slack, as she raised herself up on her toes and brought her lips closer to his neck, and in the same motion ran her hand down his chest, stomach, and stopped at his belt.

"I know you remember how it felt." She kept her voice low, and she felt his heart pound against her own chest. "I know you remember how good it made you feel." He looked down at her, and she flashed a short smile. "How good it made me feel."

His breathing grew irregular and heavy, and while his attention was focused on her, the gun was still outstretched, and his finger was still on the trigger. And with her exposed, all it would take for him to kill her would be to place that barrel against her temple and then squeeze the trigger.

Sarah kept her eyes locked on Brent's while her practiced fingers unbuckled his belt. His desire had hardened, but still he kept the gun up and aimed. She needed him to drop it. She needed him to let go. She pushed her hand into his pants and stroked him, inching her own lips closer to his until they were only a breath apart.

"If you want me," Sarah said, her voice still that whisper. "Then take me."

Brent's entire body trembled, his eyes locked on her, his breathing quickening, and then in one split second, he dropped the pistol and forced his mouth onto hers. He picked her up, his hand groping her body, and pinned her against a tree.

Sarah peeled her lips away from his and then eyed the pistol on the ground as he kissed her neck. Then, slowly, she pushed his head down, and he kissed her body as he lowered to his knees. Sarah ran her hands through his hair, hardened by the cold and all of that fucking gel he put in it. She gave it a playful tug and forced his eyes up toward her.

"Thank you," Sarah said.

And when Brent smiled, she swung Brent's head down and thrust her knee as hard as she could into his nose. The contact triggered a wave of pain all the way to her hip, which was only worsened by the cold, and blood spurted over her jeans and the ground as Brent's head popped back and he tumbled to the dirt.

Sarah sprinted for the gun, arms outstretched, and she made it three steps before a hand clamped around her ankle and pulled her to the ground.

Her chest and stomach smacked against the rocky soil, the air rushing out of her lungs with a heavy whoosh noise. She turned to look back and saw Brent's angry snarl and the flash of blood on his face.

Sarah kicked again, hitting Brent in the forehead, but he refused to relinquish his grip. He clawed forward. She squirmed, thrashing her body as viciously and wildly as she could muster. Her fingers raked the dirt and rock, the revolver just out of reach.

Desperation motivated every single movement, and when another hand clamped around her other ankle and tugged her backward, she screamed, the cry bursting from that primal place in her soul that understood the end was near.

"You bitch!" Brent screamed as he flipped her from her stomach to her back, pulling her, Sarah's back scraping against the cold and rocky terrain.

Sarah bucked and twisted her hips, kicking, fighting back with what strength remained to her, but Brent overpowered her and flung her into a nearby tree.

Sarah's back buckled harshly against the thick oak, but she was quick to bounce back when she saw him reach for the gun. Back and innards aching, Sarah sprinted toward Brent and then launched her body at Brent, spearing them both to the ground.

Shoulder, elbows, and knees violently cracked against one

another and the ground, and when the rolling ended, Sarah lay next to Brent on her back while he tried to push himself up from his stomach.

Disoriented, it took her a minute to get her bearings, but when she saw the flash of silver from the revolver, Sarah scrambled toward it. She snatched it up in her hands, and when she heard Brent roar, she spun around and fired as his body slammed against hers and they cracked against the ground.

Brent's weight grew even heavier on top of Sarah, but the pistol was still wedged between their stomachs. The pair locked eyes, and Brent's mouth was hung open in an oval shape, his tongue lolling in his mouth as he gagged.

Sarah lay still beneath him, watching the life drain from his eyes and feeling the warmth of his blood leave his stomach and spread across her body. She felt Brent's muscles relax, and then eventually blood dripped from the corner of his mouth and onto her cheek.

And finally, Brent lay his head on Sarah's shoulder and exhaled his last breath.

Crushed by his weight, Sarah struggled to get Brent off. It was her frustration that finally provided the needed strength to move him. She lay there on the ground, eyes shut, sucking in big gulps of air.

Brent's warm, sticky blood quickly dried and hardened against her clothes, and Sarah finally pushed herself to a sitting position.

Dirt and dead leaves stuck to the back of her head and back, and she stared down at the blood that covered her body and the revolver that now rested between her legs on the ground. She stared at the weapon, then turned to look at Brent.

His arms and legs were splayed out awkwardly, and a massive red stain covered his abdomen. Blood still bubbled up from the wound, and his eyes were open, his face staring up at the fading afternoon sky. He was still and quiet.

And the longer Sarah stared at the body, the more her nerves frayed and unraveled. She hyperventilated. A sourness plagued her stomach, which lurched and twisted. A warm, acidic bile crawled up her throat, and Sarah scrambled on her hands and knees away from the scene of the crime as she vomited into the bushes.

Two more rounds came up before she was finished, and then some dry heaves brought on by the sudden stench of blood that still lingered on her shirt. She wiped her mouth and then stumbled away from the pile of vomit, still struggling to catch her breath.

Sarah planted her hand on the trunk of a nearby tree to help support her, her entire body shaking from the exertion and the cold and the rundown fatigue that had crippled her body. She placed her forehead in the crook of the arm that she folded against the tree trunk, her mind throbbing and aching.

She stole one more quick glance at Brent's body. Despite the murderous thoughts that had plagued her since she was a teenager, imagining all the different ways that she wanted to kill the people who had hurt her over the years, she couldn't comprehend what she'd just done.

Brent was dead.

Sarah circled that thought like a dirty water running down a drain. She'd killed him. A man who she had slept with, a man whose body she had used, and in return given her own to him. A man who was a cop, a killer, and an asshole.

Whatever feeling of resolve or closure that she'd hoped to find with his death didn't arrive. There was no moment of clarity now that he was dead, only more questions and fear about the repercussions of what would happen to her. She'd just killed a cop, and she was the only witness to the murder. She could cry self-defense, but she knew that Brent's cronies back in New York wouldn't let his death go without retaliation.

"Fuck." Sarah slammed her head into her arm. "Fuck!" She repeated the motion, slamming it harder. No matter how hard she tried, no matter what she did, she just couldn't escape the shit loop that she'd found herself in. Any move she made was just one more scoop for her grave. It was never going to end. The pain, the suffering, the questions, the fear, it would follow her until the end of her days. Safety was an illusion, and Sarah had shattered the last of that charade the moment she put that bullet into Brent's gut.

Sarah turned back to the body, but her eyes fell on the revolver. It was still on the ground between them. Blotches of blood diminished some of the shine, but not its appeal. She shifted her glances between the gun and Brent's body.

Maybe that was the only way out. The only way to end the fear, to end the pain, was to end it all. No more running, or fighting, or struggling. All of it could be erased in the blink of an eye, the lightest pressure of her finger on the trigger.

The thought festered in her mind like a disease, and Sarah finally pushed herself off the oak tree. She scooped the revolver from the dirt, dropping it the first time, and then reaffirming her grip on the second.

It was light in her hands, and she examined the barrel and then opened the chamber. Five bullets. She closed it and then cocked the hammer back. She brought the end of the barrel to her temple without any hesitation, but she couldn't bring her finger to the trigger.

Sarah shut her eyes, trying to discover the resolve that had helped her pick up the pistol in the first place. She wanted to be done with it. No more pain. No more quests, no more struggle, no more looking over her shoulder, and no more brokenness inside of her.

"C'mon." Sarah muttered the word as a taunt and stomped her feet as she pressed the barrel harder against her skull. "Do it!" Her body shuddered in defiance, the only action that her primal instincts of survival could offer. But her mind and thoughts had traveled beyond survival.

A tenth of a second. That's all the courage she had to muster. Enough grit to squeeze the trigger, and then nothing. It would finally be over.

And then with her eyes closed, light brightened against her eyelids. She frowned, feeling the warmth of the sun on her face, which finally forced her eyes open.

The shimmer from the orb immediately caught Sarah's gaze, and she saw that it had emerged from its pillowcase and rolled onto the dirt. It must have broken free when she'd dropped it after seeing Brent. The rays of sunlight that pierced through the thick cloud cover shot down in thick streams, and the ray that cast on the orb was separate than the one that warmed Sarah.

Sarah remembered Dell and the fact that if it hadn't been for him, she never even would have had an opportunity to make that decision. If she gave up now, then everything else was lost.

Sarah lowered the pistol from her head and slouched her shoulders. She wanted to cry, but she was too exhausted to bring the tears, and the pistol dropped from her hand. She had no idea how she was supposed to destroy the portal. And she had no idea how she was supposed to stop an entire army of evil from marching into this world.

She reached into her pocket and removed the picture of her parents. She unfolded the photograph, and a tear fell on her father's face.

"Blood is the beginning. Blood is the end."

Sarah repeated the phrase like a mantra. If the gate was to be opened during the witching hour of the next early morning, then she had less than ten hours to figure out the riddle behind the words to destroy the orb. If not, then there was always the revolver.

32

$\mathcal{C}$enturies of life lived in these woods had left the witch restless and, for the first time in her tenure with the dark lord, tired. His power had sustained her for this long, and while she had unlimited access to the pools of rejuvenation, she felt the desire to sustain them slipping away.

But she quickly dismissed the thoughts with a flick of her hand, and she rose from Kegan's bed, still naked and slick with sweat. She grabbed the crystal of whiskey and poured it in one of the matching shot glasses then turned back toward Kegan, who still lay motionless and naked in bed, the same blank expression on his face as he wore when they'd slept with each other.

"Anything for you, darling?"

Kegan remained silent, and the witch chuckled to herself as she picked up her glass and took a sip.

"I do have a tendency to wear men out."

The fire in the hearth had heated the room nicely, and with her vegetative lover on top of the sheets, she walked to the window and pulled back the curtains.

Evening had begun, the sun close to setting on the horizon. It wouldn't be much longer now. Nightfall would hasten the pace toward the devil's hour, though it wouldn't matter if she didn't have the orb.

She had hoped the detective would have returned by now. She'd give him till nightfall. If not, then she'd send her new lover to fetch her prize. She turned back to him, and the fire of desire burned in her belly as she lustfully eyed his naked body. The touch of flesh helped ease her nerves.

The witch drained the whiskey and set the empty glass on the nightstand before she climbed back into bed and straddled Kegan's waist.

She placed the fingernail of her right index finger into his chest and then slowly ran it down his stomach and to his groin, her eyes locked onto Kegan's face, which remain motionless and unmoved, though he hardened in her hand.

"I've been with more men over the years than any other woman on earth," the witch said, smiling. "And I've probably been with more woman than any other man." She tilted her head to the side. "Each of them has given me what I needed, but none of them have been able to give me what I truly desire." She let go of him and then crawled toward his face and kissed him, tugging at his lip before letting it go. "But you can give me what I want, can't you?" She fell off of him, rolling to her side, and giggled. "Though I'm sure your grandmother wouldn't approve." She ran her tongue over her lips and shuddered with excitement. "No. But she won't have a say in the matter, will she? I'll force her to watch as I cut you open. Oh!" She perked up in excitement and straddled him again. "Or maybe I'll force her to cut you herself. Oooh, that would be a treat, wouldn't it?" She giggled again and then gently stroked Kegan's cheek. "Such a shame to lose such a body like yours though. And I'm confident that your innards won't be as attractive as your exterior. But I'm sure your blood will taste just divine." She ran her finger over the lips of his closed mouth and then leaned closer, a sense of wonder filling her that she hadn't felt since... well, she wasn't sure she'd ever felt like that before. She was a little girl again, her eyes wide and excited at the prospects and possibilities of the future. She would finally have everything she wanted. She would finally be able to fill that hollow pit that had gnawed at her stomach since she'd made her pact with the devil all of those centuries ago. Her role would be actualized, her mission complete. And all it was going to take was one last sacrifice. "Blood is the beginning. Blood is the end." She repeated the words like it was born from an ancient text written over millennia before her conception. Even before the dark lord whispered those words to her on the day of their pact, she could remember reciting them as a child. She whispered the words in secret to herself and herself alone. She knew that those words made her special, and if anyone else discovered that secret, then she wouldn't be special anymore. And she was special. The dark lord had shown her that. Just as Kegan Bell was special. And when he was cut open and his blood spilled upon the altar, all would be good. All would be well.

* * *

THE SEVENTH FAILED attempt at walking had left Iris crippled in the chair next to her vanity. She found it fitting that this particular chair was where she had chosen to rest. Over the years, she had spent countless hours applying rouge and foundation and eye shadow and lipstick and whatever other instruments of youth that she could buy in an attempt to conceal what nature had done to her body.

Time had marched forward, deaf to Iris's pleas to stop, or at the very least slow down. And like every other mortal, time cast her aside and stretched over the horizon and out of reach, leaving her to die along the side of the road with the other bodies decaying and picked over by the buzzards for carrion.

But the funny thing about time was that the longer it stretched, the faster it went by, and the less she cared about reaching the end. In fact, she longed for it to be over, and never had those wishes been more desired than that moment.

The sands of time had slipped through her fingers, and she knew that she only had a few grains left. And Iris was determined to make them count.

With a renewed grit, Iris gripped the back of the chair with her left hand and planted her right palm on the desk, then used the leverage to heave herself into a standing position. She eyed the door, the distance impossibly long, but she made her first step.

The more momentum she gained, the easier the trek became, and while her bones ached, and her muscles trembled, and the resolve in the back of her mind weakened to the point of failure, she didn't quit. Iris pushed past the pain and when her hand wrapped around the brass knob of the door handle, she exhaled in relief, and in that relief, she collapsed to the floor.

The loosely-held together bones cracked against one another, and a sharp, hot flash of pain spread up her spine. But despite the collapse and the pain and the exhaustion that was flooding through her body, it was the farthest that she'd gone.

Iris took a few minutes to gather her breath and find her strength, though it could have been closer to an hour, knowing how quickly time passed for Iris.

She grabbed hold of the door knob, her body trembling as she half pulled and pushed her way off the floor and finally managed to straighten out, still leaning against the door for support, though it didn't offer much.

Thoughts of Kegan and her shame provided enough grit to stand on her own two feet and open the door and step into the hallway. She used the tables and chairs that lined the walls to help her toward the stairs, propelling her closer to the stairwell.

Despite the clouds of fog brought on by her age and exhaustion, Iris had a plan. She clutched the hidden object wrapped in the cloth that Sarah had given her. The witch was only allowed inside the mansion because she believed she had been invited. Which was true.

But what Iris knew was the witch was counting on was the fact that she wouldn't expect Iris to have the strength to boot her out. And if Iris was being honest with herself, she wasn't sure if she had the strength either. But there was only one way she was going to find out.

The stairs presented their own challenge, every step of her descent cracking the bones and joints of her knee. Her body was just as noisy and defiant as the old wooden stairs, complaining with every step down. She clutched the railing like a lifeline and took the descent slow, unable to trust her rusty coordination.

What made the decay of her body even worse was the memory of what it used to be able to accomplish. Even with the decades between her mind and her abilities, she could still remember them as if they were yesterday. So with every harsh crack of her knee, or pain in her back, or swelling of her fingers, Iris used the memory of her youth to propel her forward. But the only bad thing about hanging onto the past was the sacrifice of the future.

Iris clutched one of the banister posts and hunched over, nearly collapsing as she struggled to catch her breath on the third-floor entrance. Once she had gathered her strength,

Iris crept toward the door, naturally slow, but as quiet as she could, and entered the third floor.

All the candles along the hall had been lit, flickering and causing the shadows to dance along the wall, which gave life to the lifeless. The pictures, the tables and chairs, even the dead flowers in their vases with grey, dirty water came alive.

But it was only parlor tricks. The shadows were only the zombie projections of the dead things that surrounded Iris. She clutched the walls and the chairs and the tables on her slow and painful trek down the halls. The shadows moved better than she did. And just when she felt like she was about to give up, just when she thought the end was near, she saw Kegan's door.

It was shut, and most likely locked. The light from the fire in the room glowed brightly through the door cracks. Iris shuddered at the thought of what that witch was doing behind those doors with her grandson. But she couldn't let her win. No matter the cost.

Iris clutched her fists tight, squeezing until the swollen joints ached with a pain that felt like it could burst at any moment. With what strength remained to her, Iris marched forward, forgoing the crutches of furniture on either side of the hall on her approach.

The closer she moved toward the door, the more powerful her anger became. And despite the symphony of pain wreaking havoc throughout her body, she gritted her teeth and pushed through it. She squeezed the object in the cloth tighter the closer she moved toward the door. Her heart raced and sweat broke out on her forehead.

Iris stretched out her hand, reaching for the door, expecting to find it locked, but it opened with a quick turn of the wrist, and she used the momentum to thrust herself inside, the heat in the room blazing compared to the hallway.

Iris blinked away sweat that dripped from her eyelashes,

and her skin felt as if she had plunged her entire body into the flames of the fireplace. It was like stepping into an arid desert, the heat so strong that it sucked the moisture from the air, which moved and wiggled like a mirage.

It took Iris a minute to get her bearings, but she eventually spotted the witch and Kegan in bed. She was naked, sitting upright and smiling at Iris. Even though the temperatures inside the room were sweltering, she didn't even look like she was breaking a sweat.

Thankfully, Kegan was covered with a blanket below the waist, but he still wore that vacant expression. He was still under the witch's control. And Iris had to be the one to break it.

"I'm surprised you wanted to see this," the witch said, still in bed next to Kegan and smiling. "Have you decided to expend the rest of your energy to watch me defile what's left of your family?" She cackled and placed her hand on Kegan's chest.

Iris wiped the sweat still streaming off her face. She wobbled on both legs, the heat penetrating her skin and attacking her bones, muscles, and organs. But she fought the exhaustion and the pain, still holding that covered object that Sarah had given her. It was the only thing left in her possession to draw strength from, and she clung to it for dear life.

"You will leave this house, witch," Iris said, her voice forceful and angry, but unsteady with its volatility.

But she only laughed, rolling over Kegan on the bed and placing her bare feet on the floor. Her long, dark hair cascaded over her shoulders, and her breasts bounced suggestively and matched the lustful nature of her swinging hips.

"You do not command me, hag," the witch said. "And when my master arrives, he will show you the true meaning of torture. The more you try and resist here, the harder it's going to be for you when he finally arrives."

Iris retreated, unraveling the cloth, but her fingers ached.

"What strength do you have to cast me out of this house?" the witch asked, her tone growing louder and bolder. "Your family is lost, your time is done, and your last remaining heir will provide the blood I need to open the portal!"

The joints along Iris's fingers wanted to explode as she unraveled the cloth from the object, and she slammed up against the wall near the door on her retreat, nowhere else to run.

"You have failed!" The witch lifted her arms. "Fire and blood will reign on this earth, and you are the woman who made it happen!"

The last layer of cloth fell to the floor, and Iris gripped the wooden cross in her hand, shoving it near the witch's face, a cold look of terror on her face.

"I cast you out of this house!" Strength returned to Iris's voice and flooded through her body as she held up the small wooden cross.

"NO!" The witch quickly retreated. She screamed and wailed in pain, swatting at the air with her hands and arms as if something was attacking her.

"In the name of the Father, and the Son, and the Holy Spirit, I cast you back into the hell from which you came!"

Heat and wind and fire swirled in the room, all gathering around the witch as she screamed and howled in the same hastened violence as the rest of the room.

It took all of Iris's strength and concentration to keep the cross up and not collapse into a pile of ash. The wooden cross burned in her hand as the witch continued to thrash and wail. She inched forward, moving herself and the cross closer toward the witch, which only worsened the witch's anger.

Iris glanced over to the bed and saw Kegan stir. He twitched like he was having a seizure, and she saw conflict on his face, like he was fighting something off. Finally, he woke, popping up from the bed and gasping for air like he'd been holding his breath.

The pair locked eyes for the briefest moment, and while Kegan was confused and frightened, Iris couldn't wipe the smile off of her face. He was alive. And if she wanted him to stay that way, then she was going to need to finish this once and for all.

Iris turned to the witch, forcing herself closer until it felt as though the skin was melting off of her face, but she pushed forward until she was only inches away from the witch's face and the protection of fire that had engulfed her.

The witch dropped to her knees, arms thrust out above her, and the screams were so high-pitched that Iris couldn't even hear them anymore. Iris pushed the cross a little farther, but then felt it bump against an invisible wall just before the fire. She pushed again but received the same result.

The witch looked up, her eyes on fire with rage. The beauty had faded, and weathered skin, like a snake's skin, covered her body. Her supple breasts faded and transformed into rocky lumps. The blue in her eyes morphed into a greenish yellow, and her pupils elongated to the eyes of a reptile.

Fangs protruded from her mouth, and she flicked a forked tongue as she lunged for Iris, snatching the old woman's wrists with her claws that extended from her hands in the forms of her nails.

Iris tried to move but found that her feet and her body were frozen in place. The witch's snarl worsened as she pulled herself toward closer to Iris. The heat was unbearable now, and Iris screamed as though she had caught fire.

"You will burn for this, woman," the witch said, her voice dropping an octave and ending each word with a dreadful hiss that lingered in Iris's ears long after she stopped speaking. "Your sacrifice will mean nothing. It will do nothing. And your family will still burn with the rest of the world."

The pain grew so intense that it faded and Iris felt as though she were numb to everything. She lowered her face and saw the witch's wicked smile. From there, she looked back to Kegan, who had finally removed himself from the bed, his expressions fighting between that stoic and apathetic stare to expressions of fear and sympathy.

"You must help her, Kegan," Iris said, her voice calm, but thick with grief. Tears squeezed from her eyes though she wasn't even sure how water could survive in an environment so hot. But she felt them run down her face as she continued to look at her grandson, who was fighting for his life. "You must fight the evil that you inherited." She smiled, and her grip on the cross weakened. "You must destroy what I could not."

And then, the pain from the flames returned, followed quickly by the stench of burning flesh, and Iris screamed as her skin melted, and her muscles were burned and charred into black pieces of rock and ash. Every fiber that was burned, every square inch of her body that was set aflame was felt. It was her final penance for the lives that she had taken. And as the last of her flesh and bone dissolved into ash, the only thing that remained when she was dead was the cross amongst the ash.

* * *

IT WAS LIKE A BAD DREAM. The images returned to Kegan in flashes, most of them foggy and clouded. It was like walking around in a haze so thick he could barely see his own hands in front of his face. But while he struggled with sight, he didn't have any trouble hearing what was happening outside the world.

The screams penetrated through the fog as if his grandmother was standing right next to him. And anytime he tried calling back, his tongue would turn to lead in his mouth, remaining immovable no matter how hard he tried to speak.

With his vision and his ability to speak stolen, Kegan stumbled through the haze like a drunken mute, groping for anything to hold onto. He did his best to follow the screams, but every time he thought he was close, there was nothing.

The longer Kegan wandered the hazy fields of his mind the more he wanted to scream, and the more his madness grew. He had control over nothing, and a sickness consumed his thoughts, the venom of some creature that had bit him.

And just when he was about to pull his hair out, he stopped, frozen. The fog parted in front of him and Iris stood, glimmering in light and dressed in a perfectly white gown. She was still old and frail, but there was a beauty to her even with the frailty and her advanced age.

"Kegan," Iris said. "You are the last Bell." Her voice echoed and projected like she was in a cave, but the grandmother that Kegan had always known had shouted and screamed and was so stern and emotionless. "I will help you as much as I can, but you will have to be my hands."

"I can't," Kegan said, and then jumped in surprise when he heard his own voice. He quickly started to speak, afraid that it would suddenly disappear again before he even had a chance to finish. "Whatever it is you want me to do, I can't. I'm lost." His voice caught in his throat. "I'm nothing. Just like my father."

Iris floated closer to Kegan and then lifted his chin. The tip of her hand was so warm, and it helped ease that sickness flooding through his veins, giving him a brief moment of clarity and courage.

"You are not your father," Iris said, her voice boasting with confidence. "You have the strength and conviction of your mother. You just have to reach out and grab it." Her voice faded into a whisper, and then suddenly she was floating away.

Kegan tried to follow, sprinting through the fog and haze, but the faster he ran, the quicker her ghost disappeared, until finally there was nothing but clouds.

Kegan skidded to a stop, his heart pounding, suddenly covered with a slick sheen of sweat. He spun around, trying to scream his grandmother's name, but found that his tongue had transformed back to lead, and he no longer had the strength to work it.

The sickening, poisonous rush also returned, and Kegan felt his mind slipping away. The interaction with his grand-mother started to feel like nothing more than a faded memory. He panicked, his skin turning to ice, and he shut his eyes, trying to cement the images and words to memory.

But the harder he tried, the more the images only sifted through his hands. Defeated, he collapsed to his knees. He was weak. And he had no idea how to get out of this place.

$\mathcal{T}$he sun had plummeted beneath the horizon, and so did the temperature. Sarah stomped through the forest, revolver gripped in an icy hold in her right hand, and the left holding the pillowcase with the orb. She worked her way through the forest and toward Bell.

The orb was born in that place, and it was connected to it. The priest she'd spoken to had mentioned that there would need to be a strong connection between the other world and this one, so she figured that there might need to be a strong connection to try and sever its hold on the souls that it trapped in purgatory.

Sarah periodically checked her pockets on the walk, making sure that she still had the cross and the tubes of holy water. She felt good having them, but she felt even better now that she had the revolver. It was a confidence boost, and it was one that she desperately needed.

Storming back to the Bell mansion, knowing what was there waiting for her, was madness. She still didn't fully understand what she was facing.

She stuck her hand in her pocket and her fingers nudged

the wooden cross that was tucked inside. She stopped and then glanced up. The barren tree branches provided a limited view of the night sky, but it was the first time in a few nights where it was completely clear. No clouds, just stars.

Standing there in the cold, hungry and exhausted, Sarah found herself wondering who, or what, was giving her this sudden surge in strength.

All of her life, Sarah had never believed in heaven or hell, demons or angels. To her, it was nothing more than hocus pocus, a way for adults to get kids to do what they wanted them to do lest they be sent to hell and burn with the devil.

Sarah had seen plenty of what 'religious' folks had done during her time at orphanages and foster homes. And she had determined long ago that if there was a God out there, then he wasn't the kind and forgiving God that she'd heard so many preachers and nuns talk about on the television and in church.

To Sarah, He was mean and spiteful. He was apathetic to the wants and needs of the world. He didn't care what happened to anyone, so long as people praised His name and tithed their ten percent at the weekly offering.

But the priest that she'd spoken to back in Redford had been different than any other that she'd spoken to before. There was intelligence to his words, and while he talked tough, there was love hidden in his message.

Maybe she didn't have it all figured out.

After all, with everything that she'd seen, there was proof in what she'd experienced that there were forces at work that stretched beyond the natural world. She had seen a witch, and she had felt the devil, she had seen ghosts and spirits, and she had seen more than she could probably handle.

With no watch, the passing of time was distorted. Instead of minutes or hours, Sarah measured the distance walked and the time passed by the aches that began to form along her body. Her feet were first, and then it traveled to her thighs, then her back, and finally her hips and lastly her shoulders.

And just when Sarah was about to drop the pillowcase and take a break, she saw the mansion through the trees ahead.

It was the west wing spiral that wound high into the sky. She wasn't sure how close she was to the witching hour, but since there weren't any demons flying around or fire raining from the sky, she figured she still had some time.

But while the sight of the mansion and her encounters with it had previously brought a feeling of hesitation, now she only felt a sense of urgency. Urgency to get this done, and to finish it quickly. She knew that the longer she dragged it out, the worse it would be for everyone else involved. The only thing that mattered now was ending this curse and stopping the end of the apocalypse.

Like her previous break-in, Sarah hovered near the tree line on the west side of the estate. Darkness had concealed the house in a shroud, with no light penetrating the inside. It was like no one was home.

But something didn't feel right, and it was evident by Sarah's instinct to stay put. She couldn't be sure, but she felt like something was watching her, waiting for her to—

"Hello, Sarah."

Sarah jumped, springing off the ground and covering her mouth to muffle the gasp. When she landed on her heels, she rocked backward and landed hard on her ass, the orb and the pillowcase sprawling across the frozen dirt.

Iris floated above her, all white and glowing and translucent. Sarah frowned, her breathing fast, as she examined Iris's floating projection.

"You're... dead." Sarah shook her head and then pushed

herself off the ground, still in shock at the woman in front of her. "But how did you—"

"There isn't time," Iris said, quickly floating closer. "You must destroy the orb before the devil's hour."

"I've tried," Sarah walked back and picked the orb off the ground, still using the pillowcase as a cloth between herself and the orb. "I've smashed it, I've kicked it, I've beaten it, and I haven't even given it a blemish."

"Only the blood of sacrifice upon the altar of evil can it be destroyed," Iris said. "When the witching hour approaches, the witch will sacrifice the last Bell to open the portal. But if another offers their blood, then portal will be broken, and the orb destroyed."

Sarah snorted. "Perfect."

"You can make it, Sarah." Iris floated closer, and Sarah noticed a distinct change in the old woman's appearance. She was still weathered and slightly wrinkly, but she no longer possessed that stern consternation that Sarah was greeted with every morning when she worked at the house. She looked more graceful and relaxed. Sarah felt like she was finally meeting the real Iris Bell.

Sarah reached into her pockets and fished out the cross and holy water. "Think these will help me out?"

Iris smiled, nodding as she examined the holy relics. "Yes, but you must be quick. The witch and her power will only grow stronger the closer time draws toward the devil's hour." She floated closer. "Go through the back entrance. She has Kegan watching the east wing. And remember that the orb and the blood sacrifice must be offered on the altar."

"What is the altar?" Sarah asked as Iris started to fade.

"The bed," Iris answered. "Allister's bed."

Sarah wanted to ask whose blood, but she was beginning to understand whose it would be, and the thought made her tremble and her mouth went dry. She stepped closer to Iris, wanting to reach out and touch her, desperately wanting a hand to hold in her hour of need. "What happens if I fail?"

"You are strong, Sarah," Iris said, her voice fading along with her physical body. "It was why I wanted you in my house in the first place. You have the ability to change the future." She smiled. "It's in your blood."

With Iris vanished into thin air, Sarah took a deep breath and then exhaled, her breath jettisoned from her lips in a thick stream.

She had come so far since leaving New York, both physically and emotionally. She wasn't the same person anymore, and all of the things that she had been running from were over.

Sarah hurried through the trees, keeping to the forest as she circled around to the back of the mansion and toward the rear-kitchen entrance that Iris had suggested she try.

Those skeptical bones that Sarah had relied on for so much of her life to survive rattled a little bit from the fact that Sarah realized the old woman might be leading her into a trap, but the fears quickly disappeared when Sarah opened the back door and found it clear of any foes.

Sarah worked her way through the darkened kitchen and into the hallway. She craned her neck around the door frame before she stepped from the kitchen, and once she determined that it was clear, she made her way to the staircase.

The mansion was dead quiet, even more so than the nights when she had worked here. There was no wind howling across the windows, no groans or creaks from the house settling, and no ghostly cries from the top floor.

It was as if the house itself had died, shedding its leaves and growth for the approaching winter, and had become hollow and barren.

The house was quiet. Even when she ascended the steps, the normally fussy stairs remained silent. The air was different too. While Sarah could breathe, it was hollow, and she had to inhale twice as much to catch the same amount of air as before. And the higher she ascended the staircase, the hotter it became. It was a stark contrast from her previous visits to the fifth floor.

It was always colder up here, like climbing a mountain, where the temperature plummeted. But the opposite was in effect now, and sweat poured off of her in buckets the higher she climbed.

Remembering that Kegan was still somewhere in the house, Sarah looked down and kept her head on a swivel as she scanned the staircase. But so far as she could tell in the darkness, she was alone, and she continued her trek up to the top, hoping it would stay that way.

While she had never liked Kegan, she wasn't sure if she could bring herself to kill someone again unless it was the witch. She still hadn't shaken the psychological side effects from killing Brent, and he had been someone who she hated.

Sarah took the final step up the staircase and stood on the fifth-floor platform. The door in front of her was closed, and Sarah glanced down at the orb which was still in the pillowcase. Her heart rate quickened, and her breathing grew shallow and fast.

She tightened her grip on the pillowcase and did the same to the tube of holy water clutched in her pocket. She had to let go of one of them to open the door, so she relinquished the holy water. She placed her hand on the door knob, and it vibrated.

Sarah held on and turned the knob. It gave way slowly, and the knob grew hotter the closer she moved it to open. The vibrations grew so strong that it shook her whole body, and she tightened her grip down like a clamp, her muscles straining as she struggled to open the door the rest of the way.

It wasn't until the subtle click of the lock that the vibrations ended, and the tension in Sarah's arm vanished as she pushed the door inward.

Sound returned as the hinges groaned and the door opened. Unlike the rest of the house she had passed, the fifth floor had rows of candles that lined the walls. Nearly all of the candles had been burned down to the nubs, their wax dripping from the sides in long strands as the flames flickered and waved as she passed.

She pocketed her hand again, grabbing the tube of holy water as she eyed the door at the end of the hall. While her nerves were rattled, she maintained a steady pace. She kept expecting the witch or Kegan to jump out of one of the rooms along the way, snatching her up and killing her, but the closer that Sarah moved toward the door, the more she realized just how confident the witch must have been.

After all, the witch had managed to draw her back to the house, bring her the orb, and to top it all off, she had come alone armed with only a revolver, holy water, and a wooden cross. By the time she reached the door to Allister's room, the confidence that she had boasted on the way to the house and up the stairs had dissolved.

Sarah stood there, pummeled by the heat radiating off of the door, dripping with sweat. She stared at the door handle. She had no idea what waited for her on the other side, but she knew that it could kill her and that opening the door was an acceptance of that fate.

And yet, with fear eroding her courage and the heat pummeling her senses, Sarah heard the faintest whisper in the back of her mind. She didn't recognize the voice, but she recognized the tone that went with it. And she smiled, then placed her hand on the door knob and pushed it open.

The door knocked into the side of the wall, and Sarah thrust her arm out to keep it from closing. She remained in the hallway, and from her position, she saw the witch standing at the foot of the bed, blocking her path to the altar.

The witch was dressed in a long red gown, and her nails matched the same fiery color as her dress, which was made all the more prominent by her porcelain skin and jet-black hair. She was beautifully terrifying.

Kegan stood next to her, a blank expression on his face. He wore nothing but a pair of sweat pants, standing next to the bed behind the witch.

"Curiosity always got the better of you." The witch gestured to the pillowcase. "I appreciate you bringing that back for me."

"You want it?" Sarah asked, doing her best to keep a courageous front, but her voice cracked and she wasn't sure if she succeeded. "Come and get it."

The witch smiled and shook her head, and then turned slightly back toward Kegan. "Fetch, boy."

And like a zombie, Kegan lumbered toward Sarah, his eyes focused on her own, his expression stoic. Sweat glistened off his body, accentuating his already well-defined physique.

Sarah froze, her skin crawling up her back, and she fingered the cross in her pocket. "I can't let her win, Kegan," Sarah answered, taking her first step back. "And I know you can't understand that right now, but I hope by the time this ends that you do."

Kegan stopped, then smirked. "Iris is dead. She gave her life for no reason other than to end her own suffering, but she will have her punishment when Satan walks this earth. Her soul, like all Bells, has been thrust into purgatory, and it is there she will wait until my blood touches the orb on the altar."

"So you're just going to let her kill you?" Sarah asked.

"My soul will be the key to unlock the portal," Kegan

answered. "My sacrifice will be rewarded one-hundredfold when the dark lord revives me." Kegan took one more ominous step forward, his weight thudding into the floor through his heel, and he grimaced. "I have no desire to hurt you, Sarah. And neither does my master. All he wants is to set you free." He extended his hand. "Let him give you what you've always desired."

Sarah regarded the hand, and for the briefest moment, she considered taking it. After all, the odds were stacked against her. She had literally walked into the devil's den and knew that she was unprepared to confront the evil inside. Hell, she wasn't even sure she would have the fortitude to give up her own soul to end all of this. What if she couldn't do it? What if she died anyway trying to stop all of this, and it was all for nothing? Shouldn't she at least get something out of it?

But then a whisper tickled the back of her thoughts. It was so quiet and faint that she couldn't understand the words or even recognize the voice, but that little noise immediately calmed the fears and doubts that had crawled to the forefront of her mind.

Sarah adjusted her grip on the tube of holy water in her pocket and briefly lifted her hand in preparation to strike, then she stiffened. "I can't do that."

Kegan smiled and slowly nodded. "Then I will do what I've wanted to do since the moment I saw you." He clenched his fists, and the smile faded into a snarl, but the expression wasn't his own. It was another person controlling Kegan, working his mind and body like a puppet. It was the face of the witch that she was staring into. "Your flesh will be mine. Your life will be mine." He lowered his voice to a vibrating level of bass. "Your soul will be mine."

Sarah tensed, adrenaline coursing through her veins and pulsating in every fiber of muscle along her body. "Fuck you."

"ARRGH!" Kegan charged, and before he made it two steps, Sarah pulled the tube of holy water from her pocket and cocked her arm back in anticipation to hit him with it.

But Kegan was too fast, no doubt charged up by the witch's powers, and immediately knocked her to the floor, which sent the tube flying form her hands along with the pillowcase holding the orb.

Sarah gasped for breath as the wind was knocked out of her, and before she had a chance to collect herself, Kegan gripped her by the throat and lifted her off the floor and pinned her again the wall, which made one of the picture frames crash to the floor.

"You made the wrong choice, Sarah." Kegan slowly tightened his grip, savoring the slow cutoff of air as Sarah clawed at his arm, choking to death. "You could have had everything you wanted. You could have lived like a queen."

Sarah dropped her left hand and reached back into the pocket again. Her thoughts were telling her hands to reach for the pistol, but another force guided her to the smooth and warm edges of the wooden cross.

"But now you will die like a beggar," Kegan said, those black eyes locked onto Sarah's and the witch's wicked smile spreading across Kegan's face.

With her vision starting to pepper with black dots, Sarah removed the cross from her pocket and thrust it close to Kegan's face. He released her, quickly retreating as she collapsed to the floor, coughing and hacking, but with still enough sound mind to keep the cross lifted as Kegan slammed back into the opposite wall.

Kegan thrust out his hands, grunting and groaning from the pain of the cross. And as Sarah moved to her feet, she stopped when Kegan snarled from his position on the floor.

"What do you think will happen to you when all of this is over?" Kegan asked. "You will have to kill yourself to stop this, Sarah. Do you know that? There is no happy ending for you here, there is no savior that will swoop in at the last second and rescue you from an eternity of burning in the flames."

Sarah inched closer, arm thrust out, still holding the cross, which gave herself a protective barrier, and she reached into her pocket for the other tube of holy water.

"It will be over," Kegan said, anger seething through clenched teeth, those eyes blackened and hot like burning coals. "You will know nothing but pain."

Less than a foot separated the pair of them now, the witch increasing her resistance to the cross's holy powers, and Sarah's arm started to shake.

"I've known pain my whole life," Sarah said, determination etching onto her face. "So I'm pretty fucking used to it." Sarah gathered her strength and then pushed herself forward as hard as she would go, slamming the cross into Kegan's forehead.

The skin burned and crackled as Kegan screamed and thrashed his head back and forth. He rolled his eyes into the back of his skull, and Sarah reached for the holy water and then crashed it down over his head.

Every speckle of water that connected with his skin sizzled and burned. Sarah kept as much pressure on the cross as she possibly could until Kegan thrust her backward.

Kegan lay on his side, eyes shut and breathing heavy. He trembled, every muscle of his body shaking, and sweat dripped from the tip of his nose and onto the floor.

The witch cackled and then twirled around. "You really are quite the girl. But then Iris always knew how to pick them." She arched one eyebrow. "Did she ever tell you why she always picked up women? Because they were easy." She clutched her hands together and pinched her shoulders forward, crouching in a helpless position. "So weak and fragile, afraid to make their way in the world." She thrust her chest out and flung her head back, her black locks whipping through the air. "As a woman, you'd think I'd be offended, but I thought it was brilliant. And truth be told, I haven't been a real woman in over a millennia." She gestured to the body and the dress. "I pick my form, whatever pleases me." She shape-shifted, and suddenly she was Pat again, her voice deepening to a man's. "Or sometimes if it pleases others." And then she transformed into Dell and cracked a smile. "Sarah, you could have everything you want. Even me."

"It's not real," Sarah said.

The witch transformed back into the beautiful woman that Sarah had come to know her as, and the smile faded. "So if the boy won't persuade you, then what if I could give you something else?" She strutted toward Sarah, who reached into her pocket for the cross, and the witch stopped, eyeing the hand that dove into the pocket. "I thought you might bring a few tricks with you." She flicked her eyes back to Sarah. "But I've got a few of my own."

"No tricks," Sarah said. "Now step aside."

The witch lifted her hand and wagged her finger back and forth. "No, no, no, my dear, I'm afraid that I can't let you do that."

"I told you there isn't anything you can offer me," Sarah said. "There isn't anything that can stop me."

"My master has the ability to alter time," the witch said, ignoring Sarah's words. "He can make things that never happened, happen. And he can also make things that happened... not." Those wicked red lips creased into a thin line, and Sarah's heart stopped cold.

That hollowness that accompanied sheer terror carved out Sarah's innards, and her mouth went dry. She hadn't expected the turn that the witch was taking, and as the color drained from Sarah's cheeks, the more the witch smiled.

"Your parents died when you were so little, Sarah," the witch said, her tone an over-exaggerated plea for attention. "It wasn't your fault. Drunk driver. How about I have my master never put that driver on the road? No, better yet, why not kill the drunk driver before he even gets close to your parents. We could have him veer off into a guardrail, send him straight through the window. Glass and blood everywhere." She lowered the volume of her voice. "And then your parents would drive by, slowing from all the police cars and emergency vehicles on scene, and glance over and wonder what happened."

A tear formed in Sarah's left eye, and she shook her head. "Stop it."

"Imagine it, Sarah," the witch said. "A life where you don't have to grow up in an orphanage and surrounded by people who don't care about you. Your parents would be the ones to drop you off at your first day of school, teach you to ride a bike, give you presents at your birthday and Christmas. Imagine the stability, the love. They would protect you better than any of those foster homes or social workers could, you've thought that to yourself for years. That fantasy that you've desired for your entire life could come true."

The tears flowed freely down Sarah's face as the witch stood less than a foot away. She knew that the devil woman was right. She couldn't even remember all of the sleepless nights that she used to lie awake and desperately wish for everything that the witch had said.

"It would all go away," the witch said, her voice like a sweet, singing cadence. "No more scars, or bruises. No more fear. No more pain. Just think of all of the good that would be thrust back into your life. And we could make it so you never even remember this life. You'd be in your own world, Sarah. A perfect world. You deserve that life, Sarah. Don't be afraid to take it now that it's dangling right in front of you."

The dinners, the birthdays, holidays, weekends, smiles and hugs and kisses and a love that she never knew swelled in her heart. Sarah desperately wanted all of those things. And the witch was right, Sarah deserved to be happy. Didn't she? She wasn't a bad person, never was, just someone who did the best that they could with the hand that they were dealt.

"What do you say, Sarah?" the witch asked, still keeping her distance, but offering her hand the way that Kegan had done. The fantasy of the life she'd always wanted. And an end to the life that she never did. "Let us help you, Sarah. Let us undo what God and all of his followers should have never let happen."

Sarah stared at the hand through wet and bloodshot eyes then stared down at the pillowcase that held the orb. "The social workers always told me that I needed to learn to let things go." She swung the pillowcase and flung the orb onto the bed. "But I was never good at listening."

The witch cackled, and surprise flashed over her face as she lifted her hands in triumph. "Yes, Sarah! Yes! You've made the right choice. You've made the better choice."

Sarah then dropped the cross, and the holy water, though the pistol was still in her pocket.

"Come here, child. Come." The witch waved Sarah forward, who walked slowly, stiffly.

The orb had spilled out from the pillowcase and onto the bed. She shuddered when the witch placed her hands on Sarah's shoulders, digging those red nails into her skin.

The pistol grew heavier the closer Sarah moved toward the bed, and the world around her slowed. The doubt that had plagued her mind prior to this moment had vanished. She knew what she had to do. No matter the cost.

"Are you ready to meet them?" the witch asked, her eyes

wild, not with excitement, but a joyless madness. "They have been asking about you."

Sarah stared at the bed and then slowly peeled her eyes from the white sheets and met the witch's gaze. She nodded. "There's something I've always wanted to tell them."

"And what's that, sweetheart?" the witch asked, her features slowly transforming from the beautiful woman to the demon that had taken control of her soul.

Sarah leaned close. "Fuck you." She whipped the gun out of her pocket and aimed it at the witch, who only laughed.

"You tried that once before, dear," the witch said. "You know it can't kill me."

"No," Sarah said. "But it can kill me."

The confusion on the witch's face lasted only a moment as Sarah turned the pistol toward her stomach, and when she squeezed the trigger, the witch's scream was drowned out by the gunshot.

The pistol dropped to the floor, and Sarah collapsed onto the bed on her back, clutching the wound on her stomach.

"You bitch!" The witch jumped onto the mattress, pinning Sarah down. The beauty had been wiped away, and nothing but scales, horns, and fangs looked at Sarah, the demon's true nature. "You will burn like the rest of them."

But Sarah had already extended her hand and placed her bloodied palm on the sphere. The moment her blood made contact the orb brightened, flashing white light so bright that she was forced to shut her eyes.

"NOO!" The witch howled.

And while Sarah wasn't sure what she expected, she didn't expect to feel as much pain as what coursed through her veins. Every cell and fiber of her being caught fire, and just when she thought that it would finally end, she felt hands on her face, and she opened her eyes.

The world was blinding save for one terrifying demon face that rested right on top of Sarah. The witch's head had caught fire, and Sarah imagined that hers looked exactly the same.

"There will be others! You will not stop the dark lord from his destiny! He will inherit the earth! And until then you will burn with MEEE!"

"AHHHH!" Sarah screamed and shut her eyes as the pain intensified, and it stretched on forever. She thrashed and wailed, and it repeated for an endless cycle. And just when she thought that she couldn't take it anymore, it stopped.

* * *

SARAH GASPED, waking on a smooth white floor. Her heart was hammering, and she immediately looked at her hands and arms, expecting to find them charred and burnt. But when she wiggled her fingers, she found them exactly as they'd always been, pale and freckled.

"You did well, Sarah."

Sarah turned and found Iris standing behind her. She was dressed in the same white gown that she had worn when she visited Sarah in the forest. But now that translucent look had disappeared, and she looked more like herself.

Sarah glanced down at herself and found that she wore a similar dress. She traced some of the white doilies embroidered on her stomach. She'd never felt anything so soft before. Then, she got a look at her surroundings.

An endless white stretched to the horizon in every direction. But no matter where she looked, it was only her and Iris.

Finally, Sarah ended her three-hundred and sixty-degree tour and turned back to Iris. "Where are we?"

Iris laughed. "It's not necessarily where, but when."

"When?"

"We're in a place where time has no value," Iris answered, spreading her arms wide. "I've been here forever, and I just arrived."

Sarah shut her eyes, shaking her head, unable to wrap her mind around what was happening. "That doesn't make any sense."

"I know." Iris smiled sadly and then placed her weathered hands on Sarah's shoulders. "You ended a travesty that started with my family, and for that, I can't thank you enough. I'm finally with my daughter." Tears welled in her eyes. "We're together, and there is no more pain, and that is all because of you." She smiled sweetly and then wiped her eyes.

"But," Sarah looked around. "Where is everyone?"

That sad smile returned to Iris's face, and she cupped Sarah's cheek. "You have one final choice to make, Sarah. One that will not be easy for you, though it might seem that way."

Sarah only frowned in response, and then Iris stepped back, and two doors appeared on either side of her.

"The door to my left will take you back to the mortal world, and back to Dell, who you saved with your actions. But you will awake in pain, and there is no guarantee that you will survive your wounds. If you die after you are returned, the witch's powers will consume you, and your soul will burn in hell with her just as she promised." She pointed to the next door. "This door will take you with me, and you will live for eternity with your family. You will feel no pain, you will experience no hardships."

Sarah kept her eyes on the door to the right. "My parents are there?" Her voice made her sound like a little girl.

Iris smiled happily. "Oh, yes. And they've been looking forward to meeting you."

Sarah looked back to Iris, skeptical. "Is this some kind of test?"

"No, Sarah. No test, no tricks, no hidden agendas. This is simply an offering for you to choose what path you want to take. It's a choice that you were never really given, and it's something that he wanted to give you now."

"He?" Sarah arched her eyebrows and then looked up, where again there was nothing but endless white. She looked down and stumbled, blinking rapidly. The place was disorienting. "When do I have to decide?"

"Now," Iris answered, and then she shrugged. "Or never." She laughed. "Time doesn't matter in this place, remember?"

Sarah nodded. "Right." But her tone suggested she still didn't understand. She gazed at the two doors, mulling over her options. She had so many questions for her parents. But most of all, she wanted to feel the touch of their hands on her face. That was the earliest and only memory that she could ever recall about her parents. It was something that she clung to as a child, but while she didn't think of it as much as an adult, the desire was still buried, waiting to be rediscovered.

But then her eyes drifted to the door on the left, and a mixture of terror and fascination took hold. There was still so much that she wanted to do, so much that she wanted to feel. If she walked through the other door with Iris, then she'd never be able to act on those realities. But if she did walk through that door, there was still the chance that she could die, and the witch would burn her soul for eternity.

And yet, even with all of those consequences staring her in the face, she couldn't help but wonder what tomorrow would hold. What unexpected adventures were just around the bend.

Iris laughed, and Sarah turned to find her at the door on the right, hand on the knob as she cracked it open.

"What are you doing?" Sarah asked. "I haven't told you my decision."

"I told you when I met you that I could read people, Sarah. And your desires are written all over your face. Good luck. And tell Dell and my grandson that I'm sorry."

And just like that, Iris was gone, and the door shut. But as Sarah stood there, both doors remained, and in the echoing silence and sheer vastness of this place that she found herself, Sarah couldn't help but smirk. Curiosity always did get the better of her.

34

It was the touch on her face that woke Sarah, and for the briefest moment she thought that it was her father waking her from a bad dream. But the moment ended quickly and that warmth on her cheek quickly turned cold, and she trembled.

"Sarah, just hang on. Help is on the way."

Sarah glanced down and saw a pair of hands, bloodied, on her stomach. She widened her eyes in terror, and she glanced up to the face that the hands belonged to. It was Dell.

"Everything is going to all right," Dell said, though his voice was shaking and his eyes were becoming red and wet. "Just stay with me, okay? Stay with me."

Sarah rested her head back down on the bed, and she realized that she was in the same position where she shot herself. The white sheets were soaked with blood, but the orb had disappeared.

Footsteps and shouts echoed from somewhere down the hall, and Dell turned his head toward the door while keeping pressure on Sarah's wounds.

"UP HERE!"

A few seconds later and there were more faces hovering above Sarah, who then forced Dell to step away. She tried to follow where he went, but he was quickly lost in the crowd.

"Ma'am? Can you hear me?"

"Gunshot wound to the abdomen, doesn't look like the bullet went through. We need to get her moved. Let's go. On three."

Sarah was suddenly weightless and moving. She blinked, the ceiling that passed blurred and dark. She was vaguely aware of her trip down the stairs, but the longer she stayed awake, the more cold she became. She just wanted to close her eyes and sleep. She just wanted to be warm again. But a voice kept her awake, a nagging, frightened voice.

"Don't give up, Sarah! Keep fighting!"

She was floating again, and then doors shut, and there was the wail of a siren. She suddenly realized that her surroundings had changed and a mask covered her face. Every breath fogged the clear plastic, and the people on either side of her continued to work on her stomach, wiping away blood and cutting her clothes.

Sarah wanted to ask for Dell, she wanted to ask where he was, but she couldn't find her voice. She was so tired. And as the paramedics around her shouted for her to stay awake, Sarah couldn't do it anymore. She closed her eyes and let warmth engulf her as the sirens continued to wail.

* * *

ANOTHER BURST OF WARMTH. A touch. Feeling. It was familiar, and good. Sarah's eyelids fluttered open as she awoke. At first she was blinded by white light, and she expected to see Iris again in that gown of white. But she wasn't there.

"Hey, whoa, take it easy." Dell gently placed his hand on her shoulder and eased her back down onto her pillow before Sarah could straighten herself up. "Doctor don't want you moving around."

Something tickled Sarah's nose, and she reached up to find plastic tubes. She gave them a yank and felt the thick reams of plastic slide down the inside of her nose, and she breathed freely once they were gone.

"Not sure you were supposed to do that," Dell said.

"What happened?" Sarah asked.

Dell raised his eyebrows. "Whatever you did, it got me out of that hell."

"And Kegan?" Sarah asked.

"He copped to everything," Dell answered. "The murder of the girls. Your abduction. Everything. And he named Dennis as his accomplice, who didn't deny it." He paused. "He even confessed to Brent Alvarez's murder."

"Are you serious?" Sarah asked.

Dell nodded. "But you've been summoned back to New York. Subpoena. After you're better. But…" He rubbed his palms over his thighs. "Things are looking pretty good right now."

Sarah stared at Dell, though she wasn't sure for how long. Long enough for him to smirk.

"What?" Dell asked.

And then without a word, Sarah raised her hands and cupped Dell's cheeks. She held them for a long time, and then she started to cry. And as she cried Dell embraced her, holding her gently, but protectively and firmly.

It was an embrace that she had wanted for so long, and she never could have imagined how good it would make her feel.

The moment was interrupted by the doctors, who made

their presence known by a stiff clearing of the throat. "Just need to check Sarah's vitals."

"Right," Dell said and then stepped toward the door. "I'll be right back when they're done."

"Okay." Sarah smiled as she watched him leave, and when he was out of sight, a hollowness filled her heart. But it wasn't painful. It was a promise that would be fulfilled. It wasn't a feeling she was used to.

"Okay, Ms. Pembrooke, looks like everything is healing up nicely." The doctor smiled as he checked off some boxes on her chart. "Vitals are looking strong. Responding well to medication. You should be out of here in no time at all." He placed her folder back into its slot at the foot of her bed, then rapped his knuckles on the bed's foot end a few times. "I'll send your friend back in."

"Wait," Sarah said, stopping the doctor before he opened the door. "How long have I been out?"

"A couple of days," the doctor answered. "That's normal after the type of surgery you went through, so nothing to worry about. And you're lucky to have your friend out there." He smiled as he opened the door. "He never left your side."

The door remained open for a minute, and then Dell returned. He had his hands in his pockets and a smile on his face. It was here that she realized that he wasn't in uniform. He looked more at ease. She liked that.

"Doc said that you're going to make a full recovery," Dell said. "And that you're pretty stubborn."

"Sounds like every adult who tried to reprimand me when I was a kid." Sarah laughed, but then stopped when a sharp, stabbing pain spread through her body.

Dell rushed forward and placed his hand over hers. "Yeah, you won't be able to do that for a while." He gently rubbed his thumb in a circular motion on her hand. "Better?"

Sarah smiled. "Better."

* * *

AFTER A WEEK in the hospital to recover, the doctors finally said it was time to part ways. Dell had managed to get her clothes washed, and he escorted her out the doors to his police cruiser and helped her inside.

"Oh," Sarah said, settling into the seat as Dell walked around the front to the driver's side.

"You okay?" Dell asked as he slammed the door shut hard enough to rock the car, which caused Sarah to cradle her stomach.

"Just take it easy on the speed bumps," Sarah answered.

Dell laughed and then started the car, shifting into drive. He looked at her in the passenger seat before he took his foot off the brakes. "You sure you want to go back?"

"I'm sure," Sarah answered.

Sarah kept her eyes glued to the view out of her window. All she had seen for the past week was the inside walls of her hospital room. The scenery of Redford, no matter how limited the view, was better than the off-white walls she'd stared at for the past week.

She adjusted her bag that rested between her legs on the floorboard, and she must have been staring at it for a while because Dell nudged her with his elbow.

"It's not too late to just keep going," Dell said.

"I know," Sarah said. "But it's something I want to do." She smiled at him. "And thanks for the ride."

"As far as I'm concerned, you have as many rides as you want for the rest of your life. Consider me your personal driver."

"A girl could do worse." Sarah shrugged, making sure that

Dell noticed the indifference, but then tossed him a bone as she smiled. "Thank you though."

"You're welcome," Dell replied. "All right, looks like we're here." Dell pulled up to the front of the church and shifted into park. "You sure you don't want me to come inside with you?"

"I single-handedly defeated the army of evil from marching across the earth," Sarah answered. "I think I can return a bible without your help. And besides, you've done enough." And it was true. Not only had Dell taken care of her medical bills, he'd also offered to drive her back to New York and help testify against Brent's cronies and the legal after-math of everything that occurred in Bell. And while every-thing was looking good, Sarah had learned to not trust that little sinking feeling in the back of her head that insisted on complacency. There was still work to be done.

"We're in this together, Sarah," Dell said. "And I mean that. No matter what happens, I have your back."

If her innards still weren't burning with pain, Sarah would have taken him right then in the driver seat. She'd nearly done it in the hospital, but she still wasn't fully healed, and a part of her told her to take her time with Dell. Because for the first time in her life, she didn't feel like she had to rush things. She knew that he wasn't going anywhere.

"Be back in a sec."

Sarah heaved herself out of the car and denied Dell's attempts to at least help her to the door. She needed to do it herself, and she needed to get back into the habit of normal-ity. So, despite the pain, Sarah shuffled her way up toward the church's big double doors and heaved her weight behind one of them as she pushed it open.

Panting and red in the face, Sarah step-shuffled down the center aisle, again finding the pews empty as she did on her first visit to the church. She kept her gaze focused on the statue of Jesus on the cross. For some reason, he looked different than the last time she was here, but she couldn't exactly put her finger on it.

"Can I help you, miss?"

Sarah turned to her right and found an older gentleman dressed in a priest's uniform. He had thinning white hair that was trimmed short and neat, with round glasses that complimented his plump and red cheeks.

"Yes, I wanted to return this bible." Sarah fished it out of her pack, and the priest moved closer to grab it, but Sarah wouldn't give it to him. "I was actually hoping to return it to the guy who gave it to me."

"Oh, and who might that be?" the priest asked.

"The other holy guy that works here."

The old priest smiled and shook his head. "Well, I'm the only priest at this church, and I'm sorry, but you don't look familiar."

Sarah frowned. "You're the only priest that works here?" She looked around the empty church. "So, you didn't have anybody else, like, covering a shift for you last week?"

"No, I'm sorry, I'm stationed here seven days a week. Perhaps you received that bible from another church?"

Sarah stared down at the bible and ran her fingers over the gold lettering, and then looked back up to Jesus on the cross. The disbelief spread across her face but quickly transformed into a smile as she looked back at the old priest. "Actually, Father, if it's all the same to you, I'd like to hang onto this for a little while longer."

"Of course, my child. Is there anything else I can do for you? Perhaps hear your confession?"

Sarah tucked the bible back into her bag. "No, thank you."

"Well, have a blessed day."

"You too."

The priest stepped away, and Sarah looked back up at

Jesus. A ray of sunlight penetrated the stained-glass windows high on the walls, and Sarah couldn't wipe the smile of disbelief off her face. She slung her backpack over her shoulders again and headed out the doors, knowing that tomorrow would come and that she'd be able to handle whatever life threw at her.

Made in United States
Troutdale, OR
09/13/2023

12889089R00209